BLUE COLLAR – ROMAN COLLAR – WHITE COLLAR

U.S. Catholic Involvement in Labor Management Controversies, 1960-1980

Rev. Patrick J. Sullivan, C.S.C

Department of Sociology
University of Notre Dame

UNIVERSITY
PRESS OF
AMERICA

Copyright © 1987 by

University Press of America,® Inc.

4720 Boston Way
Lanham, MD 20706

Library of Congress Cataloging in Publication Data

Sullivan, Patrick J., 1929-
  Blue collar, Roman collar, white collar.

  1. Church and labor—United States.   2. Collective
bargaining—United States.   3. Industrial sociology—
United States.   4. Church and social problems—
Catholic Church.   5. Catholic Church—Doctrines.
I. Title.
HD6338.2.U5S85   1986   261.8'5   86-24593
ISBN 0-8191-5704-X (alk. paper)
ISBN 0-8191-5705-8 (pbk. : alk. paper)

All University Press of America books are produced on acid-free
paper which exceeds the minimum standards set by the National
Historical Publication and Records Commission.

DEDICATION

to

numerous clergy, laity and religious

who served church and society

as

teachers and researchers
administrators and activists,
mediators and negotiators

in

universities and institutes,
dioceses and labor schools

ON BEHALF OF

Justice and Compassion in Labor-Management Relations.

Their number and prominence may be diminished

but their example and spirit endures.

-   -   -   -   -

Gratefully and Fortunately for All of Us!

A very special contribution were the permissions of publishers to reprint material. So gracious were publishers of America (New York), Ave Maria (Notre Dame), Catholic Mind (New York), Catholic Worker (New York), Catholic World (Mahwah, NJ), Commonweal (New York), Health Progress (St. Louis), Momentum (Washington, DC) National Catholic Reporter (Kansas City), Sign (Union City, NJ), Sociological Analysis (Storrs, CT), Social Justice Review (St. Louis), and Worship (Collegeville).

Acknowledgements

During the writing of this volume, one person's patience has been tried greatly--Dee Schlotfeldt. She has been more than a professional typist, as she deciphered my difficult handwriting, anticipated my quick changes and endured my endless composing. Occasionally, Anne Scheu showed the same kind of assistance. Also, during the researching and writing, I was ministered to graciously by the staff of the Memorial Library of the University of Notre Dame. I am especially indebted to Pam Paidle and Jayne Polega of Microtext, Kay Davies and Mimi Nee of Audio, as well as to John Liseck of Xeroxing. Circulation and reference staffs were on hand when needed with help and interest. In the Decio typing pool of the College of Arts and Letters, ever helpful were: Nila Gerhold, Nancy Kegler, Cheryl Reed, and Susie Curtis.

When the research and writing were completed several people offered invaluable critique. At Notre Dame were Rev. Thomas Blantz, C.S.C. and Rev. James Connerton, C.S.C. At Catholic University was Msgr. George Higgins.

More removed from the mechanics of research and writing were my brothers in Holy Cross. Especially supportive were so many of them, that to mention any would be to slight many. These priests and brothers made as real the kind of encouragement. I received constantly from the Sullivan family in the East and Southwest.

To all of these I am sincerely grateful!

Table of Contents

viii

Introduction

A. Origin

Ten years ago, I served as the Catholic Liaison for the Amalgamated Clothing and Textile Workers Union in its many-sided campaign to enable the workers in the J. P. Stevens Textile Company to exercise their right to organize for purposes of collective bargaining. During the three years I served in that capacity, both management and labor voiced criticism of the Catholic church. Representatives of the former claimed that the Catholic church in the United States always sided with the labor unions. Representatives of the latter claimed that the U.S. Catholic church was not doing enough to help unions organize workers in various industries. While the accusations were neither widespread nor constant, they were frequent enough to make me curious about the real situation.

Upon leaving the J. P. Stevens-ACTWU campaign in 1979, I began research on the accusations. A search of hardcover and paperback books for a twenty-year period, 1960-1980, uncovered little of any worth. So, I decided to search through U.S. periodical literature for that period.

Soon the specter of a life-time's opus began to haunt me. How to learn and share the insights of the periodical literature before the notes turned brown and brittle or someone else made my work personally academic? How to do justice to the topic of religious teaching and involvement in contemporary labor-management issues? Then, a young woman from Michigan inquired about my search. She agreed to search Protestant and Jewish periodical literature on labor-management relations from 1960 to 1980. I was to search the Catholic periodical literature on the same topic for the same span of years. After several years, I had no word about her work. So, I decided to continue my search of the Catholic role as recorded in the Catholic periodical literature. Perhaps, the young woman from Michigan or some other scholar will appear with the comparable record of Jewish and Protestant teaching and involvement. Someone should, if Catholics, Jews and Protestante are collaboratively and effectively to call labor and management to greater cooperation!

For four years, I was busy enjoying totally my intellectual romp through twenty years of U.S. Catholic periodical literature on the U.S. labor-management scene. Much of my zest was due to the fact that I missed such developments while involved in other scenes--urban affairs, student life and personnel planning.

B. Methodology

Most journals were searched page by page to find the editorials and commentaries so often missing from the monumental work of the Reader's Guide to Catholic Periodical Literature. A bonus was frequently an article whose title was not so obvious as to contain "labor," "unions," "labor-management relations." Some journals, usually those of a more popular nature, were read only with the assistance of the Reader's Guide citations. Diocesan newspapers were excluded, not only because of a sense of fairness to favor none, but also to move the project along. National Catholic newspapers, save the National Catholic Reporter, were also excluded, since preliminary search revealed relatively little on labor-management relations and without the NCR articles, the record would be very slim! A later project might be an indepth analysis of all the diocesan and national Catholic newspapers from 1960-1980 on this topic.

The dates 1960 and 1980 were chosen for several reasons. First, the period approximated the passing of most of the labor schools and activity of labor priests, about which there exists some written records. Second, the Catholic church, as well as Protestant, involvement in labor-management controversies during the period received much notice in the popular press. Third, I was curious about the details of Catholic involvement in labor-management controversies in the period during which "the social problem" was no longer "labor," as in the period prior to and immediately after World War II. Fourth, the dates coincided with a marked increase in labor-management controversy, an intensification of the attitude that unions were obsolete, and a decline in union membership. Fifth, the period was also a time when McClellan Hearings in Congress had exposed some corruption in some labor unions and led to a more negative than positive popular image of the labor movement. That image which unions still appear unable to dispel is a challenge to religious involvement. Sixth, the period also was marked by great upheavals in U.S. society and the Catholic Church. The former experienced the Civil Rights Crusade, the Anti-Poverty Program, the War in Indo-China, the assassination of leaders, corruption in government, and tremendous economic uncertainty. The latter experienced the charisma of Pope John XXIII, the Second Vatican Council, the birth control controversy, the celibacy and renewal debate, the exodus of priests and religious from their vocations, a Pentecostal Movement, a Divorced and Separated Catholic organization, and worldwide involvement in causes for the poor. Many of these events, both in society and church, distracted the Catholic church from its earlier type of involvement in labor-management issues.

My focus was usually at the point where unions and management meet the church in times of controversy. Hence, the title words "Blue Collar" (union) and "White Collar" (management). The "Roman Collar" (Catholic Church) tried to bring the two contenders into some sort of harmony, with its concern for the rights of the workers--whether skilled or unskilled, industrial or clerical. Little attention was given to internal management affairs but much attention was given to internal union affairs. This was so, because there is a burgeoning literature on "Management Ethics" and because such literature seldom alludes to labor-management relations as an ethical issue. Also, these are the contexts and emphases religious leaders must become acquainted with and respond to, if religious teaching and involvement is to make a real contribution to labor-management cooperation.

As I began to write, it became apparent that I had so much material from the research of 20 years of Catholic periodical literature on the U.S. Catholic church and labor-management relations that more than one volume was needed. Three were decided upon: the present one; one in 1985, entitled U.S. Catholic Institutions and Labor Unions (University Press of America); and one in 1987, entitled Catholic Social Teaching and U.S. Labor-Management Issues. The 1985 volume laid out the record of the U.S. Catholic institutions' reactions to the efforts of their employees to unionize. The 1987 volume will lay out the teaching of the international and national church, as well as U.S. commentators, on issues such as the economic system, collective bargaining, unions, unemployment, etc. All three volumes utilize the data from the Catholic periodical literature from 1960-1980. All three volumes hope to evoke researchers to come forth with data to fill in the lacunae of any periodical literature coverage.

C. Makeup

There are two parts to this limited history of U.S. Catholic church involvement in labor-management controversies. The first part (Chapters I-VII) presents the data found in the Catholic periodical literature about the controversies from 1960 to 1980. The events are presented chronologically by year, month and day. Numbers for the backnotes are placed at the beginning of each discussion or quoting of the data from a particular article.

In the Catholic Church involvement in labor-management controversies many individuals and organizations had come with assistance or resistance for union and management. Such assistance or resistance to either side was proferred in a variety of ways (action, writing, speaking, etc.) with respect to some industries, which experienced some serious controversies during the twenty year period. The Catholic periodicals from 1960-1980 made much of some of these industrial conflicts, especially in agriculture, clothing, mining and steel. Most of the involvement was depicted as supportive of the union side rather than the management side.

The second part (Chapters VIII-IX) presents some evaluation and suggestions. The evaluative framework is presented in the appendix and represents "a start" for others to develop in evaluating the goals, tactics, actions, and reactions as the Catholic church goes about its action on behalf of social justice. The questions represent the assumption that any judgments on the Catholic church's involvement in labor-management controversies from 1960 to 1980 must be tempered, not only in light of the great societal and ecclesial upheavals mentioned above, but also with the awareness that the selected periodical literature raised some questions it failed to answer and failed to raise some other questions at all. In offering recommendations on labor-management issues, I rely on my own background to suggest what the Catholic church might have done or might do similarly or differently in the future.

D. Purpose

My desire is to present a clear and organized compilation of the articles, editorials and commentaries on the labor-management controversies in which the U.S. Catholic church became involved during the 1960's and 70's. While the book is more than anecdotal material, it is in no way a "complete history" of Catholic involvement in some of the labor-management controversies of the 1960's and 1970's. Others, more knowledgeable and experienced, are invited to fill out the record, admittedly limited in any periodical literature's coverage of any topic in any period.

My fond hope is that this book will be a resource for more informed scholars and publicists to do better reporting, analyzing, comparing and evaluating of the Catholic, Jewish and Protestant involvement in labor-management controversies. May such better light the way and inspire the effort, on an interfaith basis, to repeat the successes and to omit the mistakes of the past. For the present and future always contain some continuities and changes. Hopefully, such writings can provide the minds and hearts of religious leaders and activists with more wisdom and courage to be faithful to the heritage while adaptive to the future. If so, then, many will see religion as more than priests and altars, rabbis and stars, preachers and spires. Be those others cutters or designers, pickers or packers, loaders or truckers, miners or electricians, mechanics or plumbers, supervisors or managers, investors or owners--or their children.

Chapter I - Migrants and Braceros

The agricultural industry's labor-management controversies seemed to occupy most of the time and energy of the Catholic church during the 1960's and 1970's. The presentations of church involvement in the labor-management disputes in the agricultural industry is treated in four chapters. This chapter describes the involvement on behalf of migrants and braceros. Chapter II treats of earlier involvement (1960s) on behalf of Ceasar Chavez' United Farm Workers Union. Chapter III treats of later church involvement (1970s) on behalf of Chavez's union. Chapter IV treats of church involvement on behalf of smaller and more disparate agricultural labor-management controversies (1960s and 1970s). First some background!

From November 21-22, 1959 the Chicago's Catholic Council on Working Life sponsored the National Conference to Stabilize Migrant Labor in the Lewis Tower of Loyola University.[1] Gathered were approximately 250 growers, canners, labor leaders, religious, government and community spokespeople. They hailed from 19 states, Puerto Rico, Canada, British West Indies and French Equatorial Africa. Among the participants there was an air of purpose, frankness and even controlled anger. What the Chicago Council on Working Life had convened was unique. For the first time, growers, canners and government sat down in a spirit of cooperation and understanding with labor, religious and community leaders to talk about the situation of some 400,000 American migrant workers and nearly 450,000 foreign agricultural laborers--mostly Mexicans admitted under Public Law 78.

There was one dissent about the gatherings' makeup. It came from Catherine Daly, partner in Daly Farms of Berrien County, Michigan, a woman of deep compassion who employed migrant workers and had a background in social work. She said,

> As I looked over the program I noticed that everyone interested in the migrant worker except the migrant workers is represented. Until the worker himself is involved in the plans and possible solutions to his problem I feel that little can be done to change his present status.

Few of those present thought an immediate answer could be given. For, more practical and pertinent was: "Who today would have adequately represented the migrant worker at the Conference?" The participants did hope that ways and means would be found to give regular employment, a steady income, a stable family life to the migrant workers; while at the same time, furnish the growers and canners with enough workers during harvest.

The editors of the Ave Maria also reported on the National Conference to Stabilize Immigrant Labor (NCSML).[2] They proposed their remedy or recipe,

> The success of such a goal is going to depend not only upon individuals of good will (such as those at the NCSML), and not only upon the individual migrant worker (who is practically powerless to help himself and has only the most rudimentary organizations under his crew leader), but also upon the good organizations of management, labor, government and the public (consumers of the asparagus, peas, apples and grapes) within a society that has proper concern for the human person.

The editors' assessment of the conference's highlights was threefold. First, there was the impassioned plea for justice from Archbishop Robert Lacey of San Antionio, Texas. He admitted that exploitation of the migrant workers was almost inevitable, due to human weakness, lack of farm organization, and absence of protective legislation. Second, there was Msgr. George Higgins' invitation to Matt Triggs of the American Farm Bureau to an "off-the-record" conference. Higgins, labor-management expert for the National Catholic Welfare Conference (NCWC), suggested a private meeting, "so we can clear the ground for more discussion at our next general conference," for Higgins thought growers did not give "a frank exposition" of their views at public meetings. Third, there was Secretary of Labor, James P. Mitchell's, summary of the migrant labor paradox.

> While the conditions of the migrant farm worker and his family might have been the lot of the human race for many thousands of years, and while it may still be the lot of many millions of people in some parts of the world today, we have come to regard it as ultimately intolerable in a society wealthy enough to correct it, and committed to such a correction because of a belief in the essential dignity of the human personality.

1960

In January 1960, there was reference to the National Conference to Stabilize Migrant Labor in the Social Justice Review.[3]

2

In addition to noting Archbishop Lucey's urging the enactment of special legislation to protect migrant workers, particularly a wage-hour law, the Review noted the following,

> To minister to the spiritual and material needs of migratory workers a national office will be set up in Chicago. This office will perform, on a national scale, functions similar to those performed by the office set up in New York by Cardinal Spellman for Spanish-speaking Catholics, chiefly Puerto Ricans. Field workers, probably priests, will be sent out by the office into communities where there is a heavy influx of migrants. These field workers will alert the clergy and organize the laity.

In December 1959, the American Farm Bureau Federation resolved in Chicago to oppose "organization for collective bargaining purposes of farm workers and the enactment of legislation, to establish collective bargaining for them."[4] In Milwaukee, the executive committee of the National Catholic Rural Life Conference met from January 26-27, 1960. It stated,

> We are scandalized at the un-Christian attitude manifested by some farm organizations and individuals toward the rights and dignity of farm workers. These workers have a God-given right to form unions and to demand wages and living conditions in keeping with human dignity. We urge legislation which would encourage the formation of such unions and the establishment of minimum wages for farm workers. We protest against those laws which makes possible a trafficking in migratory laborers in a manner suggesting that such laborers are mere chattles.

In April 1960 there were commendations in Commonweal for the heartening attitude of Secretary of Labor Mitchell in remedying the migrant problem.[5] There was also the testimony of Msgr. Higgins before the subcommittee of the House Committee on Agriculture, opposing the extension of Public Law 78 without substantial amendments and favoring its termination by 1963 or 1964, rather than by 1966 as proposed.

In December 1960 there was news in the Social Justice Review, of a newly organized Texas Committee on Migrant Workers, to be chaired jointly by Rev. John Wagner, executive secretary of the Bishops' Committee for the Spanish-Speaking, and Betty Jean Whitaker, director of the Texas Migrant Ministry.[6] The new committee was not to be confused with an existing Texas Council on Migrant Labor. The committee was to be composed of nongovernmental people and organizations interested in the betterment of Texas migrants. The council was composed of the officials of state agencies. Wagner added that Texas was the home base of migrants who cultivated and harvested crops in almost 40 other states. As such, these migrants were outside the protection of most laws and needed additional help from the citizens of Texas.

The goals of the Texas Committee on Migrant Workers were as follows. One, formation of a comprehensive statewide citizens committee to work toward the solution of problems facing domestic migrant farm workers and their families. Two, education of the public on correct information relating to the problem of the migrants and the distribution of that information to agencies, citizens and legislators throughout the state. Three, coordination and development of present state agency services for child care centers and education for the children of migrant workers. Four, stimulation of communities to provide existing and additional facilities and services of health, welfare and recreation freely to migrants. Five, consideration of long-range goals, such as free vocational and practical education for the adult migrant farm worker.

On December 29, 1960, Msgr. Higgins spoke at the annual meeting of the Catholic Economic Association in St. Louis.[7] In addition to another attack on Public Law 78, Higgins urged the enactment by Congress of legislation guaranteeing a minimum wage to farm workers, ending child labor on farms, and providing registration of the leaders of migrant worker crews. Reference was made to a U.S. Labor Department report, Higgins noted,

> ...in 1959 nine percent of the workers employed in the North Central States earned less than thirty cents per hour, twenty-seven percent less than fifty cents, and fifty percent less than seventy cents. In the Southern states, seven percent made less than thirty cents per hour, forty-eight percent less than fifty cents, and eighty percent less than seventy cents. The average annual income of the farm workers, taken from all sources combined, was less than $1,000 a year.

Higgins also noted that the presence of over 457,000 children working at those farms exerted "a downward pressure on the

4

already rock-bottom wages earned by adult workers." During the question-and-answer period, Higgins was asked whether a rise in farm wages would result in higher consumer prices. He responded by quoting secretary of Labor, James P. Mitchell,

> In this country we do not choose to keep down our bills, including our food bills, at the cost of overworking and underpaying human beings. We choose to pay the price necessary to support an adequate wage.

1961

In March 1961 the editors of America asserted that religious leaders' testimony before the House Subcommittee on Migrant Workers revealed much more familiarity with the economics of agriculture than some of the growers' familiarity with the ethical implications of Christianity.[8] As an example, the contrast was drawn between the views of the big farm organizations led by the American Farm Bureau and the views of church leaders led by Rev. James L. Vizzard, S.J., director of the Washington Office of the National Catholic Rural Life Conference (NCRLC) with respect to Public Law 78. The farm organizations supported Public Law 78 extension through H.R. 2010, claiming that the 400,000 Mexican nationals' performance of the "stoop labor", which U.S. workers avoided as unduly onerous and paying too little, enabled the farmers to sell fruit and vegetables at attractive prices to consumers and to make a profit at the same time.

The religious groups argued that the importation of Mexicans, through Public Law 78, depressed farm wages, offered unfair competition to American workers and disrupted the family and community life not only of the itinerant Mexicans, but of U.S. farm workers as well. The religious leaders were not impressed by the contention that U.S. workers would not perform the "stoop labor" if it were recompensed properly, since many of the U.S. workers already involved were of Mexican ancestry. The religious leaders also noted that no injustice was done to consumers, if they were asked to pay a price which allowed producers a decent wage and a fair profit. Vizzard himself explained to the subcommittee the relationship NCRLC thought should exist between religion and economics.

> We think that it is evident that at least a minimum of material security and well-being is required before the spiritual can flourish. Thus, in pursuit of our basic objectives and in fulfillment of our central

5

responsibilities, the organizations which I represent hold themselves obliged to come to the assistance of people in need, whoever or whatever they might be.

1962

By June 1962 the efforts to prevent the extension of Public Law 78 had failed.[9] The editors of Ave Maria viewed the defeat as cutting to the core of society, given the victimizing of migrant families,

> The lack of opportunity for social and economic advancement, the deprivations that strip migrants of a sense of self-respect and human dignity, the absence of job stabilities, future security and a home--all are usually the lot of migrant parents.
>
> Even more cruel, however, is the exploitation of children. Not only are they often denied educational opportunities, but many are forced into the fields at a time in life when they should be preparing for adulthood by the development of their minds and talents.

The efforts of Catholic, Jewish and Protestant organizations along with secular groups and the Kennedy administration through its Secretary of Labor, Arthur J. Goldberg, were extolled for the stepped-up drive to introduce admendments in the next Congressional session. The growing indignation that gave new hope to the migrants' champions was voiced by Archbishop Lucey at the 11th Conference for the Spanish-Speaking in Milwaukee in May 1962. In his keynote address Lucey exclaimed that "millions of our fellow Americans are shocked and disillusioned by the results" of Public Law 78. That law, in Lacey's words sanctioned a "ghastly international racket," the "braceros program."

The program, also known as the "strong-armed man" program, was initiated during World War II, as a result of serious U.S. farm labor shortage and serious Mexican unemployment. The two governments agreed to guarantee Mexican workers a minimum wage, plus free transportation. Despite terrible poverty, exploitation and family disruption of "braceros" the governments allowed themselves to be convinced by U.S. groups that the program should not expire in 1947, as scheduled. Instead, contractors for the "braceros" were no longer government agencies, but the groups themselves. By the late 1950s, as the ranks of the "braceros" increased to over 400,000, their conditions became even more deplorable.

1963

In February 1963, Arbishop Lucey spoke out again for the farm laborers, excluded from most social welfare programs and caught in continued child labor.[10] The archbishop's description of the migrants' plight was given by the _Ave Maria_ editors in the context of contrasting the migrants lack of union power and talk of "union power monopolies." Lucey's words about the migrant farm worker were:

> He stands before his employer defenseless and alone. He needs food and the necessities of life. He has little or no bargaining power. He must work to eat. His children need food. Until this year the employer could hire this man for 50 cents an hour and make him work 12 hours a day, seven days a week picking cotton. When payday came the grower could reduce the wage to 30 cents an hour, and if the worker didn't like it that was too bad for him. . . Prudence dictated that he be docile, silent and robbed.

On May 29, 1963 the House of Representatives defeated an almost routine motion to extend the "bracero program" until the end of 1965.[11] Vizzard of NCRLC gave to organized labor the greatest amount of credit and the rest to the various religious groups that long sought the same objectives. The 174-158 vote meant that at the end of 1963 there would be an end to Public Law 78 and with it an end to the abuses of the "bracero program" and a threat to the living standards of American farm workers.

From the time of the May 29th vote, the NCRLC spearheaded the intensified efforts of the migrant's advocates to nail down the victory.[12] Literally thousands of letters, telegrams and phone calls were directed to members of Congress, protesting the moral as well as the social and economic evils of the "bracero program." At its annual meeting in Grand Forks, North Dakota, on October 8, 1963, the NCRLC adopted a policy again condemning the program.

However, on October 31, 1963, the House of Representatives reversed itself (173-158) after the Senate had extended the bill earlier. During the floor debate, referring to bracero users-- the canning and processing industries and the American Farm

7

Bureau Federation--Representative John Fogarty of Rhode Island said,

> In the 23 years I have been a member of this Congress I have never been lobbied by so many high-handed, brazen lobbyists as I have in the last three or four weeks in behalf of the extension of Public Law 78 (the bracero program).

On the day of the vote the Washington Post carried an article on the intensive lobbying with examples like the following cited,

> One congressman was told that a big soup company would not build a new plant it was planning in his district if the bracero bill were defeated.

After the vote the New York Times editorialized,

> once again the corporate farm interests in California, Texas and Arizona are on their way to using Congress as an instrument for depressing the wages and working conditions of America's most exploited workers.

Since the Senate previously had passed a somewhat different bill, the House bill had to be resubmitted for Senate consideration. If approved there, the bill was to go to the president. The chance of victory for NCRLC and its allies in those final stages of the legislative process was not good. However, even though it lost the October 31 battle, the NCRLC could have won the war, in the assessment of the Ave Maria editors.

> Even the victorious side concedes that it cannot successfully face another such battle. During the floor debate spokesman after spokesman flatly stated that this was the last time he would vote for an extension of the bracero program.
>
> If these pledges are honored, and if the Conference's extensive efforts are continued--as they will be--the chances are that what the Washington Post called a "perpetuation of peonage" next year will be finally ended.

During this and other legislative battles, the NCRLC, the Bishops' Committee for the Spanish-Speaking and the Bishops' Committee for the Migrant Workers were also ministering directly to

8

the migrants themselves.[13] Since mid-1959 there were projects established in San Antonio, Stockton and several small cities in the North Central States for vocational training, social work and health care.

One such program was in the diocese of Madison, Wisconsin.[14] Touched and worried by the many needs of migrant and year-round farm-workers, Jerome Hastrich, the Auxiliary Bishop of Madison, initiated a ways and means committee. The Dominican Sisters from Madison took charge of an educational program, with the assistance of volunteers from Madison's Edgewood High School. The Franciscan Sisters took care of the transportation and social work. Dr. Celso Villanicenzio, a member of the staff of Divine Savior Hospital, attended to the migrant's health needs. The Salvatorian Sisters, who operated the hospital, and the Sisters of St. Mary from Madison gave professional nursing care at the weekly free clinic and where necessary at the camps.

The clinic, la Clinica en Endeavor, was a small trailer in a lot across from Our Lady of Guadalupe church in Endeavor, Wisconsin. Those who came were given a complete medical checkup, a blood test, vitamin or iron capsules, and any necessary medication--mostly from samples donated by local doctors. The hospital also established a family-centered maternity service for all the parents. An information file was kept on each clinic patient. However, Vallanicenzio realized that the clinic still needed very badly dentists and lawyers, electricians and plumbers, who could give time and service to people who could not pay the fees usually demanded. In some places the farm workers had to borrow from the growers to pay such fees. Such workers had to work-off the debt by returning the next year and probably the next. The circle of poverty had formed around them.

Realizing that such health and social services were most often short-range and stop-gap measures, Dr. Villanicenzio said,

> You have to educate them first, from mother
> to children, before things will get better.
> Then will come the reward of education: com-
> munication between two different people.

One of the sisters remarked,

> We are here to help the people spiritually,
> and if we can, materially. If we interfere in
> wages and housing, all our work here will be
> stopped. The growers say, "Why do you come
> around and make them dissatisifed? We hired
> them for a job. We made no other promises.
> Their work hours are their own business."

In spite of its help, the migrant program recalled John Steinbeck's words in the Grapes of Wrath about migrants of more than twenty-five years earlier.

> I gotta see them folks that's gone out on the road. They gonna need help no preachin' can give 'em. Hope of heaven when their lives ain't lived? Holy Spirit when their own spirit is downcast and sad? They gonna need help. They got to live before they can afford to die.

One of the foreman in Marquette County, Wisconson, remarked, "I was wondering how long it would be before the Church would do something to help these people." The Salvatorian Sisters knew it was a quarter century overdue but the Clinic en Endeavor was a start.

1964

In late 1963, Public Law 78 was defeated but a new legislative battle loomed with religious groups on one side and growers on the other.[15] The "bracero program" was defeated in Congress in late 1963 and was to end on December 31, 1964. However, at a November 17, 1964 Labor Department conference, Vizzard charged that the Labor Department scheduled a series of hearings on the plans underway to substitute another U.S. law to authorize importation of Mexicans. Vizzard continued,

> It is now becoming apparent that the growers are determined to continue to demand and get the equivalent of a slave-labor force. . .

> When we succeeded in killing the "bracero program" we thought that at last American farm employers would be forced to join the 20th century economy.

> We thought that finally they would have to offer American standards of wages and working conditions in order to get an adequate and dependable American work force. But it is now becoming apparent that the growers are determined to continue to demand and get the equivalent of a slave-labor force.

Vizzard felt that defeat of the law to extend the importation program beyond 1964,

> . . . seemed to be one of our most important
> victories, but is threatening to turn to
> ashes in our mouths.

Nevertheless, the Catholic, Jewish and Protestant groups, as well as other groups like the National Council on Agricultural Life and Labor, continued protests about the efforts to reintroduce imported Mexican farm workers.

In early December 1964, the Department of Labor hearings actually got underway to nullify the impact of Congress' decision to kill Public Law 78.[16] The strategy called for the use of provisions of the Immigration and Naturalization Act (INA)--which allowed the temporary importation of foreign workers to supply for a shortage of domestic labor--as a substitute for Public Law 78. Hence, the departmental hearings focused on "Criteria for clearance orders for aliens performing temporary service of labor." Speaking for NCRLC Vizzard said the hearings were being held in an "Alice in Wonderland" setting. While President Johnson was telling the nation that "unemployment was far too high," the hearings were saying there was "overemployment and a shortage of workers." A member of the National Council of Churches' Department of Migrant Work, Samuel A. Snyder, thought it inconsistent that a federal agency (Labor) should be working to legalize the entry of foreign workers when other agencies (HEW, OEO, etc.) were spending millions to relieve the poverty of American migrant workers.

During the course of the hearings to substitute "H-2 laborers" for braceros, through H-2 section of the 1952 U.S. immigration act, many voices were heard.[17] One of these voices was Rev. Donald McDonnell, a priest at Our Lady of Guadalupe Mission in San Jose, who claimed the substitute would be "a labor-camp system degrading the identity and life of a man." To McDonnell it was nonsense to say that Americans would not do field work. When asked why the migrants came to the U.S., McDonnell replied,

> The lure of the American buck. . . But he and
> others like him, about 40 percent, never
> return to their homes. . . This has caused a
> fearful number of broken homes in Mexico,
> something the Mexican bishops have long pro-
> tested.

McDonnell quoted from Pope Leo XIII's <u>Rerum Novarum</u>,

> Rich men and masters should remember this--
> that to exercise pressure for the sake of
> gain, upon the indigent and destitute, and to

11

make one's profit out of the need of another, is condemned by all laws, human and divine.

Quite aware of the violent opposition of the farm lobby in Washington to any legislative attempts at extending to the domestic farm workers minimum wages, unemployment insurance, meaningful social security and the right to engage in free collective bargaining, O'Donnell thought the migrants' efforts to form a good union would come to naught. Even strikes have come to nothing, said O'Donnell, ". . . because braceros were brought in to help break them in California--and men have been killed by deputy sheriffs in the process."

Another voice heard was Alice Ogle, a frequent writer on farm problems. "American workers have done and will go on doing hard unpleasant work in any industry where they are ale to earn a decent wage." She cited the experience in one of the hottest places in California, the Central Valley, where U.S. road crews tarred and gravelled highways for $2.25 an hour and stood hip-deep in slime repairing sewers for $2.75 an hour in 1964. Wages far-exceeding those of migrant workers, judged the wave of press releases by California growers' associations and their public relations firms for the renewals of Public Law 78 to be based on the fears that the crops would not be harvested and that the cost of food would be increased. She repeated the oft-quoted Secretary of Labor in the Eisenhower administration, James P. Mitchell, "In this land, we do not choose to keep down our bills, including our food bills, at the cost of underpaying and over-working human beings."

NCRLC's Vizzard, echoed Mitchell's and Ogle's sentiments,

> There can be neither moral nor economic justification for spending taxpayers' money for the antithesis of family farming, i.e. corporation or factory farming--one of the developments accelerated by the agricultural revolution.

One month later, at a National Conference on Povery in the Southwest, Archbishop Robert Lucey of San Antonio referred to Public Law 78 passing to its well-deserved oblivion.[18] Lucey remarked that the powerful growers' association did not take defeat gracefully. He noted the irony in their appeal to Public Law 414, the Immigration and Naturalization Act. "In 1923, it was used by the Congress of the United States to stop the importation of foreign industrial workers and today the growers are determined to use it to import agricultural workers."

Similar sentiments were voiced by Rev. Ronald A. Burke, an assistant pastor at St. Mary's parish in Gilroy, California, and former moderator of the Young Christian Workers, a movement in the 1940s and 1950s to involve young workers in social issues, especially in the plants and factories where they labored.[19] Several years later Burke was a member of the San Francisco arch-diocesan Spanish Missions Band, a group of priests who served both native migrants and braceros, until the band was disbanded in 1961. In October 1963, Burke helped a Presbyterian minister found the Inter-Faith Migrant Committee (IMC) and served as its co-chairperson for a time. The committee, in cooperation with the Catholic Migrant Mission Program of which Burke was the director, had approximately 75 active members. They conducted a summer school for Spanish-speaking children of farm workers, provided health clinics and had shown films in Spanish on health and welfare subjects. In late 1964, the inter-faith group pre-sented a statement in opposition to any importation of foreign farm workers to U.S. Department of Labor hearings in San Francisco. In addition to accusing the government of aiding the large corporation farms by providing "a desparately docile and readily abundant foreign labor force," the Inter-Faith Migrant Committee said,

> Low wage scales and accompanying conditions of employment in farm labor are hurting not just the laborer but the independent farmer as well, especially the farmer with a consci-ence.

> We believe that eliminating cheap labor will help break the stranglehold of corporation monopoly control of California fruits and vegetables.

The date of the statement was December 4, 1964 and in it other salient points were raised.[20]

> [We oppose] . . . the clearance of aliens under any circumstances until positive steps have been taken to improve the economic opportunities of our own people, farm laborers and independent farmers as well.

> . . . we oppose any further discussion of criteria for importation of a foreign labor force, unless such criteria should include prior enactment of laws to protect the rights of our local labor force to do farm work in the dignified fashion that we observe with

13

pride in almost every other segment of the American economy.

In the opinion of the chairperson of the Inter-Faith Migrant Committee, Rev. Mr. Ernest R. Tufft, a Presbyterian minister, opposition to the committee's work could be marked from the time of its statement.

Tufft, for the IMC, requested Archbishop Joseph McGucken of San Francisco to appoint Burke to co-chair the committee. McGucken declined by letter, saying the work of the committee was in the "temporal order" and a member of the laity could best fill the post. In expressing disappointment with McGucken's decision, Tufft said,

> In matters like the work of the committee we need clergymen today to point the way and to help lower those barriers which separate the faiths in the eyes of the laymen.
>
> We regretted Father Dwyer's [Burke's pastor] decision to ask Father Burke to resign as co-chairman of the committee. Father Dwyer's leadership in the community in the past has been both liberal and progressive.

Also, in late 1964, collections had dropped off 20 percent for several weeks in Burke's parish in Gilroy. A group of Catholic growers, angry at Burke's advocacy for the farm workers, launched the Sunday collection boycott. The same growers asked for Burke's removal from their parish.

The pastor of Burke's parish in Gilroy, Rev. John T. Dwyer, also admitted that Sunday collections dropped at St. Mary's during the Burke-growers controversy. Dwyer also admitted that he had directed Burke not to accept another term as co-chairperson of the Inter-Faith Migrant Committee upon expiration of his term in November 1964.[21] Dwyer explained again,

> Father Burke's term of office expired at the very time this dispute arose. I suggested that he not seek reappointment because I felt this was an area where a layman's participation was better particularly in view of the Vatican Council's statement on the role of the laity. Archbishop McGucken backed me up in my belief that a layman can do a better job.

A response to Dwyer's statement came in an editorial of the Inter-Faith Migrant Committee's newsletter,

> In a recent letter Archbishop Joseph T. McGucken stated his opinion that the clergy, rather than take active leadership in such work as is being done by the IMC, should offer moral guidance to the laymen. Those who are a part of the IMC feel that this is exactly what the participating clergy have been doing throughout the past year. Apparently this is also the view of the Catholic Interracial Council of Santa Clara County.

Spokespeople for the archdiocese maintained that McGucken would not intervene in the operation of a local parish and that the church's opposition to Proposition 14 in the November 1964 elections may have contributed also, to the drop in collections at St. Mary's.

Another reaction was heard from John W. Scherrer, executive of Pieters-Wheeler, a national seed company, and the alleged initiator of the economic boycott of his own parish. Scherrer denied starting the boycott and removal campaign. In a January 13, 1965 interview with the _Sacramento Bee_, Scherrer said he opposed any collection-plate pressure on the church. However, he admitted that he was one of the St. Mary's parishioners,

> . . . who expressed an opinion that they (the IMC) were entering into a field in which they are not too aware of the problems.

1965

By early May, 1965, the Burke-grower controversy was put back in the news by a challenge of John W. Scherrer, the alleged initiator of the collection boycott of Burke's parish.[22] Scherrer denied ever being interviewed by the _Sacramento Bee_, but admitted being interviewed by the United Press International; ". . . this perhaps was the source of information for the article of February 10" [NCR, A.V. Krebs]. Scherrer denied ever initiating or encouraging the collection boycott and demanding that Dwyer remove Burke from the IMC. In fact, Scherrer was not "even aware" of the existence of the "economic boycott group." However, Scherrer did admit writing to Dwyer on November 16, 1964 in protest of the IMC.'s activities. Scherrer acknowledged a welcome for the IMC.'s assistance in improving the working and living conditions of the migrant farm worker and his duty to express his opposition to the IMC.'s encroaching "on other grounds" by

15

its opposition to any further extension of Public Law 78 and continuance of Provision H-2 of Public Law 414 (Immigration and Naturalization Act). Of his letter, Scherrer said,

> I stated then, and am still of the opinion, that our parish (or any other) should not participate in or support any program designed to prohibit the use of foreign agricultural workers. I am of the opinion that clergy and laymen who have never been farmers, lived on a farm or invested in any way in agricultural crops, are not at all aware of the vast scope of problems connected therewith and therefore should not engage in this field of criticism.

Scherrer, also, levelled some charges against Burke and explained his own reaction to that behavior of Burke. Burke was charged with accusing the farmers from the pulpit of unchristian behavior, agitating workers on the farm and causing much unfavorable publicity for local and other areas. Scherrer admitted informing the pastor (Fr. Dwyer) that Scherrer did not care to support a church whose clergy were opposing the extension of provision H-2 of Public Law 414. Yet, Scherrer felt he was fulfilling his duty and desire, as a Catholic, to support his parish by contributing directly to the Sisters of the Presentation, who taught at the parish school.

Scherrer concluded by stating that the only solution could be one beneficial to both the growers and the farm laborers. He gave his reasons and issued a challenge to Burke and similar advocates. The farmer has seen. . .

> his cost of production steadily rise at a staggering rate, yet the price he receives for his product has not begun to increase in proportion--two factors over which he has no control. . .

> [The] same people who are attacking the farmer should first suggest a practical program whereby he may receive more for his product--thus enabling him, in turn, to absorb the increased cost of production entailed by raising the standard of labor.

In early June 1965, Burke broke his long silence and was happy that Scherrer's May 5, 1965 letter might be the beginnings of a dialogue--"unhappily absent in these parts at the present."[23] While Burke agreed that Scherrer and the IMC had in common agreement "that the farmer has problems," Burke had several complaints to air about Scherrer's views and charges. First, Scherrer should have taken the trouble to learn, from other than hearsay sources, that the IMF testimony at the San Francisco Department of Labor hearings, December 4, 1964, asserted that the bracero program should be eliminated in the interests of family farming, as well as domestic labor.

Second, of Scherrer's allegation that Burke "entered our farms, agitating and causing unrest among the workers," Burke asked, if agitation meant delivering baptism records, instructing children in catechism, holding devotional services, offering the Eucharist or talking with workers about their problems. He asked Scherrer if the farm workers had no rights to receive visitors, if priests needed the landlord's permission before "trespassing" when serving with the Catholic Migrant Mission Program, and if priests should refrain from talking about peoples' problems. Burke continued to pose questions about Scherrer's possible meaning of agitating and causing unrest among the workers.

> Maybe it was because we did say something about the Church's teaching on a living wage? Would Mr. Scherrer prefer that his priests be silent about the Church's teaching on these matters? Would he prefer that we say nothing about the Church's teaching that all laborers should form labor unions? Maybe he would like to see American agriculture use the Latin American patron system--where the laborer does nothing for himself, and the benevolent patron takes full responsibility for all the laborer's needs, body and soul? Or maybe this is the system we already have?

Third, of Scherrer's allegation that Burke "in speaking from the pulpit, accused the farmers of being un-Christian," Burke asserted that the celebrant of that Eucharist, Archbishop McGucken, apparently took no exception to the homily. Burke paraphrased the message. A whole litany of good deeds and financial donations cannot undo a person's neglect to reflect the spirit of the gospels and the social teaching of the church in one's business dealings. Such a person may be in good conscience and without personal guilt, but objectively, at least, is un-Christian. Burke did not want to condemn anyone. He wanted to form Christian apostles to trouble spots in the temporal order. If anyone is at fault for the general ignorance of Catholic social teaching, it must be the priests who fail to preach it. So,

17

> . . . if Catholic farmers or Catholic busi-
> nessmen remain indistinguishable from their
> non-Christian neighbors in their business
> philosophy and practice, the answer, it would
> seem to me, is _more_ preaching on this from
> the pulpit, not less.

Fourth, of Scherrer's allegation that in its opposition to "any further extension of Public Law 414" the IMC was encroaching on other grounds besides health, education and housing, Burke retorted,

> We merely endorsed a very carefully worded
> Council of Churches position paper. That
> position happens to be identical with even
> more strongly worded stands taken by Catholic
> agencies throughout the United States, a
> position by the way, which many well-
> informed, competent and Christian farmers
> from many parts of the country helped put
> together.

He quoted the 1956 policy statement of the NCRLC that condemened all legislation or agreements with other nations that arranged for temporary admission of alien agricultural workers, except in cases of absolute and objectively proven necessity.

Finally, to Scherrer's claim of interest in helping the family farmer, Burke pointed out that Scherrer was a retailer of supplies to farmers, not a family farmer. Burke insisted that the church is committed to family farming but U.S. agribusiness is not. In addition to suggestions that Scherrer read Part 3, on agriculture, in _Mater et Magistra_, Burke underlined that the state colleges in California stressed that family farming was a thing of the past and that corporate farming was the only efficient way to farm. He explained that the "efficiency" was due to the cheap, docile and unlimited labor pool of a government-subsidized bracero program. He pointed to an example in Salinas that very week, when the only strawberry grower unable to recruit workers was Salinas Strawberries Incorporated. He pointed out the dependency on the bracero program of the business patterns of such corporate farming. The assistant pastor concluded his response to his parishioner by saying that in an agricultural community and in the interests of family farming, the reference to the U.S. church's condemnation of the bracero program for 15 years was quite appropriate for the pulpit. Scherrer was described as a kind man who had the talent, mandate and grace to help the family farm greatly.

Approximately three weeks after Burke's clarification of his behavior and purposes, the Catholic Bishops' Committee on Migratory Labor and the Illinois Council of Churches Commission on Migrant Ministry declared the state of affairs "morally reprehensible."[24] Among the migrants' problems the statement listed: political disenfranchisement, haphazard and uncertain health care, educational deprivation for their children, and exclusion from the cultural advances of American society. To combat such exclusion and to bring the migrants within the pale of American society, the statement recommended legislation ". . . to assure human conditions of employment, education, health, housing and job training.

There was another account of exchanges between a priest and spokespeople for the growers over the condition of the migrant workers and the social teaching of the Catholic Church in early 1965.[25] The priest was Vizzard, of NCRLC He told of standing in the middle of the biggest strawberry farm in the world, with the manager of this 2,000 acre factory-in-the-field. The manager said to Vizzard, "Doesn't it break your heart to see these beautiful berries rotting in the field." Much to the consternation of the manager, Vizzard responded, "What breaks my heart, and has been breaking it for a long time, is to see people rotting in the field." He explained that, unfortunately, this manager was all too typical of a ". . . small group of U.S. farm employers who use migrant workers to harvest their crops" and whose concern is with profit and not with people.

The story followed Vizzard's overview of the tremendous efforts expanded to pass even relatively minor legislation benefitting the migrants. His accusation was harsh, Vizzard admitted, but it was not made with imputation of conscious evil in the growers. He acknowledged his personal acquaintance with some growers and even friendship with some. He knew them to be decent, moral and even pleasant men on matters, other than farm labor practices. He bluntly reminded the growers that their mentality differed very little "from the economic and social and moral outlook of the slave-owning proprietors of the pre-Civil War South." He found too many of the growers acting as if they ". . . have a right to use--or abuse--human beings without any consideration for decency, justice and human dignity."

After listing many of the usual responses of the growers when reminded of their responsibilities in the light of Catholic social teaching, Vizzard proceeded to counter-respond. First, to the bitter resentment and rejection of the charge of injustice, he appealed to all the ". . . responsible religious spokesmen, who are better judges of morality than the growers." The former reminded the latter of the denunciation of exploitation in the labor field by St. James' Epistle, chapter 5, verses 1-5.

19

Second, to growers' admonition that priests should confine themselves to the sanctuary and let the growers run the real world, the business world, as they see fit, Vizzard reminded the growers that the priest's vocation is also to individual and social morality. Not only is the business world subject to moral law, but the misery and poverty of the migrants recalls the words of Matthew's gospel of the final judgment scene about the least of the Father's people.

Third, to growers and others who claimed they did society a great and costly service by hiring "unemployables," Vizzard was quite frank,

> What kind of a job is it that is offered when possible earnings are often less than welfare payments? What kind of insulting libel is it to lump minors and social misfits under the term "unemployables" together with hundreds of thousands of citizens whose only handicap is their poverty? And since when can "unemployables" do jobs, as in fact they do, which the growers themselves describe as physically exhausting and demanding special skills?

Fourth, to growers who would claim that they could afford to offer better wages or working conditions, Vizzard had recourse to government reports which indicated that, in California alone, growers netted over one billion dollars in profits in 1964 on 3.5 billion dollars in sales. In light of such profits, the moral imperative for Vizzard was that if the growers cannot provide a job with U.S. wage standards and working conditions, then ". . . they have no right to be in business" in the U.S.

Fifth, the argument that growers could afford to pay more, if they could pass the increased labor costs to the consumer, was not allowed to stand. Vizzard scolded such spokespeople for trying to blame the housewives for the misery of the barceros. Even though the housewives look for bargains, they would be willing to pay more, if adequately informed about the plight of the migrants and the "troubles of the agricultural industry."

Sixth, when the assertion was made that decent housing was not available and could not be afforded for citizen farm workers, Vizzard retorted that the argument sounded like the son who murdered his parents and then pleaded for mercy because he was an orphan. As long as the growers thought they could depend on "the cheap and docile" migrant workers, the growers made no effort to develop family housing for the domestic workers, nor to take advantage of the several federal programs which could have helped the growers to do so.

Seventh and final, Vizzard attacked the cliche that U.S. domestic farm workers simply could not or would not do the "stoop or reach" labor. Many jobs in U.S. industry were as physically demanding as such farm labor accomplished by the migrants and "spurned" by the domestic farm laborers. Yet, elsewhere the wages and working conditions were such that domestic workers were attracted. Vizzard told people perpetuating such a canard to remember the 1964 resolution of the Sanat Clara County Council of Churches, which was endorsed also by the Inter-Faith Migrant Committee of the same area of California.

> If in any other industry, wages averaged 86 cents an hour, if there were no overtime, no sick leave, no unemployment insurance, no health or welfare or pension plans, weak child labor laws, no minimum wage, no worker representation, and the average worker was able to find employment only a little over a third of the year, it would not be surprising to find American citizens would prefer to work in other industries.

Beginning on June 1, 1965, two farm labor center tenants in Porterville, California, refused to pay rent in their tin, 12-by-18 foot shacks.[26] Some 179 families were on strike in the Linnel Farm Labor and Woodville Farm Centers against the decision of the Tulare County Housing Authority to boost rents in the southern San Joaquin Valley. The strike was conducted by the California Migrant Ministry, with the assistance of the American Friends Service Committee. A. V. Krebs, Jr., a frequent commentator on migrant farm conditions, supplied some facts. The buildings, constructed in 1938 as temporary emergency shelters by the federal government, had only screen doors. Minus plumbing and glass windows, the buildings were rented formerly for $18 a month. A family of four or more had to rent, for an additional $8, an extra cabin. The Housing Authority first tried to get $25 and $10 respectively, but lowered the rent to $22 and $8 respectively. Condemnation followed, after the housing and health officials cited more than fifty violations in both camps.

> At the rent strike's outset the Housing Authority stated that the hikes were necessary to pay for $82,000 in repairs made at the camps. However. . . the authority's surplus for fiscal 1965-66 before the

increase took place was expected to be
$18,166.

> It is estimated. . . that in the past 10-15
> year period the Housing Authority has accumu-
> lated over $115,000 in surpluses. Cesar
> Chavez director of the National Farm Workers'
> association, calculates that in the past six
> months the Housing Authority has taken in
> $6,000 to $10,000 from tenants who did not
> join the strike. Strikers' rent money has
> been placed in a trust fund.

1966

On November 1, 1965, a local court, in Vistula, dismissed
the charges brought against the centers by the housing authority.
In the Linnell camp case the court's judgment was that the housing authority had acted in bad faith in unilaterally breaking a
written lease and arbitrarily raising the rents. The judge
allowed the defense for the tenants to raise the issue of the
inequities of the camp. Another judge, in the same court, in a
separate action on October 26, 1965, regarding the Woodville
camp, instructed the tenants to pay the back rent. Their
attorney from San Francisco, James Herndon, seeking a re-trial in
light of the later Linnel Farm decision on November 1, 1965
remarked,

> Our position was that it was unthinkable for
> any public body, such as the Housing author-
> ity of Tulare county, to use the courts to
> collect rent from improverished farm workers
> on premises which they admitted were in
> violation of the criminal law.

1967

In Michigan, Bishop Alexander Zaleski of Saginaw, met 1,000
migrant workers on Easter Sunday morning, 1967, after 170-mile
march from Saginaw to Lansing.[27] Zaleski told the migrants he
came "to listen to what you have to say to the church in Michigan
and the state of Michigan." The migrants' march was to dramatize
their appeal to Governor Romney for a minimum wage, better housing and improved education for their children. He informed the
migrants that the Michigan Catholic Conference had asked Romney
to give serious attention to the migrant workers' problems.

Of migrants in Utah it was said that they faced "a baffling
and complicated set of circumstances" unequalled anywhere else.[28]

22

The statement was made by Paulist Father James Conway. In addition to working with California and Utah migrants several summers, Conway served in Washington, DC, NFWA office which sponsored a rally, march, and Eucharist on Easter Sunday, 1966, at the Washington Monument.

Conway explained how the followers of Brigham Young became dependent on cheap labor furnished by Mexicans from Texas, as competition increased from the corporation farms in the surrounding states. Without a government imposed minimum wage and with the steady increase of brankruptcies, the small farmers were afraid to pay better wages. Since the migrants never resided in Utah long enough to become eligible for State welfare and since Mormons took excellent care of their own members, they saw no reason to work with the community organizations concerned about migrants. The usual query was "Why don't their own churches take care of them?" Mexicans were not barred from the higher Melchizedek priesthood of the Mormon Church. Missions to the Spanish-Speaking and the Indians were always a strong tradition among the Mormons since their arrival in the land of promise. A handful of migrants had become Mormons and were supplied abundantly from the Mormon welfare warehouses. Many others were offered work for the whole winter and a chance to settle down--on the proviso that they become members of the Church of Jesus Christ of Latter-Day Saints.

Still largely mission-area, the Catholic Church in Utah did what it could for migrants by subsidizing parishes that sponsored programs for them. Some Mexican bishops had loaned a few priests for a type of worker-priest experiment. These priests travelled with the migrants in the summer from camp to camp and from state to state. In some areas of Utah, a Franciscan Mission Band with a portable trailer moved from camp to camp. Some Utah parishes had assigned to them priests for special summer work among the migrants. While the parish structure did not seem suited to the needs of the migrants at other times, parish families were helpful to some migrant families. In addition to parish families that found jobs and provided food and clothing during rough times there were parish families who were able to work with Mormons. Such not only aided the migrants but the cause of ecumenism in Utah.

Conway noted that less money had been granted under the migrant title (III-B) of the Equal Opportunities Act than under any other title. The migrants knew that the federal government had passed laws on their behalf. However, rarely did anything become visible beyond surveys and health inspectors.

Also in April 1967, Conway, who, in addition to working with and writing about migrants in Utah and California, worked with

Puerto Rican groups in New York, commented on the past and future efforts on behalf of the migrants.[29] About Catholic Church support in Wisconsin, Conway noted that clergy and nuns joined the march of the United Workers (Obreros Unidos) leading cucumber pickets eighty miles and four walking days from Wautoma to the state capitol at Madison. The workers persuaded Libby, McNeil & Libby, a large canning and processing company which employed 400 field workers, to guarantee a $1.25 an hour. The workers also were encouraged to elect farm worker leaders to represent them on the Wisconsin Governor's Commission on Migratory Labor.

With respect to the future assistance for migrants, Conway made several comments. Conway found the prospects for federal legislation on behalf of migrants rather bleak. Among other reasons, Conway noted developments during hearings in the Senate Subcommittee on Migratory Labor. While farmer and grower representatives were constant, competent and comprehensive, the church's efforts were late, limited and languishing. The success of the subcommittee was really a tribute to its membership.

Nevertheless, Conway thought that church groups might be the most active in 1968.

> We may expect to see professional social workers, hired by the churches, working as crew leaders. They will travel southward to Florida and Texas, recruit their crews and make all the contracts with the growers of the Northern states so that migrants may work their way up to the Eastern seaboard and Midwestern plains with full-time employment and adequate housing and working conditions for their crews.
>
> If a grower does not meet their standards, the crew leader will pull out and take his crew elsewhere. The crew leader will see that Social Security is withheld from the checks of his crew and he will see that adequate disability insurance is taken out for them as well.

Conway also expected northern churches to sponsor "Adopt a Migrant Family" program and families in northern parishes to help migrant families resettle in the north. Conway anticipated churches continuing their food and clothing programs, English classes in the evenings, occasional Spanish movies in the migrant camps and additional Sunday services in the language of the migrants. Conway saw the Migrant Ministry of the National

24

Council of Churches, in its fifth decade of existence, serving as a voice and umbrella organization for coordinating the church efforts to the migrants still so scattered and infrequent. He noted the October 1966 Chicago Conference sponsored by the Migrant Ministry. In addition to many government and religious participants were members of the Catholic Bishops' Committee for Migratory Labor. Finally, Conway commented,

> the real future of the migrants lies in the hands of the migrants themselves and the organizations they create to help themselves--no church, state, federal or civic effort can succeed without the grass roots support of the migrant people. Men like Cesar Chavez and Jesse Salas have had the loudest voices up to this point on behalf of their people. They will continue to be the spokesmen of the migrants in 1967.

Bill Rudd, public relations for the Brownsville diocese on the other hand, was full of praise for his ordinary.[30] Bishop Humberto Medeiros exerted major efforts in Brownsville concerning welfare reform, improved pay and working conditions, and opposition to discrimination. Since 1967, Medeiros also followed the more than 50,000 Mexican-American migrant workers who left the diocese each year to work their way through the fields of the midwest. Eventually Medeiros spent as much as three weeks visiting migrant camps in Michigan, Indiana, Iowa, Illinois, Ohio, Minnesota, Wisconsin, and North and South Dakota. In addition to celebrating the eucharist in the fields, according to Rudd, Medeiros

> . . . eats with them; he loves them; he shares everything with them. These people are part of his flock.

On one occasion Medeiros said of the migrants, "What these people want is not a dole, not a handout, but a chance to work." Medeiros' concern for prisoners was evident also by celebrating the eucharist and having dinner in the county jail. He claimed they were the people "who need me most." At Christmas time Medeiros always had open house at his home. Three mornings each week his office was open to anyone who cared to come. On the walls of that office were pictures of Our Lady of Guadalupe, a Black Madonna, and a Peanut's poster which said, "The man whose sickness is Jesus can never be cured." Medeiros travelled not only to and with his migrants but also to other places on the migrants' behalf. During an interview, he explained,

My people are poor and so the church is poor
here. We could not exist if it were not for
the help of the Extension Society and the
Board of Missions. Every year I go back to
New England and beg to Sunday masses for the
diocese. Usually Catholics there give $8,000
or $9,000.

1975

On February 1975, persons from 18 states gathered in San
Juan, Texas, for the first national meeting of workers in the
Mexican-American ministry.[31] The meeting was called by John J.
Fitzpatrick, the new bishop of the diocese of Brownsville, Texas.
Fitzpatrick, priests, religious and lay persons followed migrants
the previous summer. This practice was established by his
predecessor, Humberto S. Medeiros, who had become the cardinal-
archbishop of Boston. The 10,000 migrant workers began their
northward trek from the Rio Grande Valley to some 36 states.
Eighty percent went to 13 states such as California, Colorado,
Illinois, Indiana, Michigan, Minnesota, Nebraska, Ohio,
Oregon, Washington and Wisconsin. Upon completion of their
summer and autumn work the migrants returned to their modest permanent homes in the colonias (villages) or barrios (neighbor-
hoods) in the Brownsville diocese. Fitzpatrick and co-workers
returned from the migrant stream convinced of the need for more
widespread understanding and support of these Mexican-American
workers.

At the conference there was a call for a separate migrant
vicariate. The proposer, Rev. Virgil Elizondo, director of the
Mexican-American Cultural Center in San Antonio, saw the migrant
vicariate ". . . not as a division of the church, but as a
service of the church." He saw the vicariate, with its own
jurisdiction, solving the problems in the tremendous variation in
approaches to migrant pastoral care currently experienced from
diocese to diocese, from parish to parish. He saw a separate
migrant vicariate as able to do several things. As an
independent team it would be able to "plug priests in" wherever
needed throughout the country. It would be able to set up
training, maintain contact with dioceses dealing with migrants,
and "do some coordination." His aims were similar to those of
the first national meeting of pastoral workers among the Mexican-
American immigrants.

In early March, 1975, a more extensive report of that meeting appeared.[32] Some 120 persons were said to have participated
in the meeting, which like a PADRES' meeting earlier, was one
more manifestation of growing force within the U.S. church of the

26

Latino or Hispanic Americans familes. There were also more descriptions of church's ministry presented at the meeting.

In three counties--Hidalgo, Cameron, and Willacy--56.8 percent of the Mexican-American residents, compared to 18.8 percent of the Anglo residents, lived in poverty. The Brownsville diocese estimated 277,00 Catholics--most of them Latinos. Yet, serving these Catholics were some 30 diocesan priests, 80 religious priests, 168 religious sisters, and 34 religious brothers. That ratio of all priests to people in the Brownsville diocese was 1 to 2,500. The contrasts mentioned were 1 to 6,666 in a comparable diocese in Mexico, 1 to 1,100 in the archdiocese of Chicago, 1 to 860 in the archdiocese of Boston and 1 to 810 in the diocese of Rockford, Illinois. Pastoral workers in the Brownsville diocese viewed Latino Catholicism as a folk religion. The infrequent contact the people had historically with priests and religious had been largely liturgical--occasions of birth, baptism, first communion, confirmation, marriage, sickness and death. While the church workers admitted "Latinos love their priests and sisters," their concept of familia was so strong that a priestly or religious vocation signified a loss or separation the people were reluctant to endure. The NCR writer, deZutter elaborated,

> Sister Vicky heads the diocesan Confraternity of Christian Doctrine work in a unified Department of Education which includes Catholic schools. Sister Anne Finnerty is director of the department.
>
> Both sisters agree that another obstacle to vocations among Mexican-Americans is that the priesthood is not seen as "macho." Sister Vicky defines machismo as "what it takes to be a man: what's in it for his maleness."
>
> Apart from the obvious negative connotations of celibacy, the cassock is seen as effeminate, and devotion to Our Lady of Guadalupe encourages looking at the church as feminine.

Nevertheless, these and other people at the Mexican-American Ministry meeting sensed changes. Both sisters noted that attendance at CCD programs had risen from 1966-1974 from 11,000 to 32,000. The sisters attributed it to the rise of awareness among adults that ". . . there is more to it [faith] than just receiving the sacraments." Twenty parishes in the diocese, with 70 groups of 8 to 10 persons each, had adult education programs in Spanish, led by two or three catechists over a period of 10 weeks. The overall program was headed by Oblate Father Saturnino Lajo, a Spanish priest trained in adult catechesis in Spain. Lajo was reputed to be very sympatico, a basic requirement for successful dealings with the gente, the people. Simultaneously, the Cursillo movement with its emphasis on male leadership had been making inroads in terms of machismo. The director of the diocese of Brownsville communications, Allan Porter, described Brownsville more like a movement than a church. He emphasized the friendly, informal and cooperative atmosphere in the chancery and the operating principle of pastoral workers that the church was for the people and not vice versa. The attitude was especially prevalent in a program, Visitors for Christ, initiated by Medeiros when he was bishop of Brownsville from June 1966 to September 1970. The visitors--lay people of the parishes--visited homes to discover and to meet the spiritual, physical and financial needs of the Mexican-Americans.

Complementing the diocesan commitment, continued and expanded by Fitzpatrick, was the "caring style" of the day-to-day work at the local level. Several examples were cited. In San Juan, where the national meeting was held, there was a vibrant team in St. John's parish, counting some 1,200 families as its own. The team, Oblate Father Rene Garcia and Sacred Heart of Jesus Sister Eloisa Gonzalez, built its ministry from a foundation of personal contacts. Garcia remarked about the number of families not counted, due to the new arrivals from Mexico continually entering the migrant stream. After noting that 40 percent unemployment in Mexico drove people into migrant work, Garcia and Gonzalez pointed out that people left the migrant stream as well. Gonzalez estimated that 10 percent of the Mexican-Americans in this area ". . . move out of the migrant stream and settle down." She added that in the migrant economy a large family was an obvious asset in terms of getting ahead financially.

Another local complement to the Brownsville diocesan effort was the Shrine of Our Lady of San Juan. Its director, Oblate Father Eugene Canas, saw the shrine as an important reference point for the people. Their faith moved them to come to make petitions and to give thanks. Some even wrote letters when up north, as workers in the migrant stream or after settling out of it. Canas explained,

> We work to deepen devotion to the Blessed
> Mother by teaching about Christ, without whom
> she has no meaning.
>
> The people's idea of the church is not well
> organized, largely because of the historical
> scarcity of priests. Many of our people were

here before this was a part of the US in 1845. The first priests--Oblate Fathers-- came in 1848.

So, Canas, the sisters (Pastrano and Finnerty) and others engaged in the faith teaching or doctrina programs seized the "teachable moments"--the times and events drawing people to the church. Such would be the sacraments, fiestas and special devotion. Baptism, for example, was an opportunity to teach parents, children, and godparents with their families. For, in Mexican culture, the godparents become familia to the godchild, who is as welcome in their home as in the biological parents' home.

At that first national meeting of Mexican-American Ministry in addition to local and diocesan changes, regional and national changes were noted, especially in the image of the Catholic church. Formerly viewed with awe and at arm's length and historically often associated with social, economic and political oppressors, the church was seen more and more by Mexican-Americanas as "a church of the people." Perhaps, the single most important positive factor changing the Mexican-American's attitude toward the church on the national level was the church's support of Cesar Chavez and the farm workers' struggle to improve their working conditions.

1976

In August 1976, there were some further descriptions of the Catholic Church's ministry to migrant farm workers,[33] One was a description of Coalition of Churches for Migrant Concerns a (CCMC). It consisted of the Minnesota Council of Churches and the Minnesota Catholic Conference, as a joint commission. Executive director, Notre Dame Sister Suzanne Menshek, spoke of emphasizing "a pastoral ministry" rather than "a spiritual ministry." In fact, the team was often a referral agency for the migrants.

Another description was about the ministry of the North Dakota dioceses of Fargo and Crookston. The director of the Fargo diocesan program, Rev. Kenneth Gallagher, spoke of the original church role for migrants as active social ministry. In the early 1960's the church was the only agency aware of migrants in the area. In 1965 the dioceses of Fargo and Crookston, along with the Lutheran Church in the Red River Valley, established Migrants, Inc. For five years, with $750,000 from the federal government, the interfaith organization served the migrants many needs, until state and federal agencies took over many of the services. By the mid-1970's the church was the bridge to many agencies that did not even exist in the early 1960's.

Also a further description of the work among migrants by the Brownsville, Texas, diocise was given by that bishop's special representative to migrants, Rev. Ivan Rovira. He mentioned that there were nearly 10,000 migrant families in the Brownsville diocese, but that

> We estimate that double that number go north
> every year. The migrants are a part of our
> life here in Brownsville. For a long time we
> (the Church) have taken them for granted.
> Only recently have we begun to address our-
> selves to the farm workers.

He estimated, that in the process of healing and reconciliation, expressing concern and building, the church was 70 to 80 percent ineffective. The goal was to communicate a constant and clear message that the church visibly cares about people and effectively seeks justice. Such a focus was evident in many of the programs.

One such program, the Encuentro Conjugal or Marriage Encounter, was spoken of very highly by Francisco and Flora Cavellero, married for 23 years and migrants each year since 1968. Another program was following the migrants each spring. Four Missionary Daughters of the Pure Heart of Mary and four Missionary Sisters of Jesus, a predominantly Mexican-American community founded in the Brownsville diocese in 1972, were involved in following the migrants. One of the latter group, Sister Armida Raugel, worked during the year in Port Isabel--about 30 miles from Brownsville--with pastoral visitation, home teaching and social work among Mexican-Americans. In the spring and summer she did much the same in Minnesota, assisting with singing, home eucharists, blessing houses, and whatever else was needed.

During the summer of 1976 in Fargo, North Dakota, there was a migrant conference with the theme, "The Theology of the Land." Reactions to the conference varied. A Brownsville priest, Alfredo Garcia, who worked that summer with migrants in North Dakota and Wisconsin, did not like the conference topic. Another priest, Rev. Michael De Gerolami of the San Antonio archdiocese, told representatives of northern dioceses at the conference that in every parish none of the migrants should be strangers. There ought to be praying and visiting in the migrants homes, even in bad weather, as done down in Texas. Others at the conference were concerned over the apparent lack of unity among the migrants as to the order of priority for their needs--some wanted to be paid at the end of each week, others at the end of the season. One conference member cautioned about migrants demands "forcing the farmers into mechanization."

At about the same time as the Fargo conference, there was also a meeting of migrant organization leaders with sugar beet growers and sugar refinery leaders. All sides were concerned about "security," after an initial exploratory meeting to discuss wages and possible contracts. The employers wanted to be sure that they could rely on labor coming north. The migrants wanted assurance there would be jobs available at a decent wage.

1977

In April 1977, Msgr. Bryan O. Walsh, director of Catholic Charities for the Miami archdiocese laid out its record of ministry to farm workers.[34] First, Walsh spoke of the responsive leadership of the archbishop, Coleman F. Carroll, for many years. The policy of the archdiocese was described as

> . . . not one of paternalism, but of equal justice under the law. . . The church of Miami has always supported the dignity of each person and her main thrust has been to gain greater justice and equality under the law for these workers.

There was continued campaigning for workers' compensation, collective bargaining, and enforcement of existing federal and state legislation as well.

For example, during a 1971 Florida crop disaster, Archbishop Carroll presided at a eucharist for "God's assistance in opening the hearts of government officials at the farm workers' cry for justice." Afterwards the archbishop and a delegation of some 500 farm workers presented an appeal at President Nixon's Key Biscayne home. The result was an extension of unemployment insurance to farm workers--the first time in the history of Florida. Again, during a 1973 typhoid epidemic, Carroll drew national attention to the terrible working and living conditions of the farm workers. He appeared on television to decry the anti-union aspects of H.B. 74, which focused on frustrating collective bargaining in agriculture. He also supported a medical team to care for farm worker families and provided $100,000 in seed money and 232 acres of land for a Rural New Town Development, in the face of strong community opposition to agricultural workers. In December of 1975 the archdiocesan Rural Life Bureau took the initiative to organize a task force among the state, county and private agencies, as well as among concerned citizens, to formulate a plan of action for Dade County in the event of a farm worker crisis such as a freeze.

31

In 1976 the archdiocese requested the Florida Department of Community Affairs' Migrant Program in view of severe weather predictions to activate task forces throughout the state, in order to evaluate and adapt contingency plans. That year saw Florida's worst crop disaster. Throughout south Florida there were emergency meetings of local and state agencies. The coordinating representatives gathered in Delray Beach at Our Lady Queen of Peace Mission. The gathering's recommendation that the governor declare south Florida a disaster area was supported by the church. The call went out from Carroll for contributions of food clothing, blankets and money from the people of the archdiocese. By the end of January 1977 over 100,000 pounds of food and clothing was received and distributed by the church, as well as some $10,000 distributed for other needs. Walsh concluded with an explanation of why the archdiocese of Miami was not in favor of a national collection "aimed at Band-aid treatment." He said,

> Because the basic emergency needs of farm workers are being met on the local level, it is the judgment of the Archdiocese of Miami that it would be more beneficial for national efforts to be directed toward the promotion of equal treatment under the law for farm workers, and the reform of the whole agro-industrial system.

1979

In early September 1979, Robert Ellsberg, of the Dorothy Day's Catholic Worker movement, described the work of some migrant farmworkers on John's Island, South Carolina.[35] He spoke of John's Island as one of the better areas for migrants: new camps, food stamps, health and day care, legal assistance and other social services were available. A Migrant Division of the State Department of Labor closely monitored camp conditions. Both the community and local church were increasingly conscious of the presence and needs of the migrants.

Since the summer of 1978, the coordinator of the Charleston diocesan Migrant Ministry program was Oblate Sister Else Marie, who came originally from Cuba. She painted a most optimistic picture, although she was aware of some injustices as well. For her migrants were ". . . people of great dignity, the freest people in America. They come and go as they like, they don't owe a thing to anybody." She would never encourage anyone to leave the migrant stream. She thought that the work gave rise to a wonderful feeling of being close to God. Nevertheless, Else Marie, while wishing to burn down some of the migrant camps, focused on the limited success of raising the consciousness of the growers, ". . . in my own fashion." Migrants, she thought, did not need much money and were happy in their work. "If they get sick, they have a clinic. If they are hungry, they have food stamps." She had no doubt that Jesus was pleased with the migrants: living with a stable and strong faith in the mercy and providence of God. She attributed "the cooperation of the growers" and the making of improvements to the owners' awareness that the team did not come to agitate, expose or condemn.

Ellsberg found evidence of progress, especially in John Walpole's camp, which was built with the help of a federal loan and "could be mistaken for a suburban development." Ellsberg thought "Walpole" might represent the future, "but it is hardly typical of the present." Camps indicated as the type Sister Else Marie ". . . would like to burn" were the Fisk camp and another known even to the Health Department as the junkyard. The latter camp, unlike "Walpole," was inhabited by Black families rather than Hispanic families.

Franciscan Sister Maureen Smith, who had followed the migrant stream for ten years as part of the East Coast Migrant Health Project, pointed out some differences between the Hispanic and Black crews. The former travelled in tight family units, were well organized and acquainted with one another, and work with crew leaders who are trusted. The latter travelled as single individuals, included many winos or alcoholics, spend much free time drinking, and are exploited by the crew leaders by excessive room, board and other costs. Smith cited also a Norfolk, Virginia trial several years earlier of a crew leaders accused of "shanghaiing," virtually enslaving, beating and otherwise exploiting a crew of 40-60 men. Smith complained of such practices and violations of the Farm Labor Contractor Registration Act, by which all crew leaders were supposedly licensed.

In May 1979, she attended a meeting called by state and local authorities to inform the public about services available to migrants. She explained,

> I got up and began asking questions about housing, trying to find out who was responsible for inspecting these camps. I kept trying to tie them down. The Labor Department inspects the camps, but only at the grower's request, as a 'courtesy'. OSHA (the Occupational Safety and Health Administration) inspects the camps but only if a complaint is made. The Health Department only looks to inspect the water. In South

33

Carolina, the fact is there are no housing
regulations specifically for migrant housing.
Right now it is nobody's job to get out and
look at these camps. No one can say a camp
is violating the regulations because there
are no regulations.

Smith's commments about inadequate laws were confirmed by Charlie
Claxton of the Health Department, Bill Fields of Occupational,
Safety and Health Administration, and Charles Robinson of the
Migrant Division of Legal Services. They also noted the enormity
of the violations and paucity of staff.

[1]"On Migrant Labor," On All Horixons, _America_, v. 102, No.
6, 11/7/59, p. 147.

[2]Bernard Lyons, "Spotlight on Migrant Workers," Editorials,
Ave Maria, v. 91, No. 25, 12/19/59, p. 18.

[3]"Care of Migrant Workers," _Social Justice Review_, v. 52,
No. 9, 1/60, p. 309.

[4]"Rural Lifers on Unions," Current Comment, _America_, v.
102, No. 19, 2/13/60, pp. 571-572.

[5]"Men on the Land," Week by Week, _Commonweal_, v. 72, No. 2,
4/8/60, p. 30.

[6]"Aid to Migrant Workers," _Social Justice Review_, v. 53, No.
8, 12/60, p. 270.

[7]"Minimum Wage and Migrant Worker," _Social Justice Review_,
v. 53, No. 1, 1/61, p. 348.

[8]"Churches and Braceros," Editorials, _America_, v. 104, No.
25, 3/25/61, pp. 810-811.

[9]"New Hope for Migrants," Editorials, _Ave Maria_, v. 95, No.
22, 6/2/62, p. 16.

[10]"Help the Migrant--Now," Editorials, _Ave Maria_, v. 97, No.
6, 2/16/63, pp. 16-17.

[11]"End of Bracero Program," Editorials, _America_, v. 108 No.
25, 6/22/63, pp. 878-879.

[12]"Congress Plays Trick or Treat," Opinion, _Ave Maria_, v.
98, No. 21, 11/23/63, p. 14.

[13]"Projects to Aid Migrants," World Briefs, _Ave_ _Maria_, v. 98, No. 2, 7/13/63, p. 4.

[14]"Migrants, 'Why Do They come?,'" _National_ _Catholic_ _Reporter_, v. 1, No. 8, 12/16/64, p. 5.

[15]"Church Groups vs. Growers in Dispute on 'Braceros,'" _National_ _Catholic_ _Reporter_, v. 1, No. 3, 11/25/64, p. 1.

[16]"End Run on Braceros," Current Comment, _America_, v. 111, No. 25, 12/19-26/64, p. 79.

[17]Alice Ogle, "California Farm Labor," _America_, v. 111, No. 25, 12/19-26/64, pp. 799, 802.

[18]"Why Poverty? No Unions," _National_ _Catholic_ _Reporter_, v. 1, No. 13, 1/27/65, p. 1.

[19]"Growers Reduce Parish Giving to Punish Priest," _National_ _Catholic_ _Reporter_, v. 1, No. 9, 12/23/64, p. 3.

[20]A.V. Krebs, Jr., "S.F. Archbishop Declines Interfaith Group Request," _National_ _Catholic_ _Reporter_, v. 1, No. 10, 1/6/65, p. 3.

[21]A.V. Krebs, Jr., "Priest's Work for Migrants Cited," _National_ _Catholic_ _Reporter_, v. 1, No. 15, 2/10/65, p. 10.

[22]"Record-Straighteners," Repartee, _National_ _Catholic_ _Reporter_, v. 1, No. 27, 5/5/65, p. 4.

[23]"Farmers and Braceros, The Record Straightened," Repartee, _National_ _Catholic_ _Reporter_, v. 1, No. 31, 6/2/65, p. 5.

[24]"Join in Statement on Migrant Workers," _National_ _Catholic_ _Reporter_, v. 1, No. 35, 6/30/65, p. 2.

[25]James L. Vizzard, S.J., "Our Badge of Infamy: Substitute for Slavery in the Fields," _National_ _Catholic_ _Reporter_, v. 1, No. 33, 6/16/65, p. 7.

[26]A.V. Krebs, Jr., "California Court Backs Tenants in Rent Strike," _National_ _Catholic_ _Reporter_, v. 2, No. 3, 11/10/65, pp. 1, 3.

[27]_National_ _Catholic_ _Reporter_, v. 3, No. 23, 4/5/67, p. 3.

[28]James F. Conway, C.S.P., "Migrants in the Promised Land," _America_, v. 115, No. 11, 9/10/66, pp. 253-255.

[29]James F. Conway, "Migrants: Directions '67," Catholic World, v. 205, 4/67, pp. 31-35.

[30]"'Bishop of Poor' Succeeds Cushing," National Catholic Reporter, v. 6, No. 40, 9/18/70, pp. 1, 16.

[31]Albert de Zutter, "Migrants' Vicariate Proposed," National Catholic Reporter, v. 11, No. 17, 2/21/75, pp. 1, 2.

[32]_____ "Migrant Stream Irrigates Church," National Catholic Reporter, v. 11, No. 19, 3/7/75, pp. 7, 8.

[33]Mick Kill, "Migrants: The Church's Changing Ministry," National Catholic Reporter, v. 12, No. 37, 8/13/76, pp. 9, 10.

[34]"Miami Church Supports Farm Workers," Repartee, National Catholic Reporter, v. 13, No. 25, 4/15/77, pp. 12-13.

[35]Robert Ellsberg, "Farm Labor: Is It 'Too Tired To Stoop', or...'Beautiful Work'?," National Catholic Reporter, v. 15, No. 39, 9/7/79, pp. 8, 9.

[25]"Southern   Workers--Mississippi   Strikers,"   National Catholic Reporter, v. 16, No. 31, 5/30/80, pp. 3, 4.

Periodically, throughout the 1960-1980 Catholic literature on the "migrant-bracero" farm workers, there were evidences of interest in the organization of farm workers in a labor union.[1] The name of Cesar Chavez sometimes is linked with the National Farm Workers' Association (NFWA). Rightly so, for, although Chavez was the founder of the United Farm Workers, so widely known today, NFWA was one of the not-so-well known early union organizing efforts among farm workers. Another such organizing effort referred to in the period from 1960-1980 was Agricultural Workers Organizing Committee (AWOC).

However, as early as 1933 suspected communists appeared as labor organizers in the southern San Joaquin Valley cotton fields. The Farmers Protective League was formed. Through cooperative advertising in local newspapers, citizens were urged by the league to "drive the communists from our midst." There was violence, strike organizers went to prison, and the governor of California even appointed a committee to study the farm labor situation. A member of the committee was Archbishop Edward Hannah of San Francisco. More disputes broke out in 1939 in the Madera County cotton fields. The union, then known as the Workers Alliance, was broken up by the growers, who were later accused of using strong-arm methods. The governor's committee then worked out a wage compromise. All the early union organization efforts were unsuccessful. The Agricultural Workers Organizing Committee (AWOC) began in 1960, under AFL-CIO control. While a few growers did sign contracts, the pattern was one of grower resistance and frequent violence. AWOC moved into the San Joaquin Valley with the announced intention of organizing all the farms of the area--and, ultimately all farms in the United States.

1962

When Pope John XXIII's _Mater et Magistra_ (Christianity and Social Progress) was issued in the summer of 1961, it was noted that the San Joaquin Valley's problems made it an apt example of what John XXIII called a "depressed" sector of society. Thus, the question in many minds was:

> Will the principles set forth by Pope John actually be put into practice, or will they merely be given lip service?

In 1962, it looked to some observers as if lip service would be the only impact of the encyclical. There was a strike which brought the threat of violence between the growers, domestic laborers and braceros. The growers and union representatives threatened a continuing "life or death" struggle over the union-ization of farm workers. Many of the largest and most influential growers were practising Catholics. Many of the farm workers, especially those of Mexican descent, were Catholics. Students in the Catholic high schools of the diocese of Monterey-Fresno, which included most of central California, were being taught and were discussing the principles of Mater et Magistra. The encyclical was included in sociology courses at the diocesan minor seminary. Parish organizations and discussion groups were considering John XXIII's social message. So, it was asked, why was there no swift and positive implementation of social justice in an area where the entire economy was agriculturally based?

Charles A. McCarthy, associate editor of the Monterey-Fresno diocesan newspaper, Central California Register, remarked that Catholic scholars pointed out that it took more than 25 years for the recommendations of Pope Pius XI's Quadragesimo Anno to be adopted in industrial relations. McCarthy claimed a Catholic sociologist familiar with the central California area believed one of the biggest obstacles to the application of Mater et Magistra in the agricultural situations was "fear of economic fear." The growers saw themselves as "businessmen" who annually ran the risk of crop failure or loss through market fluctuations. If they did not make a real profit, they would not survive in a competitive economy. Until the unions came, the growers could "economize" through reducing labor costs and the workers saw the growers as "too big to fight." McCarthy quoted the annonymous sociologist:

> The growers aren't Simon Legrees. But most
> are not taking long-range means to help them-
> selves and their workers. And thus far the
> human workers don't have the bargaining
> strength that the kilowatts do.

When the union moved in, the growers decided to work together in organizations to improve their own positions. Although such a type of organization was mentioned in the papal encyclical, the letter did not intend organizations against unionization of farm workers. Labor organizers referred to "pig-headed farmers" and "barons of the land." Growers charged that the unionization movement was an attack on the American princi-ples of "free enterprise and freedom of opportunity" and claimed that the movement was supported by "misinformed do-gooders." The unions charged that braceros were being imported as strike-breakers and "scabs" to fill a nonexistent shortage of domestic labor. The average farmer claimed he was not anti-union but merely struggling to keep from going under economically. The small and medium-acreage farmers, some of whom owned family farms or family farm corporations, feared the production capacity and power of the larger farmers.

One small grower characterized the big farmer as "anyone who owns one acre more than I do." A leader of the union complained, "If a grower's dog gets sick, the growers care for him; but if a worker gets sick, they just kick him out." An AWOC organizer of Mexican descent, a mother of 12 children, claimed she watched her 19-year old son go blind in 1958 from malnutrition. She pleaded, "We are just asking for justice. I guess we got the right because we are human beings as everybody."

McCarthy concluded his article:

> Growers are among the leading and most respected citizens in their communities and in Catholic groups. Many live in spacious homes with swimming pools. They and their wives and older children can be seen driving expensive late-model cars on their way to the golf course or the country club....
>
> This is the picture in the nation's richest agricultural area some 30 years after the novel Grapes of Wrath pointed up the problem of the farm workers and one year after Pope John XXIII pointed out Catholic social principles and outlined their application to "depressed" agriculture.
>
> The growers see their very existence threatened by a cost-price squeeze. The farm laborers are struggling to attain a security they have never known. And neither side intends to quit.

1965

Rev. Victor Salandini, 34-year old priest of the diocese of San Diego and pastor of a parish in El Centro, California encouraged his Mexican parishioners in a 1965 strike in the lettuce fields.[2] He claimed that he was "silenced by the diocese, which felt that Church intervention at that time was not prudent." Salandini had helped organize workers for AWOC and allowed the AFL-CIO affiliates to hold meetings in his parish hall, Our Lady of Mount Carmel. When AWOC struck five tomato farms in the San Ysidro area, Salandini was transferred. While he explained the transfer as "pressure by influential growers", Bishop Francis J. Furey denied that grower pressure was responsible. He explained to the Los Angeles Times:

> It has been Father Salandini's own wishes that he attend San Diego State College this summer to prepare for studies next fall for his Ph.D. degree in economics at Catholic university in Washington, D.C.

Salandini acknowledged that he had wanted to attend summer school, but had hoped also to work part time in his parish.

In late 1965, Salandini told additional aspects of his experiences in an article in America.[3] He explained that after more than six years of organizing with AFL-CIO, AWOC had a membership of only a few thousand out of a total work-force that varied from 500,000 to 750,000 throughout California--the state using the largest number of seasonal agricultural labor. He judged AWOC's campaign in the Great Central Valley a failure. For, not a single major contract was negotiated there. However, AWOC had jolted many of the growers out of their complacency. The rate suddenly jumped from 70 cents to 80 cents.

In the Spring of 1965, when the AWOC organizing drive began in the Imperial Valley, Salandini discovered that the social doctrines of the church were no closer to acceptance than they were in 1891. He explained that when Al Green, the AWOC director, solicited help in organizing, the Mount Carmel parish hall in San Ysidro was put at Green's disposal for organizing meetings. Salandini himself addressed the workers about the church's social teaching several times. He explained his desire to do something about "...the impression that persisted in many of the workers minds that the Church was on the side of 'big money'."

Shortly afterwards, the growers complained to the chancery office of the San Diego diocese. Yet, Salandini left the parish hall at Green's disposal, until AWOC was able to set up its own headquarters elsewhere in the neighborhood. When Salandini preached sermons on the dignity of labor, the obligation to pay a living wage and the right to unionize for collective bargaining, the message was considered "subversive" by the big growers and their allies. To his face, Salandini was told by some of the growers that his teaching was "socialistic." Many of the latter prided themselves for their generosity to the church. Yet, Salandini persisted, despite the many questions about the worth-whileness or futility of the farm worker organizing:

> The AWOC has served--and will continue to serve--as a catalyst... Its continuing presence on the scene is an investment in human dignity that will pay rich dividends.

On September 8, 1965, nearly 3,000 workers on 36 ranches took part in the largest farm labor walkout in California since 1938.[4] The strike was called by AWOC affiliated with AFL-CIO and the other union, the National Farm Workers Association (NFWA), headed by Cesar Chavez, the farm worker trained in community organization by Saul Alinsky of Chicago's Industrial Areas Foundation. The issues were the right to collective bargaining and an increase in hourly wages.

On October 19, 1965, some 44 pickets, many of them ministers from the Northern and Southern California Council of Churches, were arrested for shouting at grape pickers, "Huelga! Huelga!" (Spanish for "Strike"). The picketing was declared "unlawful assembly" by Sergeant Gerald Dodd of the Kern County sheriff's office. He explained that the chanting was "disturbing people who were trying to make a living" in the vineyards of the W.B. Camp Jr. ranch. Rev. James Drake of the Migrant Ministry, which had been working with NFWA during the strike, charged the sheriff's department with knuckling under pressure from struck growers. He alleged that after being allowed to speak while picketing they were suddenly silenced. A democratic assemblyman, Philip Soto from la Puente, demanded that the California Attorney General, Thomas C. Lynch, investigate the sheriff department's handling of the strike situation and end what Soto termed as action which "smacks of southern justice." Fourteen of the pickets posted their own bail. The other 30 were bailed out by the American Civil Liberties Union. Hearings were scheduled for November 9, 1965.

A NFWA picket captain interpreted the arrests as follows:

> To date the growers have been placing the workers in the middle of their fields in an effort to keep them away from the pickets. As they are now almost a month behind in their harvest, growers realize that the grapes on the periphery of their property must be harvested. In their desperation they

41

are therefore seeking help from local law enforcement agencies to remove pickets from the scene.

Cesar Chavez, the NFWA director, noted that, because of the increasing number of arrests, mainly on charges of "disturbing the peace", NFWA and AWOC funds were low and that additional financial support was being sought with great urgency.

On October 21, 1965, the Central California Register, official newspaper of the diocese of Monterey-Fresno ran a front-page editorial, "Our Catholic Church Is Involved". The editors refused to take sides, but outlined employers' duties to workers and workers' duties to employers. The editors continued:

> The situation in Delano had to come... The ingredients for a change in the agricultural workers' plight have been brewing for many years. A long look at the labor problem in the vast industry of agriculture is overdue ... [The church] tries to create an atmosphere of justice and charity in which both sides can discuss their problems.

On October 27, 1965, a Cessna 180 private plane was flown by Rev. Keith Kenny, who was accompanied by a fellow priest of the Sacramento diocese, Rev. Arnold Meagher, and Cesar Chavez. Using a bullhorn on a camera mount, the three made a dramatic airborne appeal to grape pickers to join the seven-week strike of farm workers against local growers. For more than 90 minutes, the three flew over the southern Kern County vineyards, calling in Spanish to the pickets. "Join with us. This is a fight for everybody: for you and for us. Leave your work and fight for social justice."

Kenny explained that he read the account of the strike in the October 20th issue of the National Catholic Reporter. Upon reading that no local clergy were involved, he and Reverend Eugene Lucas drove to Delano. When they arrived a local priest advised them not to get mixed-up in the strike. They did become involved by walking on two picket lines, singing "Maria mia Madre" and other Spanish hymns, and being responsible for 24 pickers leaving the fields. These efforts were followed by the airplane flight. Upon landing the two priests and Chavez were met by a Kern County deputy sheriff and two growers. One grower, Jack Pandoli, said to Chavez, "I see you had the Pope with you today." Although there were no arrests, a group of growers later returned and began taking photographs of the plane.

Within a week, the Federal Aviation Agency, in response to a complaint by growers, began an investigation of the airplane flight of Kenny, Maegher and Chavez.[5] Kenny denied that any violations of FAA standards for altitude, airspeed or manuvering were committed. In a detailed letter to FAA, Kenny produced two witnesses to safe altitude, two more to pre-flight planning, one to the maintenance of the aircraft, four to his reputation as a pilot, five character witnesses (including two state senators), and a witness who Kenny said had a tape recording of "threats made against me by persons instigating this complaint." At the same time, Bishop Aloysius J. Willinger of Monterey-Fresno wrote to the Sacramento chancery officials asking that Sacramento priests not make any further flights over the area. A spokesperson for the Sacramento chancery said it honored the neighboring bishop's request by asking Kenny not to interfere "dramatically" in the strike.

The following week a letter of praise for Fr. Keith Kenny's and Fr. Arnold Meagher's dramatic support of the Central Valley striking grape strikers came from Fr. Victor Salandini, relocated to Washington, DC, at Catholic University's economics department.[6] Salandini had been asked by Chavez to serve as the NFWA's legislative representative and general liaison in the nation's capital. Salandini mentioned his gratification in the decision of the Immigration Service to increase the border patrol in the Delano area and to curb the strike-breakers' flowing across the border from Mexico. He was gratified, also, to learn that some of the success was due to his meetings with members of Congress, the Labor Department, the AFL-CIO, and Immigration Service.

Salandini also explained two days of conversation (September 12 and 13) with Chavez, along with a Brother Gilbert, F.S.C., who had been active in Delano. Among the topics discussed was the relationship of the AFL-CIO affiliate AWOC to the new union in the area, Chavez' NFWA. Chavez had placed the NFWA somewhere between a strictly economically oriented union and a "movement." In addition to collective bargaining, NFWA was interested in the social problems of the field workers, to which a credit union and a cooperative could respond. Consequently, NFWA was filling a gap to which AWOC could not respond at the time, due to its more traditional union activity, such as organizing.

On November 10, 1965, Kenny was scheduled to speak to students at Sacramento State College about the 11-week-old Delano grape strike by the 2,000 NFWA and 200 AWOC members.[7] At the last moment he canceled his appearance. There were repeated reports that Kenny and Meagher had not only been ordered out of strike activities but silenced as well. Neither Kenny nor the

43

Sacramento chancery would comment. However, Msgr. James H. Culleton, chancellor of the Monterey-Fresno diocese, confirmed some parts of the reports and said:

> We don't want outside clergy making trouble in the area. The diocese is doing what it can to bring the dispute to a just and peaceful solution.

Nevertheless, nearly a half-dozen Catholic schools in the San Francisco Bay area sent food, clothing and money to the Delano strikers. In San Francisco, Mary Anna Colwell, president of the Catholic Interracial Council, announced that members of the group had pledged $100 a month to the NFWA for the duration of the strike.

In early December 1965, the work of Kenny and other religious leaders was highlighted by Alice Ogle in an America article, entitled "Revolution in the vineyards.[8] After explaining that in expanding NFWA Chavez noticed little persecution from authorities, Ogle quoted Chavez:

> Maybe it's because members of CORE and... [SNCC] take part in the strike. I heard a police officer say: "We don't want another Selma here!"

Ogle also quoted Rev. Francis Geddes of the Religious Research Foundation in San Francisco, "But among the claims and counter-claims that swirl around this issue, the Church should not remain silent." Also, quoted was Rev. Wayne C. Hartmire, Jr., director of the California Migrant Ministry:

> Churchmen should lead the way in approaching the underlying social economic and political issues. A good beginning is to understand and give support to basic attempts to organize... We live well at the expense of these field workers and their families. Low food prices benefit all of us, but only the workers sacrifice dignity to keep these prices low.

Kenny picked up the same theme in response to growers and a deputy sheriff. He was helping because:

> ... human dignity is involved. This strike is a movement by the poor people themselves

44

to improve their position. And where the
poor are, Christ should be--and is.

A spokesperson for the California Federation of Labor described
the priests' action as one reflecting the "... continuing support
that is being generated among religious, civic and labor groups."
Finally, Ogle noted that during an interfaith meeting on November
1, 1965 at the Glide Methodist Church in San Francisco, half the
assembly were Catholic priests, nuns and lay people, many of whom
came to the meeting from agricultural areas.

On December 14, 1965, a dozen Catholic, Protestant and
Jewish leaders, forming a Committee of Religious Concern, visited
Delano to examine the farmworkers' strike, as well as the conditions that led to it.[9]   In fact, growers failed to attend a
luncheon planned by the dozen religious leaders.[10]   Cameron P.
Hall, director of the Commission on Church and Economic Life of
the National Council of Churches, surveyed the empty Delano Elks
hall and said, "This is the first time I have ever flown 3,000
miles to a luncheon and have the hosts not show up." When the
clergy concluded their luncheon a handwritten message was
received from Joseph G. Brosmer, executive secretary of the
grower-operated agency, the Agricultural Labor Bureau. The
message read:

> You have misunderstood lunch arrangements.
> Wayne C. Hartmire (director of the California
> Migrant Ministry) asked us to find a place
> for you to eat and to invite local community
> and religious leaders. No indication was
> made that you wanted to discuss local labor
> problems with us at lunch... We are still
> hopeful that you will agree to meet with us.

At 3 p.m. the committee's statement was read to the press by
Dr. Robert McAfee Brown, professor of religion at Stanford University. [cf. below]. At 4 p.m. the committee went to nearby
Slan Hall for a meeting with the growers. However, Brosmer,
speaking for some 35 growers, indicated that any attempts by the
two parties to engage in a discussion of the issues of the grape
strike would be useless in light of the statement of the committee. Although Brosmer called for the adjournment of the meeting, more than two dozen growers remained in the hall to engage
the individual members of the religious delegation on the issues
of farm labor in Delano. Brosmer called a press conference to
give the growers' views of the statement. Voicing objection to
the religious leaders' involvement in the strike, Brosmer said:

> ... there was no valid evidence that the dig-
> nity of the workers was being harmed. When
> one gets emotionally involved in a cause he
> is no longer able to be objective.

During the same visit, NCRLC's Vizzard read a strongly
worded statement meant for the Catholic Church. Asserting that
the workers had a right to expect support from the Catholic
Church, Vizzard continued:

> Very frankly, Church authorities often are
> frozen with fear that if they take a stand
> with the workers, the growers will punish
> them in the pocketbooks...
>
> When the wolf is in the fold, it's no help to
> the flock to assure them that, after all, the
> wolf needs to eat too...
>
> I think it would be more to the honor of the
> Church and infinitely more to the service of
> souls that churches, convents, rectories and
> even schools, including seminaries, should
> remain unbuilt or unfinished or even closed
> rather than that the Church should knuckle
> under to the threats of those who demand that
> the Church "keep its nose out of their bus-
> iness."

In late January 1966, an explanation of the luncheon mixup
and more details of the committee's 24-hour stay came to light.[11]
The group came at the invitation of Hartmire. It was headed by
Protestant Theologian, Robert McAfee Brown, and included such
Catholics as: Vizzard, director, NCRLC Washington, D.C. office;
Lester Hunt, executive assistant, U.S. Bishops' Committee for the
Spanish Speaking, Chicago; Msgr. William J. Quinn, U.S. Bishops'
Committee for the Spanish Speaking, Chicago; Rev. John A. Wagner,
Executive secretary, U.S. Bishops' Committee for the Spanish
Speaking, San Antonio, Texas.

After breakfast of the first full day the committee was
addressed by Cesar Chavez. He spoke of the organization's goals,
the workers' conditions, the growers, and the strike. He then
introduced two members of the Migrant Ministry who had been working for several months with the NFWA, Rev. James Drake and Rev.
David Heavens. The latter spoke about the initial reluctance but
later significantly positive response to the use of nonviolence
during the course of the bitter strike. He himself allegedly had

been dragged from an automobile by a local grower, Phil Patti, and assaulted physically. On October 17, 1965 Heavens had been arrested by the Tulare County Sheriffs Department for reading aloud to workers Jack London's classic definition of a strikebreaker:

> A two legged animal with a corkscrew soul, a
> waterlogged brain, a combination backbone of
> jelly and glue...a traitor to his God, his
> country, his wife, his family and his class.

The charges were dismissed later by a Bakersfield judge on the grounds that the minister's right to freedom of speech had been violated.

The committee next dialogued with Chavez. During this exchange of questions and answers between Chavez and the religious leaders, Hartmire, director of the California Migrant Ministry was called from the room to receive Brosmer's telephone message that the growers felt the luncheon was too informal for a meeting. The growers were willing to meet with the committee at 3 p.m., the time previously scheduled by the religious leaders for their press conference. Hartmire explained that he contacted Jack Pandol, a local grower, five days earlier and plans were made at that time for the luncheon. Brosmer explained that Pandol would be unavailable for the rest of the day, since he was tending to a friend who had a sudden attack of appendicitis. The committee agreed to send to 17 local growers the following telegram:

> National group of religious leaders inter-
> ested in hearing viewpoint of growers on
> agricultural workers' strike at noon luncheon
> today to which we were invited by you. Last
> minute cancellation of the luncheon most
> unfortunate. We shall be present at Elks
> Club as planned and hope you will be too.

Despite the growers refusal to attend the luncheon, the religious leaders proceeded to the agreed-upon round of morning activities. One part of the committee visited the Delano City Manager, Louis Shepard. He joined the local Police Chief, a representative from the Chamber of commerce, and two reporters from the Delano Record for a meeting with the group, which lasted more than an hour. Shepard felt that Delano's image was being tarnished by the conflict. So he planned to ask the City Council the following week to request that body to extend an invitation to the California State Conciliation Service to investigate the Delano strike, something the NFWA could not do since farmworkers

47

were not covered by the NLRB which allowed such appeals by unions. Even though Shepard repeated his plan two days later to UAW President Walter Reuther and representatives of the press, one week afterwards he announced that he would not make such a request. Shepard's explanation for the turnabout was that after talking with local growers he felt that requesting a California State Conciliation investigation "would be advocating the striker's cause."

Meanwhile the other half of the religious leaders' committee was given a tour of the Bruno Dispoto ranch. Dispoto, who earlier had termed the clergy's intervention in the strike "the most sickening day of my life," joined the group for the last ten minutes of the visit. He pointed out his workers were not on strike and took sharp exception to the fact that farmworkers in Delano wanted to organize. He insisted that his workers' wages were adequate, as were their living accommodations.

Hartmire continued his narrative of events by explaining that the Elks Hall officials confirmed that Pandol, a local grower, had arranged the luncheon on behalf of the growers and had taken the responsibility of inviting local clergy and business leaders. Several in the delegation felt that the growers were trying deliberately to avoid a meeting. After their own lunch the religious leaders returned to the motel and discussed their statement, based on their investigation. While the statement was being prepared for the press, Hartmire received the telephone call from, the spokesperson for the area growers, Brosmer--shortly before 3 p.m. It was later learned that Brosmer had been registered in the room directly below the religious leaders' conference.

After the religious leaders' press conference, the 4 p.m. meeting with the growers took place. Brosmer first tried to paraphrase, but finally read, the entire statement of the Committee of Religious Concern:

> As clergymen and laymen of many religious groups, Protestant, Roman Catholic and Jewish, we came to Delano to inform ourselves at firsthand about the three-month-long strike of the grape pickers. A number of us have also been here on previous occasions.
>
> The right of churches and synagogues to engage in such action is absolutely clear to us. We reject the heresy that churches and synagogues are to be concerned only with so-called "spiritual" matters. We believe that

48

this is God's world, which He not only made but continues to love. Consequently, whatever goes on in His world must be our concern, particularly when His will for the well-being of any of His children is being violated. We believe, furthermore, in the unity of the human person, made in God's image, and are persuaded that any indignity to any human person, whether to his soul or his body, must be our immediate concern.

We are not permitted to leave such considerations in the arena of pious generalities. They must be made specific, and for us they have become burningly specific in the Delano grape strike. During our visit, we have talked with strikers, union officials, city officials, and one grower. We deeply regret that other growers, clergy and community leaders failed to appear at a scheduled noon meeting, and that our sincere efforts for prolonged discussions with them were thus thwarted. We are still hoping for a later meeting with them. Nevertheless, certain things are clear to us. We are not ignorant of, nor callous to, the economic pressures on small farmers in this area and in the state and we expect the churches to stand with these farmers as change is thrust upon them. But the suffering of farm workers and their children cries to heaven and demands the attention of men of conscience.

Farm workers are men of worth. Their labor is important to the agricultural industry. It is both natural and just that they should participate in the decision-making process about wages, working conditions, and automation. Our three religious traditions have long recognized this fact and have repeatedly called for responsible collective bargaining between employers and employees, in all industries. It is apparent to us that this basic right to collective bargaining is being denied to farm workers in the Valley. We are distressed that any employer in this day and age would refuse to deal openly with his organized employees on basic grievances and turn instead to labor outside the area to carry on his business. This is a fundamental injustice which we dare not evade.

Since this right to bargain with strength as free men has been consistently denied to farm workers in this rich agricultural valley their only recourse in an effort to gain it for themselves has been to strike. We are satisfied that no other avenues of procedure have remained open to them, and that the only way which they can secure justice for themselves is to continue striking until such time as the owners are willing to enter into negotiation. Consequently, we feel compelled to identify ourselves unambiguously with the protest against such unjust treatment, and commence the pledge of nonviolence which they have faithfully fulfilled.

We therefore:

1. Urge the strikers to continue their strike until such time as their just demands are recognized, and we promise them our help and support.

2. Call upon growers to enter into negotiations with representatives of the strikers' unions, the NFWA and the AWOC, and we promise to support all such efforts by the employers as may lead to a fair and just resolution of the strike.

3. Affirm our support of the active involvement in the strike being exercised by the California Migrant Ministry and other religious groups and pledge to back them with increasing national support.

4. Call upon other unions, in particular the AFL-CIO now meeting in San Francisco, to give support to the present striking unions by active financial aid, by respecting their picket lines and by engaging in such other activity as lies within their power until such time as the present strike has been settled.

5. Call upon governor Brown and the State Legislature to enact whatever legislation is necessary to ensure the right of collective bargaining for all within the state, and to enact whatever further legislation may be necessary to ensure that the specific abuses leading to the present strike will not recur in the future, and to encourage fullest use of current state resources including the State Conciliation Service.

6. Call upon President Johnson and the Congress to enact federal legislation extending the provisions of the National Labor Relations Board Act so that it includes agricultural workers, to include farm workers under a federal minimum wage, and to initiate a Congressional investigation of the present labor dispute in Delano.

7. Call upon our churches and synagogues to support the strikers and their families, not only with their prayers, but with gifts of food, money, and personal involvement, and, acting in their capacity as citizens and as congregations, to call attention to each of the points cited above, so that power, being wisely used by them, may become an instrument of justice and love.

After Brosmer suggested adjournment of the meeting, Dr. Hall and Rabbi Herman expressed their regrets that the two groups could not conduct a dialogue. Some of the growers, nonetheless, took the floor to attack the delegation. Bruno Dispoto angrily challenged Vizzard's presence. Dispoto failed to see how Vizzard could be on a "fact-finding" tour since he had endorsed the NFWA and the strike on October 7, 1965. Vizzard replied that he had been studying farm labor problems for 25 years and considered his presence in Delano an education. Then George Lucas of Lucas and Sons Ranch, bitterly denounced the involvement of the religious leaders in the strike, "...you come here playing God and give us your wrath."

At his press conference Brosmer claimed that anyone could find hunger and poverty if he or she looked hard enough. When asked about Pope John XXIII's statement in Pacem in Terris that workers had a right to form voluntary associations and unions,

Brosmer, a Catholic, said that he was sure "...the Pope did not mean that all men everywhere should be organized."

1966

After the statement of the nationally-known religious leaders on the conditions of striking farmworkers in Delano, California, Vizzard made his own statement.[12] Insisting that the strikers have a right to expect support from the church, Vizzard continued,

> The growers really believe and expect that they can discourage or starve out the strikers. Maybe they will. If they succeed because we, the Church have failed to give the workers every support we can, both material and moral, then not only will our high sounding principles seem to the workers to be merely a sham but also we will have lost any right later to claim their loyalty and cooperation.

In January, 1966, Vizzard was attacked by the Bishop of Monterey-Fresno, Alloyoius J. Willinger, C.S.S.R., in his diocesan paper, Central California Register. In an open letter to the paper, Bishop Willinger also quoted from a letter Vizzard received upon his return to Washington from the then Monsignor Edward O'Rourke, the executive director of the NCRLC. Portions of the O'Rourke letter were in the Register. O'Rourke reminded Vizzard that on November 17th, he was instructed "...to avoid public involvement in the strike of the grape workers in Delano." O'Rourke again reminded Vizzard that the issue was not under the jurisdiction of the NCRLC's Washington office. Since the issue involved the ordinaries and diocesan directors of California, with whom O'Rourke was working directly, the issue was under his, not Vizzard's, jurisdiction. Vizzard was warned that failure to observe these instructions would be interpreted as a serious breach of duty.

Willinger characterized Vizzard's participation in the Delano strike "as an act of unadulterated disobedience, insubordination and breach of office." Willinger said Vizzard's own statement reeked of the "...self-inflicted hysteria of the priest's disposition and the autocratic flamboyant expression of the one-sidedness that preclude soundness and impartiality of justice." Willinger suggested that, if Vizzard had made his vow of obedience with any mental reservation, he should hasten to

52

invalidate it in radice [at the root]. Finally, Willinger requested the NCWC officials,

> ...to hold their subordinates within reasonable bounds, to keep them at their posts and not allow them to roam the country dictating individual ideologies or promoting personal schemes, invading jurisdictions over which a local ordinary presides and for which he is responsible. Any departure from this rule will only lead to confusion, division and scandal.

In a lengthy editorial, NCR (1/12/66) analyzed the Willinger-Vizzard controversy.[13] It was more than a local issue because the strikers needed wider support in light of the absence of adequate federal or state laws to recognize adequately a right to organize for collective bargaining, so vigorously proclaimed in Pope John XXIII's encyclical, Mater et Magistra. Yet, NCR editors found Vizzard's criticism of the institutional church biting and provocative and Willinger's reply "no less than vituperative in quality." The editors earlier thought Vizzard's judgment was correct but felt his statement, so far as the church's role, should have been less pointed or more candid. Namely, Vizzard should have been prepared to name names and prove the accusation. Otherwise, Vizzard should have said nothing about motives. With a reference to Vizzard's inner conflict between obedience to his conscience and the instructions from O'Rourke, his superior in the NCRLC, the NCR editors said. "Father Vizzard was probably under particular tension on this occasion."

The editors thought that Vizzard's and Willinger's mistakes tended to obscure the existence of an unresolved and fundamental problem, almost certain to recur.

> The problem exists because--aside from the very rare instances of papal intervention-- the bishop of each Catholic diocese is in a position to determine the witness of the Church on any moral issue rising within his jurisdiction. Yet some issues which come into focus in a given area have effects or significance far beyond the limits of the diocese concerned, so much so that all Catholics rightly feel a share of responsibility...

Therefore, the editors thought that the Delano situation called for arrangements to go beyond the control of a local ordinary. Yet, whatever the quality of Vizzard's protocol, or lack thereof, the editors' primary concern was the rights of the farmworkers and others in similar situations "...to have the justice of their cause judged by its merits and to have the support they deserve." The editors felt that Delano and Selma called for some new mechanism to handle "...such situations without bitter and unseemly public disputes."

On January 28, 1966, a Commonweal editorial called Willinger's reply "astonishingly bitter and vituperative", muscular and near hysteric.[14] The editors granted the bishop's technical point in canon law and alluded to the national moral nature of the issue. They did not think that Willinger realized the simple justice of the cause of the unorganized and exploited farmworkers. Affirming their need for every bit of support, including that of priests, the editors concluded, "Surely, there are some limitations on the view of the diocese as a walled-in private duchy."

By January 1966, the Ave Maria ran an editorial captioned "Delano--Another Selma?"[15] Vizzard's presence and statement with the fact-finding interfaith delegation was judged by the editors as an 11th hour boost to the almost hopeless cause of the striking farmworkers in Delano. The editors called them representatives of tens of thousands of U.S. citizen farmers who, using Vizzard's words, "for decades and generations have been deprived of every semblance of justice, dignity and human decency." The editors also praised the strikers' non-violent, legal and moral means, despite tremendous odds. The owners were so successful in harvesting the grape crop, through strike-breakers, that the growers would not even meet with the representatives of the strikers. The strikers' nonviolent approach had been met by growers without understanding and with opposition. The opposition was represented by local and regional press and law enforcement people. Among the odds, also, was the church. "Indeed, the local Bishop has even enjoined action by priests from outside the diocese." Finally, the plight of the farmworkers had failed to stir up and organize national support.

Vizzard was characterized as "a mature leader who has worked many years for the cause of justice for the agricultural worker worthy of admiration for his courage and honesty." Also, the editors reprinted much of the Vizzard statement, to which Willinger and some others took such strong exception.

54

No ecclesiastical superior has any right to
forbid me to be concerned with gross injustice and destruction of human dignity just
because the specific problem exists within
territory under his jurisdiction. Nor can he
rightfully forbid me to express that concern
in writings, speeches or personal presence...

It is evident that one cannot scorn the need
for money to support the parochial and
diocesan institutions. But Church institutions do not exist for their own sake. Nor
does the Church herself exist solely for the
comfortable, affluent and powerful who use or
support these institutions.

I firmly believe that just as there can be
circumstances in an individual's life where
fidelity to his Christian belief leaves him
no choice but to sacrifice everything, even
his life, so, too, circumstances can and do
arise where the institutional Church can be
faced with the same inexorable consequence of
her belief.

To be brutally frank, I think it would be
more to the honor of the Church and infi-
nitely more to the service of souls that
churches, convents, rectories and even
schools, including seminaries, should remain
unbuilt or unfinished or even closed rather
than that the Church should knuckle under to
the threats of those who demand that the
Church "keep its nose out of their business."

The *Ave Maria* editorial generated responses in its later
pages.[16] Two were severely critical. Several others were
largely supportive. The vicar General of the Monterey-Fresno
diocese, Msgr. James G. Dowling, was so severe in his criticism
that the *Ave Maria* felt compelled to print not only the criticism
but also, on the next page, the editors' point-by-point rebuttal.
Dowling began by several non-essential references to the *Ave
Maria* being published at the University of Notre Dame with its
almost fabled Spirit of the Fighting Irish, the Irish custom of
not washing dirty linen in public, and the Irish tradition of
being able to finish any fight started. The editors found such
rhetoric contributing little to communication and understanding.

Dowling branded the editors "a contankerous, fault-finding, poorly-informed lot who show little...respect for truth and justice." The editors pointed to other articles--one by the associate editor of the diocesan newspaper--which admitted there were limitations to the Ave Maria's coverage but were steadfast in Ave Maria's seriousness, honesty and continued interest in a legitimate concern. To Dowling's correction of the Ave Maria's figures--less than 300 workers on strike rather than thousands of families--the editors made no reference. Nor to Dowling's correction that Msgr. Edward O'Rourke, and not Vizzard, was director of the NCRLC.

As to Dowling's assertions that Vizzard's judgments and actions were neither informed nor worthy of reporting and approval, the editors subscribed to the statement made to the Ave Maria by Msgr. William Quinn, Director of the Chicago Office of the Bishops' Committee for the Spanish Speaking and one of the religious leaders on the Delano fact-finding tour.

> I know of no other Roman Catholic priest who knows more about the intricacies of the American agricultural problems than Father James Vizzard, S.J. His long-time concern in this area has been for all parties involved. It is not at all surprising that he should speak out on behalf of the legitimate desires of the NFWA and the AWOC to engage in collective bargaining with the growers. The on-going strike in Delano will affect the lives of hundreds of thousands of Mexican-Americans, Puerto Ricans, Negroes and poor-centered whites... The striking workers of Delano are carrying the torch for America's rural poor.

Dowling claimed that Vizzard's charges against Willinger as a shepherd who is failing in his duty to feed the sheep, were absolutely untrue, offending against charity, and demanding public apology. The Ave Maria editors responded,

> We feel no need to defend the rhetoric of Father Vizzard's original statement; the choice of wording was his and he is quite capable of speaking for himself.

Dowling proceeded to extol Willinger's service to the poor, especially the Spanish-speaking. Dowling also characterized most of the growers as hardworking but with human faults like the rest of us. Dowling characterized as unfair any assumption that the leaders in Monterey-Fresno diocese refrained from protesting the injustices visited on the farmworkers because of any possible reprisal "...from those best able to support our churches, schools and institutions." Finally, Dowling invited Vizzard and Ave Maria's editor, Father John Reedy, C.S.C., to leave their ivory towers and

> ...come out to this vineyard of the Lord where people are and where there are souls to be saved. They would accomplish far more for the poor by honest labor where priests are needed than by carping criticism and destructive comments.

The Ave Maria editors devoted most of the editorial to what they considered the more serious issue of Dowling's criticism-- the as-yet unresolved problem of "ecclesiastical jurisdiction over a national issue which happens to come into focus in a particular diocese." Hence, the caption of the New Year's Day editorial, "Delano--Another Selma?" The presence or absence of Catholic clergymen in Selma had national effects in the struggle for civil rights and in the church's communication with blacks. Delano was viewed as another test-case of a national problem. The problem touched upon, not only the images or effectiveness of the church in Selma, Delano, Watts or St. John's University, but also the consciences of priests and religious torn by conflicting pressures.

The editors confidently called for the addressing this problem by the first convocation of the U.S. bishops for the purpose of restructuring their Conference in conformity with Vatican II's demands for regional or national conferences. The editors saw a real and pressing need for a new definition of the rights and limits of local ordinaries over issues that have national significance. In both the civil rights and farmworker causes, the jurisdictional problem was an impediment and the Protestants arrived earlier and in larger numbers than Catholics. Consequently, the editors suggested that when the National Conference of Catholic Bishops met, "the Conference might well formulate policy and legislation for the effective handling of situations that concern the interests of the entire Catholic community in this country."

Also, in mid-February, 1966, Ave Maria was able to produce further support, not so much for itself, but for Vizzard and the strikers.[17] The editors quoted from an article of Msgr. George Higgins, "The Right to Strike." After quoting Vatican II's decree, Church in the Modern World about the right of workers to organize and their right to strike under certain conditions, Higgins discussed Delano,

> The question as to when and how clergymen should get involved in socio-economic controversies is admittedly difficult to answer, but in this particular case the moral issues involved are so clear that clergymen, it seems to me, simply have to take a stand.

Almost simultaneously, the NCRLC officials, meeting in Oklahoma City, endorsed the strikers in a strong statement. One of the signers was O'Rourke, whose original attack on Vizzard was interpreted by Willinger as support for his own views. In his original statement to Vizzard, O'Rourke said,

> Your performance was a complete contradiction... The issue at stake is not whether agricultural workers have a right to strike (italics ours). It is a question of how a lasting improvement of their lot can be won and what is the proper role of the NCRLC in such efforts.

The more recent statement, signed by O'Rourke and the NCRLC's president, Bishop Frederick W. Freking of La Crosse, avoided any reference to the controversy between Willinger, Vizzard, and the Ave Maria. It limited itself to support of the strikers,

> The failure on the part of most of the growers to recognize the right of workers to organize and conduct a peaceful strike shows that much must be done to develop a Christian conscience toward such issues.
>
> The National Catholic Rural Life Conference will continue its efforts on the national and local levels to assist workers, growers and Church leaders to fulfill their respective obligations in this crucial issue.

The largely supportive responses to the New Year's editorial in Ave Maria came from several places and in different weeks. In mid-February, 1966, a Mother M. Assumpta, O.S.U., wrote from Los Angeles.[18] She praised Ave Maria for its courage and charity in supporting, like Vizzard, what is true and right in the strikers' fight for justice. She felt that one need be in Delano for only a short time,

...to see clearly the issues which have
caused the farm workers there to risk literally everything to pursue their right to collective bargaining. One, too, sees immediately how poorly these people are served by
their Church, and one wonders why they are
not bitterly anticlerical. But if the clergy
in the area will not commit themselves to the
problem which is moral as well as social, the
Church will carry on her struggle for social
justice in the persons of her lay people, her
Mystical Body.

In March there were several responses to the _Ave Maria_
editorial.[19] The first, from Mathew Ahmann, Executive Director
of National Catholic Conference for Interracial Justice (NCCIJ),
wrote to correct the record as follows:

[To] ... our knowledge Catholics who were in
Selma were never ordered by Archbishop Toolen
to cease participation in civil rights demonstrations in that state.

Ave Maria made such a correction in its response to Dowling,

At Selma, a number of the Bishops gave permission for their priests to be present even
though the opposition of Archbishop Toolen
was public knowledge.

A frequent writer on migrant workers, Alice Ogle, wrote from San
Francisco the following response,

YES, Delano is another Selma. What else can
you call it when an oppressed people fight
for civil rights as well as human rights?
Monsignor Dowling's contention (Jan. 29) that
Father Vizzard (and Father Reedy too!) have
a lot to learn about what's going on in the
"vineyard of the Lord" just doesn't add up.
Even if the Jesuit had not seen for himself
what is taking place in Delano, he'd have to
be illiterate not to know that the public
conscience has been challenged for--lo--many,
many years in relation to the long-term deg-
radation of farmworkers and their families,
and that the explosion in Delano can be compared with attempts in the South to secure
justice.

Another supportive response came from an Anne Rosen of San Bernardino, California. She complained of the absence of clergy of any faith from the community's Inter-Faith Social Action Council. After arguing that without proper guidance the Delano situation might well become another Selma, Rosen pleaded,

> It makes little sense to me to read of the glorious work our Maryknolls accomplish and then to recognize in my own community that priests are in hiding from the problems surrounding them. Genuine humanitarianism should begin in our communities, and we should be able to solve some problems without total reliance upon politics. The solution of problems through politics is too easy and eliminates the need for any majority of citizens to participate.

However, there was, also, Carl V. Kolata of Watertown, Wisconsin, who agreed with Dowling that the Ave Maria editor was "not objective" and saw Delano "from his leftward window of the Ivory Tower."

The columnist, John Leo, spoke of Vizzard as the most prominent "house Catholic" to identify himself with attempts to improve the miserable condition of the farm workers.[20] Referring to Vizzard's trouble with Willinger, Leo noted,

> Both the ministerial association and the Diocese of Monterey-Fresno have washed their hands of the affair, thus assuring that a struggle which they ought to lead will be conducted as a secular movement. The question is: where does the danger of "secularism" lie--with the Church's decision to align itself with the business interests and the status quo, or with the secular forces which do the Church's work without the Church's help?

Later in March, Vizzard himself answered Leo's column.[21] All of Leo's points were granted, save that Catholics were absent from the grape strike. For, there was considerable public and private assistance provided by the Bishops Committee for the Spanish Speaking, under the direction of Msgr. William Quinn of Chicago. Also, the NCRLC gave much unpublicized leadership in developing and applying the principles and attitudes which Vizzard hoped would lead eventually to a Delano solution. In the same issue of the National Catholic Reporter there were stories about support from Archbishop Lucey of San Antonio and Bishop Hugh A. Donohoe of Stockton. In fact, as a representative of eight California bishops, Donohoe said, "Those who seek to organize farm laborers are not to be looked upon as outside agitators."[22]

Much about Vizzard's work appeared in a Sign article.[23] Doing the work of a lobbyist for the NCRLC--without high-powered sales pitches, parties, pressures and bribes--Vizzard viewed himself as "a spokesman for some otherwise neglected viewpoints" and for clients having trouble paying for food and clothing. In representing the U.S.'s poorest people, farm-workers and their families, he became known, not so much to the public, but to legislators on both sides of the aisles in both houses of Congress. In being sought out for leadership in rural problems by Lyndon Johnson and Hubert Humphrey, Vizzard could have expected to be not just one of the most influential but also one of the most controversial men in Washington with regard to rural life. Foremost in his record were battles over the abuse of Mexican and migratory farm workers, unionization of farm laborers, and the 160-acre limitation on the use of land irrigated from federal water systems.

In 1955 he went to Washington as director of the NCRLC's office there. Although the NCRLC had only four thousand members in the late 1960's, it spoke with considerable weight on national affairs and was a leading spokes group of the Catholic Church on International affairs--especially when Msgr. Luigi G. Ligutti was its international director in Des Moines, Iowa. Through Vizzard's work in its Washington office, the NCRLC played key roles in foreign aid and trade, the Peace Corps, soil and water conservation, civil rights, redevelopment, and the war on poverty. Much more was accomplished through a "coalition of conscience and power" (religion and government and other institutions). Vizzard referred to the coalition of 42 national organizations (labor, farm, civic, women, social and religious groups), the National Council on Agricultural Life and Labor, of which he was chairman.

The NCRLC team attempted to implement a philosophy that entailed liberal, progressive, and international interpretations of papal declarations on social justice. As the Washington "lobbyist," Vizzard drew more attention than other members of the team. In a sense, he was a throwback to the "labor priests"-- this time for the farm workers. He pulled no punches when he talked about the permanently depressed "clients." In a speech widely quoted by the press, he charged,

61

I contend that the consumer has no right to
eat tomatoes and strawberries if the price of
bringing them to the table is the most des-
perate kind of human misery. I contend,
moreover, that no employer has the right to
stay in business if he can do so only by
beating down the workers' wages and keeping
them at a level far below the minimum
required by law and decency in other occupations.

Such talk did not endear him to the nation's leading
farmers. For, the growers held him chiefly responsible for
recent congressional action to improve the farmworkers conditions. They blamed him, more than anyone else, for killing the
"bracero program." Hence, the growers' anger was focused
personally on Vizzard. He persevered when so many others had
left the field in the fight for the dignity of the farmworkers.

On occasion, his blunt language and devastating analysis got
him in trouble with superiors, support in the national press, and
threats from big growers. Such fearsome tactics did not bother
him after awhile. For, he had the backing of most of the hierarchy and had friends among the growers as well. Examples were
given. One growers' association fired its lobbyist because
Vizzard was more accurate on a consistent basis. To growers who
would not or could not agree with him, Vizzard would tell them
they did not know what was good for their industry. Usually, he
would prevail. Despite being hospitalized for a variety of
physical illness nine times from 1963-66, he bounced back and
talked of work still to be completed.

We must wipe out, at least, the disgraceful
discrimination which has exempted farmworkers from practically every piece of
protective and welfare legislation passed by
Congress or the state legislatures in the
past thirty years... They are the excluded,
the forgotten, the silent ones in our
society. But speaking for them is a voice
which cannot be ignored with impunity. It is
the voice of organized religion, which calls
on farm employers, the Congress, and particularly the President to right these wrongs.

About two months after the issuance of the statement of the
Committee of Religious Concern, the Ave Maria cited six items
from several issues of the Monterey-Fresno diocesan newspaper,

Central California Register.[24]   First, there was a very abbrevi-
ated "Diary of a Grape Strike."   There were several entries by
Charles A. McCarthy about church involvement.   He noted that
families of growers and strikers were estranged by bitterness,
yet worshipped in the same churches each Sunday.   He remarked
that Cesar Chavez had been called by some as "the walking embodiment of the principles in the encyclicals."   Yet, a spokesperson
for the growers warned the clergy that they could not organize
unions, if they were "going to serve the Lord."   Warning of such
involvement doing irreparable harm, the grower representative
accused the churches of treating farmworkers like children and
forcing them into the union.

Second, there was also a Central California Register
editorial.   Among other things the editorial praised the vast
majority of the farmers and ranches as honest, hardworking and
anxious not to take advantage of the workers, even though there
would be greater need in the future for a more skilled and stable
labor supply.   The unjust and self-defeating nature of sweeping
generalizations about either growers or workers was underlined.
Also, there was a warning that outside groups joining in the dispute for their own selfish interests could be disastrous.   The
editorial ended with a call for reconciliation,

> The Church has no simple solution to offer
> which will magically end the Delano dispute
> overnight.   But she has clearly outlined the
> guiding principles of social justice and
> charity which are essential to a sound
> solution.   She stands ready to meet with both
> sides in an effort to begin the discussion
> needed to arrive at a just and peaceful
> solution.

Third, there was another editorial, about farm laborers and
just wages,

> If prices are so low that the farmer cannot
> pay the minimum wage, then he should not be
> farming.   If, on the other hand, the farmer
> is making a greater profit due to the market
> demand, it is only just that the workers
> should share in the good fortunes of the mar-
> ket.

Fourth, there was an October 28 letter to the Central
California Register editor, signed "A Christian (I Think)."
Deploring the fact that the Catholic social service agencies in

Fresno and Bakersfield sent food to hungry workers' families in the strike area, the writer said, "...let the loafers starve if they don't want to work...no work, no eat." Fifth, there was a note that on November 1, Catholic youth groups, social workers, ministers and students--as members of the Congress of Racial Equality (CORE) and the Students Non-Violent Coordinating Committee (SNCC) did earlier--supported the strikers on the picket lines. The ranchers complained about the "outside agitators" and "beatniks" in the November 1 demonstration.

Sixth there was a November 4, another front-page editorial. Among other things the editorial said,

> Granted there have been mistakes made by both sides in the past. To focus attention on such abuses and to continue to make accusations, however, serves no purpose in reaching agreement in the present dispute. Such antagonism can only separate the two sides even further.

In mid-March 1966, the U.S. Senate Subcommittee on Migratory Labor held three days of hearings in Visalia, California, on pending farm labor legislation.[25] Before taking testimony the subcommittee visited the Linnell Farm Camp, which had been termed in 1965 by Secretary of Labor, W. Willard Wirtz, as the filthiest the subcommittee members, California Republican Senator George Murphy, said he hoped no one would ever have to visit the camp again and that it would be torn down as soon as possible. On March 14, Chavez testified before the subcommittee that the growing unrest among the farm workers could lead to a state wide labor strike during the summer of 1966. Chavez added,

> I am hoping we don't have to go as far as the Negro revolution and its resulting bloodshed to prove that we are tired of occupational discrimination and that we are ready for our freedom.

Chavez, also, accused Kern County sheriff's deputies of harrassing pickets repeatedly during the grape strike. Chavez specified that he objected to deputies taking pictures of strikers and making unnecessary arrests.

During Chavez' testimony, a guest of the subcommittee, Harian Hagen, the Democratic Congressman from the Delano area, charged that the NFWA was under Communist influence. Chavez challenged Hagen to prove his charges. Senator Murphy objected to the line of questioning and asked the chairperson of the sub-committee, Democratic Senator from New Jersey, Harrison B. Williams, to rule Hagen out-of-order. Williams did and noted, "...some committees may tolerate this type of questioning, but not this one." In later sessions the Kern County Sheriff, Leroy Gaylen, was questioned by another subcommittee member, New York's Democratic Senator, Robert F. Kennedy, about Chavez's charges against the police in the County, in which Delano was located. Gaylen responded that he often had pickets arrested "because when people are being threatened to have their hearts cut out we go out and arrest them." The former U.S. Attorney General, Kennedy, acidly told the sheriff to "review his procedures" and start by "reading the Constitution of the United States."

On March 15, Bishop Hugh A. Donohoe of Stockton, California, testified before the subcommittee on behalf of the state's eight bishops. Donohoe urged the adoption of federal legislation insuring collective bargaining and a minimum wage for farm workers. Donohoe added, "Those who seek to organize farm laborers are not to be looked upon as outside agitators." The Bishop's testimony was greeted with applause by the subcommittee. Prior to Donohoe's testimony Senator Kennedy asked workers who testified before the subcommittee if, at any time, they had been helped by the clergy. Later, Kennedy told a reporter that he considered a bishop's first responsibility to be with the poor and the oppressed. Kennedy said he would be "surprised and considerably shocked" to hear of a bishop not allowing priests to go out and help farm workers. Kennedy added,

> Bishops should encourage their priests to work with the farm laborer. They themselves should leave their homes and live among these workers.

In mid-March also, a small army of 200 striking grape pickers began a 300-mile trek to the California state capitol in Sacramento to obtain legal protection and implementation of collective bargaining rights. As the pilgrimage moved even one city-block into Delano toward the capitol, it was detained at the city limits by the Chief of Police, James Ailes. Ailes told the NFWA's legal counsel, Alex Hoffman, he could not "control the route," if the striking farm workers marched through the city. Ailes suggested the pilgrimage bypass Delano. Clifford Loader, Delano Mayor and dentist, when Chavez telephoned him to break the deadlock, claimed permission for a the march through the city was not his responsibility. The Delano City Manager, Lewis Shepard, however, alleged that the workers had failed to give the police any warning of the march and that the NFWA was trying to "create an incident for an incident's sake." Hoffman responded that the police had been notified of the march and its intended route through Delano. After some further discussion, the pilgrimage was allowed to proceed.

Singing hymns and "We Shall Overcome" in Spanish and English, the marchers were accompanied by priests from four dioceses and moved 12 to 15 miles each day. The banner of Our Lady of Guadalupe canied by the marchers was explained by Louis Valdez, a native of Delano, "In their desire for freedom the Mexican people have not always had the backing of the Church or of the bishops or the priests, but the virgin is ours." Chavez also explained.

> In every religious-oriented culture the pil-
> grimage has had a place, a trip made with
> sacrifice and hardship as an expression of
> penance and of commitment--and often involv-
> ing a petition to the patron of the
> pilgrimage for some sincerely sought benefit
> of body and soul. Since this is both a
> religious pilgrimage and a plea for social
> change for the farm worker, long advocated by
> the social teachings of the Church, we hope
> that the people of God will respond to our
> call and join us for part of the walk just as
> they did with our Negro brothers in Selma.

More than one week into the pilgrimage, the striking workers were greeted in West Fresno by more than 1,000 people--mostly local farm workers--who crowded into the local Aztec theater.[26] Rev. Ephrem Neri, an official representative of Monterey-Fresno's Bishop Alyosius J. Willinger, stated that it is an unquestioned right of workers to achieve social justice and that the Catholic Church encouraged the farm worker's efforts.

Priests from the San Francisco Archdiocese celebrated the eucharist daily throughout the pilgrimage. Seminarians from San Francisco's St. Patrick Seminary, as well as Franciscan and Immaculate Heart sisters in the Bay area, joined the march, as the 100 or so Delano farm workers passed the half-way mark in their 300-mile, 25-day pilgrimage to Sacramento. The NFWA officials estimated that more than 1,000 San Joaquin valley farm workers, clergy, religious and other sympathizers had partici-pated in the pilgrimage. The number was expected to increase sharply as the pilgrimage neared its completion. The marchers were to arrive in West Sacramento, at Our Lady of Grace Church, early in the evening of Holy Saturday. On Easter morning the eucharist was to be celebrated at 8:30 and followed by a Protestant service. After the religious ceremonies the pilgrimage was to begin the final four miles of the march--to the west steps of the State Capitol.

At the Capitol steps the farm workers hoped to present Governor Edmund G. Brown Sr. with "The Plan of Delano", which the workers drew up during their march and had been signed by local workers in the various communities through which the pilgrimage had passed. For that Easter, the Catholic Ed Brown had indicated that he would be vacationing in Palm Springs when the pilgrimage arrived in Sacramento. He promised to "pay his respects" to the workers along the pilgrimage route and acknowledge the dedication of the farm workers. NFWA leaders said that if Brown was not present in Sacramento when the pilgrimage arrived, "The Plan of Delano" would be read aloud from the Capitol steps to an expected group of California State legislators. Chavez replied to Brown's statement by saying,

> We are not interested in respect from the governor, we are interested in action.

> We want laws which will grant farm workers collective bargaining rights, unemployment insurance, a minimum wage and other legal protections which cover most workers.

During the course of the pilgrimage, the Delano farm workers received a letter on congratulations from San Antonio Archbishop Robert E. Lucey.[27] Writing directly to Chavez, Lucey congratulated him on his "magnificent leadership" in the Delano strike. Lucey continued,

> Unfortunately a great many poor people here in San Antonio are afraid to join a worthwhile union because the people who control Texas and particularly San Antonio don't like labor unions.

> I greatly admire the courage you and the other men have shown in the face of the powerful and wealthy growers in California. You and your associates have been good soldiers.

> A great deal of public opinion in the United States is on your side. You are winning friends constantly and I hope nothing will

discourage you in the long battle for justice.

On the 20th day of the pilgrimage news arrived from Los Angeles of an agreement between Chavez for NFWA and Sidney Korshak, attorney for Schenley Industries, Inc., the second-largest grape grower in the Delano area.[28] The marchers were jubilant and tore up signs calling for the boycott of Schenley products. The news came as 200 farm workers, priests, ministers and other sympathizers paused for a brief rest beside a Lodi vineyard. Rev. Donald Postum, a Christian Churches-Disciple of Christ minister, offered a brief prayer of thanksgiving. Elated over the agreement with Schenley Industries to initiate collective bargaining and to discontinue the boycott, Chavez rejoined the pilgrimage. He said,

> We recognize the great help that civil rights workers and the clergy have given us.

> But without the courage and desire to win on the part of the workers, our victory over Schenley would never have been possible. Their willingness to suffer has made this victory possible.

Even though the Council of California Growers charged that Schenley was "not of California agriculture" and NFWA did not represent the vineyard workers, 24 hours after the Schenley-NFWA settlement, the Delano area's largest ranch--the 4,800-acre Sierre Vista--owned by DiGiorgio Fruit Corporation, called for a secret ballot election on its properties. In a letter to Governor Brown, Robert DiGiorgio, the company's president, called upon the California Mediation and Conciliation Service to assist his company and labor organizations in setting up the representational election. Chavez noted that NFWA had made the same proposal several months before, but had received no reply from DiGiorgio. Chavez also expressed concern about DiGiorgio's attempt to dictate the conditions for the election.

When the pilgrimage finally reached Sacramento it was with Chavez' message ringing in their ears, "Now that Schenley Industries has seen the light, we hope that Governor Brown will see the light."[29] Brown was scheduled to meet with the farm workers' delegation, joined by members of the clergy and representatives of other supporting groups. As Schenley capitulated and the pilgrimage ended, Chavez was the hero. One priest who watched Chavez in action commented,

68

It is simple for us as clergy to enunciate
the social doctrines of the Church, but if
someone doesn't put shoes on it and make it
walk around in the fields, the papal encyclicals may as well not have been written.

Ave Maria editors said of Chavez:

If there was some doubt that Ceasar Chavez of
Delano, California, would be for the Spanish
speaking of this country what Martin Luther
King has been for the Negro, there probably
isn't anymore...But it would be interesting
to speculate how much farther they would be
away from their rights had not the Church--
and especially including its representatives
from outside the state of California--backed
the movement for human rights and dignity...

Around the same time, a reader of the NCR, a Helen M. Sugg
of St. Louis, Missouri, emphasized the point.[30]

The thousands of us who synpathize with the
just cause of the NFWA were joyous at the
news that the march of grape workers had met
with a degree of success... Let each of us
write to the company; and to use a Trumanes-
que phrase, assure them we will "put our
money where our mouth is" and buy Schenley
products whenever possible as proof of our
thanks.

On April 17, 1966 some 900 farm workers had completed
another march through the west end of the San Joaquin valley community of Delano and were preparing for an open-air eucharist in
a local park.[31] They were confronted by some 60 sign-carrying
pickets, led by Rev. James Dillon, pastor of St. Mary's parish
and his assistant, Rev. Weneceslas H. Van Lun. The signs read,

Keep the Mass Sacred! Keep the Mass in
Church! Has This Mass Been Authorized by the
Bishop? and How Can You Use Our Lady of
Guadalupe in a Labor Dispute?

After conferring with Chavez, Rev. James Bishop, of Our Lady of
Guadalupe parish in Sacramento, decided not to celebrate the
eucharist in the park. Bishop explained,

The situation was too explosive and rather
than risk open conflict we asked the workers
to adjourn to the Agricultural Workers Organizing Committee's hall for a rally.

Chavez expressed regrets that the tense conditions of the Sunday
demonstration prevented the celebration of the eucharist. He
noted that many of the workers had not attended a morning eucharist in anticipation of the evening celebration. He added, "Mass
is sacred wherever it is held."

Msgr. James V. Dowling, Vicar General of the Monterey-Fresno
diocese, said,

We advised the pastor and his assistant not
to demonstrate and let the priest who was to
celebrate the mass face the consequences of
coming into another diocese without the
bishop's permission.

Dillon, the pastor, claimed that he had remained neutral during
the eight-month old grape pickers strike. He estimated that
between 20 and 25 percent of his parishioners were "workers who
have remained in the field during the strike." Some 97 southern
Tulare and northern Kern county growers were also members of his
parish. He decried what he called,

...bally-hoo and circus atmosphere...

The Mass belongs in church and should not be
used in a phony local situation. The strikers have been attempting to use every gadget
to make people believe the Church is behind
them.

At the time of this Delano demonstration Commonweal ran an
article by Jerome Wolf about earlier incidents of church conflict
over the farm workers.[32]   Referring to the farm workers' eight-
month strike and the announcement of the Schenley Industries'
agreement to enter into collective bargaining talks, Wolf set the
framework for an understanding of the earlier incidents,

Priests from the area who had hoped to remain
neutral have bitterly attacked priests from
outside who have come to the support of the
agricultural workers. And these priests in
turn have raised the question of the Church's
social mission...The particular nature of the

70

> communities involved, often remote from large
> urban centers and under the virtually
> unchallenged social and economic leadership
> of growers and landowners, makes certain pat-
> terns of conflict almost inevitable. Union
> influence, for example, either in town or in
> the fields, is usually absent. A strike
> almost always means the presence of "outside
> agitators."

The "historical precedents" selected by Wolf were two, dating back to the beginning of the 1960's. The first involved several priests. The second involved a doctor and his wife.

In 1961 during a joint-organizing drive by AWOC and the United Packinghouse Workers of America among the lettuce workers in California's Imperial Valley, a one-day work stoppage was called when the growers refused to bargain. A large rally was planned in the city of Calexico and Rev. Victor Salandini was asked to speak. In the valley, since 1957, Salandini was sophis- ticated enough to understand the "class forces" at work in the dispute. He suggested that the speakers be two priests from Northern California who had been involved there with the farm workers for many years and who would not be subject to local pressures in Southern and Central California. The two priests, McDonald and McColough, flew in their own private plane directly to San Diego to request permission of Bishop Buddy to speak in his diocese. The permission, according to Salandini, was granted. After delivering their speeches, McDonald and McColouth spent the night at Salandini's rectory and flew out of the valley the next morning--the day of the work stoppage.

The two priests were criticized for their sympathy with the union and for their "outsider agitating" by a wide variety of sources. One source of criticism was Rev. Joseph DiCristina, a wealthy and influential priest in El Centro and the Dean of the priests ministering in the Imperial Valley. Specifically, DiCristina was quoted in the January 8, 1961 issue of the Imper- ial Valley's News-Press,

> When I heard of the demonstration and the
> participation by these priests, I contacted
> the Bishop and asked him whether he had auth-
> orized it. His answer was that he was quite
> upset by their actions, that I should repri-
> mand them severely and ask them to leave the
> area.

As a young and involved priest, Salandini was quite taken by the character, social responsibility and "prudence" of McDonald and McColough. He was shocked and his faith was shaken by DiCristina's claims. He felt that the bishop's actions "almost make him look like a liar." After finally being removed from his parish, Salandini remained a critic of the church authorities and cited with a mixture of humor and bitterness which priests in the valley got large contributions from the growers.

The other example Wolf gave of "the absolute loyalty demanded of local officials by the agricultural industry" involved Dr. Paul F. O'Rourke, the county Public Health Director and his wife, a pacifist and Quaker. Dr. O'Rourke had given up a successful practice in Northern California's Marin County to study public health. Upon completion of his degree work, he decided to come to the Imperial Valley, to what he called "California's most unhealthy county." Although quite aware of a direct relationship between the poverty of the agricultural workers and the high incidence of disease in the valley, he was determined to remain neutral during the strike. However, one incident after another, soon made O'Rourke a cause celebre!

First, the growers demanded that the Health Department, which O'Rourke directed, prevent pickets from urinating along the irrigation ditch bank. The Health Department took no action. For, previously growers successfully opposed local ordinances calling for mobile sanitary facilities for workers during harvest season. Second, when the request was made that the Health Department close the labor temple kitchen for sanitary reasons, he made it clear that his department would remain neutral. Third, when the local jail, filled with strikers, was denounced by the union attorney as a heath hazard, the sheriff demanded a sanitary inspection. O'Rourke conducted an investigation and found hazardous plumbing defects, very inadequate diet, seriously overcrowded and dirty jail cells. Even though the newspapers headlined the investigative report as an attack on the sheriff, O'Rourke had made clear his loyalty as the Health Officer of his community.

Fourth and finally, a "Communist smear" campaign was then focused on Dr. O'Rourke and his wife. She was engaged in several types of activities which fitted neatly into what a "paranoid mind" would call subversive. Her adopted family included a Hoopa Indian daughter and a Chinese-Hawaiian son. She aided underpriviledged farm workers. Occasionally she frequented a black church. She attempted to find a home for a black psychiatrist. Along with her husband, she was a member of the American Association for the United Nations and the American Civil

Liberties Union. An explosion was touched off however, when she abstained from the Pledge of Allegiance at a Democratic Club meeting.

Under intense and continuing pressure, O'Rourke resigned as director of Public Health. However, the Board of Supervisors rescinded their acceptance of the resignation and reinstated him, under mounting criticism and protest against them throughout the state of California. However, exactly one year from the time of his arrival, he again resigned and left the valley "with a sense of tragedy"--convinced that relationships had been so strained that effective work was impossible.

In concluding his account of the experience of the priests and the O'Rourkes, Commonweal's Wolf called cries against "outside agitation" specious. He was not surprised that local workers called for outside support, in view of hundreds of growers and allies being deputized in 1961 roaming the Imperial Valley with shotguns across their arms. Wolf concluded,

> it appears that any successful challenge to the corporate agricultural power structure in California's farm communities will be as dependent upon the aid of "outside agitators" as the civil rights movement in the South was dependent upon the freedom riders, student groups, priests, nuns, ministers and all others who had the courage to invade that closed security.

Some support and comfort came in April 1966 to many alleged "outside agitators" from the Catholic Bishops' of California.[33] The editors of Ave Maria evaluated the bishops' pastoral letter as masterful an application of Catholic social doctrine to a particular situation as they had ever seen. Although the pastoral was late in coming, still the bishops were congratulated. For, the pastoral was issued at a most propitious time. Without prejudice to the health of the agriculture industry, the revolution for the dignity of the farmworkers had begun to be effective. The pastoral also offered people concerned about both the workers and the industry some "sympathetic and wise counsel of a concerned Church."

The Ave Maria editors thought that the pastoral letter was bound to play a major part in the hopeful emergence of better relationships between contending forces in the migrant labor dispute. That major contribution of the letter, however, was contingent upon its suggestions being followed. The suggestions

73

included a national minimum wage law for farm labor, the uniting of family farmers for the common good, the self-determination for the workers through organizations for bargaining, the injection of Christian judgment on both sides, and the responsibility on the part of the "agribusiness" giants. Finally, the _Ave Maria_ editors referred to "a previous statement by the Bishops foreshadowing the pastoral" as instrumental "in helping to bring about the monumental agreement" between Chavez and Schenley.

One week later the editors of _America_ saluted the pastoral as "notable for its down-to-earth application of moral principles to the changing face of agriculture."[34] _America_ added that in defending the family farm, the bishops, like the NCRLC, insisted that the family farm must be made a viable economic unit, not a fantasy of well-meaning folk. To insure that family farms be as efficient as corporate agribusiness, the bishops called for a variety of co-operatives, continued government assistance, and retention of the basic objective of the federal reclamation law. The editors noted, "at least implicitly" that their recommendations would not be popular among farm owners. Furthermore, , that applications of the NLRA and unemployment to farming would necessitate some adaptation of existing laws, and, in the case of Catholic farm owners and workers, the atmosphere of conflict was due largely to ignorance of the church's social teaching. The bishops looked forward to the time when well-instructed lay people, intent on existing a Christian influence in agriculture, would take whatever action necessary in their vocational field. Then, the bishops added, with an almost audible sigh of relief, "the hierarchy and clergy will no longer have to be involved in the front lines of the social apostolate." The hope of the editors of _America_ was that in all the U.S. farm states the California Pastoral would receive the widest possible circulation.

However, one month later the same editors had to indicate confusion over--not the circulation--but the sponsorship of the California farm statement.[35] It seemed that Bishop Aloysius J. Willinger of Monterey-Fresno did sign the document and assumed that the other California bishops would ratify the document at a meeting the next day, April 13. They did not do so. The statement had been approved on March 17, 1966, by the rural life directors of the eight California dioceses. Even though the Monterey-Fresno diocesan paper, _Central California Review_, characterized the directors' statement as a "pastoral letter" on April 14, the California bishops never issued one. Subsequently, the document was published in the San Francisco _Monitor_ as "A Pastoral Letter From the Priest-Directors of Catholic Rural Life in California." The diocese of Oakland's _Catholic Voice_ similarly described the statement. The document was not published by the official church organs of Los Angeles, San Diego,

74

and Sacramento. Nevertheless, <u>America</u> repeated its hope for "the widest circulation" and judged that the sponsorship flap "in no way detracts from the intrinsic merits of the statement."

Also, of the opinion that there was a "California Bishops' Pastoral" was Vizzard.[36] He commented on the document and other aspects of the growers' workers' dispute in two different publications with basically the same language. After noting the joy on Easter as the pilgrimage ended in Sacramento and the news of the Schenley announcement, Vizzard noted that a few days after Easter, Mt. LaSalle Vineyards (owned and operated by the Christian Brothers) and Los Gatos Novitiate Winery (owned by the Jesuit California Province) announced that they too were recognizing the NFWA and were prepared to negotiate and sign a contract. Vizzard identified the promotion of national legislation with Christ's injunction to assist the hungry, thirst, naked, etc. The Jesuit farm expert likened a letter to a Congressman or Senator on behalf of such legislation to a cop of cold water given in Christ's name.

In early June 1966, there were strong protests when the U.S. Department of Labor allowed the importation of 1,000 braceros for temporary farm work in California.[37] A new law permitted "emergency" admissions. Along with Chavez' union and the Santa Clara County Council of Churches, the San Francisco Archdiocesan Commission on Social Justice protested the invoking of the "emergency" provisions. Rev. Eugene Boyle, the commission's chairperson, described the decision of the government as a step backward. He attributed success in collective bargaining, among the farmworkers, to the January 1, 1965 decision of Congress to end the "bracero program." Its restoration, whatever the legal rubric, was seen as a blow to the legitimate rights of domestic farm workers.

On June 1, 1966 the International Brotherhood of Teamsters (IBT) announced that it secretly had signed contracts with eight major California growers which hired 2,000 workers, but declined to name the growers.[38] The announcement followed indications from the Council of California Growers that it disliked the Teamsters less than the NFWA. However, on June 6, 1966, the spokesperson for the Western Conference of Teamsters, Elnar O. Mohn, said the Teamsters would stay away from the huge DiGiorgio Corporation's ranch in Delano "solely in response to the entreaties made by Roman Catholic clergymen on behalf of the National Farm Workers Association." The growers immediately charged that priests in Chicago, San Francisco and elsewhere had thwarted "free democratic practices" by their pressure.

From his Washington office, Vizzard, said,

> The Council of California Growers is merely
> defending its own selfish interests by con-
> demning Church leaders' efforts to bring
> legal and social justice to farm workers.

By the end of the week a Teamster spokesperson claimed the union had received petitions from 400 to 500 DiGiorgio workers expressing regret that the union had "succumbed to the entreaties made by the clergymen." However, the union planned no immediate action, according to the spokesperson. Nevertheless, after a 15 minute meeting between Mohn and the 80-year old Bishop Willinger on June 17, a statement issued by the bishop called for free elections which would give every farm worker the right "to accept or reject a plan of union organization or membership." Agreeing in general with the bishop's sentiments, an NFWA spokesperson thought the remarks at the time,

> ...are evidence that he [Willinger] has
> become a dupe of both the DiGiorgio Corpora-
> tion and the Teamsters.
>
> The current dispute between the Teamsters and
> the NFWA at the DiGiorgio ranch is not a
> jurisdictional dispute. The NFWA cannot
> ignore its original responsibility to those
> hundreds of our members who have lost their
> jobs to join the strike.

On June 22, 1966, Robert DiGiorgio at a press conference in San Francisco, revealed that he had written Bishop Willinger to mediate the nine-month strike by the NFWA against the DiGiorgio firm.[39] So, DiGiorgio announced a June 24 union recognition election, "in accordance with Bishop Willinger's recommenda- tion...(of) free, democratic elections." The election would be conducted by a secret ballot asking the workers to state their preference for representation by AWOC, NFWA, IBT or any other union. The election was to be supervised by a national account- ing firm. Serving as "impartial observers" would be Rev. Roger Mahoney of the Monterey-Fresno chancery office and Rev. R.B. Moore, pastor of St. Paul's Baptist Church in Delano.

DiGiorgio's plan was challenged at the press conference by William Kircher, national director of organization for the AFL- CIO. He compared DiGiorgio's announcement to "the treachery at Pearl Harbor" and revealed that no indication of the June 24 election had been given to NFWA, which had reopened informal talks with DiGiorgio regarding elections on June 16 and June 20. Procedures worked out at the meetings had to be discussed with the NFWA membership. There was also an agreement to meet again on June 24 and to place a moratorium on all statements to the press. Less than 24 hours before the June 24 election, the San Francisco Superior Court Judge Gerald S. Levin issued a temporary injunction sought by AWOC and NFWA to keep their names off the ballot.

So, to protest the unilaterally established election procedures, AWOC and NFWA boycotted the June 24 election. In addition to picketing the election sites--two DiGiorgio ranches-- the unions charged voting irregularities. Ironically, the day before DiGiorgio called for elections, NFWA and Schenley Industries announced the signing of a one-year agreement including a minimum wage of $1.80 an hour, improved working conditions and hiring employees through the union hall.

Around this time, Robert DiGiorgio responded to a request of the Ave Maria editors to state the DiGiorgio position on its controversy with the NFWA.[40] DiGiorgio stated his support for the inclusion of agricultural workers in the NLRA, the negotiations with NFWA, and the proposal for the election. Before concluding with an expression of appreciation for the opportunity to present DiGiorgio's side of the story, the corporation's spokesperson added two additional elements.

First, during meetings of DiGiorgio and NFWA there were several modifications of DiGiorgio's proposals for the elections, in order to overcome NFWA objections. New objections were found and finally DiGiorgio asked Chavez to bring to the May 10th meeting election conditions that would be satisfactory to NFWA. At the May 10th meeting, Chavez once more insisted that DiGiorgio recognize the NFWA without elections. Said Di Giorgio's spokesperson, "When we asked him point blank if there were any conditions under which he would agree to hold elections, his answer was a flat no."

Second, during the dispute DiGiorgio had sought counsel from religious leaders. Subsequently, Bishop Willinger sent Reverend Roger Mahony as an observer. After introductions to both grower and union representatives, an NFWA attorney said, "When we want the Church involved we'll call them." When Mahony asked Chavez if he was of the same opinion, Chavez said, "Yes." Mahony left the meeting.

Nevertheless, within a few days of the June 24 election, Governor Brown announced that he had asked President Johnson's

Commission on Equal Opportunity Consultant, Ronald W. Haughton of the University of Michigan, to conduct an "impartial investigation" of the disputed election.[41] The move by Brown was hailed by Senator Harrison B. Williams (D-NJ), chairperson, and Senator Robert F. Kennedy (D-NY), member of the U.S. Senate Subcommittee on Migratory Labor. Both senators urged the DiGiorgio Corporation to delay any further discussions with the Teamsters until the investigation was completed. Although DiGiorgio announced it would bargain with the Teamsters, the latter group made no comment.

There were two other investigations of the election--conducted by religious groups. The bishop of San Diego, James J. Furey, appointed the diocesan rural life director, Rev. Terry Sims, to investigate the DiGiorgio's Barrego Ranch portion of the election. The official impartial observer there, Rev. John Desmond of Julian, California, refused to sign the certification papers. In Delano, on June 26, a 14-member Inter-Faith Committee for Just Farm Labor-Management Relations heard testimony from more than 25 non-NFWA DiGiorgio employees. These non-union workers charged that DiGiorgio personnel used pressure, intimidation and fraudulent election procedures.

On June 29, four days after the election, Chavez, Hartmire, Salandini and nine farm workers were arrested for trespassing at the DiGiorgio's Barrego Ranch. The twelve escorted DiGiorgio workers to retrieve their personal belongings from the workers' barracks after leaving their jobs in protest of the DiGiorgio handling of the June 24 election. Earlier the former DiGiorgio employees were refused a sheriff's escort into the ranch. Although Chavez, Hartmire, Salandini and the nine workers were released on bond the next day, on June 29 they were subject also to citizens arrest by other DiGiorgio employees. In addition to being manacled and confined in a truck most of that night, the 12 were driven 50 miles by San Diego County sheriff's deputies to Ramona for an afternoon arraignment on June 30th.

About the same time, there was a three-day prayer vigil and protest in the Sacramento diocesan cathedral of the Blessed Sacrament.[42] Some 400 people protested Bishop Alden J. Bell's restrictions of the boycott picketing of DiGiorgio products by Rev. Eugene Lucas, assistant pastor of Our Lady of Guadalupe parish. In the fall of 1965, Lucas, Rev. Keith Kenny, Administrator of Our Lady of Guadalupe parish, and another priest were restricted to activities within the Sacramento diocese, after visiting Delano, 300 miles away in the Monterey-Fresno diocese. At the cathedral in late June, 400 persons signed a petition to the bishop, asking that "Father Lucas be given freedom to serve the needs of his ministry." A spokesperson for the social justice committees said that Lucas had picketed stores handling DiGiorgio products on four different occasions.

The social justice committee, a group of Mexican and English-speaking Catholics, had requested the bishop to come to the cathedral on the first night. They had been informed that the bishop had left for vacation the previous day. However, he was known to have been in his office on the morning of the first day of the vigil. The protestors were met at the cathedral by Msgr. Raymond Renwald, the rector, and two other priests appointed by the bishop as official greeters. Renwald approved the use of the cathedral for the vigil and assured the protestors he would be happy to receive the petition. The petition was placed on a table at the altar rail. For approximately one half hour, the petitioners processed up the aisle to sign, all the time singing Spanish and English hymns. The petition contained other points, in addition to the request on behalf of Lucas. Besides a call for a collegial-type diocesan senate of clerics and laity, clear approval for the Cursillo movement and assistants to be treated as "mature and responsible adults," the petition requested that priests and laypeople be allowed to choose their own position on the grape strike, the bishop speak out on social issues, pressure against people in social action be ended, and the bishop make clear that preaching the Good News is the principal work of the Church and that buildings are secondary.

On August 22, 1966, the National Farm Workers Association (NFWA) formally merged with the Agricultural Workers organizing Committee (AWOC), to become the United Farm Workers Organizing Committee (UFWOC)--AFL-CIO with headquarters in Delano.[43] Eventually, UFWOC was referred to simply as United Farm Workers (UFW). Around the same time, Governor Brown's chosen investigator of the DiGiorgio election, University of Michigan labor management relations expert, Ronald W. Houghton, issued his report. In addition to his recommendations that a new election be held on August 30, 1966--there were three key provisions of Houghton's report,

> The election should be held under the supervision of the American Arbitration Association. (Farm workers are presently excluded from all National Labor Relations Board jurisdiction.)

> Workers eligible to vote would be those who had been employed by the DiGiorgio Corporation in Delano before September 19, 1965,

and in Borrego Springs before June 23, 1966 (the days prior to the beginning of the strikes at those properties), or who had been on the payroll for 15 working days prior to the August 30 election day.

All field workers were to vote on a white ballot while nonfield workers were to vote on a green ballot. The winner of each ballot would then be designated as the sole bargaining agent for those particular workers.

All parties--DiGiorgio, the Teamsters and UFW agreed to Houghton's recommendations. On the August 30, 1966 election the UFW AFL-CIO won jurisdictional and bargaining representation rights over the farmworkers, with only 19 of the 1,319 who voted rejecting Chavez's union. Krebs called the vote "a dramatic rebuke to the long-used grower argument that agricultural workers do not want unions." However, during the campaign there were verbal attacks on the religious and other UFW supporters, especially from the Teamsters, despite praise and pledge of support from Teamster president Hoffa's special representative, Jack Goldberger, at the end of the 25-day pilgrimage from Delano to Sacramento, April 10.

Chief Teamster organizer for the southern San Joaquin Valley, Bill Grami, circulated in August an article by Gary Allen, a Los Angeles screenwriter, entitled "The Grapes", which appeared in the June 1966 issue of American Opinion, published by the John Birch Society. Grami defended the use of the article, which he found distasteful, on grounds that the UFW "persisted in calling us criminals." However, some of the items in the article, which Grami found helpful for his purposes, focused on the church's involvement. For example, the author, Allen, found one common denominator among the Migrant Ministers in Delano. They were all graduates of the same school, the "University of Alinsky," which had a rather narrow curriculum--offering classes only in revolution. Also, "the phony strikers' were supported by the California Council of Churches and the "Liberal-dominated Central California diocese." Allen proceeded to his evaluation that the situation in Delano was a textbook example of the classic "united front." Communists and "non-Communists fellow travelers, opportunists and dupes" worked together and make "strange bedfellows."

On the other hand, there was additional religious support for UFW. In addition to laudatory wires from New York Democratic Senator Robert Kennedy and AFL-CIO president George Meany, UFW was notified that it was the recipient of the award

80

for the promotion of social justice by the National Catholic Social Action Conference (NCSAC). The UFW election victory over the Teamsters and DiGiorgio was also a source of encouragement to migrant workers elsewhere.

In Wisconsin, Jesus Salas, leader of an independent chapter of UFW, was successful in organizing a seven-day march to the state capitol in Madison.[44] Clergy support was led by Rev. Michael Gerrigan, assistant pastor of St. Joseph parish in Wautoma and a full-time official for the Migrant Apostolate. The apostolate was sponsored by the Green Bay diocese and also provided during summer months, clinics, thrift shops and teaching.

In Texas' Stan County about 1,000 persons, including many farm workers, were gathered in the cafeteria of the San Juan shrine, after a five-day 48-mile pilgrimage from Rio Grande City.[45] They heard the Bishop of Brownsville, Humberto Medeiros, call for a minimum wage of $1.25 an hour for striking farm workers and support unequivocally the right and duty of workers to form unions for their own protection and to strike when conciliatory talks failed. Medeiros called the existing farm wages in the Lower Rio Grande Valley unjust and a direct cause of substandard housing, malnutrition and disease. He asserted that such conditions were the rule and not the exception among farm workers in the valley. He received a standing ovation when he claimed that those who received less than $1.25 an hour were not receiving what they needed to live decent lives according to American standards of living.

Although Medeiros also supported the management right to unite and expressed the hope that both sides would meet and bargain for a just outcome, he did not specify whether he believed the strike was justified. He outlined the church's stand.

> In the present dispute between workers and growers the role of the bishops and priests is...to preach the justice and charity of the Gospel...
>
> We can act as mediators, as conciliators; we can meet as I have met with labor union leaders representing labor and with growers representing management and bring them to the light of the Gospel in the hope that they will meet and bargain for what is just for all and not only for one side...

81

> It is not fair to expect the bishops and the
> priests to be experts in all matters concern-
> ing the affairs of the world...(they) serve
> the people by teaching and inspiring them
> with the truth of the Gospel, but the laymen
> must see to it that what they learn from the
> bishops and priests is put into practice in
> the world in which we all live. They have
> the competence, the ability, and should have
> the zeal and the will to do it.

During the question and answer period Medeiros said about the
dispute, "...until both sides ask me to mediate, my hands are
tied."

Two months later, the pilgrimage, which included eucharists
in Catholic churches and food served in parish halls, had completed its 400-mile march to the Texas capitol in Austin.[46] Even
though the marchers' demand for a $1.25 an hour minimum wage was
not met, they resolved to picket the capitol until the demand was
met--despite the fact that the Texas state legislature would not
meet again until January 1967. Awaiting the marchers who carried
religious banners and the red "huelga" (Spanish for strike) flags
was a rally of some 8,000 people. Democratic Senator, Ralph W.
Yarborough, of Austin, Texas, led the march the last six blocks
to the capitol building calling it "the greatest march in the
history of Texas." Democratic Senator, Robert F. Kennedy of New
York sent a telegram of support from Washington, D.C.

The Texas governor, John Connally, Jr., earlier said he
could not lend the dignity of his office to their cause by greet-
ing the marchers at the capitol steps. Instead, Connally met the
marchers in New Braunfels, 50 miles outside Austin. His surprise
appearance came after eight of the Texas Catholic bishops sent
the governor a letter urging him to meet the strikers when they
reached Austin. In a separate letter, San Antonio Archbishop,
Robert E. Lucey, one of the eight bishops, urged Connally to consider the marchers' plea. Referring to the celebration of
a Pontifical mass on August 27th in San Antonio's San Fernando
Cathedral, Lucey told Connally,

> I met with these people last Saturday...They
> are honest, God-fearing farm laborers, whose
> social status is low and whose financial con-
> dition is desperate.

During the New Braunfels' meeting Connally was cheered upon
his arrival and jeered upon his announcement that he would not be

in Austin when the marchers arrived. Connally responded, "You don't need a march to see me. The door of my office is open and was open on July 4." The marchers' request for a special session of the legislature to pass the minimum wage law was denied by Connally, as well as the Attorney General, Waggoner Carr, and the House Speaker, Don Barnes. When Connally began listing the amounts of federal money spent on anti-poverty programs, he was interrupted by Antonio Gonzalez, one of the chairpersons for the pilgrimage, who shouted,

> We don't want charity...The Mexican-Americans
> have been suffering for 100 years...We don't
> want talk; we want action.

Connally retorted, "I'm answering you by my presence here today."

1967

Some seven months after this confrontation and rally, the Texas Catholic bishops spoke out even more forcefully.[47] At the close of a two-day meeting during the week of March 31, 1967, ten Texas Catholic bishops issued a joint-statement on "the critical controversy between farm workers and growers." Among other things, the bishops asserted

> We...would remind farm workers that among the
> basic rights of the human person is the right
> of freely founding associations or unions for
> working people. These unions should be able
> to truly represent them and to contribute to
> the organizing of economic life in the right
> way. Included is the right of freely taking
> part in the activity of these unions without
> risk of reprisals. In view of the present
> depressed state of farm workers and the need
> for organization in order to bargain effec-
> tively in our economy and to rear their
> families in frugal and decent comfort, we say
> that generally they have a duty to form and
> join unions or associations of the type
> mentioned.
>
> On the other hand, farmers in general, and
> especially farm families also need to cooper-
> ate more closely together, forming associ-
> ations that will safeguard their interests
> and secure for them a just share of the gross
> national product of this country...

It would seem reasonable that legislation similar to the NLRA which has proven benefic- ial to the economy and culture with modifi- cations taking into account the special characteristics of this segment of the economy.

On April 20, 1967, Humberto Medeiros, whose Brownsville, Texas, diocese was the scene of a 10-month strike by migrant workers, issued a pastoral letter to all Catholics in the diocese and in effect to most of the population of the area.[48] The pastoral letter, issued much earlier in the strike, contained many quotes from Pope John XXIII and Pope Paul VI on the right of farm workers to a decent living. Medeiros noted that American farmers "live out a precarious existence" and urge both farmers and workers to organize in their own interest. He elaborated,

> The present plight of the migrant farm work- ers of America is a constant reproach to our way of life.
>
> They do not ask for charity. They demand what is theirs by natural right. When the affluent farmers pay a just wage to the migrant worker, when they make it possible for him to support himself and his family in frugal comfort and to provide education for the whole family, they are not making a gift of their possessions to the farm worker; they are simply handing over to him what is his, for they had arrogated to themselves what had been given in common for the use of all...
>
> Given the national and even international depressed condition of agriculture and of farm workers and of many farm owners in par- ticular, it is urgent that they be aware of their right to join associations which alone can procure for them the means of development which in the words of Pope Paul VI signifies peace.
>
> We know that every man has a basic natural right to form and join workers' unions which contribute to economic progress by defending his rights. But the circumstances of the times the world over indicate that for the common good it is also the duty for both

84

migrant farm workers and for farmers to form associations.

Consequently, Medeiros reminded the country of its duty to the migrant laborers and to the farmers,

> ...by passing appropriate legislation and using other suitable and democratic means of assistance so that not only our tables, but the tables of the world may be blessed with the abundance of the fruits of the earth.

The pastoral was a happy climax to a diocesan flap.[49] For, in early February, 1967 five Texas priests were arrested, along with ten members of UFW AFL-CIO, on charges of disturbing the peace at La Casita Farms, near Rio Grande City, Texas. The priests responded to the request for church support from workers who had been on strike for about eight months, in order to gain the right to organize and bargain collectively. The five priests also took part, at various times, in the 1966 600-mile march to the state capital, Austin, to dramatize the plight of the farm workers and their need for a minimum wage. The priests and ten strikers were merely shouting to workers in the fields and were not on La Casita Farms property nor in violation of any law. Tony Orendain, chief UFW organization in Texas, said the strikers were "pleased to have the priests here" and that the local priests had not responded to pleas for support.

Yet, several complaints were registered about "interference."[50] One Brownsville priest said in an interview by the _Alamo Messenger_, when asked if farm workers needed a union in Starr County--17 poorest of 3,130 U.S. counties,

> No, but if they ever do, and if they go about it properly, they will receive all the support they need.

When asked if the principles of the papal encyclicals were involved in the dispute, the same priest, Monsignor Dan Lanning of Mission, Texas, answered,

> I am not able to say. I was ordained to offer Mass and bring the sacraments to the people.

Some of the priests accused of "interference" were from San Antonio. Its ordinary Archbishop Lucey twice defended his priests. Immediately after the incident, he said,

> Father (William) Killian and the others who
> went down to Rio Grande City were acting
> largely as individuals, but at the same time,
> no one doubts that they are Catholic priests
> belonging to this Archdiocese. They saw
> human beings in distress and they went to
> help them. In view of this help, they went
> with my blessing.

Some days later in Brownsville, Lucey preached at the installation of the new bishop, Humberto Medeiros. In speaking of the farm problem, Lucey said

> It is the clear and constant teaching of the
> Church that labor must be organized and
> strikes sometimes are necessary. This teach-
> ing is dangerous heresy to businessmen who
> are blind to the necessity of labor organi-
> zation...Woe to those who would keep the poor
> downtrodden.

Approximately seven months later, however, two of the priests who went into Brownsville were punished, along with three other priests, by Lucey for trying to encourage lettuce workers to strike and were arrested on February 2 near Rio Grande City.[51] The two "recidivists", William Killian, editor of the Alamo Messenger, and Sherrill Smith, archdiocesan director of Social Justice, were ordered to spend a week at a Jemez Springs, New Mexico retreat house.

For, soon after his installation as ordinary of Brownsville, Bishop Medeiros let it be known that he did not welcome priests from other dioceses coming to the aid of strikers in his diocese. He vigorously protested the "intrusion" of such priests on several occasions.

Killian and Smith stated that the punishment for their disobedience was just. However, they also issued a joint-statement,

> We ask for the people, why can't they have
> priests they want and trust? Why can't they
> have priests who will not sit on diocesan
> fences but will stand on them? How do we get
> the church's "alliance" with the poor out of
> rhetoric and into reality?

Seconding their plea was the national field representative of the Bishops Committee for the Spanish Speaking, Father John McCarthy. He asserted,

> It seems essential that the Church set up new structures that would give freedom to movement to those engaged in social action. The organizational structure of the Church is still built completely around totally autonomous dioceses.

When the priests' punishment was announced, 18 members of the Valley Farm Workers committee picketed Lucey's residence. Though the pickets' signs criticized the archbishop, the spokesperson said they were supporting the priests, not attacking the archbishop. Such picketing was a sharp change in behavior accorded Lucey, who had been a staunch defender of labor and Mexican-American farm workers for most of his 75 years.

Similarly, Lucey's behavior was a sharp contrast to some additional remarks he made two months earlier in Brownsville at Medeiros' installation,

> In our day Christ could say, "I was a compesino near Rio Grande City working 10 hours a day under the burning sun. I was tired and weary and you did not comfort me. My children were hungry and you bought us no food, although you were well fed.
>
> "Three priests came from afar. They walked with me and they talked with me. They offered me their love and loyalty, and you called them imposters.'

A priest from Notre Dame University, Richard J. Grimm, C.S.C., compared their action to that of the Good Samaritan.[52] He also complained about the virtual silence about "negative heretics" who had neither studied nor implemented the teachings of Ecclesia Docens in Vatican II.

In early May, 1967, Smith was suspended by Archbishop Lucey after voicing support of three other priests who criticized Lucey in a secular newspaper, The San Antionio Express-News.[53] This was the first suspension of Smith by Lucey. In late May all four priests were reinstated by Lucey. In late June 1969 Father William A. Killian, wrote a clarifying letter to National Catholic Reporter.[54] Writing, as the reinstated editor of the Alamo Messenger, Killian insisted.

> ...just for the record and once and for all,
> the archbishop never suspended any priests
> for their involvement with the huelguistas in
> the Rio Grande Valley...Archbishop Lucey has
> supported us wholeheartedly in this work.

Admitting that the Archbishop's prohibition came after the local bishop preferred to handle the situation himself, Killian remarked.

> In the midst of the controversy...many in the
> church and news media implied that Archbishop
> Lucey has reversed his stand regarding the
> farm workers in particular and thousands of
> other poor people in this part of the coun-
> try.

> Nothing could be further from the truth.
> In this entire effort, we have been applauded
> and supported by Archbishop Lucey.

Smith returned in Autumn of 1972 from a two year assignment as an assistant in a small farming community, El Campo, on the edge of the San Antonio Archdiocese.[55] Less than a month after being entrusted with the pastorate in Crystal City, he was arrested with four others on the charge of obstructing a public highway in the course of a farmworkers' strike.[56] When Lucey's successor, Archbishop Francis Furey, was asked about Smith's arrest he responded, "I expect something like this. I'm not surprised." Several years later, when Smith heard of Medeiros' appointment as archbishop of Boston, he even called Medeiros "a holy man in the true sense of the word." He said Medeiros had opposed the presence of the priests from outside the Brownsville diocese, because Medeiros "thought his own priests and/or he could take care of the matter."

Further praise of Lucey was raised in 1967 when Reverend James T. Conway, the Paulist Father cited above, commented on church support of strikers in Texas.[57] Conway remarked on the support of Archbishop Lucey mentioned when he met strikers who marched to San Antonio's Cathedral of San Fernando. After accepting their offering of a basket of melons and a bushel of cotton, Lucey mentioned that his father had been a union member. He stated, "We endorse and approve your demand for an hourly wage of $1.25. This objective of yours is a step in the right direction." Noted also was that the Bishops' Committee for Migratory Labor, which Lucey chaired, had shipped more than 10,000 pounds of food to the strikers during the first three weeks of the strike.

By July 21, 1967 the spotlight was once again on the California migrants.[58] On that day, R. Perelli-Minetti, a Delano grape grower, acknowledged UFW as the collective bargaining agents for their farm workers. The original controversy began on September 8, 1966 when UFW struck the grower. On September 16, 1966, the growers signed what the UFW called a "sweetheart contract" with the Teamsters. During five months of negotiations between the company and union representatives, seven clergymen served as an arbitration board. The July 21, 1967 agreement gave UFW jurisdiction over field workers and the Teamsters over workers in canneries, creameries, frozen food processing plants, dehydrating plants, producers markets and warehouses.

However, the president of the Council of California Growers, O.W. Fillerup, accused the interfaith clergy committee of...

> bludgeoning growers in behalf of farm union organizers (and following) the whims of the powerful bosses of organized labor.
>
> These church leaders have now appointed themselves the ultimate authority as to who will decide what contracts are valid, who should be boycotted, who should be picketed and literally who does what to whom.

The chairman of the Episcopal diocese's Department of Social Relations, Rev. Richard Byfield, responded to Fillerup's criticism,

> The committee was working at the request of, or with the concurrence of, all three parties to the dispute. Mr. Fillerup has mistaken reconciliation for dictation.

Chavez, on the other hand, announced that other large California wineries were also expressing a willingness to recognize UFW. He claimed, "We now have several contracts signed and we are preparing for representation elections at several other companies."

1968

In early March 1968, it was announced that Chavez would end a 25-day "spiritual fast to rededicate his union to justice through non-violence."[59] Union spokespeople emphasized that this action of Chavez was not a "hunger strike" but a "spiritual fast"--

A hunger strike usually follows some sort of specific demands. Cesar Chavez's fast was entirely different. It was simply an action of rededication to those ideals of non-violence which the union has sought to maintain throughout the Delano strike.

...(Chavez's fast) is a powerful call for faithful and effective leadership so that present hopes will not turn to frustration, frustration to despair, despair to violence.

Early in the fast Chavez took only about a gallon of water a day, but on March 5th, his doctor, James McKnight, advised Chavez to take a clear medication with his water to correct a dangerously high lactic acid content in his blood which could cause premanent kidney damage. McKnight remained with Chavez throughout the fast making periodic tests and examinations. During the day Chavez rested on a cot in a 10-by-12 room adjacent to a chapel in the UFW's nearly completed co-op gasoline station. Each evening Chavez joined his wife, eight children, mother and father, UFW members and friends in the eucharist.

UFW spokespeople reported that more than 100 telegrams were received urging Chavez to abandon his fast. One of the telegrams was from Senator Robert Kennedy of New York who stated his support for Chavez' commitment, but added that was the very reason "...why your active leadership is so badly needed not only for the future but right now as well." The plans to end the fast by mid-March included the news that Chavez would take sweet Mexican bread during an outdoor eucharist celebrated by Rev. Mark Daly, a Franciscan assigned to work with UFW.

By early June 1968, the bishops of the eight Catholic dioceses in California issued a statement on farm labor, highlighted by a unanimous call to the U.S. Congress to include all farm workers in the NLRA.[60] Deploring the plight of U.S. farm workers as belonging to "that vast number of poor, forgotten and neglected Americans," the California bishops also cited the "anguish, bitterness and even despair" of the three-year old farm labor dispute in Delano. The bishop recalled previous occasions on which they had stated.

...the right of all men--both farmers and farm workers--to organize themselves for purposes of collective bargaining and mutual protection.

90

We now reaffirm those teachings, motivated by
the knowledge that the entire agricultural
industry will benefit from such organization.

Declaring their judgment firm because they had witnessed chaos
and human suffering all too clearly, the bishops called for a
change of heart, encouragement and sponsorship of more public and
private discussions between growers and farm workers and union
organizers --a true ministry of reconciliation. The call to the
U.S. Congress was no less insistent:

> We feel strongly that genuine, lasting peace
> will never come to farm management-labor
> relations, until farm workers are included
> under the NLRA . . . The majority of our
> nation's farm workers belong to that vast
> number of poor, forgotten and neglected Amer-
> icans. Both government and private agencies
> have given no more than token response to
> their cries for help. Farm workers have been
> seeking a basic right accorded almost all
> other workers in this country. . . Congress
> has found reason to exclude (farm workers
> from the NLRA) since 1935. We cannot in con-
> science allow another year to pass without
> effecting social justice for the farm worker.

By late July 1968 statements endorsing Cesar Chavez' and the
UFW's boycott of California grapes began to arrive. One such
endorsement came from the Chicago meeting of the National Association of Laymen.[61] Another such endorsement came in mid-August
1968 from a group of 25 persons in Los Angeles who formed an
interfaith, interracial coalition to support the nation-wide boycott against California table grapes.[62] The coalition's sponsoring committee included social action leaders of several denominations, including representatives of the Los Angeles Association
of Laymen and Catholic Human Relations Council. Also included in
the coalition were the Southern California Board of Rabbis, the
Presbyterian Interracial Council and the Southern and Northern
California Councils of Churches. One member of the coalition,
Sister Mary Corita Kent, I.H.M., issued a statement from Boston,

> I recognize that a boycott, though non-
> violent, causes much economic disruption.
> This disruption is not necessary and it can
> end quickly if only agricultural employers
> will recognize the worth of their workers and
> bargain with them as men.

91

In late August 1968, Gerard Sherry, editor of the Central California Register, official publication of the diocese of Fresno, testified before the U.S. House Labor and Education Subcommittee hearing in Delano.[63] The subcommittee hearing was one of several held throughout the U.S. to study the impact of the one-and-one-half year old federal minimum wage law on farm workers and to consider other types of protective legislation. Sherry alleged

> ...grower-supported people have been harrassing and picketing and threatening those firms which advertise in our newspaper. . .

> We have taken no sides in the dispute between growers and the union, but we have urged conciliation in keeping with the position of the Catholic Church.

Stating that the paper's advertising revenue reached its lowest point in 20 years, Sherry claimed that growers and members of the Agricultural Workers Freedom to Work Association (AWFWA) were displeased about the newspaper's free distribution in July of pamphlets on the Delano strike to 50,000 families in the Fresno diocese. The pamphlets contained the California Bishops' statement, interviews with Chavez and interviews with Martin Zaninovich, president of the South Central Farmers Committee of Delano. The newspaper's editorials coincided with the California Bishops' statement also.

On July 17, 1968 letters were sent to the diocesan newspaper's advertisers by Jose' Mendoza, general secretary of AWFWA, accusing the Central California Register, the church and Fresno's bishop, Timothy Manning, of "helping to promote an illegal boycott against certain California vineyards" and indicated that any firm advertising in the Central California Register would be picketed. UFW officials charged that the pro-grower AWFWA was composed mainly of local business leaders and merchants who in the past formed organizations such as Citizens for Facts on Delano, Mothers Against Chavez, and Men Against Chavez. In June 1968, AWFWA picketed a Fresno conference called by Bishop Manning on the problems of the Spanish-speaking. During the noisy demonstration pickets burned an UFW flag.

In late November 1968 some other officers of the South Central Farmers' Committee, Louis Lucas and John Bree, were critical of religious support of Chavez' union in Delano.[64] Both spoke at a Young Republicans and Interfraternity Council discussion at Stanford University, whose student body, in October

1968, voted 1,030-409 to support the California table grapes boy-cott. Both Lucas and Bree said the UFW had failed to win sub-stantial support in the Delano area and had "made an atrocity" of its bargains with the Di Giogio Fruit Company and the Schenley Industries. Both claimed that the grape workers around Delano earned about $2.30 an hour rather than the $1.69 average for California farm workers. Both claimed that a full-time grape worker's annual earnings ranged from $4,000 to $10,000 depending on the type of job. Both alleged that the publicized statistics on earnings usually lumped together full-time workers with house-wives, students and other part-time employees. Lucas and Bree asserted that Chavez never produced proof that 30 per cent of the workers had signed cards indicating a desire for a union within NLRA guidelines and that in the vote to unionize the Di Giogrio operation union members were bussed round-trip from El Paso, Texas.

Lucas criticized clergymen supporting the grape pickers strike for "adding dignity to a cause which is without dignity." Lucas also claimed that in some areas the boycott had been successful. Noting that vineyard owners had filed suits against unions involved in the boycott and had considered legal actions against stores supporting the boycott, Lucas quipped, "It's been used as a good excuse for a lower price" by chain stores negoti-ating with growers. Bree said

> . . . many church leaders are taking a second look at Delano. I'm not so naive as to stand here and tell you we're all great guys--but we're not demons, either.

Bree indicated that growers were considering picking grapes by machines even though it may cost twice as much as now paid to laborers.

In early September 1968, the AWFWA, South Central Farmers Committee and national legislators received some strong criticism from the America editors.[65] Recalling the AWFWA's picketing of advertisers in the Central California Register and the divisive-ness and bitterness in the California vineyard communities, the editors quoted from the pastoral letter of the bishop of Fresno, Timothy Manning. Issued on the feast of St. Joseph the Worker--Labor Day--and to be read at all church eucharists, the pastoral pleaded,

> In God's name, let us meet at the altar and beg for the charity of reconciliation, remove all bitterness and begin once more to cooper-ate, to forgive and understand.

The editors could understand the strong feelings in the Congress over all questions of farm labor legislation and even the reluctance before the 1968 election to place one's party in a precarious position for control of the White House and both houses of Congress. Nevertheless, the editors of America felt that Congress should rise to the challenge from California over the basic issue in the farm laborers' and growers' controversy-- the right of farm workers to organize for the purpose of collective bargaining. The editors elaborated,

> There would be fewer strikes out there, less employer-inspired violence, fewer boycotts, if farm employers acknowledged that right. Most of them, banded together in the South Central Farmers Committee, refused reconciliation simply because the right is not legally protected...(They) will not recognize or negotiate with unions representing their employees until they are compelled to do so by law.

> Whatever justification there was originally for excluding farm workers from the Wagner Act...there is none now. The shape of agricultural enterprise has so changed... that over large areas employment relations are comparable to those existing in industry- ...Unless it acts before the end of the present session, it (Congress) must assume, therefore, full responsibility for the largely unnecessary strife in California and elsewhere.

Just before Christmas 1968, Commonweal printed an article quite critical of the NCCB's failure to support by name the striking UFW or its national consumer boycott of California table grapes.[66] A. V. Krebs, Jr., who wrote the article, labelled "lack-luster" the NCCB statement calling for federal legislation to allow America's 1.5 million farm workers the legal right to organize and bargain collectively. Krebs pointed out that there were reports that an original draft of the bishops' statement specifically noted the strike and the boycott's significance. However, bishops Hugh A. Donohoe of Stockton and Timothy Manning of Fresno objected to such specifics. To a reporter, Bishop Donohoe replied, "The bishops had to put out a statement with which we can all live." Krebs recalled the statement in 1966 from a chancery official, when a union pleaded for the then bishop of Fresno to mediate a strike. Declaring the church's

94

neutrality, the Fresno spokesperson used language different from Donohoe's: "It is unfair to assume that we hesitate to speak out against injustice because of the reprisal from those best able to support our churches, schools and institutions." However, offensive and unlivable or unfair and unfounded, Krebs, not only accused the bishops of "allowing local diocesan economics to dictate to them to what degree they should support the nation's farm workers," but also accused the NCCB of ignoring some important facts.

First, the bishops ignored an important part of their own statement by turning a deaf ear to agricultural employees from Florida to California who looked to the Delano strike and California table grape boycott as a last ditch effort to help themselves achieve economic and social justice. The important part of the NCCB statement that was ignored read, " ... for 30 years the disadvantaged field workers of this nation have stood by helplessly and listened to other Americans debating the farm labor problem." Second, the NCCB ignored President-elect Richard M. Nixon's making it abundantly clear that he did not favor NLRB coverage for farm workers. Nixon's preference was for, " ... farmers and farm workers discussing mutual problems in good faith and always within the framework of law that protects the individual interest and public interest. Third, the U.S. Catholic bishops ignored the loss of pro-Chavez supporters from the Senate Labor Committee: "[The] ... the loss of Pennsylvania's Joe Clark, Oregon's Wayne Morse, Alaska's Ernest Gruening, and particularly Robert Kennedy will make passage of appropriate legislation doubtful if not impossible." Fourth, the NCCB ignored its efforts in 1965 on behalf of the Civil Rights Act, when they did detail a "specific program to mobilize a grass roots campaign." Fifth, the bishops' failure to advocate "all available just means" to achieve the basic right to organize made empty promises of the assertion of that right in the social documents of the Church. The bishops' lack of specifics reminded Krebs of Vizzard's criticism of the local church's non-involvement in the beginnings of the Delano strike,

> When the wolf is in the fold it's no help to
> the flock to assure them that, after all, the
> wolf needs to eat too and that besides
> efforts are being contemplated to build--at
> some time in the indefinable future--a more
> secure sheepfold or perhaps even to attempt
> to tame the wolves.

Finally, Krebs expressed his bewilderment over the contrast between the NCCB and NCC. The NCC, "far more vulnerable to economic pressures than the Roman Church", had endorsed the strike and boycott strongly. Krebs cited the closing of the Fresno Council of Churches administrative office for "budgetary reasons". Krebs alleged that when the NCCB was willing to "suffer," it would begin to end the real suffering of millions of the rural poor in the U.S.

A further contrast and comparison was provided in late 1968 between the efforts of bishops and priests working in the Mexican-American community.[67] It was an attempt to study the crucial role of support or opposition provided by neighboring institutions in accounting for the success or failure of priests involved in social and economic protest. Data came from interviews with, and newspaper accounts concerning, thirteen priests known as "social action priests," who had devoted substantial amounts of time and interest to activities aimed at improving the socioeconomic status of Mexican Americans. The thirteen priests formed two sub-groups. Eight were directors of anti-poverty programs. Five took part in direct action on behalf of striking Mexican American agricultural field workers, such as marching and picketing.

There were three striking conclusions from the study. First, unlike priests involved in the "War on Poverty," priests assisting the farmworkers had no network of support in the larger community,

> Their actions touched not upon community supported enterprises such as curbing delinquency, teaching migrant workers new job skills, or improving English usage among preschool children. Union organization threatened to restructure an entire regional economy and do so quite rapidly.

Second, the priests assisting the farmworkers collided directly with the Catholic church's desire to be accepted by the larger society, since the favorable reception of Vatican II. There were threats of economic reprisal at the local, regional and state level. Third, in addition to being vulnerable in the secular realm, the priests assisting the farmworkers were vulnerable in the ecclesial realm also. Not only was their work considered barely pastoral, but appeals to the higher law of charity were dismissed because of challenges to ecclesiastical law. That is

> ...direct disobedience to one's bishop; usurping the jurisdiction of the local clergy; crossing diocesan boundaries without approval of both bishops concerned. Thus the burden of legitimating this action fell

96

squarely upon the priests themselves, whose pleas for involvement" and "relevance" and "social justice" were hardly sufficient to ward off the cross-fire of criticism and counter action from both secular and religious institutional representatives.

1969

In early January 1969 the editors of America noticed the complaints of California grape growers that church folk were biased and ill-informed and compounding a grave injustice by backing Chavez, since the failure of the long Delano strike proved that workers did not want Chavez.[68] The editors passed on the advice of Floyd L. Begin, bishop of the Oakland, California, diocese that all the growers needed to do was to agree to "impartially supervised elections." Begin alleged that the growers' continued refusal to do so "can only question the integrity of the growers' contention and induce more and more people to support the boycott." America restated the endorsement by the U.S. Catholic bishops and the California religious leaders of the "legitimate demand of farm workers for legislative protection of the natural right to organize for purposes of collective bargaining." With rather blunt finality, the America editors concluded that the growers' stand was morally indefensible and that the bishops were not insensitive to the owners' problems.

In early April 1969 the Priests' Senate of the diocese of Davenport endorsed the Chavez boycott of California table grapes.[69] From the diocese of Pittsburgh's Fund for the Aid of Neighbors in Need came $1,500 to provide materials for promoting the boycott. In mid-June 1969, UFW received overtures from ten growers in the Coachella Valley for talks about the four-year old Delano strike of farm workers.[70] The explanation was financial loss and moral pressure. The latter was implied by Fresno bishop, Timothy Manning,

> I commend the leaders. . . in the Coachella Valley and in the Arvin area. . . for their courage to respond to the farm workers' repeated calls for discussions.

The former explanation was admitted more readily by the leaders of the breakaway. Lionel Steinberg of David Freeman Company, who joined John Kovacovich K.S.G., a major grower in the Arvin area, admitted the union-inspired boycott of table grapes was "definitely hurting." A third Coachella grower told a reporter,

97

"We have to settle this thing to survive." The influence of the talks was not likely to be decisive for the standpatters: growers in the San Joaquin Valley and the South Central Farmers Committee of Delano. For, the San Joaquin growers produced a type of grape that readily could be converted into raisins or wine. Consequently, they probably were not hurt as badly by the boycott as the southern producers.

In mid-July 1969 a telegram of support from Chavez and demonstration of assistance from the AFL-CIO and other area organizations encouraged Rev. Stanislaus Pack, a Trinity Missions priest, and eight young men and women who conducted a sit-in the Cleveland Offices of the Great Atlantic & Pacific Tea Company (A & P).[77] The sit-in was in support of the UFW boycott of California table grapes sold in the A & P. Pack was the director of the Spanish Catholic Mission Office, which was supported almost entirely by the Cleveland diocese. Cleveland's auxiliary bishop, William M. Cosgrove, attempted to mediate in the second week of the sit-in. Pack, however, turned down the A & P's conditions: sit-ins leave and an agenda be established before any discussions take place. His reason for refusal--"The only point at issue is the removal of the grapes."

Also, in July 1969, Bishop A. Donohoe of Stockton, spoke at the Newman Center of the Berkeley campus of the University of California.[72] In addition to approval and support of Chavez' change of tactics in retaining exclusion of farm workers from the NLRA, Donohoe underlined the need for such a tactical change. For, the NLRA excluded the secondary boycott so helpful to the UFW cause. The bishop also defended the failure of the U.S. bishops to endorse the boycott, despite the March 1969 NCCB support of farm labor legislation in California. Donohoe, one of the principal drafters of the NCCB statement, responded to the criticism thus:

> Our purpose was to put forth proposals, to build bridges between people. . . Many of the growers already feel the church has "sold out" to the workers. There was no reason to wave a red flag and further raise the hackles of the growers. . . The fact, however, that the bishops did not condemn the boycott, I feel, is significant.

In late August 1969, America printed an article, "The Clergy and the Grape Strike," by the Franciscan priest, Mark Day, who served for some time as a chaplain to UFW.[73] Although he cited mostly incidents involving Protestant clergy, Day said the same conclusions could be drawn about the behavior of the Catholic clergy as well. Those conclusions were:

> Few of the local clergymen have made even the most notorious strikebreakers look respectable. . . I am convinced that no self-respecting rancher would share the contempt these men of the cloth have shown for the impoverished workers. . .

> Not only have most of the churches in Delano failed in their duty to be the conscience of the community, they have taken upon themselves the task of articulating and authenticating the prejudices and bigotry so embedded in this conservative and rural community. It would be fair to say that the churches have assumed the function of being the cornerstone of the status quo. . . And . . . they have become an effective countersign of the gospels. . .

> The statements and actions of some have been unchristian. The silence of others has been a malignant cancer. Had they spoken out for justice earlier, the strike would have ended long ago. . .

> I am convinced that there is a need for "outside agitators" to remind all of us of our responsibilities.

In late September 1969, Bishop Hugh A. Donohoe of Stockton, wrote in the Oakland diocesan newspaper, Catholic Voice.[74] The topic was collective bargaining for farm workers. He asserted Catholic social teaching that on the inalienable right to organize for any good reason is as proper for the farm owners as it is for farm laborers. If farm owners seldom choose to exercise the privilege, it does not entitle them to deny it to farm workers. Anyone attempting to organize either owners or laborers should not be looked upon as "outside agitators." Donohoe reminded the readers of the Catholic Voice that in the 1930s Harry Bridges was more obnoxious than Chavez. Yet, the San Francisco waterfront employers would hate to lose Bridges. Donohoe cautioned that, if Chavez did not do the organizing of the farmworkers, someone else would be on the scene. Chavez was said to be still a learner, so it was not correct to call him "an impossible man" with whom to deal.

Donohoe then proceeded to explain why he and the new arch-bishop of Los Angeles, Timothy Manning, opposed NCCB unholding the legitmacy of the grape boycott in its November 1968 statement on farm labor. In addition to saying something positive to both sides--without red flags or condemnations of the boycott--Donohoe took pains to point out:

> It was not because I felt that I would lose the farmers' economic support because...I have already lost much of that...The Church in general, as far as the farmer is con-cerned, is looked upon as having sold out to the workers...Our object as bishops was to build a bridge. That is our basic function and it isn't always easy to keep this stand.

To stress his point Donohoe drew the contrast between the bishop's stand on farm labor legislation and that of California Republican Senator George Murphy. Donohoe called Murphy's pro-posal "consumer legislation" rather than farm legislation.

> The way Senator Murphy has advertised his bill is that the product comes first, the farmer comes second, and the employee comes third. Having thrown protection around the product with no strikes at harvest time, hav-ing protected the farmer against strikes and offered him other securities, then and only then would the workers be allowed to organ-ize.

In addition to characterizing Murphy's proposal as "putting the cart before the horse," Donohoe contrasted Murphy's with that of the National Industrial Recovery Act in the early 1930's. It forbade employers to interfere with the worker's right to organize, a secret ballot election was mandated. Donohoe pre-ferred this type of legislation to the paternalism the Senator Murphy proposed.

A further echo of the NCCB 1968 call for true farm labor legislation was voiced by Msgr. George Higgins in November 1969.[75] Higgins, in his syndicated column Yardstick, referred to a book sponsored by the editors of Twin Circle and written by a Rev. Cletus Healy. In the book, Battle for the Vineyards, Healy claimed that Cesar Chavez did not begin "truly to represent" the ordinary California grape pickers. Higgins could not imagine

...why Fr. Healy and his sponsors, the
editors of Twin Circle, have yet to commit
themselves to this (NCCB) legislative objective.

For Higgins the one sure way to decide if Chavez truly represented the farm workers was the secret election, for which the NCCB
called.

[1]Charles A. McCarthy, "Farm Crisis in Central California,"
Ave Maria, v. 96, No. 12, 9/22/62, pp. 9-13.

[2]"Pressure Caused Transfer, Priest Says," National Catholic
Reporter, v. 1, No. 35, 6/30/65, p. 2

[3]Victor Salandini, "Union Organizing in the Fields,"
America, v. 113, No. 15, 10/9/65, pp. 400-401.

[4]A.V. Krebs, Jr., "Priests Fly Over Fields, Sound Call to
Strike," National Catholic Reporter, v. 2, No. 2, 11/3/65, pp. 1,
3.

[5]A.V. Krebs, Jr., "California Court Backs Tenants in Rent
Strike," in loc. cit.

[6]Repartee, "Money and Farm Strikers," National Catholic
Reporter, v. 2, No. 4, 11/17/65, p. 4

[7]A.V. Krebs, Jr., "Priests Who Aided Strikers Ordered to
End Involvement," National Catholic Reporter, v. 2, No. 6,
12/1/65, p.12.

[8]Alice Ogle, "Revolution in the Vineyards," America, v.
113, No. 24, 12/11/65, pp. 747-748.

[9]"Grapes of Wrath in California," Current Comment, America,
v. 114, No. 2, 1/8/66, pp. 33-34.

[10]A.V. Krebs, Jr., "Announce Boycott in Grape Strike,"
National Catholic Reporter, v. 2, No. 8, 12/15/65, p. 10.

[11]A.V. Krebs, Jr., "Top Clergy Offer Backing for California
Strikers," National Catholic Reporter, v. 2, No. 9, 12/22/65, p.
12.

[12]"California Bishop Attacks Priest's Strike Comments,"
National Catholic Reporter, v. 2, No. 11, 1/12/66, pp. 1, 10.

[13]"The Bickering in Delano Obscures a National Issue," National Catholic Reporter, v. 2, No. 11, 1/12/66, p. 3.

[14]"Dispute in Delano," Editorials, Commonweal, v. 83, No. 16, 1/28/66, p. 491.

[15]"Delano--Another Selma?," Editorials, Ave Maria, v. 103, No. 1, 1/1/66, p. 15.

[16]"Delano Views," Editorials, Ave Maria, v. 103, No. 5, 1/29/66, pp. 16-17.

[17]"Support for Delano Strikers," Editorials, Ave Maria, v. 103, No. 7, 2/12/66, pp. 16-17.

[18]"Boycott Delano Grapes," Letters, Ave Maria, v. 103, No. 8, 2/19/66, p. 3.

[19]"Delano's Vineyards," Letters, Ave Maria, v. 103, No. 11, 3/12/66, p. 3.

[20]John Leo, "Values from the 'Outside' World," National Catholic Reporter, v. 2, No. 19, 3/9/66, p. 8.

[21]"Catholics Not Absent from Grape Strike," Repartee, National Catholic Reporter, v. 2, No. 21, 3/23/66, p. 4.

[22]A.V. Krebs, Jr., "Grape Strikers Begin 300-Mile 'Pilgrimage'," National Catholic Reporter, v. 2, No. 21, 3/23/66, pp. 1, 10.

[23]Burton H. Wolfe, "Enemy of Exploiters," Sign, v. 45, No. 9, 5/66, pp. 16-18.

[24]Charles A. McCarthy, "Diary of a Grape Strike," Ave Maria, v. 103, No. 3, 1/15/66, pp. 19-22.

[25]A.V. Krebs, Jr., "Grape Strikers Begin 300-Mile 'Pilgrimage'," National Catholic Reporter, v. 2, NO. 21, 3/23/66, pp. 1, 10.

[26]A.V. Krebs, Jr., "Marching Strikers at Half-Way Point," National Catholic Reporter, v. 2, No. 23, 4/6/66, p. 3.

[27]"Texas Bishop Congratulates California Grape Strikers," National Catholic Reporter, v. 2, No. 21, 3/23/66, p. 10.

[28]A.V. Krebs, Jr., "Farm Union Gets Revolution," National Catholic Reporter, v. 2, No. 24, 4/13/66, pp. 1, 10.

[29]"Delano: Victory for Migrants," Editorials, _Ave Maria_, v. 103, No. 17, 4/23/66, p. 4.

[30]"One Way to Endorse the Schenley Decision: Put Money on the Line," Repartee, _National Catholic Reporter_, v. 2, No. 26, 4/27/66, p. 4.

[31]A.V. Krebs, Jr., "Priest-Pickets Help Stop Mass for Farm Workers," _National Catholic Reporter_, v. 2, No. 26, 4/27/66, p. 3.

[32]Jerome Wolf, "The Church and Delano: Social Witness," _Commonweal_, v. 84, No. 6, 4/29/66, pp. 168-169.

[33]"California Bishops Speak," Editorials, _Ave Maria_, v. 103, No. 18, 4/30/66, pp. 4-5.

[34]"Farm Pastoral from California," Editorials, _America_, v. 114, No. 19, 5/7/66, p. 642.

[35]"Farm Statement from California," Current Comment, _America_, v. 114, No. 23, 6/4/66, p. 790.

[36]James L. Vizzard, S.J., "A Cup of Cold Water for the Farm Workers," Repartee, _National Catholic Reporter_, v. 2, No. 28, 5/11/66, p. 4, and "The Grape Strike," Correspondence, _Commonweal_, v. 84, No. 10, 5/27/66, pp. 295-296.

[37]"Protest Approval of 1,000 Imported Braceros," _National Catholic Reporter_, v. 2, No. 32, 6/8/66, p. 3.

[38]A.V. Krebs, Jr., "Teamsters Eye Delano Farm Labor Contracts," _National Catholic Reporter_, v. 2, No. 34, 6/22/66, p. 10.

[39]A.V. Krebs, "Teamsters Lead in Di Giorgio Election," _National Catholic Reporter_, v. 2, No. 35, 6/29/66, p. 3.

[40]Robert Di Giorgio, "Statement of Di Giorgio Corporation to Ave Maria," _Ave Maria_, v. 104, No. 1, 7/2/66, pp. 13, 25.

[41]A.V. Krebs, Jr., "Chavez, 11 Others Arrested," _National Catholic Reporter_, v. 2, No. 36, 7/6/66, p. 5.

[42]"400 Protest Priest's Removal from Picketing," _National Catholic Reporter_, v. 2, No. 36, 7/6/66, p. 5.

[43]A.V. Krebs, Jr., "Ganamos!," Ave Maria, v. 104, No. 19, 11/5/66, pp. 11-14.

[44]Brad Niemczk, "Wisconsin/Migrants Find a Voice in 7-Day March . . . at Least Temporarily," National Catholic Reporter, v. 2, No. 42, 8/24/66, p. 5.

[45]"Bishop Medeiros Backs $1.25 Wage for Strikers," National Catholic Reporter, v. 2, No. 38, 7/20/66, p. 1.

[46]"Texas Workers Vow to Keep Marching," National Catholic Reporter, v. 2, No. 45, 9/14/66, p. 13.

[47]Kay Durate, "Texas Bishops Say Unions a Duty for Farm Workers," National Catholic Reporter, v. 3, No. 23, 4/5/67, p. 3.

[48]"Medeiros Tells Texas Farm Owners to Improve Pay, Living Conditions," National Catholic Reporter, v. 3, No. 26, 4/26/67, p. 10.

[49]"Five Texas Priests Arrested Aiding Strike," National Catholic Reporter, v. 3, No. 15, 2/8/67, p. 12.

[50]"Chavez Farm Revolt," National Catholic Reporter, v. 2, No. 36, 7/6/66, p. 1.

[51]"Two Priests Punished for Helping Strikers," National Catholic Reporter, v. 3, No. 16, 2/15/67, p. 10.

[52]"The Texas Priests Parallel With Parable," Repartee, National Catholic Reporter, v. 3, No. 17, 2/22/67, p. 4.

[53]"4 Suspended Texas Priests Reinstated," National Catholic Reporter, v. 3, No. 30, 5/24/67, p. 6.

[54]"Lucey and the Farm-Worker Pirests," Repartee, National Catholic Reporter, v. 5, No. 35, 6/25/69, p. 4.

[55]"Sherrill Smith Back From Limbo," National Catholic Reporter, v. 8, No. 12, 1/21/72, p. 17.

[56]"Sherrill Smith Arrested in Texas Labor Dispute," National Catholic Reporter, v. 8, No. 15, 2/11/72, p. 3.

[57]James F. Conway, "Migrants: Directions '67," Catholic World, v. 205, 4/67, pp. 31-35.

[58]A.V. Krebs, Jr., "Grower Assails Clergy Efforts as Farm Union Reports Gain," National Catholic Reporter, v. 3, No. 39, 8/2/67, p. 12.

[59]A.V. Krebs, Jr., "Chavez Ends 25-Day Fast," National Catholic Reporter, v. 4, No. 20, 3/13/68, p. 2.

[60]"Bishops Back Farm Workers Plea for NLRA," National Catholic Reporter, v. 4, No. 33, 6/12/68, p. 7, and "California Bishops and the NLRA," Current Comment, America, v. 118, No. 24, 6/15/68, pp. 764-765.

[61]Doris Grambach, "Last Look or First Hope," Commonweal, v. 88, No. 17, 7/26/68, pp. 487-489.

[62]"Los Angeles Group Support Grape Boycott," National Catholic Reporter, v. 4, No. 42, 8/21/68, p. 5.

[63]A.V. Krebs, Jr., "Delano Catholic Editor Says His Critics Cut Ad Revenue," National Catholic Reporter, v. 4, No. 43, 8/28/68, p. 2.

[64]"Grower Hits Clergy Support of Strike," National Catholic Reporter, v. 5, No. 7, 12/4/68, p. 10.

[65]"An Appeal to Congress," Editorials, America, v. 119, No. 7, 9/14/68, pp. 176-177.

[66]A.V. Krebs, Jr., "The Bishops Stay Out of the Vineyard," Commonweal, v. 89, No. 12, 12/20/68, pp. 393-394.

[67]Patrick H. McNamara, "Social Action Priests in the Mexican American Community," Sociological Analysis, v. 29, No. 4, Winter 1968, pp. 177-185.

[68]"Churchmen and Table Grapes," Current Comment, America, v. 20, No. 1, 1/4/69, p. 4.

[69]"Rights for Farm Workers," America, v. 120, No. 17, 4/26/69, pp. 492-493.

[70]"Sundering of the Grape Growers," Current Comment, America, v. 121, No. 1, 7/5/69, p. 2.

[71]"Grape Boycotters Stay Two Weeks at A & P Office, National Catholic Reporter, v. 6, No. 39, 7/23/69, p. 5.

[72]"Bishop Backs Chavez," National Catholic Reporter, v. 6, No. 39, 7/23/69, p. 5.

[73]Mark Day, O.F.M., "The Clergy and the Grape Strike," *America*, v. 121, No. 5.

[74]Hugh Donohoe, "Collective Bargaining for Farm Workers," *Catholic Mind*, v. 68, No. 1239, 1/70, pp. 24-27.

[75]"For a Vote in the Vineyards," Current Comments, *America*, v. 121, No. 17, 11/22/69, p. 482.

Chapter III Later Cesar Chavez and Farmworkers, 1970's

By 1969, Chavez had become the recognized leader of the widely-known effort to unionize the farmworkers. He had much church support, much grower opposition, much governmental interference or indifference and a few small victories. By 1970, his troubles were far from over but success would be coming. There would be many more contracts with grape growers and the initiation of a lettuce boycott, but also further troubles with the Teamsters and the law.

1970

Yet, the call for farm labor law truly helpful to the workers was still being pursued. In February 1970, there was the widely circulated testimony of Reverend John E. McCarthy, USCC Director for Poverty and assistant to Msgr. Higgins, given on Mexican workers before the special subcommittee on labor of the U.S. Congressional Committee on Education and Labor on August 18, 1969.[1] McCarthy spoke in support of HR 12667 which was to amend the NLRA to make it an unfair labor practice to employ certain aliens ("green card commuters") in circumstances that would destroy the rights of workers to organize and bargain collectively. McCarthy pointed out that the "green card commuter" workers from Mexico were unorganized and were used to defeat the efforts of workers to bargain collectively for better wages or working conditions. McCarthy pointed out that the June 1967 Immigration Service regulation prohibited the entry of the "green carders" who intended to take employment in situations where a certified strike was in effect. HR 12667 did not discriminate against green card holders who established residence in the United States. However, HR 12667 extended to the NLRB and to the employers the enforcement of the June 1967 Immigration Service regulation. McCarthy then proceeded to describe the opponents and supporters of HR 12667--on one side the growers, employers, merchants and Chambers of Commerce; on the other side labor union, church, Mexican-American and people-oriented groups.

The latter side sought reasonably to protect U.S. citizens from exploitation. The former side, fearing increased costs, in the past had fought to retain Public Law 78, minimum wage coverage for farmworkers and inclusion of farmworkers in the National Labor Relations Act. The claims of the growers, employers, merchants and Chambers of Commerce that such measures would harm the agricultural industry were wrong, according to McCarthy. For, in the long run, poverty profits no one but creates an incalculable social cost.

Around the time McCarthy's testimony appeared, another USCC official testified before the U.S. Senate Committee on Agriculture.[2] He was John E. Cosgrove, Director of Social Development. His testimony was about S. 2203, the bill of California Senator George Murphy.   While deploring the exclusion of farm workers from most labor and social legislation, Cosgrove rejected S. 2203 as being just non-workable.

First, the purpose of the bill was to restrict severely the activities of farm labor unions.   Second, the enactment of Section 201 of the bill would set aside years of NLRB experience and precedents.   The section would have created a separate Farm Labor Relations Board (FLRB).   The USCC's fear that the proposed FLRB would be prejudiced in favor of farm employers was based on the USCC's reading of the policies of the U.S. Department of Agriculture.   Cosgrove also listed "unwarranted restrictions on the rights of agricultural workers" contained in Section 101.   Namely, that farm produce is highly perishable did not justify restrictions on farm worker's rights "to strike, to picket, to publicize their cause and to enlist the support of persons in other occupations."   Cosgrove took exception to S. 2203's definitions of "employees" and "employer."   Restrictions of the former term would leave only a fraction of all farm workers entitled to participate in farm union elections.   Extension of the latter term would permit the majority of employers to refuse collective bargaining to their farm workers.

Cosgrove saw solid reasons for employees and employers to bargain in good faith and to enter the harvest season protected with a solid contract.   Nevertheless, Cosgrove called the many restrictions on freedom of expression "clearly unwarranted" and "probably unconsitutional."   He closed by a plea to remedy the severe cost-price squeeze experienced by many farm employers,

> ...by appropriate collective bargaining at
> the market place, not by an effort to prevent
> collective bargaining by farm workers.

These efforts of the staffs and members of the United States hierarchy were not lost on one Commonweal observer.[3]   In late April 1970, John Deedy noted,

> . . . one day the strike will be settled
> fully, and on the side of justice.   When it
> is, a measure of credit will belong to the
> NCCB.   The settlement which the bishops'
> mediation committee helped arrange between
> the AFWOC and three Coachella Valley grape
> growers is the first real breakthrough in
> that four-year period.

108

> The three growers represent only 1/8 of the growers and only about 1% of the California crop. . . Inland Steel is a relatively small producer, but its decision turned around the 1962 steel crisis. The same thing could happen here. With luck, it will.
>
> For the bishops, meanwhile the. . . settlement stands as a quiet triumph. The grape strike is the kind of controversy that bishops as a body would ordinarily shun. This time they involved themselves and their institution. It was no mistake. Maybe, even it will set a pattern. That's the sort of social work episcopal bodies should be about.

One week later, words of praise for the NCCB Committee's mediation role came from Rev. Victor Salandini, a very knowledgeable and early advocate of the union organizing efforts of Chavez and his predecessors.[4] The contracts were hailed as a major breakthrough in Chavez' five-year campaign to organize the approximately 400,000 California agricultural workers. A key feature in the contracts was a clause that ruled-out the use of dangerous pesticides. That issue led to termination of the 1969 negotiations in the Coachella Valley because of the growers' adamant opposition to such a clause. Salandini summarized a 1968 independent study of Richard A. Fineberg, a doctoral candidate in the Claremont Graduate School. In addition to giving the lie to the California Growers' Association, the Farm Bureau, John Birch Society, the California branch of the American Independent Party, and numerous other ultra-conservative groups, the data substantiated the bishops' realism. Chavez was not "the head of an illusory army created by press releases," as alleged by spokespeople for some growers.

Salandini also repeated several encomiums on the bishops' role in the unexpected settlements. Jerome Cohen, UFW attorney, also was cited about the ad hoc committee of Catholic Bishops entering the discussions in November 1969, at the invitation of both the growers and union supporters. In crediting much of the success of the breakthrough to the committee members, Cohen said, "Their presence created an atmosphere for conciliation." Speaking for the committee its chairperson, Joseph Donnelly, auxiliary bishop of Hartford and veteran labor-management mediator, said they were ". . . confident that this breakthrough would serve as a pattern for others." Chavez was quoted as saying simply, "This is a very important day." Finally, Salandini quoted Lionel Steinberg, who signed for the growers, as saying.

> I have some concern that [the union shop
> clause] may not be completely workable, but I
> am convinced that I will try and they will
> try. It is my hope that we have commenced a
> historical breakthrough.

Approximately two weeks later, another <u>Commonweal</u> observer
cited the ad hoc committee's chairperson, operator of the three
vineyeards (Lionel, Coach, and Valley Hi Grapes), and UFW
representatives as present for the contract signing in the chancery office of the Los Angeles archdiocese.[5] Lawrence King, a
frequent commentator on California migrant labor problems, noted
the prophetic nature of some of the negotiators' comments that
the April 1, 1970 breakthrough would serve as a pattern for
others in the grape fields. On April 12, 1970, K. K. Larson and
C. C. Larson, operators of two vineyards in the Coachella Valley,
announced that they had signed similar contracts with the UFW.
The surprise in such an announcement was intensified by knowledge
that K. K. Larson had spent much time in 1969 traveling across
the nation, appearing on TV talk-shows and speaking to any group
willing to listen to his argument that the grape workers did not
want a union.

When the first three contracts were signed in the valley,
K. K. Larson was approached by a number of workers who previously
picked grapes during the early harvest on the UFW contracted
vineyards operated by Lionel Steinberg, David Freedman and
Charles Freedman. These grape pickers told K. K. Larson that
they could not work as union labor on some farms and as "scabs"
on the others. K. K. Larson said,

> I felt the only way to really determine the
> will of the workers was with a secret ballot,
> and since there is no law in agriculture
> which sets up election procedures, I asked
> the Bishops' Committee of the Roman Catholic
> Church if they would help out by conducting
> an election.

According to King, the bishops, eager to help, immediately dis-
patched Msgr. Roger Mahony, chancellor of the Fresno diocese, to
the Coachella Valley. With the help of Rev. Lloyd Saatjion,
pastor of the First Methodist Church of Palm Springs, election
machinery was set up and balloting was conducted at the two
Larson vineyards on April 11, 1970. On the next day, Chavez
announced the results: 146 votes for UFW and two against.
Immediately afterwards, the Larson brothers and Chavez signed the
contracts.

In the April 1970 meeting of the NCCB at San Francisco, Bishop Donnelly, chairperson of the bishops' ad hoc committee spoke out during a news briefing.[6] The 25-year veteran of exposing and undercutting the communist caucus in the original CIO said,

> . . . no matter what paper makes such charges against Chavez, the committee finds him to be a good and sincere advocate of social justice.

The charge was stated and rejected also by Msgr. George Higgins, the NCCB committee's principal consultant engaged in the breakthrough. Said Higgins,

> The Bishops' Committee totally disassociates itself from the view that Cesar Chavez is a Communist organizer! [He is]. . . an honorable and dedicated man in the field of unionism.

About three weeks later, C. C. Crawford, a Catholic and small farmer in Bonsall, California, questioned the nature of the "breakthrough" Salandini and others had extolled.[7] Crawford noted Salandini's reference, in the May 2, 1970 issue of America, to "more than one third of 85" small farmers abandoning an average of 33 acres each as a result of the boycott of California grapes. The three growers who settled with UFW, through the mediation efforts of NCCB ad hoc committee, were big farmers with an average of 376 acres. Crawford asked if boycott supporters wanted to bring about the rather rapid demise of family farming and the inrease in large corporate farming. The latter had the access to adequate financing to withstand pressures the farmer could not withstand--". . . high costs, low prices, property taxes, labor problems and--in California--the grape boycott."

Crawford found possible relief "in a fair and proper federal agricultural labor law." For him that meant a law that would protect the farmer from work stoppage at harvest time. Such stoppages could bring on financial destruction for the family farmer. Such a one needed the crop for borrowing. If it rotted, lost would be profits, a family's livelihood and a way of life. However, Crawford found part of his church contributing to the loss.

> Agriculture under the NLRB would doom family farming. The Murphy bill (S-2203), opposed by labor, provides a fair solution. Unfortunately, the Catholic Church--at least, the USCC--appears to oppose the Murphy bill,

too. Why do so many Church leaders involve
themselves in an economic power play that is
bringing so many good people--30 Coachella
families--to ruin?

Crawford concluded his letter on an ominous note.

When the collection plate comes around each
Sunday, I wonder to what extent I am financing the cutting of my own throat. I don't
think my church should be trying to do me
in.

Three months later, Rev. Edward J. Holleran, O.F.M. of
Lafayette, New Jersey, wrote America a letter furthering the
cause Crawford would dismiss.[8] The Franciscan priest said,

The whole story of the last five years of the
grape pickers' heroic struggle for social
justice should be made the subject of compul-
sory study in every seminary in the world.

Also in September one member of the ad hoc committee,
Humberto S. Medeiros, bishop of Brownsville, Texas, was named by
the Holy See to succeed an ailing Richard Cardinal Cushing as the
archbishop of Boston.[9] The assignment was described as a "leap-
frog from a small diocese with many poor Mexican-Americans to the
second largest Catholic archdiocese in the U.S." The Portuguese-
owned Azores native and later naturalized American, returned to
Massachusetts where he had served as chancellor in the diocese of
Fall River. He did so with high praise from Texans. From his
McAllen office in the Brownsville diocese, Antonio Orendain,
national secretary-treasurer of UFW and its chief organizer in
Texas, praised Medeiros' support of collective bargaining, a
minimum wage and UFW "...in Delano every year since he arrived."
Chavez had great respect for Medeiros, who reciprocated with the
comment that Chavez was more than a union leader.

He is a symbol of unity; this is 12 million
people with Spanish names on the road to
recognition. I think we should thank God
that it is a man of peace and non-violence
who happens to be in his position.

Upon leaving Brownsville, Medeiros was reported as giving 10
acres of diocesan land and $3,000 to UFW to commence building a
union center on the land.[10]

112

Around the time Medeiros was moving from Brownsville to Boston, attention was turned again to Chavez and the California growers by Catholic Mind.[11] The Jesuit documentary service reproduced an editorial, "Chavez Reaps Bitter Harvest," by the editor of Twin Circle, Rev. Daniel Lyons, S.J. of July 12, 1970 and responses to it. The Jesuit editor of a lay Catholic newspaper charged that grape pickers were not oppressed, were the highest paid agricultural workers in the United States, were not clamoring for a union, were not striking against growers, were as fond of Chavez as of a seven-day itch, and were receiving less take-home pay under UFW contracts than before. Lyons also charged that Chavez failed miserably as a union organizer to get workers behind him; introduced hippies, members of the Students for a Democratic Society and other characters from the Berkely campus; launched a nationwide boycott that failed until late 1970; agreed cynically to waive the "pesticides weapon" if the majority of growers would sign contracts with him, even though the California Department of Agriculture proved his charges were untrue; profited from fires set in scores of sheds and hundreds of tires slashed on the cars of grape pickers; was importing thousands of workers from Mexico; was advertising constantly on the radio for workers from Mexico; threatened sometimes to have the Internal Revenue Service harass grape pickers opposed to his union. Lyons also claimed that UFW made no attempt to contact workers before it "forces an employer to sign a contract" and construed ratification as "telling the workers they will be fired that day, or at least within three days if they do not sign a union card." Of the U.S. bishops' involvement, Lyons said.

> The committee intends to dedicate its efforts
> to organizing all of the farm workers in
> America. . . When the bishops' committee
> talks about "negotiations" they mean compul-
> sory unionism.

The first response to Lyons' Twin Circle editorial was that of the U.S. Bishops Ad Hoc Committee on the Farm Labor Dispute, issued on July 15, 1970--three days after Lyons' remarks about the committee, UFW, Chavez and grape pickers. Medeiros, Manning, Donnelly, Donohoe and Curtis (Bridgeport) found it incredible that a publication calling itself "Catholic" should publish

> . . . such a collection of untruths, inuen-
> does, distortions and plain inaccuracies in
> interpreting the views and motives of ad hoc
> committee members, all of whom are bishops,
> speaking for and acting in the name of the
> entire American hierarchy.

113

They accused Lyons of never giving the committee the courtesy of seeking its views or studying its findings and of consistently using limited sources of information hostile to the committee and totally misinformed about its role of mediation and conciliation. The bishops who constituted the ad hoc committee claimed that the July 12, 1970 editorial was only one among many in Twin Circle which consistently impeded the peaceful resolution of the California labor dispute. The bishops were quite angry, "This bungling interference of Twin Circle has injected an added, unnecessary note of bitterness to the dispute."

The bishops' committee was meeting in Fresno, in order to initiate negotiations, at the written invitation of the Western Employers Council, which represented the growers with more than 50 percent of the table grape acreage. The committee members noted that during the NCCB semi-annual meeting in April 1970 at San Francisco, the U.S. bishops "unanimously endorsed the work of this ad hoc committee" and voted to support the committee's "ministry of service to growers and workers" and its attempts to resolve the dispute through the process of collective bargaining. The committee of bishops concluded their statement with an appeal.

> We hope that he [Lyons] and his associates at Twin Circle . . . will return to the path of charity and brotherly love. . . that the readers of Twin Circle will reject Fr. Lyons' negative tone. . . and they will urge upon him and his associates a more objective policy in covering the social justice issues at stake.

The second response to Lyons' editorial which the Catholic Mind presented was the July 24, 1970 statement of "Padres," an organization of priests of Mexican-American descent and priests serving the Spanish-speaking in the U.S. They were appalled and disgusted at the anti-farm worker stance of Twin Circle "[It]... claims to be Catholic but appears constantly to practice a subtle form of bigotry. The "Padres" learned in Delano that Lyons and another Twin Circle writer, Reverend Cletus Healey, S.J., obtained most of their information from growers long opposed to Chavez, a few Mexican-Americans who were also labor contractors, and the pastor of an Anglo parish to which most of the growers belonged. The "Padres" accused the priest-writers of neglecting to visit the Franciscan priests who ministered to most of the Mexican-American farmworkers in Our Lady of Guadalupe parish. Finally, the "Padres" alleged that Lyons and Healey never contacted "...the two priests appointed by the Bishop of Fresno to minister to the grape workers on strike in the Delano area."

In October 1970 the Benedictines' journal, Worship, printed an account about Chavez by one of its Collegeville, Minnesota, monks.[12] Chrysostom Kim, a Benedictine from St. John's Abbey, spent some time in Delano observing and interviewing Chavez and others. Kim first tried to convey the relationship of Chavez' strategic sense of non-violence and fasting to his Christian morality deeply rooted in the ancient soil of Mexico. In doing so, Kim quoted from Peter Matthiessen's Sal Si Pudes: Cesar Chavez and the New American Revolution, about the strike, "We've always suffered. Now we can suffer for a purpose."

Kim also quoted Chavez himself from an April 1, 1969 interview with Look magazine. After the 300 mile, twenty-five day peregrinacion from Delano to the capitol steps in Sacramento, Cesar explained the beginning with 75 workers and the climax with 8,000 people. In addition to carrying the Virgin of Guadalupe and the flags--UFW, U.S. and Mexico--Cesar mentioned the rally each night and the joyful eucharist each morning for the local workers. All was focused on the theme of the march, "Penitence, Pilgrimage, and Revolution." Cesar noted that on Holy Saturday, one big company had agreed to negotiate with them.

Kim was also in the joyful union hall on July 29, 1970 when Chavez signed with John Giumarra, the world's largest table grapes producer. Also there was Bishop Donnelly representing the U.S. Bishops' ad hoc committee. At that point in time, UFW, after five years of bitter strife, had signed approximately seventy-five percent of California's growers. Giumarra represented twenty-six Delano growers, who produced half of California's table grapes. Twenty-five percent of the California growers had signed previously.

After indicating the UFW's unmet challenges in the oranges, melons, peaches, cotton, lettuce and nectarines areas of California, Colorado, Florida, New York, Ohio, Texas and Washington, Kim spoke of Chavez' future plans for "The Forty Acres." More than envisioning the country's first migrant workers' center, Chavez had the vision of psychologically and spiritually healthier Christian communities, not so contaminated by materialistic life styles. Once during a car ride, Kim asked Chavez if someday he would be someday like "one of the biggest union leaders. Cesar almost gagged, said Kim, "...so repugnant was the thought."

After explaining that Chavez had an impact on questioning youth because Chavez was devoid of the seeming disparity between rhetoric and reality which made institutional Christianity so suspect, Kim quoted Chavez extensively about the earlier work and sporadic support from priests and bishops. This contrasted with the early and continued support of the California Migrant

Ministry in the camps and the fields. Cesar recalled that when the strike started in 1965, most of "our friends" forsook the workers. However, despite tremendous pressure on the Protestant churches and significant loss of money by the Migrant Ministry, Chavez told of their deciding that the strike was a matter of life and death to the workers. The workers asked, "Why ministers? Why not priests? What does the bishop say?" Answering that the bishop said nothing, Chavez elaborated his expectations of his church,

> What do we want the Church to do? We don't ask for more cathedrals. We don't ask for bigger churches or fine gifts. We ask for its presence with us, beside us, as Christ among us. We ask the Church to sacrifice with the people for social change, for justice, and for love of brother. We don't ask for words. We ask for deeds. We don't ask for paternalism. We ask for servanthood.

> When poor people get involved in a long conflict, such as a strike, or a civil rights drive, and the pressure increases each day, there is a deep need for spiritual advice. Without it we see families crumble, leadership weaken, and hard workers grow tired. And in such a situation the spiritual advice must be given by a friend, not by part of the opposition. Thus, what sense does it make to go to Mass on Sunday and reach out for spiritual help, and instead get sermons about the wickedness of your cause? That only drives one to question and to despair.

In November 1970 Chavez got a mixture of advice and good news from fellow Catholics. The indirect advice came from Patricio Flores, Auxiliary Bishop of San Antonio, in the form of encouragement for retraining migrant farm workers.[13] Judging organizing of farm migrants as too late because within five years some 70,000 migrants would lose jobs due to automation, Flores stated that in the San Antonio area only strawberries could not be picked by machinery. In calling for training programs for the migrants, Flores lauded the foresight of Puerto Rican groups who left the fields and enrolled in training programs for other types of work.

The indirect good news came from Patrick Frawley, chairman of the Board of Directors of Twin Circle, who effected the resignation of Rev. Daniel Lyons, S.J., from the newspaper's top editorial position.[14] In addition Lyons discovered that his Twin

116

Circle--sponsored television program was suspended and his syndicated radio program was placed on a self-sustaining basis. The
editors of Commonweal commented,

> Lyons' travail began during the summer when
> he failed to heed Frawley's counsel to cool
> it on the U.S. Bishops' Ad Hoc Committee on
> the Farm Labor Dispute and present both sides
> of the issue.
>
> Frawley has been Lyons' angel, but angels, it
> seems can have poor tempers.

By December 4, 1970, Chavez was not only in a campaign
against lettuce growers but also in jail for refusing to abide by
a superior court injunction ordering UFW to call off its strike
and boycott of the lettuce growers.[15] The ruling was based on a
California law prohibiting strikes or boycotts in inter-union
jurisdictional disputes. UFW spokespeople indicated there would
be a court challenge of the state law. A group of twenty religious leaders, representing eleven Catholic, Jewish and Protestant
boards and agencies from the United States and Canada, came to
Salinas to "stand with Cesar Chavez in a time of crisis." They
found themselves cast as mediators in this bitter labor dispute
between UFW and the majority of the lettuce growers in
California's Salinas Valley. The group of religious leaders, who
came in response to an invitation from UFW which sought further
religious support for the lettuce boycott, met with the UFW
staff.

The twenty religious leaders then met with Bud Antle and his
son Bob. The Antles were growers of about eight percent of the
valley's lettuce. During the amicable discussion, the religious
leaders voiced their confidence in Chavez and UFW, while the
Antles maintained that the real battle was between UFW and the
Teamsters. Insisting that the Teamsters would not release his
company from its contract, Bob Antle told the religious leaders,
"This is a true jurisdictional dispute and we are unwilling participants." The UFW position was that in July 1970, the Antles
and other growers signed "sweetheart" contracts with the Teamsters covering field workers to prevent organizing efforts by UFW
and that the contracts were signed without secret elections.
Under insistent questioning by Rabbi Joseph Glaser of San
Francisco, Bob Antle said his company would be willing to negotiate with all parties involved and would welcome religious leaders
as mediators.

Glaser and Rev. Eugene Boyle, a long-time Chavez supporter
from San Francisco, were selected by the religious leaders to
serve as mediators. Bud Antle chose a third mediator, Rev. Paul

Stauffer, assistant general secretary of the United Methodist Board of Missions.

Several of the religious leaders were cautious of the outcome, pointing out that Antles had offered nothing new and one of them said, "There was going to be a meeting with Antle Saturday but Cesar went to jail on Friday." The Rev. Wayne C. Hartmire, director of the California Migrant Ministry, was skeptical, "If there's a breakthrough, great. But, if not, it makes the work of the boycott harder since people may relax." Boyle thought of the outcome of the meeting between the Antles and the religious leaders as at least a partial breakthrough. The group of twenty religious leaders issued a formal statement from Salinas saying, among other things, that UFW's and Chavez' "long, determined, non-violent battle exemplifies what is best in spirit" and has been "an inspiration to people around the world."

Speaking from a cell in the Monterey county jail through Boyle, chosen by the religious leaders as an intermediary, Chavez indicated willingness to negotiate on the part of UFW. Calling himself a "non-person" in a jail, Chavez delegated the UFW associate director, Delores Huerta, to represent him. Of Chavez' conversation with him in the jail, Boyle said he spoke, not only as a mediator, but as a priest giving words of spiritual comfort.

Across the street from the jail, the eucharist was offered every evening as a part of a 24-hour vigil for Chavez. Many of the religious leaders joined, as did Mrs. Ethel Kennedy on December 6, 1970. After her visit with Chavez, supporters of the growers criticized the jail authorities for permitting the visit by the widow of Senator Robert Kennedy.

Later in the month, December 15, 1970, Chavez visited for an hour with Auxiliary Bishop Patrick Flores of San Antonio.[16] Flores, the first Mexican-American in the U.S. hierarchy, once picked cotton in south Texas as a farm laborer. He described himself and Chavez as "old friends." Flores, who was participating in the San Diego diocesan celebration of the feast of Our Lady of Guadalupe, was first refused the permission to visit. Initially, Sheriff Ralph Davenport vetoed Flores' request because jail regulations permitted only Saturday visits. In the previous week the same regulation was cited in response to a request by an Episcopal bishop for a visit to Chavez. In the case of Flores, the authorities eventually relented. Of the visit, Flores' aide characterized the meeting as "a friendly pastoral visit." After the visit Flores told newspeople that he was "concerned, puzzled and a little surprised" by the contempt-of-court decision.

Flores also chatted with Chavez supporters, including several from his own diocese, in the parking lot opposite the jail where UFW members and others were maintaining a vigil for Chavez. In addition to praising Chavez as a "great man . . . attacking the problems of injustice without becoming unjust himself," the bishop indicated his support for both the union and the boycott. Although unable to remain for the nightly vigil eucharist, Flores had a statement read for him. It said that he found Chavez "very content, optimistic and a great sense of enthusiasm." Of the farm workers, Flores declared,

> You have been for us a great inspiration. You have been able to organize yourselves in the vineyards, and you have been very successful without having recourse to violence.

1971

In late March 1971 an agreement was signed between the Teamsters and the UFW, with the help of the U.S. Bishops' ad hoc committee.[17] The stipulation was that in general the UFW would organize the field workers while the Teamsters would organize the drivers and food processors. On specific points of difference the pact provided for binding arbitration, especially the Teamster contract with Bud Antle, Inc. Even though labor would be able to face the growers in closed ranks, America's editors did not think UFW "home free yet." Nearly 200 growers had contracts with Teamsters and were reluctant to relinquish them. The Teamsters made it very clear that they were being hurt by those contracts and would like to withdraw from them. Even though Chavez agreed, on March 26, 1971, to a 30-day suspension of the lettuce boycott, the editors of America concluded there would be even greater pressure on the growers at harvest time.

In early April 1971 the first grants from the U.S. Bishops' nationwide fund drive, the Campaign for Human Development (CHD), totalled $586,000.[18] The specific funding was determined at a Washington, D.C. meeting of the National Committee on Human Development and were announced by Bishop Francis J. Mugavero of Brooklyn and chairman of the U.S. Bishops' Committee on Human Development, along with Dr. Albert Wheeler of Detroit, and chairman of the campaign's national committee. The NCCB committee, which had ultimate approval authority, concurred with the national committee's funding recommendations. The UFW in Delano received $55,125 to strengthen its effort in California and four additional states. The UFW group in McAllen, Texas, was granted $31,000 to develop educational radio programs directed at poor Mexican-Americans in south Texas. There were several other grants to Mexican-American groups and, in the words of a campaign

119

spokesperson, other projects funded "affected all areas of the country and virtually all ethnic groups among the poor."

In late May 1971 there were protests in the Monterey diocese against the $86,125 grant to UFW from the Campaign on Human Development.[19] Rev. Michael L. Cross, an assistant pastor at Sacred Heart Parish in Salinas claimed ". . . at least seven or eight parishes" out of 43 in the diocese refused to take up an annual Catholic Charities collection because of the grant. Asserting that the decision was made "spontaneously by the pastors," Cross continued,

> It's pretty difficult to ask Catholics to contribute to charities when the Campaign for Human Development money, which was designated for anti-poverty groups, ends up in the hands of a labor organizing committee already funded from various other sources.

Cross also spoke of approximately 30 persons being invited to a meeting at which a letter was drafted and sent to Bishop Harry Clinch of Monterey. Actually, 104 people, among them five priests, attended the meeting and represented approximately 14 parishes. The letter asked the bishop to "publicly denounce" the allocation to UFW. It was also requested that UFW return the $17,924 contributed by Catholics of the diocese to the development campaign. If that request was not met, the letter stated that Catholics in the diocese opposing the allocation would withhold funds from the diocesan office, until the amount donated by the parishes "has been reclaimed for legitimate charitable efforts within our diocese." Finally, the letter of the 104 Catholics said the allocations violated the conditions under which the funds were solicited because UFW was not poor, was not lacking for funding, and was not using the monies to eliminate poverty.

Approximately at the time the bishop of the Monterey diocese was the recipient of a letter of protest against CHD grants to UFW, the bishop of the San Diego diocese had a meeting with farm owners.[20] Some farm owners emerged to announce that Bishop Leo T. Maher recognized the right of workers to organize but endorsed no specific action. The owners' statement declared

> We were in mutual agreement that the Church should keep a neutral stand and keep to the middle road rather than siding with any particular group.

Maher could not be reached to comment on the owners' statement.

The bishop, two months later, had another controversial situation on his hands.[21] A long-time supporter of the farm workers, Rev. Victor Salandini, on leave as associate professor of labor economics at Fresno State College, had been tramping the dusty roads with the Chicano pickets and celebrating the eucharist at makeshift altars in front of the homes of farm owners being picketed. The workers had been picketing the Egger-Ghio produce farms of southern San Diego county for five months. Salandini, on these occasions, had been consecrating corn tortillos instead of bread and wearing a vestment with a black eagle, the symbol of the UFW. The bishop suspended Salandini. Initially, Salandini defied Maher with the judgment, "The UFWOC symbol and the tortilla 'host' are of special significance to the Mexican farm workers." One week later, Salandini relented after a meeting with the bishop. The teacher-activist priest agreed no longer to use the tortillas and vestment with the black eagle. The bishop lifted the suspension. As Salandini left for a four-day retreat, he explained that he wanted to take the emphasis off the controversy with his bishop and to focus attention on the farm workers' problems.

In Manchester, New Hampshire support of the boycott brought an attack in the press upon that diocese's social action director, Reverend Philip Kenny.[22] The attacker was the editor, Loeb, of the Manchester <u>Union Leader</u>. The issue was support of the boycott of the California table grapes. The charge was, "How can our communist enemies weaken this country much more effectively than by gaining control of the production and distribution of food."

1972

Throughout 1972 there were many developments in church support of the farm workers in a variety of locales, culminated by very significant support from the top religious leaders in Washington, California and Rome. From Salt Lake City, "Mormon Land," there was the story of Rev. Jerald Merrill, who strove to help through the Spanish-Speaking Organization for Community Integrity, Opportunity (SOCIO).[23] Used to describe Merrill were words once used by a Chicano about Chavez,

> Burning with a patient fire. . . talking
> quietly, moving people to talk about their
> problems first and suggesting never more than
> that--solutions that seemed unattainable. We
> didn't know it until we met him, but he was
> the leader we had been waiting for.

In Florida in early March 1972, Chavez reported a contract, after less than a month of negotiations, with Coca Cola.[24] Such a quick settlement was aided by the backing of the archdiocese of Miami and the full support of the AFL-CIO. In the estimation of the editors of America,

> More important was the enlightened attitude of Coca-Cola officials toward unionization and their honesty and fairness in negotiating. . .
>
> In addition to a raise. . . there were provisions for insurance, pensions, paid holidays and other benefits. Also, the time between the use of poisonous pesticides and the time when the workers have to re-enter the field had been lengthened. DDT and some other pesticides were banned altogether.

However, elsewhere in Florida, the Citrus Industrial Council, an organization of growers, had declared against Chavez and claimed that most independent growers would not follow the Coca-Cola contract. These growers were reported to be considering importing seasonal help from the West Indies.

In the Spring of 1972, Cardinal O'Boyle, archbishop of Washington, D.C., issued public statements supporting the lettuce boycott of the UFW.[25] His support coincided with a letter to President Nixon from USCC officials.[26] They protested the decision of the NLRB to seek an injunction that would prohibit the UFW boycott as an organizing tool. The officials were: John Cosgrove, director of the urban life division; Paul Sedillo, Jr., director of the Spanish-Speaking division; and Rev. John McRaith, co-director of the rural life division. The text of their letter highlighted the following points.

> In view of the fact that the protection and benefits of the National Labor Relations Act have not been extended to agricultural workers, this action clearly lacks the evenhanded approach one has a right to expect from the agencies of our federal government.
>
> The low incomes and harsh working conditions faced by our farm labor force make progress for farm workers a requirement of social justice. The strengthening of their union is an important aspect of this effort. We therefore urge you to intervene to halt this

wholly unfair action of the National Labor Relations Board's general counsel.

We sincerely believe this question merits your prompt, personal attention.

In June 1972, the USCC Social Development Committee endorsed the boycott of head lettuce called by UFW "to bring about collective bargaining and a just settlement of the dispute."[27] The committee discovered a "fundamental issue of social justice" in the boycott begun in May 1972. The issue was the efforts to organize workers and to negotiate with lettuce growers in California and Arizona. In addition to the failure of negotiations with the growers the committee's statement added,

> Further complicating the problem is the fact that severe and repressive anti-labor legislation has already been enacted in Arizona and similar legislation is being sponsored in several other states. . .

> Without strong, honest representation such as can be provided by the United Farm Workers the plight of agricultural workers and their families will remain desperate.

In late July 1972 word came from Colorado that three members of the hierarchy had endorsed the UFW lettuce boycott.[28] They were: Archbishop James V. Casey and Auxiliary Bishop George R. Evans--both of Denver--and Bishop Charles Buswell of Pueblo. They declared their endorsement was an effort to

> . . . consider the plight of the farm workers in terms of our Christian responsibility as a means of helping these workers obtain a just and equitable scale of wages and living conditions. . . Support given to the unionization of farm workers is not intended to jeopardize in any way the rights and prerogatives of the farmer-grower. This is not a farmer versus farm worker situation, but rather the farmer and farm workers--each working within its own organization--seeking a just price from the market. Farmers throughout the country are united in such unions. Their right should not be impeded; nor should the right of the farm worker.

123

To the Colorado hierarchy's endorsement of the lettuce boycott was added that of the University of Dayton and the national board of the Leadership Conference of Women Religious (LCWR). The national board included the officers of the LCWR and one representative from each of the 15 regions in the United States. The statement called for the LCWR members to boycott all lettuce except that containing the Black Aztec Eagle trademark of UFW, and to support the farm workers in other ways.

On August 13, 1972 an Arizona law became effective, only to aggravate the two-year lettuce dispute in that state.[29] The editors of America recalled Msgr. George Higgins' judgment on the legislation in his June 1972 discussions between representatives of Arizona growers and laborers,

> The tragedy here in Arizona seems to be that Arizona is on the verge of repeating all the mistakes made in a similar controversy which raged in California . . . Until there is negotiation you will experience nothing but grief and that grief will be greater now that there is a law on the books that the workers believe is a bad law.

The editors also recalled the USCC's Social Development endorsing the lettuce boycott and describing the Arizona law as "severe and repressive anti-labor legislation."

In late August 1972, Raymond J. Gallagher, the chairman of the USCC's Social Development Committee, and bishop of Lafayette, Indiana, sent a letter to all the U.S. bishops.[30] In addition to urging the bishops to issue Labor Day expressions of support for UFW, Gallagher told the bishops that it would be appropriate to express support for the farm laborers in homilies, parish bulletins and prayers of the faithful on Labor Day and the preceding day, Sunday, September 3rd. The letter was authorized by the Social Development Committee at its August 17, 1972 meeting.

In late September 1972 all fourteen of California's bishops, chaired by archbishop Timothy Manning of Los Angeles, signed a statement urging voters in the state to reject Proposition 22, a proposal to restrict unionizing activities by farm laborers and to outlaw secondary boycotts of agricultural products.[31] The proposition, called the Agricultural Relations Act of 1972, was sponsored by the California Growers Association, the state Chamber of Commerce, and agri-business groups. Other opponents of the proposition, UFW, state trade unions and the California AFL-CIO Council called the measure "oppressive" and "unjust." Released by the California Catholic Conference in Sacramento, the bishops' statement based its conclusions on the "bedrock social doctrine of our church," as proclaimed in the Vatican II <u>Pastoral</u> <u>Constitution on the Church in the Modern World</u>. They noted that that document called for freely founded and representative labor unions.

Calling their opposition to Proposition 22 a matter of conscience, the California bishops declared the act was so unjust that, if it were passed, more serious tensions and difficulties would be created than the proposition attempted to resolve. They continued by outlining several of their specific objections to the proposition:

> -The election criteria and procedures proposed in the initiative so restrict the farm workers' freedom of choosing to join a union that they must be declared in direct opposition to the basic right of free choice. -The criteria for worker eligibility are so worked as to deny the vast majority of farm workers the right to vote.

> -The proposed act grants to the employers management rights which make it virtually impossible for the farm workers to negotiate many issues affecting their basic working conditions.

> -The basic right of workers to strike is so conditioned by the act as to render this right meaningless.

This California bishops' statement also responded to some of the claims of the proponents of the bill. Although proponents said the California bill followed closely the guidelines of the NLRA, the bishops said, ". . . the provisions of Proposition 22 actually deprive or restrict the (present) rights of the state's farm workers."

Also, the fourteen California bishops backed the "consumer boycott . . . [as] the only means available to the farm workers in the absence of appropriate legislation." In conclusion, the bishops expressed sympathy for the problems of the growers-- especially those with small farms--but maintained that Proposition 22 would not bring peace, while restricting the rights of the farm workers. "Legislation is needed," the bishops said, "but it must respect the legitimate rights of the farm workers as well as the growers."

There was also opposition to Proposition 22 from two other religious groups: the National Federation of Priests' Councils and San Francisco's Interfaith Committee for Justice for Farm Workers. Speaking for the NFPC, Rev. Eugene Boyle, its Director of Justice and Peace Office, told a San Francisco press conference that Proposition 22 would destroy unionization for the farm workers and " . . . is extremely disenfranchising of the poor--the poorest and weakest workers in the state." The Interfaith Committee had started an informational campaign against the proposal. The committee charged that the sole backers of the proposition were agri-business interests and that fraud was involved in obtaining the necessary signatures to get Proposition 22 on the Fall 1972 ballot.

At the end of 1972 support for Chavez came from Rome in the form of appointing him to the Pontificial Commission on Justice and Peace.[32] He was not actually made a member, but an invitation was extended through a priest in Mexico and conveyed through Patricio Flores, Auxiliary Bishop of San Antonio. Chavez declined the appointment for several reasons. First, there was the " . . . personal commitment to live, eat, pray, work and sleep with the Farm Workers Union." Secondly, there was his policy to decline membership in any group that would bring him " . . . personal prestige and honor" apart from the union effort. Third, there was the requirement of travelling abroad if he accepted the membership. Stating that he would reconsider when the farmworkers were organized, Chavez expressed gratitude for such an expression by the Vatican of genuine concern for farm workers. He also asked the Vatican to choose another representative of a union that dealt with poor workers, " . . . if possible, with farm workers."

1973

In early 1973 there was a dialogue at UFW offices in LaPaz--near Bakersfield, California--between Pablo Freire, the educator of the poor, and Cesar Chavez, the organizer of the poor.[33] The audience was mostly farm worker organizers, urban community activists and educators. Chavez spoke of organizing in terms of a symphony, stressed the importance of persistence in organizing and referred to the need of coalition between urban and rural movements. Chavez concluded with an insistence on strict solidarity between the church and the struggle of the farm workers. Chavez also insisted that the processions and fasts were not gimmicks, rather an integral part of the farm workers' culture and piety.

126

Also, in early 1973, officials from the Baltimore archdiocesan Catholic Charities and Social Action Committee testified in a Maryland State committee hearing.[34] Two Catholic state senators attacked them for opposing a bill that would have outlawed boycotts against seafood and agricultural products. The officials from the archdiocese also heard the Pope berated and a lecture on the Ten Commandments.

In March 1973 the Catholic bishops in the state of Florida affirmed the right of farm workers to form unions and to engage in collective bargaining, in order to improve their working conditions.[35] The bishops did so as part of their criticism of a proposed bill to amend the state's already existing right-to-work law by further prohibiting the use of a hiring hall for farmworkers. The bishops' statement also urged the state legislators to use "great prudence" in their implementing of the state constitution's right-to-work provisions and to insure that workers not be exploited further.

In June 1973, during a review of the UFW-Teamster controversy, mention was made of the role of religious leaders, especially the U.S. Bishops' ad hoc committeee.[36] It was said that the committee originally assisted in bringing UFW and growers together in mediation during negotiations in 1970 and in bringing Fitzsimmons, President of the Teamsters, and Meany, President of AFL-CIO into a jurisdictional agreement. It was also stated that Msgr. George Higgins, consultant to the U.S. Bishops' ad hoc committee, along with 25 other religious and civic leaders, had conducted an informal poll which revealed that the great majority of the field workers favored UFW over the Teamsters.

Also, in June 1973, there were outcries over the alleged beating by a Teamster of Rev. John Banks, a priest of the Youngstown diocese on leave to work with UFW.[37] Charged with the assault and released on $600 bond was Mike Falco, a Teamster employee. He was said to have beaten Banks whom he accosted while at breakfast in Coachella with Bill Wrong, a Wall Street Journal reporter. One outcry came from Banks' superior, Bishop Malone of the Youngstown diocese. In a telegram to Teamster president Fitzsimmons, Malone protested, asked for a public apology, and urged Fitzsimmons to

> . . . lead your union to dialogue with UFWU
> and call for and support free and secret bal-
> lots for union representation by farm workers
> in California, Arizona, as well as my home
> state, Ohio.

Another outcry came from Msgr. George Higgins who called on the Teamsters to repudiate the "unprovoked assault" and who scolded Teamster oficials for "neither having condemned the assault nor repudiated the guilty party."

In the midst of this Teamster assault on the UFW, Auxiliary Bishop Flores of San Antonio and Auxiliary Bishop Arzube of Los angeles flew to Palm Springs, the nearest airport to Coachella. Coming to be witnesses to the cause of social justice and to lend their support to UFW, Flores and Arzube were met at the airport by a caravan of several hundred strikers.   The two bishops then concelebrated the eucharist for some 400 strikers and their families.

While Meany and Fitzsimmons and their top aides were reported to have been working out a jurisdictional agreement, Chavez and others called for secret elections.[38] Charging that Teamster agreements with grape growers in the Imperial and San Joachin Valleys, due to expire in Spring 1973, were "sweetheart contracts," Chavez called for secret ballot elections to prove or disprove the Teamsters' and growers' claims that the farmworkers preferred the Teamsters to UFW.   A call for secret ballot elections also came from prominent Catholic and Protestant religious leaders and fourteen California Democratic congressmen.   On June 20, 1973, Hugh A. Donohoe, bishop of the Fresno diocese, also called for secret elections. In Chicago the 16th annual assembly of the conference of Major Superiors of Men was attended by some 150 members during the week of June 17-21, 1973.[39]   Almost routinely, the assembly approved two telegrams.   The first supported the UFW's call for free elections to determine union representation for farm workers by either the UFW   or the Teamsters.   The second telegram was sent to Safeway Stores, applauding the food chain's call for free elections in the dispute.

During the same week of June 1973, as the dispute between the UFW and Western Conference of Teamsters heated-up, the National Council of Churches, all the Catholic bishops of New England and the U.S. Bishops' Committee on Social Development and World Peace added their support to the UFW by urging a national boycott of table grapes and iceburg lettuce.[40]   The executive committee of the NCC criticized the Teamsters for being

> . . . strongly dominated from the top down,
> with little grass roots participation. . .
> [because it] does not provide or encourage
> union leadership for Mexican-Americans.

The NCC also asked for elections to be supervised by an impartial third party. The bishops' Social Development and World Peace Committee condemned the Teamsters' actions as " . . . in violation of all canons of trade union ethics." The same committee stated the "dominant moral issue" w a s the free elections.

On July 13, 1973, George Evans, Auxiliary Bishop of the Denver archdiocese, Msgr. George Higgins and 45 members of the Conference of Major Superiors of Men joined pickets in Lamont, California, and held a press conference afterwards.[41] There was agreement among all that the dispute was one of self-determination, the plight of the small and independent growers caught in the middle was appreciated, the imposition of "alien leadership" on the Mexican-American farm workers was deplored, and the principles and nonviolent tactics of the protest advocated by Chavez was supported.

Also on July 13, 1973, Chavez received the 1973 Reinhold Niebuhr award and an accompanying $5,000 grant. The citation, presented by John Bennett of Union Theological Seminary, and James L. Loeb, president of the fund, read,

> He is deeply involved in the struggle on behalf of men and women who have suffered great wrongs in our society, and have used economic and political power nonviolently and effectively, in ways consistent with Reinhold Niebuhr's social philosophy and ethics.

By the end of July 1973 the picketing of Teamster-controlled fields in Kern, Tulare, and Fresno counties had occasioned more than 2,000 people arrested for ignoring injunctions against the use of bull horns, communicating with workers still in the field, and standing less than 100 feet apart.[42] Of these farm workers, religious, clergy and others, America's editors said,

> While many of these supporters could be released in their own recognizance as first offenders, most have decided to stay in jail and fast until the farmworkers . . . are also released . . . Only by going to jail, by urging more support of the nationwide boycott can church leaders and other dedicated Christians and Jews play the vital role they must in this fight for social justice.

By early August 1973, the number arrested had increased to almost 3,500.[43] In addition to the farmworkers there were some 60 priests, religious sisters and brothers, and members of the laity. Among them were Rev. Eugene Boyle, NFPC Director of

Justice and Peace; Rev. Juan Romero, Executive Director of PADRES; and Dorothy Day, founder of the Catholic Worker Movement. Boyle remarked, "Could you imagine United Auto Workers pickets marching in front of General Motors and being arrested like UFW members?" Dorothy Day remarked, "I'm happy to be here--to be part of the greatest thing that has ever happened in the labor movement yet."

While in jail the religious and clerical supporters helped the strikers to avoid a difficult time. The former even complained that Judge James Pago, who handled the bail hearings, was trying to handle each case separately in order to split up the strikers and their religious supporters. In an addition to the unconstitutional court injunctions, they were protesting a breakoff in the UFW-Teamster jurisdictional negotiations, when it was learned that 29 Delano grape growers, whose contracts with UFW ended in July, had signed or were about to sign with the Teamsters. The contracts were signed on August 9, and Fitzsimmons sent a letter of repudiation on August 21. On August 23 Chavez agreed to resume the talks, stating that the repudiation was "extremely important" and noted a need for "guarantees" without any specifications.[44] Chavez resumed the negotiations despite the statement of Guimarra, who represented the 29 growers.

> We'll have to analyze this before we respond, but as far as we're concerned, we've got a legal binding contract regardless of what anybody says. . . I don't think Mr. Fizsimmons has any information that will substantiate invalidating contracts.

While in the area, Dorothy Day was interviewed by Gerard E. Sherry.[45] Among other things, she spoke of her admiration of Chavez and meaning of the presence of the religious, clergy and hierarchy on the picket line and in the jail. Of Cesar Chavez, Dorothy Day said,

> One has only to visit Cesar's home. . . There is no sign of the opulence normally attached to the homes of other leaders of labor unions. Chavez' salary is well below the poverty level and his associates, including the union attorneys, exist under the same substandard conditions. Whatever money comes into the union is used mainly for its members, not for its leaders.

Of the presence of religious leaders, Dorothy Day said,

It is good to see priests, nuns, seminarians
and novices joinging the pickets. They are
getting a first-hand experience of what it
means to work in the fields--what a long way
the farm workers still have to go. I hope
they go back to their rectories and convents
and colleges and tell the story. I hope that
they can encourage their superiors to divest
themselves of unnecessary riches in land,
buildings, stocks and so on, and that such
assets are put to the use of the poor.

Delighted with the turnout of these religious leaders, Dorothy
Day hoped for more " . . . putting themselves squarely on the
side of the poor and oppressed," and stirring great inspiration
in the farm workers by " . . . joining them in their struggles to
be free men and women, directing their own lives through their
own God-given talents."

One of the religious jailed was the theologian, Sr. Carol
Frances Jegen, who described her impressions of the scene in
Fresno on the day of the picketing, July 30, 1973, and the day
after in jail.[46] Jegen spoke of Sidney Metzger, bishop of the El
Paso diocese celebrating the eucharist outside the prison barracks, joined by Juan Arzube, auxiliary bishop of Los Angeles and
Walter Schoenherr, auxiliary bishop of Detroit and special delegate of the Michigan Catholic Conference. Dorothy Day was
depicted in prison comparing Chavez with Martin Luther King, Jr.
and Ghandi. Finally, Joan Baez was seen and heard strumming "De
Colores," the Cursillo theme, as the prisoner's song.

Throughout the remainder of 1973 demonstrations of religious
support for the UFW came from many sectors and groups. For
example, at a social justice institute at St. Thomas More College
in Covington, Kentucky, one hundred-fifty lay people, priests and
religious urged Catholics across the United States to see that
parish altar wines came from vineyards having contracts with
UFW.[47] From Davenport, Iowa, under the auspices of the Iowa
Catholic Conference's Social Action Department, pledge cards for
the UFW boycott were distributed to stores and restaurants.[48]

In Washington, D.C., there was a eucharist and luncheon com-
memorating two slain UFW members.[49] The homilist of the
eucharist at the USCC headquarters was Bishop James Rausch, General Secretary of the USCC. He asserted that the farm workers
movement was receiving "unprecedented support" from Protestant
and Catholic church groups, because,

. . . the cause is just . . . the manner is
Christian . . . Time is on the side of the

131

UFW. There is hope because there is faith--
belief in men and the rights of man . . .
because there is commitment to spend all time
and energy in a cause that is so right.

Rausch continued by praising the commitment to nonviolence
throughout the dispute with California growers and the Teamsters
union. Rausch announced that the USCC Committee on Social Development and World Peace telegrammed the U.S. Department of Justice
to investigate the slaying of the two UFW members and to prevent
future acts of violence. At the luncheon attended by Archbishop
William Baum of Washington, D.C., Chavez said, "The continued
support of the church is very important to us." The luncheon
host, Msgr. George Higgins, made a strong plea for reconciliation
between the Teamsters and the UFW. Higgins noted that he
observed that sympathy and support of the vast majority of
Catholics was with the cause of organized labor in the entire
controversy.

Around the same time, a cross-country contingent caravan of
more than 30 cars and a bus made its way from Delano, Kansas
City, St. Louis, Chicago, Toronto, Detroit, Pittsburgh,
Washington, New York and other cities.[50] The purpose was to pro-
mote the boycott and the ultimate destination was the return to
Delano for the September 21, 1973 national UFW convention. On
September 4, the eastern move reached St. Louis. Some 420
workers and families received overnight shelter in the Hillel
House (Jewish ministry center) at Washington University; in resi-
dences on the St. Louis University campus for Jesuits, Resurrec-
tionists and School Sisters of Notre Dame; in two Jesuit and
Redemptorist inner-city parishes. Meals were provided in the
Jesuit parish, St. Matthew. The food was provided by local UFW
supporters, as well as the $300's worth donated by the National
Food Stores, Inc. In the St. Louis Cathedral a special eucharist
was concelebrated by two dozen local priests and approximately
800 persons. Joseph A. McNicholas, auxiliary bishop of St.
Louis, presided and offered words of support and encouragement.
Unfortunately, the public impact of the one-day stopover in St.
Louis was slight due to intermittent drizzle, a strike against
both daily newspapers by the local Teamsters, and the failure of
the major television stations to provide coverage.

At the University of Notre Dame, in mid-November 1973, during the annual meeting of the Catholic Committee on Urban
Ministry, praise came for the announcement of the settlement of
the jurisdictional dispute between the UFW and the Teamsters.[51]
The speaker was Rev. Eugene Boyle, director of the NFPC's Justice
and Peace Office and a member of the newly created UFW public
review board. He summarized the settlement, similar to the 1970
one, in which the Teamsters agreed not to organize field workers

and the UFW agreed not to organize canners, drivers and others normally organized by the Teamsters. The Teamsters thus agreed to rescind their table and wine grape contracts and their other contracts signed in the summer of 1973 with two lettuce growers and not to try to renew current lettuce contracts that were to expire in 1975. The UFW agreed not to boycott lettuce until 1975. The legal tactic by which the Teamsters rescinded their contracts was to disavow that they represented the field workers.

Boyle expected the growers initially to accept such moves unwillingly; even though, eventually they would have to deal with the farm workers. Chavez said that Teamsters who had not yet signed were having second thoughts but he was personally certain the agreement would be signed. Boyle himself thought the agreement would be successful because it called on Teamsters to rescind their contracts unilaterally, whereas in 1970 the rescinding was bilateral--only when the growers let them. He also thought success was guaranteed because of the high-level and extensive publicity of the negotiations. It was reached by Chavez, Fitzsimmons and Meany. The rest of the labor movement was watching. Boyle noted that the original "timetable" of the growers and Teamsters called for the elimination of the farmworkers' union by the summer of 1973. This was prevented by organized labor and religious support groups. Singled-out for special praise was Msgr. George Higgins, who was instrumental in getting Meany to intervene.

From St. Paul-Minneapolis, in the archdiocesan newspaper, the Catholic Bulletin, a septuagenarian Monsignor, Arthur D. Durand, paid for a full-page ad to protest the Minnesota Catholic Conference's championing the UFW cause.[52] The ad was an open-letter to the state's Catholic bishops.

> I received with amazement and sorrow your undated letter. . . in which you urge your priests "to support and enforce the boycott" by Cesar Chavez's UFW union. . . It is for the great "silent majority" that I protest . . . although at the same time again professing my humble obedience and submission to my archbishop in those areas of true Catholic faith and morals wherein I have never once disobeyed him.

The appearance of such a letter, which would have been strictly taboo in 90 percent of the diocesan press, was deemed to have said much about the openness of the archbishop, Leo C. Byrne, in the judgment of a veteran Catholic newspaper man like Msgr. Salvator J. Adamo of Camden, New Jersey. The editor not only published, in a later issue, form letters in favor of Durand, but did not invent a hundred excuses for not accepting the ad.

In late November 1973, James J. Magee, Coordinator of Social Work at the College of New Rochelle, New York, analyzed the Catholic church's involvement in the farm worker's cause and suggested further steps.[53] Magee began by quoting the rationale of the people jailed and fasting in late July:

> We are fasting to accentuate our support for farm workers as they seek to express their basic constitutional rights and free assembly on the picket line. We are fasting because we believe they are some evils which, as Jesus said, can be cast out only by prayer and fasting.

Magee, commended editorials in diocesan papers, statements from chanceries and episcopal conferences, resolutions passed by conventions of religious men and women, and participation in picketing and jail-ins, as evolving elements for an effective, non-violent movement to change the migratory labor system.

Yet, Magee did not think such protests, programs and personnel investments achieved substantial changes in the migrant system. In fact, he feared they would amount, not just to works of mercy, but also palliative interventions, if a sustained campaign did not go beyond publicizing the issues, extending social services, lobbying for legislation, and instituting litigation. He urged mobilization steps to lift the oppression of farm labor, but not before praising the hierarchy's tenacity, in spite of dissent. He quoted the protest of the Delano Ministerial Association in the late 1960s,

> We're here as spiritual leaders to bring people to God. We are not to give advice on economic matters. We resent highly the fact that other clergymen have come into this area and destroyed the image of the Church. There's no moral issue involved. The clergy have no business to be involved.

He also quoted the 1970 _Twin Circle_ attacking the USCC ad hoc committee for

> . . . not listening to the pastors involved or their parishioners . . . Large numbers of Catholics have already been alienated from the Church and thousands of non-Catholics

134

have been embittered by the arbitrary, high-
handed action of the bishops' committee.

He also asserted that the bishops persevered even when growers
withheld their parish contributions and forced one diocesan paper
to fold because it supported the grape boycott. Most of the
parishes had not distributed the bishops' statement and had no
intentions of implementing its contents.

To fill both voids Magee suggested several action steps.
First, priests should deliver homilies treating the migrant condition and motivate organizations they moderate to examine the
issues and to assist in strategizing. Second, social studies
courses in parochial schools should incorporate content exposing
the migrant system. Third, high schools and colleges should
offer students the opportunity to participate, for academic
credit, in social services reaching migrants. Fourth, parish
councils should subsidize volunteers to work in health stations
or day care centers with migrant families and to report developments to the parish. Fifth, religious communities should sponsor
some of their members in similar types of experience.

Magee's sixth action suggestion was for a more ecumenically
involved humanitarian service to migrants, in light of the under-
staffing of existing projects under parish, diocesan and religious community. Such projects included education and leisure
programs, liturgy and socializing opportunities, coordination
with county health and social service projects along the migrant
stream, and transportation of workers from inaccessible camps to
local community services.

A seventh suggestion was that urban parishes and schools
should provide housewives and students to assist UFW boycott and
picketing campaigns at stores selling non-union lettuce and
grapes. Eight, religious and clergy should expand their presence
among the striking migrants, in order to diminish hostility
against Mexican-Americans, to witness the church's mission outside the sanctuary and to dramatize the church's role as reconciler. Ninth, the church should pull from the ranks of its
celibate members--lay and religious--cadres of lawyers, community
organizers, industrial relations experts, and social scientists
to abet the passage of legislation and to foster litigation aimed
at changing the migrant system in favor of the workers rather
than the agribusiness interests. Magee lauded the relentless
efforts of the National Catholic Rural Life Conference to lobby
for laws to ensure that the agricultural industry behave like
other industries. He specified legislation pertaining to wages,
job security, union organizing, due process, unemployment compensation, workers' compensation, health and safety codes, and
educational services.

Concluding his action steps, he repeated his call for a sustained, informed and coordinated campaign of social action at each and among all levels and sectors of church. The fasting and imprisonment of religious leaders would be meaningless, he felt, until the resolutions of episcopal conferences and the plans of the national coordinating bodies gave rise to ongoing projects at local levels and a movement for profound social change.

Shortly after Magee's plea, a report was given by the Executive Secretary of the Ohio State Catholic Conference, Dr. Joseph Gibboney.[54] He was sent to the Coachella Valley by the conference's chairperson and archbishop of Cincinnati, Joseph Bernardin, to collect facts and to demonstrate support. In a press conference after a tour of the area, Gibboney stated his findings.

Almost all the workers were Chicano. They wanted to be represented by the UFW, because the Teamsters represented Anglos and because the Chicanos wanted self-determination. The UFW hiring hall was noisy, dirty and lacked sophisticated machinery. However, it was the Chicanos' place. The police evidently were not enforcing the injunction preventing pickets from standing closer than a hundred feet from one another and prohibiting the use of bull horns on the picket lines. Apparently, the mass arrests had been counter-productive. The number of non-striking workers was not sufficient to complete the harvesting. Those picking appeared inexperienced and quite slow. They were very attentive to the activities of the strikers. The strikers showed no real hostility and made no attempts to cross the line. Neither the state police nor the pickets provoked any incidents. Gibboney's concluding remarks were:

> One could not but conclude that La Causa had a significant number of enthusiastic supporters, especially when we recalled that this was a relatively small area within the valley and another large group of strikers were present some two hundred miles north in the Fresno area.
>
> As we left the scene, I was convinced that such persistent, non-violent activity must necessarily achieve success in the long run and that justice will prevail. At the same time, I thought how unfortunate it was that such a struggle was even necessary in order to obtain a basic human right.

In November 1973 another eye-witness report of the events surrounding the prison and picketing experience appeared.[55] It was written by Sr. Camilla Shea, chairperson of the Social Concerns Committee for the midwest province of the Sisters of Christian Charity. In addition to a description of the picketing, arresting and jailing situations, she indicated where many of the religious leaders came from and what kinds of questions they had about their involvement. About one-hundred of the 600 participants at a two-week institute at the University of San Francisco left by private cars and a chartered bus on the five-hour ride south into the San Joaquin Valley. Said Shea,

> In every case, the decision to join in this expression of solidarity was a personal choice influenced by a seen need and the freedom to adjust plans at the close of the symposium.

The questions were:

> Why disobey? What action was planned? Would harm come to anyone? How long would violaters be in jail? What about those from out of state?

When the outdoor liturgy began at 5:35 a.m. with the main celebrant, Rev. William Byron, S.J., surrounded by farm workers, priests, religious brothers and sisters, there were answers to many questions. As the bi-lingual liturgy ended, as the sun brightened the sky enough to forecast a clear and hot day, there was little need for further discussion. Each had assessed the situation and accordingly chosen the commitment each would follow.

1974

Throughout 1974, among the many developments in the farm workers campaign, the first was an appeal from the National Farm Workers' Ministry Board for religious groups to publicize the struggle during the week of April 28, either in worship services or through film and other special programs.[56] The specific concern of the board was that the battle for survival against the Teamsters had taken the UFW's attention away from their struggle to correct working conditions that other sectors of American labor banished years ago.

In May 1974 the California state assembly committee on labor relations heard testimony from Msgr. Roger M. Mahony, spokesperson for the California Catholic Conference and Catholic

Charities Directors.[57]   Mahony spoke on behalf of state law that would "bring peace and justice." He stated that ideally the U.S. Congress should establish regulations and procedures to protect all parties but he did not expect that soon.   Without furthering any specific state law, Mahony enuciated some principles his groups supported. They supported a guarantee for workers to establish unions which truly represented their needs, freedom for workers to choose a union without interference of organizers or growers, and the right to a secret ballot elections to decide union representation.

In July 1974 more than thirty priests, sisters and brothers-members of the Conference of Major Superiors of Men and the Leadership Conference of Women Religious-reaffirmed their support for the UFW.[58] They also called on U.S. religious and priests to join in prayer and personal commitment to the UFW's elementary demand for justice. However, the major superiors also noted that their organizations' resolutions on behalf of the farm workers were approved in various and diverse groupings of religious communities. A report was given on talks with farm workers and Teamster officials whom they called upon to join UFW in arranging for secret ballot elections with the growers--even before any proposed legislation was enacted.

A few days before the major superiors' visit, Bishop Clinch of Monterey, in whose diocese Salinas was located, strongly disapproved their impending visit.   Within a week it was reported that their call for support was heeded.[59]   From various cities, approximately 100 volunteers arrived in Los Angeles to work full-time on behalf of the UFW.   The volunteers included twenty-one priests, seminarians and sisters. Their tasks included talking to individuals and groups, conducting house meetings, organizing support groups, circulating petitions and distributing leaflets at grocery stores.

By early September 1974 Ernest Gallo wrote of his distress over the position of some religious groups on what he considered was merely a "jurisdictional dispute."[60] He claimed that inflammatory statements originated from zealots in various committees. He had trusted that it was another administrative problem to be corrected internally by the executive level of the UFW.   He also assumed that the statements were so patently lies, distortions and exaggerations that few would believe them.   Finally, Gallo called the religious endorsements of boycotts sincere but based on the mistaken belief that the Gallos were cruel and inhuman exploiters of farm workers and their families.

Also in early September 1974, it was apparent that the California legislature would not pass legislation guaranteeing a secret ballot election for union representation by farm

workers.[61]   Although such a bill passed the assembly, it died in
the senate which refused routine action to permit the proper committee to take up the measure immediately.   Such a procedural
decision was accorded thirty other bills on the same day.   However, the proposed legislation was fought by the growers and the
Teamsters.   Yet, a new governor (Jerry Brown, Jr.), increased
organized labor support, and the   resignation of Nixon who had
spoken against the bill were seen as signs of hope.   The chancellor of the Fresno diocese and secretary of the bishops' ad hoc
committee, Msgr. Roger Mahony was "confident such a measure can
pass in 1975."   The principle of the secret ballot election, of
course, was consistently hailed by the Catholic bishops in the
state and around the nation.

In September 1974, while Chavez toured western Europe and
Scandinavia where U.S. grapes were shipped, he was received in a
private audience by Pope Paul VI.[62] Of the audience on September
25, 1974, Chavez spoke of the Pope's thanks

> . . . for the work we are doing for social
> justice for farm workers and he spoke warmly
> of his appreciation of the Mexican-American
> community.

Part of Pope Paul's statement to Chavez and his party during the
private audience was as follows.[63]

> Our welcome goes this morning to Cesar Chavez
> whom we are happy to receive as a loyal son
> of the Catholic church and as a distinguished
> leader and representative of the Mexican-
> American community in the United States.
> We know in particular, of your sustained
> effort to apply the principles of Christian
> social teaching, and that in striving to do
> so you have faithfully worked together with
> the support of the bishops of your country
> and with the support of their authoritative
> representatives, the members of the United
> States Catholic Bishops' Ad Hoc Committee on
> Farm Labor.

The next day some 200 representatives of religious communities heard Chavez' appeal for their support of the lettuce and
grape boycotts.[64]   The superiors were gathered at a special
meeting arranged by the Vatican Justice and Peace Commission.   At
that reception for Chavez, an address was given by Archbishop
Giovanni Benelli, papal undersecretary of state.   Part of the
text follows and contained praise for many others, as well.

139

We are all indeed grateful to Mr. Chavez for the lesson which he brings to our attention. It is a very important lesson: to know how to be conscious of the terrible responsibility that is incumbent on us who bear the name "Christian." His entire life is an illustration of this principle; it shows a laudable endeavor to apply this principle, which means expending the effort that is required to put the gospel into practice.

What attracts our attention in a particular way is the commitment that is manifested: the commitment to work for the good of one's brothers and sisters, to be of service to them in the name of Christ, and to render this service with the full measure of all the energy one possesses...

Gratitude is also owed to those who have counseled Mr. Chavez and those who have supported him in faith in God, and love for his people. Particular gratitude goes to the Bishops' Ad Hoc Committee on Farm Labor, represented here today by Bishop Donnelly and Monsignor Higgins.

An expression of appreciation is owed likewise to the rest of the group: to Cardinals Manning and Medeiros and to Bishops Donohue and O'Rourke, as well as to the dedicated secretary, Monsignor Mahony. Congratulations to all of you here today for your interest in the church's social teaching and your desire to see the gospel live.

Near the end of 1974 there was more support around the United States for the UFW. In New York the director of the USCC Division of Film and Broadcasting, Rev. Patrick J. Sullivan, S.J., criticized the content of a CBS television show, "Chavez and and Teamsters: An Update," which was telecast on October 20, 1974 nationally.[65] The "updated" program was shown in the Sunday morning time slot of the long-running national "Lamp Unto My Feet" religious series. Sullivan faulted the program for not identifying in full a California Catholic priest who was said to oppose the UFW and who was a spokesperson for farmer growers. Sullivan also complained of CBS's editing of old footage of picket-line skirmishes with police in a way that gave the impression that the UFW were the initiators of violence.

In Livingston, California, a priest and three religious sisters visited the E & J Winery.[66] They challenged the U.S. Border Patrol's claim that no aliens were employed. In Grand Rapids, Michigan, the director of the diocesan Catholic Information Center, Paulist Father Joachim Lally, ended a 78-day fast.[67] The fast, on behalf of the UFW was ended on December 1, 1974 because Lally felt so drained he couldn't be responsive to people." While the fast did raise the consciousness of many people, it did not influence the officers of Meijer's, Inc., a supermarket chain, and the immediate focus of the fasting and boycott effort.

1975

Continued church support of Chavez and the farm workers was evident throughout 1975 in the United States. In Philadelphia, Rev. James T. Ryan, O.S.A. of Villanova University, voiced his protest against the feigned ignorance and repeated arrogance of A & P food chain officials, relative to the UFW boycott of grapes and lettuce.[68] In Chicago, Sr. Maggie Fisher, R.S.C.J., an official of the National Assembly of Women Religious, voiced support for the UFW.[69] She found the silence of the media the most insidious aspect of the UFW campaign. She deemed the most essential element in renewing the labor movement was disproving the myth of one's own powerlessness through the UFW battle. Fisher reported the assignment by NAWR of Sr. Patricia Dryryk, O.S.F. of Milwaukee to coordinate the activities of women religious in support of the UFW. To pay her expenses, sisters "scraped up $1,400" and a group of religious priests donated several thousands of dollars. The Vice-President of UFW, Dolores Huerta, at the convention of the National Catholic Education Association, told the assembled delegates that the Gallo Wineries were hiring workers under the legal age limit.[70] The 300 delegates also heard Richard Martell respond for Gallo Wineries that the charges were false.

On March 1, 1975, 15,000 people rallied in Modesto, California, in support of the UFW strike against Gallo Winery.[71] It was, perhaps, the largest single gathering of UFW members and supporters in the movement's ten year history. It was the climax of a week of marches--one from Stockton, a second from Fresno, and a third from San Francisco--all converging on the Gallo homebase in Modesto. Amidst the weariness, harrassment and fasting there were moments of refreshment too. Jan Adams, a member of the Catholic Worker was so impressed by the courage and honesty of the farm workers that she quoted the words of a campesino, Caetano Nani, at a liturgy in Livermore, California, during the pilgrimage:

141

When I see all of you here, mothers with
strollers, students, all of you, I know that
I need you in La Causa. That is what I have
learned with the union. I know that I want
to go on in the struggle with you--to go on
until we win together or till we die
together, if we must, until we are victori-
ous.

As Oregon attempted to pass a bill allowing 5 to 12 year-old
youth to work in bean and strawberry fields, America's editors
urged its readers to take seriously National Farm Worker Week May
4-10.[72]

That Farm Worker Week is now institutional-
ized into an annual affair is an eloquent
commentary on the slow pace with which social
reform is being accomplished on this land.

The editors recalled the November 1973 NCCB endorsement of the
grape and lettuce boycott and the bishops' 1974 call for elections for farmer workers and legislation to assure the same.
Around the time of America's reminders the Catholic bishops of
California supported that state's legislative bill for secret
ballot elections to assure collective bargaining for farm
workers.[73]

During National Farm Worker Week some 80 religious leaders
issued a statement of solidarity with Chavez and the UFW and
pledged their commitment to boycott grapes, head lettuce and all
Gallo wines.[74] They commented,

[We] look to Cesar Chavez and UFWA as
important ethical and spiritual leaders in
our time . . . [We] will not forget the cry
for bread and justice . . . [from] hungry
farm workers in America who feed us all.

Among the signers were representatives of the National Catholic
Rural Life Conference, the National Federation of Priests' Councils, PADRES,and the Conference of Major Superiors of Men.

In California, speaking for the California Catholic Conference, Roger Mahony, auxiliary bishop of Fresno, hailed the passage of the state farm labor bill. The bill was supported, not
only by California's 17 Catholic bishops and "others who supported the farm workers over the past ten years," but also by the
California agribusiness, including Gallo.[75] The bill, popularly

known as Governor Jerry Brown, Jr.'s bill was not supported by the International Brotherhood of Teamsters.

In Connecticut, The Teamsters Local and 443 and International Union of Operating Engineers Local 478 withdrew each $25,000 pledge made toward the construction of St. Raphael's Catholic Hospital in New Haven in June 1975.[76] They were protesting the involvement of one of the hospital board members, Bishop Joseph Donnelly, in the Teamster dispute with the UFW.[77] However, by early July 1975 the pledge of the International Union of Operating Engineers was reinstated. The Construction and General Laborers Union had withdrawn their $25,000 pledge earlier but had announced no further decision.

On May 26, 1975 ten UFW demonstrators were wounded near Hidalgo, Texas, by a grower when he admittedly "opened season" on them with an automatic shotgun.[78] On May 29, another angry grower, brandishing a pistol, drove his car through a group of UFW pickets, ramming a truck and scattering the workers on the ground. Offers were made to meet with the melon field farmers and union representatives in the Rio Grande Valley, in order to identify the disputed issues and to map out a strategy of reconciliation by John J. Fitzpatrick, bishop of Brownsville; O. Eugene Slater, bishop of the United Methodist Church of San Antonio; Harold C. Gosnell, bishop of the Episcopal Church of West Texas. In Fitzpatrick's estimation, such incidents of violence had generated an atmosphere of

> . . . fear over the possibility of further, even more large-scaled violence [and created] disgust that men, concerned about their livelihood, their families and the welfare of our community, cannot or will not sit down and discuss issues, even though they know--as we all know--that continued violence and threats are not and never will be the answer.
>
> Someone . . . must seek to clarify the issues at stake. Because of my Christian concern that justice be done on all sides, I wish to volunteer to be such a catalyst, such an "enabler."
>
> I offer my services . . . not at this moment in the role of mediator, but in the role [of a clarifier]. This seems to be the necessary first step, without it other steps seem to be almost impossible.

Fitzpatrick told National Catholic News by mid-June that he already had met separately with representatives of the workers and farmers because "they won't talk to each other." From that meeting and later meetings, Fitzatrick compiled a statement on "what each one thinks" and was to submit it to both sides to get them to agree about what they disagreed. If the negotiations ensued, then, Fizpatrick would try to "shift into a mediator" role and ride the middle of the road between the farmers and the workers. He noticed that the violence had ebbed, but that formal negotiations were unlikely at the time because the farmers had refused to recognize the workers' attempts to organize.

In late August 1975, as the National Assembly of Women Religious renewed its support for the UFW, religious leaders' attention was focused on the pending Teamster-UFW election in California.[79] At a UFW convention Msgr. George Higgins, holding a new position as USCC Secretary for Research, told the members that the UFW would win at least 85 percent of the field workers' votes in that election.[80] When he pronounced the prediction and promised the continued support of himself and the U.S. bishops, Higgins received a rousing ovation. Later, during an interview, Higgins was asked whether the bishops at their November 1975 meeting might withdraw their unofficial support of the UFW now that California had passed legislation for secret ballot elections for farm workers. He responded,

> I doubt it. My recommendation to them will be that they take no action or make no change until at least after November. You see, the support of the bishops is promised until free elections are held, not just guaranteed, and few if any elections will be held until well into September and even later.

He continued by indicating that Chavez already had raised the issue of whether the elections would be "free and fair." Chavez cited three procedural problems: the right to free access to farms to organize workers, the use of symbols on the ballot for farmworkers who cannot read well or at all, and the use of Teamster dues checkoff cards as a means of claiming that 50 percent of the workers on a farm want an election. Chavez said that if these problems were not resolved fairly,

> We will have to go to Sacramento and stage sit-ins until the board (to supervise elections) understands how important the rule changes are to free and fair elections.

On August 29, 1975 the first California Agricultural Labor Relations Act was to become effective.[81]   With an overwhelmingly Democratic state legislature, Governor Brown won a stellar achievement with the passage of the law. The law created a five-person board to channel farm labor conflicts into a legal process.   Its first test would be to supervise the election. Hearings were to be scheduled within a few days on the question of union organizers' right of access to farm workers--hotly contested by the growers.   On August 20 the governor's appointees underwent polite but needling challenges to their "impartiality" during a hearing before the California State Senate Committeee. The Governor's appointees included: Roger Mahony, secretary of the bishops' ad hoc committee since 1970 and auxiliary bishop of Fresno; LeRoy Chatfield, a close Brown aid, a key assistant of Chavez and a teacher for 15 years as a Christian Brother in California's Central Valley; Joe C. Ortega, executive director of the Center for Law and Justice, a poverty-law agency in Los Angeles; Joseph R. Grodin, San Francisco professor of law at Hastings College of the University of California and a specialist in labor law; and Richard Johnsen, Jr., executive vice-president of the Agricultural Council of California.

Farm spokespersons indicated that "thousands"of growers considered the new board "pro-labor or pro-Chavez." Yet, despite open animosity from such major farm groups as the California Farm Bureau Federation, which wanted new names proposed, and much skepticism in Teamster cirlces, the state was so weary with the 10-year disruption in the California legislature that prompt State Senate approval of the Governor's appointees was expected.

Mahony, chairperson of the board, was asked by rural senators how he could take a fulltime state job.   Noting that his state-appointment was for two years, Mahony replied, ". . . it would take about that long to get another auxiliary bishop from Rome. I'll be through and return to Fresno."   One of the most challenging senators, Howard Way, grilled Chatfield and Mahony. Mahony was asked how he would deal with an election if it should be marred by a low-flying airplane piloted by a Catholic priest dropping UFW leaflets on the fields.   Alluding to an actual episode of that sort, Way asked Mahony, "Does the church have control over low-flying priests?" The bishop responded,

> No, we really don't. A lot of Catholic
> priests are out these days climbing
> mountains, running boats, walking alleys,
> doing their own thing and I guess some are
> flying. They don't clear their flight plans
> with the bishop.

145

Mahony also said during the Senate hearings that the bishops' ad hoc committee did not take sides with any faction, but aimed to win the right of representation and secret ballots for agricultural workers. All the board members, except Johsen, executive vice-president of the Agricultural Council of California, were challenged by the rural area state senators for suspected "prejudice." When Johnsen was asked if he didn't "feel lonesome" in the group, he replied, "all seemed in agreement about working objectively and fairly with the new law."

Nevertheless, the center of the conflict in late 1975 was neither the farm worker nor Cesear Chavez out walking the state of California rallying supporters. It was the five-member board, chaired by a Catholic bishop and ensconced in state capitol offices, so new that its members were working out of cardboard boxes instead of filing cabinets. So tense was the scene that peace officers in rural areas were bracing themselves for an eruption of countless conflicts. One union expert had predicted demands for 200 to 300 elections all at once in September 1975. Large amounts of factual data had to be verified and new procedures applied by a state agency that sprung into life just as harvests peaked. Two unions were fighting for the right to represent the workers. The Teamsters had contracts with more than 400 growers since 1972. Earlier, the UFW had represented the farm workers in the hiring of some by those growers. Likely to erupt anew in September in lettuce fields, vineyards and vegetable rows were some of the fist fights, bleeding heads and angry confrontations of the past decade at California harvest time.

By late September 1975 many fears were realized and articulated by a delegation of more than 70 Catholic, Jewish and Protestant religious leaders from 17 states.[82] Among the interfaith delegates were representatives of the National Federation of Priests' Councils, Commission on Justice and Peace of the Archdiocese of Denver, the Catholic Worker, Sisters of Mercy, the United Methodist Commission on Race and Religion, New England Province of Jesuits, Unitarian-Universalist Migrant Ministry, PADRES, Fellowship of Reconciliation, National Assembly of Women Religious, Union of Hebrew Congregations and the National Council of Churches. These religious leaders returned home "shocked, saddened and angered" after three days in Delano investigating allegations that California's Agricultural Farm Labor Relations Act was being misused or not enforced. They returned to their constituencies to call on people to re-emphasize the boycott of non-UFW lettuce, grapes and Gallo wines until the law was administered both in spirit and in the letter, until elections were certified and until the contracts were signed. Before leaving the Delano area and after talking to farm workers, state board agents, growers, Teamsters, and UFW members, the inter-faith religious leaders issued a joint statement. Admitting that "there is nothing more frustrating than a good law badly administered" the delegates called on Governor Brown to take immediate steps to enforce the law and to protect the rights of the farm workers. They added,

> . . . if he is unwilling to do that, then he should not continue a process that fools the people of California and the nation into believing that his law is working.

During their investigation the religious leaders were told that the supposedly secret ballot elections allegedly did not prevent growers and Teamsters from knowing who voted for UFW and who did not. Systematic reprisals then took place. It was also learned that workers were being threatened before elections. Post-election reprisals included the eviction of farm worker families from their homes, physical and mental abuse, wage cuts, and reassignments to harder and dirtier jobs without regard to seniority. It was known that agents of the Agricultural Labor Relations Act had not made a decision on even one of the 137 unfair labor practice complaints filed at the Salinas regional office of the ALRB. In Oxnard, board agents stated clearly that they were concerned only with the election--not with what happened before or after the elections. The posting of an election notice sign at the M. Zaninovich ranch took place three hours after the election had begun. When questioned board agents admitted they allowed the growers to determine who was eligible to vote on the ranches. Access of UFW organizers to growers' property, in order to talk with farm workers, was denied routinely, even though the California Supreme Court had overturned a lower court decision and clearly stated that all union organizers should have access. It was abundantly clear that security guards and local sheriff's deputies were used to enforce the growers' will, rather than the law. One of the religious leaders, Sister Clare Dunn, an Arizona state representative, stated in a Los Angeles interview,

> The growers and others with power in rural California are still using that power to try and keep the workers intimidated.

Another member of the delegation, Angie Calvert, of the Catholic Worker, added more details.[83] A call went out from the Farm Worker Ministries to religious leaders late Friday night, September 19, 1975, as the expected violence erupted in the fields of California. As the UFW began winning the secret ballot elections, Calvert said,

147

> . . . more and more violence was directed
> towards the voters . . . I have seen the
> dogs, the rifles, the muscled Teamsters, the
> local smiling sheriff . . . I have felt the
> fear as police cars approached, the spit of
> hate. And I know that still, farm workers
> are struggling for their own union without
> using the tactic of violence.

Blatant violations among board agents were also observed by the Catholic Worker representative,

> Board officers take full ballot boxes on
> vacation with them--the ballot boxes are
> cardboard, quite unable to be locked. A
> board officer leaves the election site with
> the ballot boxes, and gets into the same car
> as the grower and Teamster observers.
> Fraudulent lists of employees are given to
> UFW organizers.

Calvert concluded her account by pleas to readers to substitute leaf lettuce or cabbage, to avoid lettuce "on McDonald hamburgers, in salads when you eat out," to ask grocery stores to remove boycotted items from their shelves, to refuse to order such items for schools or hospitals or other organizations, and to make sure Gallo wines were not used on church altars and at parties. For,

> The Catholic Bishops in this country, as well
> as the Conference of American Rabbis, have
> renewed their pledge of support for the UFW.
> More than on any other issue, churches have
> been supportive of the struggle of the United
> Farm Workers and the leadership of Cesar
> Chavez, who holds out to us a basic under-
> standing of nonviolent philosophy.

In late September 1975, also, Bishop Roger Mahony was confirmed by the California Senate as Chairperson of the Agricultural Labor Relations Board.[84] In late October 1975, Mahony was theatened and jostled and his car damaged by Teamster demonstrators after a two-hour talk on the charge that the CALRB members were biased against the Teamsters.[85]

Just before Christmas 1975, a parish priest in Mecca, a tiny town in the Coachella Valley, Rev. Joseph F. Pawlicki, C.S.C., wrote about his parishioners--farm workers and small growers.[86] He told his readers about the poor wages and profits, the hard work and long hours of those he called "Small Fry in the Valley."

Pawlicki told of the help both small growers and farm workers could gain from organizing. He pointed to the loans, advice and aid the small growers needed from government agencies to form marketing cooperatives, but also to the price of noncooperation--extinction. He pointed to the farm workers devotion to Cesar Chavez and the UFW, and to the "immigrant mentality," traced to times when no unions protected workers' rights to a decent wage in the United States, yet which said to the newcomers in the 1970's, work hard and be thrifty, be thankful and quiet yourselves and the next two or three generations will arrive. The parish priest, from Mecca, concluded with some frank comments on Chavez and the Teamsters, growers and workers,

> If his dispatch office in Coachellas has been run poorly by the kind of misfits who seem to gravitate to causes, if there has been violence by the same types, then he must try to put his house in order.

> Inexperience in union administration had undoubtedly weakened the UFW and made it vulnerable to the Teamsters' assault on their contracts. The struggle is not over. It has now entered a new phase, although, unfortunately, not all of the violence has been left behind. I have little doubt that the future happiness of the people of Mecca in the Coachella Valley is linked to the success of Cesar Chavez. The vision of the Teamsters for the future quite clearly focuses on a union of big business and big growers. But it is the small people that the battle is really all about.

1976

In early 1976, Governor Jerry Brown received some good press and one example was an article in America magazine.[87] The former Jesuit novice was characterized as the "Gadfly Governor." Too many of the gushy reports on Brown's anti-government crusade omitted his opinion on business. For example, on one occasion Brown said,

> . . . too often people point to the infirmities of government, but they neglect the obeseness of business . . . People in private enterprise have to begin to limit themselves and their excesses.

149

Brown's greatest legislative accomplishment to date was the ALRA. Yet, the law worked no magic. Charges and counter-charges flew back and forth. State-appointed observers estimated that the UFW lost 15-20 percent of the votes cast in early elections because of fraud and incompetent regulation. That the law and the board, under the leadership of Fresno's Bishop Roger L. Mahony clearly had made a major contribution to a just settlement was attested to by California's AFL-CIO Executive Secretary, John F. Henning. He called Brown,

> . . . the best Governor California workers ever had, mainly because of the farm labor law, his support of collective bargaining for teachers and state employees, his help in increasing maximum unemployment benefits and his pro-labor appointments.

At the time plaudits were sounded for the ALRA and Jerry Brown, Jr., an appeal went out from Rev. Chris Hartmire, director of the National Farm Worker Ministry.[88] The long-time advocate of farm workers first laid out the record of election results since August 28, 1975 when the law went into effect. The UFW's two-to-one lead was growing. While the UFW had won 113 elections, the Teamsters had won only 24 and very few elections went "no union."

However, on January 1, 1976, the ALRB gave 30-day termination notices to its staff, because operational funds were running out. The unprecedented number of elections and unfair labor practice hearings made the administration of the law more expensive than originally estimated. Teamsters wanted no funds extended until after an investigation of the board. The growers opposed any provision of funds unless changes were made in the law.

Hartmire elaborated on the changes. The growers wanted to lengthen the time between filing for an election and holding an election from the seven days stipulated in the ALRA to twenty-one days. Such a change would not only disenfranchise seasonal workers, but also would increase the time for intimidating workers. The growers wanted to strip the ALRA of its powers to punish growers for firing or intimidating workers, to demand payment of back wages, to allow union organizers access to the workers in the fields, to order apologies to workers, and to make other forms of restitution for unfair labor practices.

The growers wanted labor contractors to be considered as employers. Bishop Mahony, chairperson of the board and Governor Brown stated that the law needed a longer period of time than five months, to be judged fairly. Hartmire indicated that the

150

farm workers were reluctant to get into the political process
(". . . it has not served the poor very well") and made compro-
mises in order to gain the new law. The law served the growers
well, since there were few, if any, strikes since June 5, 1975
when the law was passed. In 1975 when the growers agreed to
California's ALRA provisions, they told the public that the boycott was unncessary because "now we have the law." While talking
peace they intimidated workers and obstructed legitimate union
organizing activity. The leading opponent to refunding the board
was State Senator Clare Berryhill, a Modesto grapegrower.
Hartmire noted that the NLRA was not amended for twelve years.
He concluded with an appeal to readers to write to the governor
and Berryhill and an admonition:

> If they succeed, the UFW drive in the
> Imperial Valley would be halted. In addi-
> tion, the unfair labor practice hearings on
> hundreds of elections would not be certified
> and negotiations could not begin; the growers
> would not have to face charges for unfair
> labor practices; the Gallo election result
> would remain undecided.

In mid April 1976, Joseph Early of Sacramento, wrote some
protests to America magazine.[89] In addition to complaints about
several attacks on growers and support of farm laborers, he
claimed Bishop Mahony favored the farm workers. The writer
asserted the California assembly leader, Leo McCarthy, and
Senator Albert Rodda were fed up with Chavez' excessive
demands. Early also accused the archbishop of San Francisco,
John Quinn, of using tactics America condemned, when

> . . . the Catholic teachers struck for better
> working conditions. . . using priests, nuns
> and students as strikebreakers.

May 2-8, 1976, was the third time the NCCB announced "Farm
Worker Week."[90] Tracing the roots of the farm workers' union
movement back to 1962, the America editors judged that the UFW
had,

> . . . done the most to bring the situation of
> farm workers into the public consciousness
> . . . the UFWA and Farm Worker Week are both
> aimed at counteracting the defenselessness
> that generally characterizes farm workers.
> As Cesar Chavez has said: "We want suffici-
> ent power to control our destinies. This is
> our struggle. It's a lifetime job."

151

Back in California there were some farmworker developments in the 1976 presidential campaign.[91] Jimmy Carter, Democratic presidential candidate, called Chavez at a UFW political session. Carter told Chavez and the listening audience of farm workers

> I feel close to you in spirit. You have added a great chapter in the history of American labor.

The Fresno meeting erupted in a tumult of applause when Carter stated he endorsed the UFW initiative, Proposition 14, which would have written California's basic agricultural labor relations law into constitutional status, untouchable by the legislature. If successfully passed at the ballot box, the measure would be safe from punitive politics and would have added a few stiffer rules, especially one mandating operational money.

After Carter's announcement, the UFW formally endorsed his campaign. However, Fred Heringes, president of the California Farm Bureau Federation, labeled Carter's announcement his "first major campaign mistake." California growers already had pledged some $2 million to defeat the measure. On September 12, 1976, the San Francisco Examiner political writer, W.E. Barnes, reported a prevailing sentiment that San Francisco Catholics voted on socio-economic issues rather than on moral issues. So, Carter's new identification with Chavez was likely to be more persuasive than objections to Carter by right-to-life forces. It was learned also that after Brown's unsuccessful nomination, backed by the UFW, he urged Carter to review the initiative rather carefully.

In early June, Chavez' initiative qualified to be on the ballot. For, within 29 days twice the necessary one-third of-a-million signatures were garnered, so powerful was Chavez' appeal. The new target, the intiative, took attention off the board. By July 1, a new budget quietly provided the entire $6.68 million Mahony had requested for 1976-77. More than 40 administrators and 100 attorneys began, once again, to conduct hearings and enforce the law. Mahony and three new Brown appointees oversaw the administration of the law.

Mahony spoke of the California experience as a prelude to sound labor relations in agriculture throughout the United States and as a stabilizing factor in California farm labor relations,

> I don't find any grower organization that wants to go back to pre-1975 conditions without a legal process for worker representa-

tion. The opinion in the agricultural
industry is that this is the better way to
go. Our agency is a vehicle to handle the
problems. . .

The progress can be illustrated in wage
rates. In 1965 farm hands earned $1.25 an
hour. Today contracts are being negotiated
for $3 an hour and the latest contracts are
scaled to $3.50. This represents a serious
movement to upgrade farm worker living
standards.

Mahony also reflected on the religious aspect of the law and the
church's involvement. He viewed the law as an implementation of
some of Jesus' teaching. "I cannot think of any area in our
times where the support of the Catholic bishops had such pronounced and successful follow-through." Indicating that no
bishop had spoken negatively of his role as chairperson of the
state board, Mahony added,

I don't see such direct government participation as a pattern for many to follow, but I
can conceive of other situations where it
might be desirable. If we can serve, we
should serve. We cannot ask the people to
undertake responsibilities if we, as bishops,
back away from committing ourselves to implement social justice where we see the necessity for action.

Finally, Mahony had informed Governor Jerry Brown that on
December 31, 1976 he would return to full-time pastoral responsibilities in the diocese of Fresno. He also indicated that he
proudly took with him from his office the wall-sized tapestry
stitched for him by some religious sisters. The message on it
was from the first California Agricultural Labor Relations Act,
". . . to ensure peace in the agricultural fields by guaranteeing
justice for all agricultural workers."

1977

There was also a commentary on the work of Mahony in early
1977 in the context of a discussion about Governor Jerry Brown.[92]
Mahony never thought the permission for the appointment would
come from his archbishop, the apostolic delegate, and the president of the NCCB/USCC. He and two other board members were
"pegged" as pro-UFW. "I am pro-farmworkers. I am for his right
to organize and choose his own union." Mahony found the policy

of the State of California stronger than that of the federal labor law. The former encouraged the right to organize. The latter merely protected the right to organize. Very mindful that the bitterness of the farm labor controversy in Fresno was so great that its Catholic newspaper was closed because of a boycott by advertisers and that probably he would head the diocese before long, Mahony commented:

> I think if the bishop is pastorally oriented in any diocese, that the very extensive involvement in the life of the parishes would create a very different atmosphere than what we have. The more removed the bishop is, the more people misinterpret what he says and does.
>
> I would see a beautiful opportunity in the blessing of the fields and harvest-time liturgies in the fields that would involve both workers and growers and highlight our gratitude to God for giving us the richest valley in the world.

Remarking that the growers reacted to the idea enthusiastically, Mahony favored greater organization among the farm growers. He expanded,

> The growers are organized, but not for the right purpose. They are organized to buy fertilizer and tires and machinery, and to fight the unions, but not to deal with the middlemen who squeeze their profits.
>
> The church should help push this. Chavez wants to support this, too.

Around the same time Mahony commented on the farm situation, the new archbishop of San Francisco, John Quinn, was in the news for touching the issue of the plight of the smaller farmers.[93] The editors of America noted that, as archbishop of Oklahoma City, Quinn marked the Bicentennial Year by issuing a pastoral letter on family farms in June of 1976. Quinn noted that it was the position of the American Catholic bishops that farms and ranches ought not be any larger than necessary for efficiency. The editors added,

> But it is precisely the family farm . . . that is generally speaking, more efficient than corporate farming, provides more care of the land and produces a better general

environment in rural America. . . . All Americans ought to hope that the Young Farmers Homestead Act of 1977 . . . will become law, because family farms, as Archbishop Quinn said in his pastoral, make an indispensable contribution to the whole nation.

In April 1977, the editors of America again focused on farm workers.[94] The editors stressed the continuing need of farm workers, especially during harvest season. Yet, they had been so neglected over the last several decades that in California, Texas, Florida and other states they had to resort to marches and boycotts to dramatize the "dehumanizing conditions of their precarious existence." The sponsorship of Farm Worker Week by the USCC, NCC and Synagogue Council of America was emphasized by a reminder of its enduring importance.

> While significant victories have been recorded in the past few years, mainly in California, much remains to be done. Farm Worker Week provides a good opportunity to learn about the people and their issues and to help them achieve their goals.

On June 18, 1977 Spanish-speaking migrants began a march, under the auspices of the Texas Farm Workers (TFW) whose president was Antonio Orendias.[95] The purpose of the march was to protest inhumane conditions suffered by migrants in the Rio Grande Valley, exclusion of farm workers from the NLRA, child labor violations related to the low wages paid to farm workers, and the need to repeal Section 14-B of the Taft-Hartley Act--the "Right-to-Work" laws. Said Orendais, "We march because we would rather die on our feet than on our knees." By August 23, 1977, approximately 44 migrants, including 13 children, as well as supporters were met at Lourdes Church in Raleigh, North Carolina, by Christ Scott, labor adviser to Governor James B. Hunt, and North Carolina AFL-CIO chairperson, Wilbur Hobby.

Bishops Michael J. Begley of the Charlotte diocese and F. Joseph Gossman had requested that North Carolina parishes welcome the TFW, participate in the 1,450-mile March for Human Rights, and "give them the aid the Samaritan gave the traveller." All the parishes, with one exception, responded enthusiastically. The lone exception was St. Paul's parish in Henderson, North Carolina. The call for the repeal of 14-B caused some controversy in the Catholic community because of North Carolina's "Right-to-Work" law and a number of nonunionized plants employed Catholic personnel in management positions, who had moved from Northern states.

In a telephone conversation, the president of St. Paul's parish board, John Piccioli, declared that it was the "political" side of Orendias' proposals that caused the six-member parish board to vote unanimously against providing housing for the marchers in Henderson. Piccioli speculated that the buses following the marchers might have been provided by local union funds. The three battered buses actually belonged to the TFW. Ted Quant, an advance organizer of the march, said, "The unions haven't given us a dime. I wish they would help us."

After a noontime rally on Capital Square, the migrants began anew their march to Washington, D.C. If they could maintain their pace of 20 miles a day, they would be in the nation's Capitol on Labor Day, September 5, 1977. Orendias' letter to President Jimmy Carter, asking for a meeting, remained unanswered.

On August 26, 1977, Bishop James Rausch of Phoenix addressed the UFW Biennial Convention.[96] During a press conference after his address, Rausch said, "What I know of (Arizona) state law is that it impedes the right of collective bargaining." He called for a study of Arizona union laws to make sure they,

> . . . make it possible for people to exercise what is a very fundamental right (collective bargaining) and to exercise that right without impediments being thrown in their way.

One such impediment for Rausch was the state's "right-to-work" law.

There was a quick and strong response in the press. Two Phoenix newspapers said Rausch "isn't going to produce jobs. . . by attacking Arizona's labor laws." The first paper was the Phoenix Gazette which was controlled by the second, The Phoenix Republic. The Republic asked why Rausch was questioning the "right-to-work" law when "the unions themselves have shown no concern" about repealing it. The Gazette defended the law and attacked Rausch.

> The right of an individual to. . . participate in collective bargaining is beyond question, but surely there is an equal right for an individual to choose not to join a union.

By Labor Day 1977, Rausch was the new chairperson of the U.S. Catholic Bishops' ad hoc Committee on Farm Labor.[97] Rausch, a former General Secretary of the NCCB and the newly appointed bishop of the diocese of Phoenix, Arizona, replaced bishop Joseph

Donnelly, the first chairperson of the committee, who fell very ill only to die shortly afterwards.

In November 1977, as many U.S. farmers went on strike and moved on Washington, D.C., they received a message of support from the National Catholic Rural Life Conference.[98] The message declared that NCRLC was, ". . . in sympathy with your cause in seeking a just price for your products." The NCRLC approved a call to "church leaders, farmers and all people who eat" to seek producer-consumer justice. The NCRLC staff was directed to study and to disseminate information on the issues underlying the proposed nationwide strike.

1978

On November 26, 1978, Rev. Henry Wasielewski, director of the diocese of Phoenix' special ministry to farmworkers, was stopped from conducting a eucharistic liturgy by Juan Torres, a field boss at Chandler Heights groves east of Phoenix.[99] Torres produced a temporary restraining order, issued against the Maricopa County Organizing Project (MCOP) in the fall of 1978, and ordered Wasielewski off the property. When a sheriff's deputy was called, he said the farmworkers had the right to have visitors and allowed the migrant ministry director to stay. However, a week later one of Wasielewski's parishioners, Paul Hernandez, visited the groves to bring clothing to the workers. The sheriff's deputy this time told Hernandez he could be charged with criminal trespassing if he went into the groves. Later, Hernandez submitted a sworn statement to a local court that Torres had threatened him with a rifle during the visit.

In November 1978 the MCOP leader, Guadalupe Sanchez, was arrested for violating the court order. He was charged by citrus grove owners of using harrassment in an attempt to organize the workers. At a later hearing, Wasielewski offered evidence that he was not a member of MCOP and verified MCOP's claim that his visits to the groves had not violated the temporary restraining order. The owners of the groves, Blue Goose Growers, Inc., had accused Wasielewski of being connected with MCOP and had alleged the connection in an attempt to keep the priest from visiting the groves and celebrating the eucharist for the illegal aliens who lived under the trees in the groves. The director of field operations at the Chandler Heights groves, Ross McElhaney, testified that Wasielewski was seen frequently associating with MCOP organizers.

Wasielewski's response was that in his minstry he met with many organizations and agencies concerned with the workers' welfare. Wasielewski also argued that anyone should be able to

157

visit the farmworkers because the groves are their home. He stated that the illegal aliens eat, sleep and work in the groves and they know they risk deportation if they leave the property. Wasielewski told the judge that it never occurred to him to obtain the grower's permission to go to the fields and celebrate the eucharist. The priest added, "I also don't get permissions from landlords when I go to say mass in people's apartments."

Nonetheless, on January 5, 1979, Superior Court Judge Robert J. Corcoran issued a permanent restraining order. He ruled that MCOP did not need to enter any of the groves having contracts with Blue Goose Growers since the illegal aliens could leave the fields whenever they wished. Although MCOP was barred from any property associated with Blue Goose Growers, Inc., McElhaney invited Wasielewski to celebrate the eucharist in the fields.

1979

In early March 1979, as UFW in California and Arizona neared the end of the second month of striking, a report appeared on the sparse Catholic support for the farmworkers.[100] Negotiations had been cut off, no plans were made for future negotiations, and striking workers moved north as the lettuce harvest wound down in California's Imperial Valley and in southern Arizona. The UFW centered its efforts on garnering support for the strike by fund-raising and food collection and for the boycott of Chiquita bananas, products of United Brands--parent company of one of the largest struck growers. A special effort concentrated on gaining boycott support from the AFL-CIO, the Canadian Labor Council and the International Conference of Free Trade Unions. On March 1, Chavez addressed about 500 UFW members and sympathizers in a union hall in Phoenix. He told the audience that California farmworkers, who usually came to Arizona when work ran out, probably would stay in California. Chavez expected more Arizona farmworkers to join the strike.

At the time, in California, there was little Catholic support for the striking farmworkers. Aside from auxiliary bishop Rogery Mahony of Fresno and several other bishops who were working behind the scenes to bring the opposite sides together, there were no reports of support from other official church circles. The only California diocesan agency known to support the striking farmworkers was the Social Justice Commission of the archdiocese of San Francisco. It was busy striving to raise money and collect food for the farmworkers. Several parishes in the diocese of San Jose and Sacramento, as well as the San Francisco archdiocese, were holding fund-raising efforts and collecting food. A major fund-raising effort, attended by Chavez, was held in Our Lady of Guadalupe parish in Sacramento in early March. Church activists were unable to raise any support for the farmworkers in the Monterey diocese, where much of the strike activity was taking place. The National Farm Ministry leaders asserted that less support was coming from the Los Angeles area and practically none from the San Diego area. The Los Angeles support came primarily from Catholic Churches in the East Los Angeles barrios. Said Alice Barnes, spokesperson in San Diego for the NCC agency, the churches in San Diego, ". . . are dragging their feet" and the most significant support there came from Tom Hayden's and Jane Fonda's Campaign for Economic Democracy.

There were three additional accounts about dubious support of Chavez in early September 1979. The first was about some alleged "tests" or "errors" of Chavez.[101] Some of the alleged errors were: Chavez' acceptance in the summer of 1977 of an award from Philippine President Ferdinand Marcos, purges of staff members, inability to tolerate internal opposition, friendship with Synanon leader Charles Dederich, use within the UFW of the Synanon "game," antagonism that led to creation of the Texas Farmworkers Union (TFU), and a forceful UFW campaign to urge a crackdown on illegal aliens. Only in the next few weeks or months would it be evident how much these alleged errors had damaged Chavez' traditional sources of support--religious, minority, and liberal groups. During those weeks UFW would seek to mobilize for the lettuce boycott the massive support enjoyed from these groups during the famous grape boycott. Chavez and other UFW leaders denied both the alleged errors or loss of traditional support.

Yet, some solid UFW backers thought otherwise. For example, John Henning, California AFL-CIO executive director and former undersecretary of labor in the Kennedy administration, said "Chavez doesn't have the friends in the liberal community he once had." Nevertheless, Henning and other labor leaders thought it might not matter, since weakened ties within the liberal community might be more than compensated by the strengthened ties Chavez had forged within the labor movement. Furthermore, once the California Agricultural Labor Relations Act was enacted in 1975, the UFW was less in the public eye and was caught up in the work of administering a union from the UFW new headquarters, a former tuberculosis sanitarium in La Paz, California. There Chavez was attempting to form UFW into an effective union.

Surrounded by a fiercely loyal cadre of supporters, Chavez was alleged to ignore or silence critical voices that challenged his and UFW actions. In 1977, allegedly a major purge took place within the UFW. One union worker who quit during the period of the purges, Michael Yates, became an instructor of economics at the University of Pittsburgh. Yates said people were fired en masse with no reason given. Even though it often would take people a few days to find transportation out of the isolated LaPaz community, Yates claimed that Chavez guards would threaten people in the middle of the night, if they refused to leave. Yates also told about one fired worker who refused until the charges that he was a grower spy could be proven. The police were called and allegedly the fired worker did not want to talk about the incident, lest it harm the farmworkers.

Julie Loesch, a Catholic activist in Erie, PA, who had worked several times for the UFW in California and the East, spent several months trying to find out why UFW abused so many of its members. Her conclusion was,

> Although Cesar is democratically elected, he is a one-man leader, above criticism, if you criticize him, you are accused of being an elistist. . . against farmworkers. . . a de facto grower agent.

Loesch claimed her efforts were useless because UFW supporters were reluctant to challenge Chavez. She cited as an example a letter she received from Msgr. George Higgins. In addition to indicating he was aware of the problems, Higgins did not care to confront Chavez face-to-face and was even more reluctant "to go public." A northern California priest and close friend of Chavez acknowledged the UFW leader may have lost some credibility. The priest-friend said people were used to seeing,

> . . . smiling Chavez, they don't realize that he is as tough as nails. . .

> Chavez lives, breathes and sleeps farm-workers; everything else is extraneous. People are to be used as long as he or she remains useful.

Another Catholic activist said of the UFW internal problems,

> Chavez has let it be known that these are his problems and nobody else's business. Outside supporters are just that, outsiders who support the UFW for whatever therapeutic reason they might have.

In early 1979, Chavez was said to have tightened even further his control over the union. There was a bitter internal struggle waged about whether top staff should be salaried or allowed to serve only on a volunteer basis. Chavez won--top staff would receive $10 a week plus expenses. Chavez defended the volunteer basis as insurance for a highly "motivated" staff.

Critics inside and outside UFW contended that volunteerism insured a dependent staff. Some former UFW workers went so far as saying that Chavez' attraction to the "group encounter sessions" of the nationally infamous Synanon leader's, Charles Dederich, was used as a possible tool to crush dissent in UFW. Chavez in August 1979, said that Dederich would be exonerated of charges of corruption and attempted murder of a lawyer who won a suit against Synanon, Dederich's drug-rehabilitation program.

Alfredo Avila, Texas Farm Worker leader, at odds with Chavez since the mid-1970's, said the UFW ". . . is a very, very top-heavy union, to say the least. Everything must come from Chavez." Of these charges from the Texas Farm Workers, Chavez said,

> How can people say we're not democratic; the
> workers feel this is a democratic union
> . . . We have not attacked them, but they've
> attacked us.

The rift among UFW leaders, which led to the creation of the Texas Farmworkers Union in the mid-1970's, was thought by leaders of the Texas Catholic Conference to make success unlikely in winning collective bargaining rights for farmworkers there.

The criticism of Chavez' and UFW's stand on illegal aliens stemmed from efforts of the union to urge a firmer crackdown by the U.S. Immigration and Naturalization Service on illegal aliens in California. UFW regretted taking such a position, since illegal aliens were also oppressed people. However, growers in California were employing the illegal aliens as strikebreakers. Among activists working with the illegal aliens and who expressing anger toward Chavez, was a priest in southern California, who said, "Cesar's losing a lot of credibility. He's going after his own people."

No criticism of Chavez, however, was as strong as that focusing on Chavez' acceptance of an award from Philippine President Marcos. Philip Vera Cruz, a union vice-president of UFW, resigned in protest. Calls came from within the union for Chavez to admit he had made a mistake. Asked in August 1979, if he had made a mistake in accepting the award from Marcos, Chavez responded that the only people upset were the intellectuals. The workers were not upset. However, several folks thought otherwise. Sister Rena Paz of Maryknoll, who worked closely with Philippine farmworkers, said the workers were most angered by Chavez' action. Ed Diokno, an editor of the Philippine News, a national newspaper, said Chavez' action still rankled the Filipino community in the U.S. Rev. Eugene Boyle, a long-time UFW supporter, said he and other UFW supporters within the

Catholic community deeply regretted Chavez' acceptance of Marcos award. Another northern California Catholic activist said,

> It's never been the same (our relationship with the UFW) since then; we were deeply hurt.

Whatever the source and nature of the criticism and however Chavez had bruised or disillusioned his supporters, many UFW supporters would not criticize Chavez publicly. Chavez and the UFW, for many were "the only game in town" and farmworkers were perhaps the nation's most oppressed group. Chavez' support within the labor movement seemed more important to him. If the 1979 strike ended soon, it would be the result of manuevering by other labor union leaders. After 30 years of building a labor union from scratch, Chavez was close to control of the largest labor union in California.

The second account about dubious support for Chavez, centered around an August 1979 UFW march to Salinas which was launched in San Francisco's Union Square.[102] Msgr. James Flynn, the chairperson of San Francisco archdiocesan Commission on Social Justice, proclaimed the church's support for social justice, the farmworkers, the strike and the boycott. Yet, the call did not echo time and time again, as in earlier UFW struggles. Most religious leaders in California and the United States were silent. One UFW supporter was very angry. Dr. Armando Navarro, a southern California layman who headed the National Institute for Community Development said,

> Not one bishop in California [or] in the U.S., is saying anything to support the strike or boycott. Our leadership still thinks we're going to be saved by the middle-class approach.

Many asked what happened to Catholic Church support. Few other social causes shared as much U.S. religious support as the long battle of farmworkers in California to gain collective bargaining rights.

Namely in 1973, 60 priests, religious brothers and sisters were arrested during one UFW civil disobedience campaign. Also that year, Bishop James Rausch, General Secretary of the U.S.C.C., said of the U.S. Catholic Church support for farmworkers, "There is commitment--commitment to spend time and energy in a cause that is so right." The Vatican played its part when Pope Paul VI personally praised Chavez and his work. Cardinal Benelli proclaimed the Vatican's support for U.S. church

162

efforts to support farmworkers. Continually U.S. bishops were celebrating the eucharist with the farmworkers.

Nevertheless, in August 1979 during the march to Salinas, Catholic presence was thin. Rev. Richard Garcia, of the San Francisco archdiocese, was the only priest celebrating the eucharist for hundreds of farmworkers. Throughout the long march from San Francisco, only a few clergy could be seen, and only periodically. Garcia, like many other Catholics throughout California who were involved deeply in earlier farmworker struggles, wondered what had happened to Catholic church support, not only during the march, but also throughout the seven-month-old strike. Although numerous parishes and church groups in California helped the UFW in the strike, the level of support did not reach that of the earlier UFW campaigns. There were several explanations.

Garcia said, "Well, you know maybe its just because there aren't as many priests as there were 10 years ago." Others thought the lack of enthusiastic Catholic Church support for farmworkers was due to the change in the times. Rev. Eugene Boyle, who spent time in jail during previous farmworker struggles, found it difficult to drum up support for UFW among the students with whom he worked at Stanford University's Newman Center. Oakland, California, activist Rose Lucey, said, "It's hard to get the people who were involved before out again. People are getting older, more tired, cynical."

Yet, during the 1979 march and strike, as in other matters, UFW officials did not admit the existence of any problems. Rev. Wayne C. Hartmire, United Farmworkers Ministry leader, called the 1979 church support "impressive." In August 1979, Chavez claimed not to be dissatisfied with the church support. Others close to UFW said the union might not want or need massive church support. Fresno Bishop Roger Mahony, former chairperson of the California Agricultural Labor Relations Board, said UFW, in trying to become more of a union than a social cause, wanted to be able to operate successfully without depending on churches and other "outside" groups.

The third account of dubious Catholic church support for Chavez, described the ninth day of the eleven-mile march from San Francisco to Salinas.[103] The marchers were weary as they moved through Castroville, a tiny agricultural town between Santa Cruz and Monterey that calls itself the "artichoke capital of the world." The day's march ended in a baseball field across from a Catholic church. Among the prominent symbols dominating the gathering was the images of Our Lady of Guadalupe. Comments were made about the purpose of the march; the role of an organizer and son of a rabbi, Marshall Ganz; and later moves to enlist the strikebreakers in the UFW. The account also included comments about Chavez and his talk to the marchers.

> Catholicism has always provided succor for farmworkers and for Chavez, although he revealed earlier this year that he is not as strict a Catholic as many of his followers. He has developed a keen interest in Eastern religion, an interest about which few of his followers are aware.

> Chavez spoke about hope, about faith, about the rightness of the cause. He spoke slowly, rarely raising his voice. His manner was restrained; his tone soothing, paternalistic. Observers said this is how Chavez speaks when his is fasting. The fast heightens discipline, dissipates anger and helps maintain Chavez' single-minded devotion to the strike.

In May 1979, Msgr. George Higgins presented the position of the U.S. Catholic Bishops' Committee on Farm Labor to a U.S. Senate Committee on Labor and Human Resources during hearings on on the revival of the Mexican "bracero program."[104] Explaining that the Mexican government was pushing the exportation of its workers on a contract basis "to relieve its own unemployment problem," Higgins asserted that revival of the "bracero program,"

> . . . would inevitably have a disastrous effect on the wages and working conditions of the American labor force and might well destroy the only viable union ever to be established in the history of American agriculture.

> If the U.S. has an obligation to assist Mexico in solving its domestic economic problems, there must be a way of doing this without cutting the ground out from under the United Farm Workers and without undermining the wages and working conditions of American agricultural workers.

In elaboration of his reference to UFW, Higgins noted that from 1954 to 1964 the "bracero program" was at its peak. More than 500,000 Mexican contract workers were brought into the U.S. in a single year. They were recounted by the U.S. Labor Department at the expense of taxpayers. That was before the UFW grew to be a strong counter-force.

164

[1]John E. McCarthy, "USCC's Statement on Mexican Workers," Catholic Mind, v. 68, No. 1240, 2/70, pp. 3-5.

[2]John E. Cosgrove, "USCC Supports Farm Labor Rights," Catholic Mind, v. 68, No. 1243, 5/70, pp. 5-6.

[3]John Deedy, "The Grape Strike," News and Views, Commonweal, v. 92, No. 6, 4/24/70, p. 130.

[4]Victor Salandini, "Breakthrough in Coachella Valley," America, v. 122, No. 18, 5/2/70, pp. 470-471.

[5]Lawrence King, "Bishops in the Vineyard: The Grape Strike," Commonweal, v. 92, No. 9, 5/15/70, p. 214.

[6]"Bishops Support Cesar Chavez," Current Comment, America, v. 122, No. 21, 5/30/70, p. 574.

[7]"Whither Family Farming?," Letters, America, v. 122, No. 23, 6/13/70, p. 619.

[8]"Social Justice Studies," Letters, America, v. 123, No. 6, 9/12/70, p. 133.

[9]"'Bishop of Poor' Succeeds Cushing," National Catholic Reporter, v. 6, No. 40, 9/18/70, pp. 1, 16.

[10]"Going-Away Gift," Reporter's Notebook, National Catholic Reporter, v. 6, No. 44, 10/16/70, p. 2.

[11]"Three Statements on the California Grape Strike," Catholic Mind, v. 68, No. 1246, 10/70, pp. 1-7.

[12]Chrysostom Kim, O.S.B., "Cesar Chavez in Delano," Worship, v. 44, NO. 8, 10/70, pp. 488-96.

[13]"Bishop Asks Retraining for Laborers," National Catholic Reporter, v. 7, No. 5, 11/27/70, p. 13.

[14]"Lyons' Dropping Stock," News and Views, Commonweal, v. 93, No. 9, 11/27/70, p. 210.

[15]Robert Herhold, "Clergy Group Intervenes for Chavez," National Catholic Reporter, v. 7, No. 8, 12/18/70, pp. 1, 17.

[16]"Bishop Flores Visits His 'Old Friend' in Jail," National Catholic Reporter, v. 7, No. 9, 12/25/70, p. 13.

[17]"Temporary Halt on Boycott," Current Comment, America, v. 124, No. 14, 4/10/71, p. 362.

[18]"Bishops' Campaign Aids Chavez Union," National Catholic Reporter, v. 7, No. 28, 5/14/71, pp. 1, 14.

[19]"Catholics Oppose Grant to Chavez," National Catholic Reporter, v. 7, No. 31, 6/4/71, pp. 1, 7.

[20]"Neutrality," National Catholic Reporter, v. 7, No. 30, 5/28/71, p. 2.

[21]"Farm Workers' Militant Priest and Maher Agree," National Catholic Reporter, v. 7, No. 36, 7/30/71, p. 3.

[22]"Fighting Loeb on His Home Ground," National Catholic Reporter, v. 8, No. 24, 4/14/72, p. 5.

[23]Gloria Skurzynski, "Chicanos in Mormon Land," America, v. 126, No. 11, 3/18/72, pp. 290-293.

[24]"Farm Workers in Florida," Current Comment, America, v. 126, No. 11, 3/18/72, p. 274.

[25]Edward Glynn, "A Changing of the Archbishop," Washington Front, America, v. 128, No. 11, 3/24/73, p. 254.

[26]"Protest Backs Farm Workers," National Catholic Reporter, v. 8, No. 23, 4/7/72, p. 24.

[27]"Committee Backs Boycott," National Catholic Reporter, v. 8, No. 32, 7/21/72, p. 3.

[28]"Nuns' National Board Backs Lettuce Boycott," National Catholic Reporter, v. 8, No. 33, 8/4/72, p. 16.

[29]"More of the Same for Farm Workers," Current Comment, America, v. 127, No. 4, 8/19/72, p. 79.

[30]"Farmworkers Support Asked," National Catholic Reporter, v. 8, No. 35, 9/1/72.

[31]"California Bishops Oppose Farm Workers' Curb," National Catholic Reporter, v. 8, No. 38, 10/6/72, p. 4.

[32]"Chavez Refuses Vatican Invitation," National Catholic Reporter, v. 9, No. 7, 12/9/72, p. 3.

[33]Mark Day, "Freire and Chavez: Educator (of Poor) and Organizer (of Poor) Rap," National Catholic Reporter, v. 9, No. 15, 2/9/73, p. 1.

[34]"Boycott Stand Raises Ire," National Catholic Reporter, v. 9, No. 16, 2/16/73, p. 22.

[35]"Florida Bishops Back Farmworkers," National Catholic Reporter, v. 9, No. 21, 3/23/73, p. 5.

[36]Ron Taylor, "Chavez Heads for Showdown Strike," National Catholic Reporter, v. 9, No. 28, 5/25/73, pp. 1, 6, 15.

[37]"Bishop Malone Protests Priest's Beating," National Catholic Reporter, v. 9, No. 30, 6/22/73, p. 5.

[38]"Unions Work on Vineyard Agreement," National Catholic Reporter, v. 9, No. 32, 7/20/73, pp. 1, 6.

[39]Kenneth Guenterl, "Men Religious: Pluralism Antidote to Polarity," National Catholic Reporter, v. 9, No. 31, 7/6/73, p. 5.

[40]"The Bishops and the Boycott," Current Comment, America, v. 129, No. 1, 7/7/73, p. 1.

[41]"Grand Jury Investigates New Data on Payoffs," National Catholic Reporter, v. 9, No. 33, 8/3/73, p. 5.

[42]"Going to Jail for the UFW," Current Comment, America, v. 129, No. 4, 8/18/73, p. 78.

[43]Ron Taylor, "3,000 Arrested Backing Chavez," National Catholic Reporter, v. 9, No. 34, 8/17/73, pp. 1, 17.

[44]Ron Taylor, "Teamsters Repudiated Contracts: Move Seen Bid Toward Peace," National Catholic Reporter, v. 9, No. 35, 8/31/73, p. 15.

[45]Gerard E. Sherry, "Jail Is Almost Like a Motel to 75-Year Old Dorothy Day," National Catholic Reporter, v. 9, No. 34, 8/17/73, pp. 1, 17.

[46]Carol F. Jagen, "Where the Church Is: Present on the Picket Line," National Catholic Reporter, v. 9, No. 6, 8/31/73, p. 15.

[47]"Use UFW Grapes for Altar Wine," Reporter at Large, National Catholic Reporter, v. 9, No. 35, 8/31/73, p. 20.

[48]"Reporters' Notebook," National Catholic Reporter, v. 9, No. 36, 9/14/73, p. 2.

[49]"Boycott Gets Church Support," *National Catholic Reporter*, v. 9, No. 36, 9/14/73, p. 5.

[50]"Farm Worker Caravan Promotes Boycott," *National Catholic Reporter*, v. 9, No. 36, 9/14/73, p. 5.

[51]"Boyle Hails Settlement," *National Catholic Reporter*, v. 9, No. 41, 10/19/73, p. 15.

[52]Salvatore J. Adamo, "Knight of the Midwest," The Press, *America*, v. 129, No. 12, 10/20/73, pp. 295-296.

[53]James J. Magee, "The Church and the Farm Workers: From Palliatines to Root Change," *America*, v. 129, No. 13, 10/27/73, pp. 302-304.

[54]Joseph Gibboney, "Huelga: A Morning in the Coachella Valley," *Catholic Charities Review*, v. 57, No. 9, 11/73, pp. 20-22.

[55]Camilla Shea, "I Was There," *The Sign*, v. 53, No. 3, 11/73, pp. 12-15.

[56]"Solidarity with Farm Workers," Current Comment, *America*, v. 130, No. 15, 4/20/74, p. 300.

[57]"California Bishops Ask State Farm Labor Law," *National Catholic Reporter*, v. 10, No. 31, 5/31/74, p. 17, and "Free Elections for Farm Workers," Current Comment, *America*, v. 130, No. 23, 6/15/74, pp. 470-471.

[58]"Major Superiors Renew Farm Worker Support," *National Catholic Reporter*, v. 10, No. 36, 8/2/74, p. 20.

[59]"Religious Volunteers in United Farm Worker Movement," Reporter at Large, *National Catholic Reporter*, v. 10, No. 38, 8/30/74, p. 17.

[60]"Boycott of Gallo Disillusions," Repartee, *National Catholic Reporter*, v. 10, No. 39, 9/6/74, p. 14.

[61]"Farm Worker Secret Ballot Action Hailed," *National Catholic Reporter*, v. 10, No. 39, 9/6/74, p. 2.

[62]"Pope's Praise of Chavez," *National Catholic Reporter*, v. 11, No. 2, 11/1/74, p. 16.

[63]"Religious in Rome Hear Appeal by Chavez," *National Catholic Reporter*, v. 10, No. 44, 10/11/74, p. 2.

[64]"Text of Vatican's Support for Chavez," National Catholic Reporter, v. 10, No. 45, 10/18/74, p. 5.

[65]"CBS-TV Program on Chavez Criticized," National Catholic Reporter, v. 11, No. 2, 11/1/74, p. 16.

[66]"Priests, Nuns Charge Winery," National Catholic Reporter, v. 11, No. 4, 11/15/74, p. 6.

[67]"Priest Ends Fast for Farm Workers," National Catholic Reporter, v. 11, No. 8, 12/13/74, p. 15.

[68]"Philadelphia A. & P.," Letters, America, v. 132, No. 10, 3/15/75, p. 181.

[69]"Agribusiness and UFW," Letters, America, v. 132, No. 11, 3/22/75, p. 201.

[70]"NCEA Delegates Hear Gallo Defense," National Catholic Reporter, v. 11, No. 25, 4/17/75, p. 3.

[71]Jan Adams, "UFW March on Gallo," Catholic Worker, v. 41, No. 1, 3/4/75, p. 1.
[72]"Justice Delayed," Current Comment, America, v. 132, No. 17, 5/3/75, p. 333.

[73]"Catholic Bishops of California," News Desk, National Catholic Reporter, v. 11, NO. 29, 5/16/75, p. 6.

[74]"Church Leaders Support Chavez," National Catholic Reporter, v. 11, No. 29, 5/16/75, p. 16.

[75]"Hope in California," Current Comment, America, v. 132, No. 20, 5/25/75, p. 392.

[76]"Unions Retract Fund Pledges," National Catholic Reporter, v. 11, No. 33, 6/20/75, p. 4.

[77]"Union Reinstates Hospital Pledge," National Catholic Reporter, v. 11, No. 34, 7/4/75, p. 20.

[78]"Fear Growing in Texas Melong Fields," National Catholic Reporter, v. 11, No. 33, 6/20/75, p. 6.

[79]Albert de Zutter, "NAWR: Power in Church Sisters' Aim," National Catholic Reporter, v. 11, No. 38, 8/29/75, pp. 1, 3, 13.

[80]Kenneth Ingang, "Higgins Predicts 85% of Vote Will Go to United Farm Workers," National Catholic Reporter, v. 11, No. 38, 8/29/75, p. 16.

[81]Mary Ellen Leary, "Conflicts Expected as Farm Vote Approaches," National Catholic Reporter, v. 11, No. 38, 8/29/75, p. 16.

[82]Vernon Schmid, "Farm Election Investigation 'Shocks' Religious Leaders," National Catholic Reporter, v. 11, No. 44, 10/10/75, p. 4.

[83]Angie Clavert, "Injustice Continues in the Fields," Catholic Worker, v. 41, No. 3, 10-11/75, p. 1.

[84]"Bishop Roger M. Mahony," National Catholic Reporter, v. 11, No. 42, 9/26/75, p. 6.

[85]"Bishop Roger M. Mahony," News Desk, National Catholic Reporter, v. 12, No. 1, 10/24/75, p. 6.

[86]Joseph F. Pawlicki, C.S.C., "Big Fish and Small Fry in the Valley," America, v. 133, NO. 18, 12/6/75, pp. 399-401.
[87]Edward J. Cripps, "California's Gadfly Governor," America, v. 134, No. 6, 2/14/76, pp. 108-112.

[88]Chris Hartmire, "Justice for Farmworkers," Catholic Worker, v. 42, No. 2, 2/76, pp. 1, 6.

[89]"California Labor," Letters, America, v. 134, No. 15, 4/17/76, p. 322.

[90]"Third Farm Worker Week," Current Comment, America, v. 134, No. 18, 5/8/76, p. 399.

[91]"Auxiliary Bishop Roger Mahony," National Catholic Reporter, v. 13, No. 11, 1/7/77, p. 5, and Mary Ellen Leary, "UFW Strong Factor in California Politics: Farm-Labor Strides Told," National Catholic Reporter, v. 12, No. 42, 9/24/76, p. 5.

[92]"Politically The Church Is On Both Sides of the Fence," National Catholic Reporter, v. 13, NO. 19, 3/4/77, pp. 1, 4, 16.

[93]"Sharecroppers on Family Farms," Current Comment, America, v. 136, No. 10, 3/12/77, p. 207.

[94]"Where Have the Farmers Gone?," Editorials, America, v. 136, No. 17, 4/30/77, p. 388.

[95]Lois Spear, "Farmworkers Reach Raleigh," National Catholic Reporter, v. 13, No. 39, 9/2/77, p. 3.

[96]"Arizona Bishop's Labor Law Remarks Draw Fire," National Catholic Reporter, v. 13, No. 41, 9/16/77, p. 4.

[97]"Bishop James S. Rausch," National Catholic Reporter, v. 13, No. 39, 9/2/77, p. 2.

[98]"Rural Life Body Backs Strike Cause," National Catholic Reporter, v. 14, No. 5, 11/18/77, p. 17.

[99]Melissa Jones, "Farmworker Mass Brings Ban from Grove Owners," National Catholic Reporter, v. 15, No. 15, 2/2/79, p. 3.

[100]Bill Kenkelen, "Catholic Support Sparse for Farmworker Strike," National Catholic Reporter, v. 15, No. 21, 3/16/79, p. 3.

[101]_____"Chavez Tests . . . Could Jeopardize UFW Support," National Catholic Reporter, v. 15, NO. 39, 9/7/79, pp. 3-5, 36.

[102]_____"Looking for Church UFW Support," National Catholic Reporter, v. 15, No. 39, 9/7/79, p. 5.

[103]_____"Farmworkers' Lament: 'Will You Join Us Today?,'" National Catholic Reporter, v. 15, No. 39, 9/7/79, p. 4.

[104]"Higgins Raps Bracero Plan,'" National Catholic Reporter, v. 15, NO. 29, 5/11/79, p. 15.

Chapter IV - Some Other Food Laborers

Once Chavez' "farmworkers cause" caught the attention of the U.S. society, difficulty arose in differentiating clearly what was UFW, migrant, farmworker, and food laborers. The "Chavez phenomenon" brought new dimensions to some areas of the church's involvement in the plight of agricultural workers and highlighted old or new church assistance to union organizing among them. Chapters I-IV attempt to sort things out. Earlier chapters dwelt mostly with migrants in the west, southwest and southeast - many of whom stayed in "the migrant stream." This chapter deals with migrant workers who attempted unionization in the midwest and agricultural workers involved in food-processing, who attempted unionization in the southwest and midwest.

A. FLOC

In the state of Indiana the beginnings of organizing among migrant farm workers was somewhat imperceptible, yet nonetheless real, when the Indiana State Advisory Committee to the U.S. Commission on Civil Rights held hearings on migrant labor conditions in May, 1967.[1] In support of these workers throughout the state were several Catholic religious leaders. Testifying at the public hearings of the state committee was Brother Raymond Vega of Divine Heart Seminary in Donaldson, Indiana. Vega was employed as a public health nurse in northern Indiana's Marshall County each summer since 1964. He called conditions in the migrant camps in Marshall County "subhuman, substandard and abominable." He elaborated by alleging that upper respiratory diseases and diarrhea were very common among the migrant children in these camps. Vega concluded that his frequent reports filed with the state board of health on camp conditions generated no results whatsoever. Also testifying at the hearings was a Catholic seminarian, who told of a priest being allowed to celebrate the eucharist in one camp, only on condition that the local anti-poverty program enroll no migrant children in its day school.

However, following the hearing, Alfred J. Hernandez of Houston, Texas, national president of the League of United Latin American Citizens (LULAC), called for a national boycott of the products of the H.J. Heinz Company, to protest the conditions of its labor camps. The Pittsburgh-based food company had been in Indiana since 1884 and had operated eight migrant camps in the region since 1941. From May to September the Heinz camps housed approximately 600 Mexican-Americans, who picked primarily tomato and cucumber crops. Instead of a personal appearance, Heinz sent the hearings' official a statement from its Indiana representative, Gerald F. Smith, which cited the company's "fair, effective, and workable migrant labor policies." However, two days after Hernandez' call for a boycott, Heniz announced that it would close all its Indiana camps immediately. Contracts were canceled with Indiana growers who depended on Heinz to house migrant pickers. Farmers who could provide other housing for the workers were given the opportunity to re-write their contracts. Heinz critics called its actions "buck-passing." In some cases, the critics' fears were realized when some farmers moved the migrants' shacks from the Heinz camps to their own properties. Although Heinz was an easy target at the public hearings, it was not the only one.

The Farm Labor Service of the Indiana Employment Security Division placed work orders for migrant laborers when housing for them had not been certified. State laws had watered down federal minimum housing requirements for migrants. Despite this allegation, a representative of the Chicago office of the U.S. Department of Labor testified that housing, which met Indiana standards was considered in compliance with federal regulations. The state advisory committee also heard claims that decrepit, combustible buildings with numerous health hazards were used to house large families in clear violation of building codes, fire regulations and local health laws. The enforcement powers of local agencies were allegedly unused.

Such complaints were similar to those of migrant workers throughout the country. Despite the fact that living conditions in 1966 for Indiana's 21,000 migrants were miserable, with few exceptions, the migrant labor union movement gaining momentum in California had barely touched Indiana. In South Bend, Indiana, the Centro de la Communidad aimed to train migrants to be leaders, to send them back to the farms in order to acquaint fellow workers with their rights and opportunities, and to leave the migrant stream altogether. The Centro's director, Arnold Solomon said,

> These groups are a pretty passive people as a
> group. . . The civil rights movement really
> hasn't gotten to Mexican-Americans as much as
> it has to the Negro. LULAC is not as power-
> ful as the Urban League.

Supportive of Centro's classes in English and efforts to help migrants find other jobs - especially in face of increasing agricultural mechanization - was James F. Walsh. He was director of South Bend's Catholic Social Services and a member of the

Friends of the Migrants, a group of South Bend residents and students involved in shaking up Indiana growers and the state legislature. Walsh, who grew up in Texas with children from a Mexican-American orphanage, referred to most of the migrant councils, ministries, and apostolates as "company stores" and characterized those who ran them as "tremendous people, but they're too damn tame." He said day care programs for migrant children and the lack of efforts to change adult migrants' status perpetuated a Christian myopia: "If you can teach a kid to read and write, he's going to be much better off."

In an effort to change the migrants' situation, Walsh lobbied the Indiana legislature in the 1967 session for the passage of three bills. One, prohibiting children under the age of 10 from working in the fields, passed. Prior to 1967, it was not unusual to see five-year-olds working in the fields. A second bill, to establish a minimum wage for migrants, passed the state senate but died in the house. The third bill, to eliminate the bonus system through which a grower withheld some of a worker's wages to guarantee the worker's remaining until the end of the harvest season, never got out of committee. Walsh and the other friends of the migrants hoped for more protective migrant legislation in the following legislative sessions.

Meanwhile, they concentrated on applying pressure to solve the most glaring problem: migrant housing. The building commissioner of St. Joseph County, where South Bend is located, finally condemned the migrant shacks on four farms in his jurisdiction. Migrant families, however, continued to occupy those shacks, since there was no other housing available. Still being considered was the possibility of grower and agency representatives forming a non-profit corporation to build new migrant housing with the help of federal grants available through the Farmers Home Administration.

There were later efforts to assist and organize migrant workers in other parts of Indiana when migrant workers struck for better wages and working conditions on August 24, 1976.[2] The workers' demands of the Morgan Packing Plant included: minimum 10 working hours a day; base pay of 26 cent per 30 pound basket of tomatoes, up from 22 cents per basket; better camp care; and better health facilities. In a mailgram to plant owners, the six Catholic bishops of Indiana and the Indiana Catholic Conference expressed support for the migrants. Appealing to the owners to "recognize the reasonableness" of the demands, the bishops and conference called for early relief of the workers' grievances and for "immediate and sincere negotiations between the parties so as to reach an equitable agreement." The bishops and conference also appealed for donations and contributions of food and

174

clothing for the migrants to be sent to the Fort Wayne-South Bend Department of Spanish-Speaking.

By early October 1976 the movement for the midwest migrant farmworkers appeared more organized as the Farm Labor Organizing Committee (FLOC), founded several years earlier under the president, Baldemar Velasquez.[3] The occasion was a march by more than 200 migrant workers and their supporters to the Toledo office of the U.S. Immigration and Naturalization Service (INS), protesting the "barbaric and terroristic tactics" allegedly used by the federal officers when seeking aliens. The agents were accused of entering the Maag Brothers Farm near Ottawa, Ohio, 50 miles southwest of Toledo, without identifying themselves, seizing and fighting with workers, and hauling three away in unmarked cars. Workers who tried to follow the cars were stopped by a Putnam County sheriff's roadblock and sprayed with Mace. The FLOC president, Velasquez, said none of the workers spoke English and none of the sheriff's deputies spoke Spanish. Consequently, the workers could not find out what was happening to the three fellow workers. The director of the Department for the Spanish-Speaking of the Toledo diocese, Sylvester Duran, Velasquez, and other supporters met with Edward Doherty, office-in-charge of the Toledo INS office. Duran claimed that the immigration officers had not been showing identification when confronting farm workers throughout northwest Ohio during the summer of 1976 and had taken legal citizens as well as aliens into custody. Doherty said he would forward the letters of protest to the Cleveland district office which had jurisdiction over the area.

Meanwhile, FLOC had filed a $700,000 lawsuit against law enforcement officials of neighboring Fulton County, two farmers and a work crew leader in the U.S. District Court in Toledo. The suit was filed after FLOC organizers were held at gunpoint by crew leader Guadalupe Hernandez and arrested by sheriff's deputies who were called to the farm by owner Rene Victor. The latter claimed the FLOC organizers refused to leave in violation of no trespassing signs posted, despite the fact that none of Victor's workers told him they had invited the FLOC organizers to the farm's camp. Two other FLOC workers were arrested and jailed and three others were detained several hours when they went to the county jail in Wauseon to inquire about the other two. Unlike southern and southwestern states where no trespassing policies at farm labor camps had been overturned in the courts, such policies in Ohio previously had not been challenged. Consequently, in addition to compensatory damages ($200,000) and punitive damages ($500,000) the FLOC lawsuit sought a permanent injunction barring the defendants from interferring with FLOC's efforts to speak with migrant workers.

175

In January of 1978, the FLOC president, Baldemar Velasquez, addressed a mini-pastoral course for people working with Latinos, held at Mundelein College in Chicago.[4] He spoke of locating and plotting 358 camps employing about 20,000 migrants in northeastern Indiana and northwest Ohio in 1977, of talking to the workers and getting names of canners from the workers' crates, and of planning to focus a strike on one region and one cannery. He spoke of a kind of tomato belt from Toledo in Ohio (22,000 acres) into mid-northern Indiana (14,000 acres) and indicated that the 358 farms supplied six firms - Campbell, Del Monte, Heinz, Hunt and Libby. Valesquez continued,

> Some people say, "Why don't you demand what
> you want from the growers and then have them
> get it from the canneries?" But that's what
> we tried in '69 and it didn't work. The
> growers simply switched their crops from
> tomatoes to corn and wheat.

The 12 Ohio growers who made the switch had signed contracts with FLOC in 1968. The growers, Velasquez explained, contracted in advance with one cannery, selling their produce at an agreed upon price. The grower had to get his profit out of that price, after labor and other costs were met.

The FLOC president continued to lay out the plans.

> We'll probably start putting on organizers in
> March. We'll start by going to Texas and
> Florida where the workers come from. We want
> to have it organized before workers get up
> here. We'll use people from the camps as
> organizers.

> We'll need 40-50 full-time organizers who
> we'll pay $60-$70 a week, enough for food and
> gasoline.

He also mentioned that FLOC had raised $30,000 on its own and had a grant pending from the USCC Campaign for Human Development (CHD), which would cover the remaining costs. Stressing an increase of support in 1977 because of endorsements from "the bishops' conference" and Chavez' UFW, Velasquez added, "People don't have any reason not to support us now." He claimed as crucial the initial support of the organizing proposal from William A. McManus, bishop of Fort Wayne-South Bend, with other bishops following his lead. During 1977 the Toledo diocese denied CHD funding three times. So, for Velasquez, "Support from the bishops really helped make the CHD grant possible." He concluded with comments about Lakewood Greenhouse, near Toledo, which allegedly fired seven women for reporting unsafe working conditions, including pesticide problems, to OSHA.

On August 25, 1978 in Belmore, Ohio, there was an outdoor rally and prayer service, attended by 200 farm workers and conducted by Rev. Richard Notter of Toledo, one of the many clergy supporting negotiations between area farmers and the Libby Cannery in Leipsic, Ohio, with striking FLOC workers.[5] Libby's cannery was chosen as a striking and picketing target because of a lack of success in more and disparate targets in 1968. FLOC's secretary-treasurer, Roy Santiago, claimed that the strike had received support from the bishop of Lafayette, Indiana, Raymond Gallagher, and the Spanish-Speaking Office and Human Relations Office of the Toledo diocese, as well as from several individual Catholic and Protestant clergy. Sister Ann Weller of the Lafayette diocese and a member of the Indiana State Migrant Action Committee raised money for FLOC's strike fund. Bishop Gallagher informed FLOC that he would do what he could to assure that the strikers would be fed and clothed properly. In addition to support from UFW's Chavez, FLOC's organizing campaign was funded $89,000 from the U.S. Bishops' CHD office, $5,000 from the Toledo diocesan CHD office and $2,950 from the Lafayette diocese. Velasquez estimated that of the 9,000 farm workers in the 18,000 acres of tomatoes in northwest Ohio, 2,000 were officially members of FLOC.

In April 1979 there was more than 200 people gathered in the basement of a parish church to testify before the Toledo diocesan CHD committee.[6] Some were Mexican-American farmworkers and their families. Others were farmers and their families. Previous CHD awards of $40,000 and $89,000 to FLOC had embittered area parishes with both Hispanic and farm families. For 1979, FLOC sought $97,300 for an organizing campaign. Even though the money was not to be used for strike benefits, talk at the hearing did turn to the 1978 strike during the peak of the tomato harvest season and to FLOC's promise to do similar action in the future. Many asked why the church should help fund the union that had caused the migrant workers to walk out of the fields. An agriculture extension agent said,

> Basically, the church has been for the family
> farm. And this is the one that has been
> employing farm workers in the past.

He added that the processors reacted to the 1978 strike by favoring contracts with farmers owning mechanized tomato harvesters.

However, Velasquez, claimed that the farmers refused to face the real issue - the economic control that large corporations have over the farmer. He maintained that only after farmers ignored union requests to bargain together against the processors did FLOC announce its boycott of Campbell's and Libby's products. The FLOC president continued,

> Mechanization is going to come whether there is a union or not. That's inevitable.
>
> We have to do what's right for our people, and we can't wait on you (farmers) forever.

Another farmer said after the meeting that he did not object to the union itself, but he did not think that the church should be involved in funding he organizing effort. "When I first heard of that," he said, "I really felt betrayed. I never felt so bad about the church." Also, after the meeting the CHD committee voted unanimously to recommend top priority to FLOC out of the four applications it had to consider for 1979. The national CHD committee was not to decide on the FLOC application until June 1979.

In its Agust 4, 1979 convention, FLOC officially announced new targets for a national boycott: Campbell Soup Company and Nestle Company subsidiary, Libby.[7] FLOC wanted a contract signed by the two processing firms and local farmers. Key demands were health insurance, restrictions on pesticides, minimum pay of $3.50 an hour, and a guarantee of 28 hours work every two weeks during harvest season. According to a FLOC report in the Detroit-based newsletter Labor News,

> Migrant pickers earn roughly $2.50 an hour, pay their own way North, and get no guaranteed minimum weekly income. . . They live in two-room shacks without plumbing . . . are exposed to pesticide. . . have skimpy health insurance or none at all. Their average life expectancy is about 49 years.

The director of the Toledo diocesan Office of Communty Relations, Rev. Charles Ritter, said, "FLOC is an essential effort to provide some self-determination for the farm workers." Ritter and officials of the Ohio Council of Churches had tried, without success, to convince the processing firms to negotiate with FLOC, since a 1968 victory was turned into a defeat when the processors dropped the union farms and bought tomatoes from unorganized farms. Campbell's public relations manager, Scott Rombach, denied the charge and said,

178

> FLOC is attempting to force us to intervene
> in the affairs of our suppliers. We feel
> that could raise serious legal questions.

In February 1980, a member of the Latin America Task Force in Detroit, Rev. Joseph E. Mulligan, S.J., spoke of the "modest but significant contribution" of liturgies, prayer services and scripture to the spirit and commitment of the cause of FLOC.[8] Referring to of the summer 1979 religious celebrations of migrant families encouraging FLOC in the struggle, Mulligan mentioned how the celebrations were shaped by the theology of liberation developed at the grassroots level in Latin America and discussed in many seminars for middle-class North Americans. For Mulligan, liturgies celebrated "the organization and liberation struggle" that actually took place among the farm workers in Ohio. However, without the long, hard and capable work of FLOC, without the strike and boycott, without a 60-mile march from Toldeo to the Libby cannery, and without the sit-in by 28 farm workers who peacefully blocked the mechanical harvester -"technological strikebreakers" - Mulligan maintained that there would have been no "history of salvation" to celebrate and no human struggle to nourish. Mulligan then proceeded to list a summary of facts which made the "justice of FLOC's cause" evident. He also told of 28 farm workers arrested for the sit-in blocking the farm machinery; the attack by sheriff's police on their attorney, Jack Kilroy, after his visit to the jail; the F.B.I. investigation; and 200 farm workers' protest outside the Ottawa, Ohio, sheriff's office and courthouse.

Mulligan devoted most attention to describing several liturgical events. The first was a eucharist, celebrated in Saints Peter and Paul Church the night before the march from the Toledo barrio parish to the Libby cannery. The service began outside where the church steps, sidewalk and street were illuminated by the lighted candles held in the participants hands. The first reading from the fifth chapter of St. James Epistle contained, for Mulligan, some prophetic words which required little homiletic explanation.

The five farm worker families were recognized as the leaders and the heart of the march that was about to commence. Mulligan explained,

> We called them up before the assembly and
> anointed them, explaining that this was an
> ancient ritual to designate prophets and
> leaders, that there was nothing magical or
> miraculous about it but that it was an
> affirmation and celebration of their action

and message. As far as we could tell, this
liturgy was indeed "efficacious."

Toward the close of the service, hands were imposed on FLOC's
president as an affirmation of his leadership of the organization.   He was prayed over, as he began a four-day fast.   The
final part of the eucharist was a procession through the barrio
led, as was the march, with a banner of Our Lady of Guadalupe,
symbol of the Mexican's "struggle for liberation."

After the march, there was a rally involving approximately
300 people.   There was a "paraliturgical" ceremony.   It celebrated Velasquez' breaking his fast.   After scripture readings
and songs bread was distributed and everyone joined Velasquez,
sharing the bread and showing solidarity with him and one
another.   On later occasions when the echuarist was celebrated
the experience of this ceremony would be felt by all.   Mulligan
then mentioned that after the march, FLOC intensified its
efforts.   On one occasion, Mulligan met with some non-striking
workers who came to a solidarity rally on their day-off from
farms not targeted by FLOC.   Mulligan reflected on the risk they
took of being fired, "Like the disciples, could they cast their
lot with someone who was challenging the status quo?"   Mulligan
told of unwittingly venturing over an obscure property line
dressed in his clerical black shirt and being ordered off
promptly by the farmer.   Mulligan described the rest of the
dialogue, which had not begun very propitiously:

> He and his friends then told me that religion
> had nothing to do with all this, that priests
> and sisters should stay in church and that if
> the Auxililary Bishop and other church folk
> continued to support FLOC, the farmers would
> stop contributing to the collections.
> Nothing subtle here. I replied that that was
> his decision but that we would not be
> deterred by such considerations.

The following day, a eucharist was celebrated at the farm
workers' request, in the big tent that served as FLOC's strike
headquarters, nearby the Libby cannery.   There was a baptism,
planned some two weeks earlier, of a farm worker's child.   After
realizing there had been no classes of preparation, instructions,
etc., Mulligan discussed the pastoral considerations with the
pastor, Sr. Jean, and a Hispanic deacon. Mulligan expanded their
discussion about the paraliturgies and homilies during the march
and the strike.   Baptism as the incorporation of the person in
the community and the passage from sin to concern for others was
related to FLOC's efforts to help the poor and oppressed and to
provide examples of love in action.

As the eucharist began, the first reading was a passage from the first chapter of Philippians, where St. Paul made it clear that he was writing from prison and that his incarceration was actually helping to spread the good news, because others were gaining courage from him to speak loudly. The gospel passage presented Jesus breaking the letter of the Sabbath law by healing some. After this "catechesis" the families, godparents and children to be baptized came forth to be baptized. The families, godparents and children were asked if they intended to continue to grow by sharing with one another, to assist each other by reaching out as the community did, and to inculcate the challenges and values of the Gospel. One of the vice presidents of FLOC then anointed the foreheads of children, godparents and families - symbolizing their call to be prophets and leaders of the community. All then picked up a banner or picket sign to march around the tent to the tune of "We Shall Not Be Moved" ("No Nos Moveram"). It was their expression of their identity as a Christian community struggling for justice. The actual baptizing was done by a deacon who was a worker in the fields.

On February 25, 1980 there was a student referendum at the University of Notre Dame.[9] The vote was 2,012 to 1,321 for banning from campus food outlets, all the products of Campbell's and Libby's. The FLOC boycott endorsement by the students followed an endorsement from William McManus, bishop of Fort Wayne-South Bend diocese, active support of the campus ministry staff, and a student group which electioneered door-to-door in all of Notre Dame's 22 residence halls. There was also a letter from FLOC's president and a report for the boycott elsewhere. Velsaquez' letter characterized the migrant farmworkers as,

> . . . one of the most violently exploited groups of workers in this country, whose life expectancy is 49 years, whose infant mortality is double the national average, whose wages are the lowest of any group of workers.

The report of activities claimed schools had been asked to drop Campbell's "labels for education" campaign by bishops in Fort Wayne-South Bend and Lafayette, Indiana; Orlando, Florida; and Wyoming. At least 50 Catholic elementary schools, most in the midwest had done so. Velasquez explained an additional reason for targeting schools,

> Ohio farms are the number one violator of child labor laws in the entire U.S. We have hordes of children working in the fields because the whole family - mother, father,

grandparents and children - all have to work
just to make ends meet.

The University students' endorsement of the FLOC boycott was
the first by an institution of higher education. The referendum
was held under a Notre Dame policy which permitted students to
decide whether the university would join a consumer boycott. In
1979 a similar referendum was held and a majority of the students
who voted supported FLOC. However, the turnout was below the 50
per cent required for adoption of a boycott proposal. Also, in a
separate 1979 referendum, the Notre Dame student body supported
the international boycott of the Nestle Company. That boycott
was organized by social justice activists who charged that Nestle
caused infant deaths in the Third World by distributing baby
formula to mothers not trained to use it safely. From 1973 to
1978, Notre Dame students also participated in the UFW boycotts.

In early May 1980 there were comments on Notre Dame students' support of the FLOC boycott, in a large story about the
university.[10] Among the many Notre Dame "credits," which contributed to the university's excellence in the minds of many
observers were projects such as the "Urban Plunge" and efforts
such as the FLOC boycott. However, such projects did not get
publicized as much as Notre Dame's academics and athletics. One
of the student organizers on the Notre Dame campus was Anne
Huber, a philosophy major. She recalled,

> . . . we got 50 people to work door-to-door
> in the dorms. It seemed that people really
> were ready to do something to help somebody -
> almost as if they were waiting for something
> to do . . . If you approach the people here
> personally about these issues, they're intel-
> ligent enough to respond.

However, another FLOC campus promoter, who had written his
doctoral dissertation on the UFW for the Economics Department,
Rick Coronado, found the boycott support incredible,

> It is incredible that we got Notre Dame to
> back a union. . .because there is a tre-
> mendous anti-union mentality here. [We also
> had to contend with] . . . people like this
> one kid who said to me, "I'm a realist. If I
> begin to worry about the farmworkers, then
> I'll have to worry about the garment workers,
> the other service workers - I can't worry
> about all these things."

In mid-1980 FLOC received further significant support from two quarters.[11] First, the National Catholic Educational Association decided that its 1981 convention would not provide an exhibition booth for the Campbell "labels for education" program. The decision followed criticism from FLOC for the NCEA's allowing such an exhibit in its April 1980 convention in New Orleans. Said NCEA convention director, Rev. Richard Elmer, "I would have denied them a booth if I had known about the boycott in time, just as we denied Nestle's a booth because of its Third World sales practices."

The second source of support was the outcry from FLOC supporters - Hispanic civil rights groups, social service agencies, religious groups, such as the National Farm Workers Ministry - against the Ohio Council of Churches' (OCC) negotiations with Campbell toward creation of a company-funded social service program for migrant workers. FLOC supporters charged that such negotiations reflected an unwillingness of the Ohio Council of Churches to do for FLOC what it had done for California farmworkers and J.P. Stevens' textile workers, namely, endorse their boycotts.

In 1979 the Ohio Council of Churches' executive committee had narrowly rejected the endorsement of the FLOC boycott. The state council had tried, unsuccessfully, to mediate among FLOC, tomato farm owners and tomato packing firms. Campbell made an offer of a quarter million dollars to finance job-training for farmworkers displaced by machines and day care for farmworkers' children. The Ohio Council of Churches responded with a "compromise" plan that pleased no one. For, there was not sufficient input from the Hispanic and migrant workers' groups. Yet, Campbell was offered help in planning a different program in conjunction with such groups - including FLOC. The leaders of such groups were named by the church council as possible participants, but denounced the council for suggesting collaboration with Campbell. One Campbell official, on the other hand, said he could not work with FLOC, an organization which unfairly made the company a protest target.

In May 1980, the Ohio Council of Churches' executive director, Dr. Carleton Weber, received a sharply worded letter from the director of the National Farm Workers Ministry, Rev. Wayne C. Hartmire.

> People in the churches may not agree with FLOC's strategy, but the people of FLOC are the ones who have put their lives into this struggle and they are therefore the only ones with a right to determine strategy. The

issue for churches is now "yes" or "no" on
boycott. . .

Campbells is seeking credibility as a way of
fighting the boycott. If OCC can't support
the farmworkers the way they need most, why
turn around and aid their oppressors? You
may not see your actions as aiding Campbells.
But my experience tells me that they will
skillfully put to use your openness.

The associate director of the state council, Rev. Keene
Lebold, responded to Hartmire and other critics by conceding that
Campbell might have been spurred by the bad publicity of the
FLOC boycott to propose the training and day care programs but
maintaining that such was not adequate reason for unconditional
rejection of the company's funds. Lebold insisted on the state
council's commitment to justice,

Our sympathies lie with FLOC, but it has been
such a controversial group in the northwest
part of the state that we feel it would
jeopardize the relationships we have with
growers, many of whom are members of our
churches, if we identified with FLOC. We
don't want to alienate ourselves from any
party as long as there is a chance for
reconciliation.

A response to the FLOC supporters, also came from Campbell
public relations director, Rodger Duncan. He denied that the
consumer boycott had had any noticeable effect on sales. In
fact, he claimed that participation in the "labels for education"
program had increased 15 per cent in 1980, despite FLOC's
campaign to persuade schools to drop out of the program. Duncan
said the training and day care programs were not designed to
short-circuit support for the FLOC boycott. The programs, suggested by officials at the Campbell plant at Napoleon, Ohio, were
examples of other such programs sponsored by Campbell near its
U.S. factories. When questioned further, Duncan admitted the
criticized programs were the first Campbell had designed primarily to aid migrant workers.

In late July 1980, the Wisconsin Women for Agriculture
sponsored a forum on farm labor at De Pere, Wisconsin.[12] One of
the speakers was a holder of a doctorate in agricultural history
from Catholic University, Sr. Thomas More Bertels, a member of
the Franciscan Sisters of Christian Charity. She blasted as
"wrong" and "potentially tragic" the FLOC boycott of food growers

and processors. She rapped farmworker boycotts in general. "They don't work. The United Farm Worker boycott didn't work. It's just propaganda." Several members of the Wisconsin Women for Agriculture seconded Bertel's complaint that several Catholic organizations addressing the farmworker issue did not listen to both sides of it. Specifically mentioned was the FLOC boycott, allegedly endorsed by the National Conference of Catholic Bishops, the CHD, the Leadership Conference of Women Religious and other Catholic groups. One farm woman said, "I resent bishops telling us how to run our business." Another member of the state farm organization added,

> I have children who go to Catholic school. As a parent, I resent having our children being taught to . . . see us farmers as the problem. We battle bad weather, mechanical failures. . . now we have to battle even the church.

Another speaker was FLOC's president, Baldemar Velasquez. Formally invited at first to address the group, Velasquez was later "disinvited." He was allowed finally to speak when some of the 75 audience members complained that the forum was weighed in favor of farm owners. Velasquez emphasized,

> We don't see the farmers as our enemies. [In pressing for three-way negotiations] we are really doing the growers a favor. The grower has become a worker of the canneries under his contracts, being told when to plant, spray, harvest, mechanize. . . [Three-way negotiations] will give growers the power to demand what they need.

Another speaker was Rev. Patrick J. Sullivan, C.S.C., formerly Catholic Liaison in the J.P. Stevens Textile controversy and later a researcher on church-labor-management issues at the University of Notre Dame. In addition to insisting that papal teaching maintains that "social action is as integral to the church as the sacraments," Sullivan suggested a future imperative of grower-farmworker cooperation. His reason - "farmers are getting poorer too, and more powerless." However, the Wisconsin Women for Agriculture offered little response to Velasquez' and Sullivan's suggestions that a co-operative alliance between family farmers and farmworkers might have been the only way to deal with new conditions in the agricultural industry, which were created by the large corporation farms and food processors.

185

B. Sugar Cane Workers

In 1973, the NCR told of the expulsion from the diocese of Baton Rouge, Louisiana of Rev. Vincent O'Connell, a Marist priest.[13] The occasion was the New Orleans States-Item publication of a May 21, 1973 letter from the bishop of the Baton Rouge diocese, Robert E. Tracy, to the Marist provincial of the same O'Connell. The letter, ordering O'Connell out of the Baton Rouge diocese in 30 days, among other things, said,

> I find no need to explain to Father O'Connell or to anyone else the rationale for this decision. . . I do not believe Father O'Connell's ministry or residence in our diocese is in the best interests of the people. . . My reasons are personal. . . All concerned are agreed that Father O'Connell's misguided efforts are a hindrance rather than a help.

Previously, Tracy had endorsed the Southern Mutual Help Association (SMHA) for which O'Connell had worked for four years. However, even though the headquarters of the SMHA's Plantation Adult Education Program of which O'Connell was the director was in Thibodaux, part of the New Orleans diocese, he followed his provincial's instructions. So, O'Connell moved out of the Baton Rough diocese rectory and into the home of a sugar-cane worker in Ladadieville, which was in the Baton Rouge diocese.   Thus, O'Connell was not subject to the bishop's authority and did not appear to be "giving in to his directive."   O'Connell received some public support from the Council of Nine Marists in Washington, D.C., who were all in non-church-related jobs.

Two months later O'Connell received additional testimonies of support, and the sugar-cane workers were spotlighted.[14] Although the dispute ended when O'Connell moved into the sugar-cane worker's home, there were exchanges about the 30 year champion of unionizing efforts, education, food stamps, improved housing, better wages and working conditions of the sugar cane workers, most of whom were black. Tracy claimed a jurisdictional problem since O'Connell had moved into the Baton Rouge diocese without permission.   Of O'Connell's work, a diocesan statement said, it

> . . . appeared to be harmful to the interest of the people. . . [So] it was necessary to make it clear that he [O'Connell] in no way represented the Baton Rouge diocese.

Nevertheless, Ray Scott, executive director of the diocesan Social Responsibility Board, agreed with Sr. Aline Boutle, a SMHA staffer, who said that before the dispute with Tracy, "There was apathy and ignorance. . . Now there is knowledge and under-standing." Scott, also, said that O'Connell had put sympathetic people in contact with SMHA, despite some disagreement about what was said about the cane workers' conditions. Scott also admitted that SMHA's request for funds for a communications' director, necessitated by a cutback in federal funds, was turned down by the diocesan Social Responsibility Board, due to its lack of funds. He also admitted that he was directed to work with Dominican Sister Anne Catherine Bizalion, but could never come up with a program. O'Connell quoted his superior, Rev. Charles J. Barrett, that a wealthy grower in St. James Parish (county) and a large contributor to the church, forced Tracy to expel O'Connell. Tracy denied the charge. Privately, a church leader said the dispute was a matter of personalities as well as jurisdiction.

A defender of O'Connell, Associate Professor James Bolner, in the Political Science Department at Louisiana State University in Baton Rouge, said,

> The official church has all too often been a tool of rich farmers. . . Instead of siding with those who would obstruct Father O'Connell's work, the Catholic hierarchy should be actively supporting it. . . Opposition to him is based precisely on the proposition that he is effective.

Sr. Lorna Bourg, who founded SMHA with Sr. Bizalion, stressed that there was more early support from Protestant and Jewish groups than from the Catholic church. She added,

> We applied three years in a row to CHD. Last year our proposal was rewritten to their standards. But they say sugar cane workers are a low priority. . . The Catholic church is responsible for the problem. Most growers are Catholic. But the church hierarchy has done nothing to change the situation. It has condoned it.

Opposition to SMHA's Plantation Adult Basic Education Program was due not only to its content - basic education, wages, food stamps, the Sugar Act, etc. - but also to the involvement of two sugar cane union organizers as early as the 1950's. They were O'Connell and Henry Pelet, president of the Amalgamated Meat Cutters' local. The daughter of a sugar cane worker fired after

187

a 1968 union meeting in his home, Joyce Westbrook, pointed out the need for SMHA,

> Growers feel workers can't do anything else.
> If people feel they have help, they figure
> they can get off the plantation and get a
> better job. They know they have food stamps
> and a little money. All they have to find is
> a home.

Yet, due to alleged pressure from growers, state officials withdrew approval for a promised federal funding for a $300,000 Migrant Resettlement Program that would have included manpower training.

In October 1971, the beginning of the harvest season, Department of Agriculture officials told O'Connell, Pelet, and Bizalion in Washington that the setting of minimum wage rates would be delayed until December 28, 1971 and they would not take effect until January 10, 1972 - the end of the harvest season. However, SMHA filed and won a suit making the wage increase retroactive to October 1, 1971. The Department of Agriculture held up all subsidies to the growers until the back pay was given. SMHA hoped to create changes in the Department of Agriculture's laxity in administering the Sugar Act and hoped to work with the small growers - to pull together, to be more productive, and to obtain their subsidies promptly. Said Bazilion,

> We don't want to destroy the industry. That
> would be foolish. Where would the workers
> work? We're concerned with a healthy
> industry. But the industry can't be healthy
> if only one part of it is healthy.

Healthy or not, one part of the industry in Louisiana, the growers, were pleased that Bishop Tracy ordered O'Connell out of the diocese in May 1973. Some of the growers, several weeks later in Houma, Louisiana, applauded when O'Connell mentioned the expulsion during his testimony at Department of Agriculture's hearings on sugar cane wages. Nevertheless, it was revealed how the growers were squeezed from more sides than SMHA. Mills that needed to refine sugar cane before it could be sold were closing in many places. Land owners held on to ownership for mineral rights. The leasing cost to growers was 20 per cent of their gross income. Mechanization costs were estimated at $20,000 for every 100 acres of sugar cane harvested. Finally, the U.S. government not only fixed the amount of sugar cane to be grown but paid a subsidy for cane not grown in the U.S. The government also set the minimum wages on the testimony of growers and

188

others.   It was noted that some growers did pay approximately 10 cents above the minimum.

O'Connell   may have   been laughed   at by   some   growers, but another priest, Msgr. John Kemps, pastor of Sacred Heart Parish in Broussard, Louisisana, very early on July 3, 1973, was shot at by someone unknown at the time.[15]   Fortunately, the four or more shots, which were fired through the bedroom window in the rectory in the heart of southern Louisiana's sugar cane region, missed the priest.   Kemps and Bishop Frey of the Lafayette, Louisiana, diocese had supported the right of the parish school principal, Sr. Robertine Galvin, S.D.P., to assist SMHA.   Quite an uproar was caused in the 600 population town, when Galvin had invited Bazilion to address a group of sugar cane growers and to explain SMHA's court decision on the minimum wage payments. Many persons with ties to large sugar cane plantations began a move to oust Galvin as principal of the school.   Before the shooting, Kemps had read at all the Sunday eucharists a letter of support for Galvin from her religious community, the Sisters of Divine Providence.   After the shooting, which Kemps refused to discuss and to reveal to his Ordinary, Kemps said, "I'm just a victim of someone who has been subjected to something."   He added that neither before nor after the shooting incident had he received any physical threats.

In early March 1974, there were some national demonstrations of support for the sugar cane workers.   The executive board of the National Assembly of Women Religious stated its support of the Sugar Cane.[16]   In the U.S. House Agriculture Committee, Stephen E. Bossi announced the support of the National Catholic Rural Life Conference for decent wages, housing, education, health care, comprehensive health and accident insurance, and some workers' input in adjusting wage rates for sugar cane workers.[17]

Later in March 1974, along with others, three religious sisters testified before the U.S. Congress on behalf of the sugar cane workers.[18]   The first to testify was Sr. Carol Coston of Network. She indicated that some 15,000 farm workers were caught behind the "cane curtin" in Louisiana's sugar fields, with their fate decided, by the Sugar Act of 1937. The goal of that act was to help growers, workers, and consumers benefit from tight regulation of domestic production and foreign imports.   They benefitted from a market price 5 cents below the world price.   The growers annually enjoy about $90 million in subsidies.

However, while unionized sugar workers making from $2.85 to $4.80 per hour in Hawaii, the largest sugar-producing state, benefitted from and welcomed tight government control, the mostly

189

black and poorly educated sugar workers in Louisiana had the 1937 Sugar Act working against them. In 1973 the average family of six made about $3,250 a year, more than $1,600 below the 1972 poverty level for farm families, according to the estimates of the Office of Economic Opportunity. Most of these farm workers performed skilled jobs, such as driving trucks and tractors, and earned between $1.90 and $2.10 an hour. That figure was described as very deceptive, since there was little work from January to August and since there was an increase in mechanization. Furthermore, since so much owed to druggists, utilities or plantation-run stores was deducted from wages, said Coston, "Some workers never see any cash." She also indicated that to lose a job, along with wages deducted for such bills, made the workers helpless. For, there were no savings. Although the housing was supplied free by the growers, it was substandard. Usually there was a four-room shack, one-third of the time cold running water, an open chimney for wood-burning fire and 13 per cent still lacking indoor toilets.

The second religious sister to testify was Loren Marie Guilloux of Rutgers University Law School in New Jersey. She spoke of Louisiana having the highest rate of illiteracy in the U.S. Much of that was attributed to the low education level on plantations and to the plantation system having developed a separate culture and almost a language of its own. To remedy the overall situation of the workers Sr. Guilloux had several suggestions. There had to be some protection from fear of recrimination for testimony given by sugar workers. There had to be workers input in the wage-hearings. There had to be the use of verified and current data and representative sampling assured, due to prevalence of slanted data. There had to be Department of Agriculture hearings to determine the growers' ability to pay workers, given the market conditions.

The third religious sister to testify was Bazilion of the Southern Mutual Help Association. She spoke of unionization for the sugar workers, "if and when the people are ready, they will choose." Also testifying was Steve Bossi, representing the USCC and NCRLS. Bossi said the

> . . . minimal impact of wage increases on consumer prices would be a minor adjustment in a system as complex and massive as the sugar industry.

Also testifying were Tulane University medical students. They showed that two of 37 adults were found to be medically normal and eight of 37 needed no immediate medical attention. There was also a high level of mental retardation among children due to

190

malnutrition.   Also, the overall health of children was slightly better than adults.

Later, in May 1974, Bossi, as director of the USCC's Division of Rural Life, sent a letter to all the members of the U.S. House of Representatives, urging approval of several amendments to improve the farm labor provisions of the Sugar Act.[19] Bossi pointed out the need to apply more reasonable and fair criteria in determining the minimum wage rates to provide insurance protection comparable to workers' compensation laws, to set piece rates at levels comparable to the hourly minimum wage rates, and to provide compensation to workers for illegal actions taken by employers.

By June 1974, the U.S. House of Representatives defeated H.R. 1290-175, Sugar Act's Extension Bill.[20] Decrying the defeat of the bill, as well as several amendments, which would have improved the wage-setting procedures and given the sugar workers' a modified form of workers' compensation insurance were Rev. Vincent O'Connell and Sr. Anne Catherine Bizalion. They stressed that the prime purpose of the extension bill was the guarantee of a fair and reasonable wage, about to be realized before the defeat of the bill. They also stressed that the defeat would put many small growers out of business.

In June 1979, both Bizalion and O'Connell were back in the news, along with two other sugar worker advocates.[21] The four advocates were criticized by the growers and some differences of opinion appeared among the advocates themselves.   Cane growers who were Knights of Columbus had written the Catholic bishop to call off Bizalion, "this federally-funded nun."   In the U.S. since 1956 and co-founder of SMHA in 1969, Bizalion helped bring hundreds of thousands of federal dollars into the Louisiana sugar cane area.   Thanks to federal grants, the sugar cane workers were the beneficiaries of free clinics, education, job skills programs, low-interest housing loans and housing construction assistance.

Bizalion was criticized also for media manipulation, internal handling of SMHA issues and grievances, and over-emphasis on "Band-Aid" social service programs.   Some SMHA staffers contended that Bizalion "choreographed" a visit of NCR people in early March 1979, a visit of Southern Christian Leadership Conference (SCLC) President Joseph Lowery, and a CBS "Sixty Minutes" visit.   The critics contended that such visitors were taken on plantation tours but were dissuaded from stopping at workers' houses, because Bizalion did not "want the bosses coming along afterwards to harass the workers."   CBS producer, Joseph Wershba, said he also gathered from Bizalion that the camera team "shouldn't stop" at the worker's houses.

191

At the end of his March 1979 tour, Rev. Lowery charged that the cane plantation ". . . is an Auschwitz without gas chambers. . . it really is a concentration camp." Cane worker advocate, Divine Providence Sister Imelda Maurer talked to workers on the planation Lowery toured and found that the workers were ". . . generally insulted by his characterization of their lives." Sr. Berni Galvin, another Divine Providence Sister, said that when Lowery returned, after his speech, to talk to the workers, they told him no stories of gross mistreatment," . . . only that they needed more money."

A former SMHA staffer said that Bizalion, ". . . by exaggerating an image of the sniveling, abused worker . . . sets up a straw man which growers can easily blow down." Bizalion denied that she tried to influence media coverge, "We are not trying to tell people what to write or not to write." She showed one particular plantation. ". . . because it is the worst, and we want people to see how bad it is. But we tell them that it is the worst." Her emphasis, said Bizalion, is that ". . . it's not either/or - the holy farmworkers versus the ugly farmers - it's good and bad on both sides." SMHA concerned itself with social service programs, not labor organizing. Many who left SMHA expressed the desire "to work more directly with people."

The long-time organizer of cane workers, 67-year-old Marist priest, Vincent O'Connell, expressed some irritation,

> . . . we can't get it through some people's heads that social service projects won't do. We have to get down to the causes of the leaky roofs and the hurt people.

Referring to the local Catholic churches usually accepting growers' contributions and ignoring the workers' problems, O'Connell confessed that, if it was simply a labor dispute, he would not expect church assistance. However, he would, in case of the violation of human rights. O'Connell stated that since the 1940's, during organizing campaigns, the sheriff would move people from jail to jail so that they could not be gotten out on bail. When a man left a plantation to get a job in town, the town employer would call the grower and say, "One of your boys is here". There would be no town job and upon return to the plantation the "boy" would be moved down the job ladder for "misbehaving". These and other evidences of the plantation system's continuance were protected by the area's bankers, machine merchants, politicians and others.

Also, seeking basic changes was Henri Pelet, 59 year-old president of the refinery and mill employees' union, Local 1422 of the Amalgamated Meatcutters and Butchers International, AFL-CIO. Pelet frequently housed O'Connell since he was ordered to give up his rectory residence by Bishop Tracy. Pelet worked for the Supreme Sugar refinery since high school. In 1945 he organized the union at Supreme and in 1953 he promoted a strike by 3,000-4,000 cane workers against more than 50 operators.

The strike failed after four weeks, said Pelet, ". . . because the workers had no more food and money, and it was apparent the strike was not going to succeed." He noted that the mill and refinery workers did not walk out. For, Pelet was convinced that no field hands' strike could succeed, unless the possibility existed of withholding the entire crop. This necessitated cooperation of mill and refinery workers and could be done only in harvest and processing time, when they controlled demand. Aside from fighting "the whole power structure of the community", the field workers had to fight hard times. The farmers and the people in the area were not so sure that they were making a lot of money and willing to let the field workers have "a piece of it". Seventy-five per cent of the 10,000 residents in Assumption Parish (county) involved in some aspect of the sugar industry were close to the poverty bracket. The other 25 per cent were "growers and such." Another 10,000 residents were not involved in sugar fields, but in factories or subsidiary services: stores, repairs, machinery sales, etc.

However, short of a strike, the only way Pelet saw to upgrade the workers' conditions would be an NLRB election. Pelet explained the slim prospects for such an option. The farmers were not willing to agree to the NLRB coverage. So, the organizing was easy in Pelet's mind. The recognition was the real rub.

Sisters Galvin and Mauer saw organizing simply as a matter of ". . . educing the power and courage and dreams that are in them already." Maurer, a 40 year-old Texas native said, "Everyone's afraid at times - but that doesn't mean the workers don't take steps to improve things." Galvin, a 44 year-old Oklahoman added, "When the time comes that the workers see it's possible to significantly change their lives by risking, they do." On one occasion, workers, in twos and threes, refused to operate their cane machinery until they got a raise of a nickel or dime an hour. However, said Sr. Maurer, ". . . they got their money and didn't get kicked off the plantation. They won."

Both of the religious Sisters of Divine Providence maintained the growers' treatment of the workers had improved throughout the 1970's. Whereas ten years ago the workers were

193

always in debt, in 1979 many of the workers refused to borrow from the boss and stated that there were only five company stores left in the sixteen sugar cane parishes. Whereas in the past growers refused to pay the field workers during the grinding season, such a practice was illegal and not done very often in 1979. "When the food stamps don't come in, the people eat cush-cush (cornmeal mixed with grease)." As for low wages, Sr. Galvin said,

> We don't accept the basic assumption that the
> farmers are so hard up they can't pay a
> decent wage - look at their fine brick homes
> and boats and campers. . .

> Besides which, if they respected the workers,
> the farmers wouldn't say, "I'm having a hard
> time; I'm only going to pay you half as
> much" - they'd never say that to their
> machinery dealer or their tax collector.
> Church teaching says that if an industry
> can't support its workers, it has no right to
> exist.

On October 31, 1979 a letter was sent, to the U.S. Departments of Health, Education and Welfare, Housing and Urban Development, Labor and Engery by several southwest Louisiana religious and social workers involved in aiding sugar cane workers.[22] The signers of the letter, asking for a review of the funding of SMHA, were six former agency employees, board members and founders. Specifically, they were: Sisters of Divine Providence Imelda Maurer and Bernie Galvin (SMHA workers in 1973-75); Bernard and Rose Mae Broussard (SMHA co-founders who left in 1974); Richard Sauder, a Mennonite volunteer SMHA fired in June 1979 after eight months; and Alice Drefchinski, who worked in an SMHA-sponsored clinic from 1972-73.

The statement said,

> SMHA has not only been unfaithful to its
> goals of helping sugar cane field workers in
> southwest Louisiana become more self-
> sustaining, but . . . SMHA has actually
> hindered the development and self-
> determination of the sugar cane field
> workers.

Specifically, the call for funding review was based on five points:

The exploitation and manipulation of sugar cane field-workers in the name of justice.

The distorted portrayal of the field-worker as helpless and servile.

The exploitation of staff members within SMHA.

A pattern of poorly administered programs resulting in a waste of both federal and private money and enriching least of all the field-workers themselves.

A long history of serious yet unresolved intra-agency conflicts.

Mauer added that the group drafted the letter, ". . . after repeated futile attempts to work out the problems with Sister Anne Catherine [Bizalion]."

Noting that half of the SMHA board were farmworkers and a large majority of the staff were farmworkers, Bazilion added that none of them raised such complaints. She concluded by asserting that any further statement would have to come from the organization's board and that she had "no idea" what effect the call for funding review would have on the U.S. government grants SMHA received.

C. Corn Processing Workers

On June 13, 1980, Local Six of the American Federation of Grain Millers was decertified as the bargaining agent for the workers in the Clinton Corn Processing Company.[23] The move climaxed a bitter 10-month strike marred by charges of violence, undue church interference, and union-busting that sharply divided the Iowa town's residents. The mood was somber when the final vote on retaining the 43 year-old local as the bargaining agent: 48 in favor, 567 opposed, 41 ballots challenged. Said Maryknoll Father and Justice and Peace Director for the National Federation of Priests' Councils, Thomas Peyton,

A pall went over the room as the results were announced. Several people wept openly. . . it was one of the worst moments I have ever experienced as a priest.

Peyton was part of an interfaith "pastoral task force" which travelled to Clinton to investigate the obstacles to the strike.

Also in the task force: Rev. James M. Reed, a Methodist minister from Joliet, Illinois; Rev. William Mundy of the DuPage, Illinois, Unitarian Church; and Dominican Sister Mary O'Keefe, co-director of the National Assembly of Women Religious. The Task Force's report had been released on May 21, 1980. The company was accused of engaging in union-busting tactics that provoked the strike and decertification vote. The report called for binding arbitration as an alternative to the decertification vote and, failing that, recommended a boycott of products made of Standard Brands, parent company of Clinton Corn since 1956.

Tom Massion, director of the Davenport Diocesan social action office, said that the Social Action and Catholic Charities directors of Iowa's four dioceses would meet on August 10, 1980 to initiate a year-long study of Iowa labor-management relations, the state of the union movement, the recent upsurge in decertification of unions, and any factual basis to charges of union-busting in the Clinton and other strikes. Massion claimed a need for more concrete evidence of union-busting:

> The national trend toward management consulting firms giving assistance to companies to prevent unions is well established; but to prove it in an individual case is difficult.

Although Local Six received support from a number of local, state and national church leaders, one observer said they moved too little and too late and failed to address the key issue in people's minds - whether the strike was legal. Another observer noted that while many local clergy privately supported the strike, they feared alienating church contributors and other sectors of their parishes. For example, when the bishop of the Davenport diocese, Gerald O'Keefe, spoke at a May 1980 rally in support of Local Six, no local Catholic clergy attended. Other people analyzed what they thought went wrong. Several said the union waited too long to try to "woo" strike-breaking and replacement workers into supporting the union, thus allowing the company to play on their fear that retaining the union would jeopardize their jobs.

The Local Six leadership contended that, since 1975, the company had tied the local in costly grievance negotiations and hired non-union workers under Iowa's "right-to-work" laws. Departing in 1975 from an earlier amnesty policy following wildcat strikes, the Clinton Corn Processing Company fired 13 of Local Six's 14 executive board members and stripped 133 workers of their seniority - some of them 25 year veterans with the company. An August 1, 1979 disagreement was primarily about non-wage issues, including reinstatement of seniority rights for the workers penalized in 1975. Since the NLRB judged that issue to be a non-mandatory negotiating issue, the company continued to describe the 1979-80 strike as illegal, despite Local Six' signing of an agreement with the NLRB removing that issue from contention. Furthermore, the Local Six executive board had recommended that the union members who had been fired in 1975 place their names on the company's preferential hiring list - as mandated under NLRB regulations - and return to work when called. The local had no strike funds and only indifferent support from its international. However, other area local unions contributed more than $100,000 - including more than $40,000 from United Auto Workers locals. Finally, Local Six call for a boycott of products of parent company - Standard Brands - was a weighty decision. Not only did Standard Brands have an array of more than fifty products to boycott, but Standard Brands was also a transnational food-processing giant, which ranked 123rd in sales in 1978 and 261 in return on equity in 1978. Furthermore, Clinton Corn was the town's largest employer, the third largest corn refiner in the U.S., and had set the pace for wage agreements throughout eastern Iowa.

Whatever the relative weight of these or other factors in the course of the strikes and the final decertification vote, the results for the town's people, whether supportive or non-supportive of the local, were evident. As striking workers watched friends and relatives cross the picket line, there were deep community scars, broken marriages, savings wiped out, several confrontations, and charges of worker violence and police brutality.

As noted, several national religious figures and organizations attempted to rally local and regional support for a settlement of the Clinton strike. In addition to the National Federation of Priests' Councils and the National Assembly of Religious Women assistance, there were pleas from Msgr. George Higgins and the Catholic Committee on Urban Ministry. For example, on Palm Sunday, 1980, a march of approximately 100 strike supporters moved from a prayer rally in a city park to the gates of Clinton Corn Processing Company.[24] The prayer rally, the third during the course of the strike, was planned by Mary Ellen Eckellberg, a local resident, and Rev. William O'Connor, 73, a former pastor of Clinton's Sacred Heart Parish and long time labor advocate at St. Ambrose College in Davenport, Iowa. The rally was addressed by Rev. Patrick J. Sullivan, C.S.C. a labor researcher at Notre Dame University and a representative of the Catholic Committee on Urban Ministry. The march was interspersed by hymns and prayers reminiscent of the Way of the Cross.

197

At that time in late March, 1980, it was estimated that only 350 of the 700 member Local Six remained on strike. In the midst of the bitterness and violence, there were the unsettled grievances, concerns about wages and safety, complaints about women and minorities being hired as replacement workers, and worries that the union would be "busted." In fact, at the end of the march, there were reports that the father of a woman replacement worker drove to the plant to pick up his daughter and was heckled by stragglers from the march. When his car was kicked, he left it to throw a punch. Allegedly, he suffered a broken arm and his tires were slashed.

[1]Mary Papa, "Indiana Migrants Rumble," National Catholic Reporter, v. 3, No. 35, 6/28/67, pp. 1, 5.

[2]"Migrant Canners Get Support," National Catholic Reporter, v. 12, No. 41, 9/17/76, p. 2.

[3]Jerry De Muth, "Migrants Protest Search for Aliens: Lawsuit Contests Organizers' Eviction," National Catholic Reporter, v. 13, No. 1, 10/22/76, p. 22.

[4]Jerry De Muth, "Canners Target of Strike Plan," National Catholic Reporter, v. 14, No. 14, 1/27/78, pp. 1, 15.

[5]Jerry De Muth, "Ohio Tomato Pickers Strike Farms; Church Groups Help," National Catholic Reporter, v. 14, No. 41, 9/8/78, p. 17.

[6]Robert L. Rose, "Catholic Farmers Ask Why Church Aids Migrants," National Catholic Reporter, v. 15, No. 27, 4/27/79, p. 9.

[7]Steve Askin, "FLOC Tackles Canners," National Catholic Reporter, v. 15, NO. 38, 8/24/79, p. 21.

[8]Joseph E. Mulligan, S.J., "Liturgy and La Lucha," America, v. 142, No. 7, 2/23/80, pp. 144-147.

[9]Steve Askin, "Notre Dame Joins FLOC Food Boycott," National Catholic Reporter, v. 16, No. 12, 3/28/80, pp. 3, 28.

[10]"Campus Activities: Notre Dame," National Catholic Reporter, v. 16, No. 29, 5/16/80, pp. 1, 4, 5.

[11]Steve Askin, "Church Groups Rap, Help Campbells," National Catholic Reporter, v. 16, No. 33, 6/20/80, p. 18.

[12]"Growers 'Battle' Church, Laborers on Farm Issues," National Catholic Reporter, v. 16, No. 36, 8/1/80, p. 24.

[13]Patsy Sims, "Bishop Ousts 'Sugarcane' Priest; Pressure by Growers Charged," National Catholic Reporter, v. 9, No. 31, 7/6/73, pp. 2, 3.

[14]Jerry De Muth, "Dispute Spotlights Plight of Cane Workers," National Catholic Reporter, v. 9, No. 36, 9/14/73, pp. 1, 16.

[15]"Shots Fired at Priest in Rectory," National Catholic Reporter, v. 9, No. 36, 9/14/73, p. 16.

[16]"Nuns Back Sugar Cane Workers," Reporter at Large, National Catholic Reporter, v. 10, No. 18, 3/1/74, p. 20.

[17]"Rural Life Unit Backs Aid Measure for Sugar Workers," National Catholic Reporter, v. 10, No. 19, 3/8/74, p. 13.

[18]"Three Nuns Testify for Cane Workers," National Catholic Reporter, v. 10, No. 21, 3/22/74, pp. 1, 6.

[19]"Pending Sugar Law Not Enough," National Catholic Reporter, v. 10, No. 31, 5/31/74, p. 17.

[20]"Priest and Nun Deplore Rejection of Sugar Cane Law," National Catholic Reporter, v. 10, NO. 32, 6/21/74, p. 3.

[21]Patty Edmonds, "Cane Worker Advocates Battle Growers, System," National Catholic Reporter, v. 15, No. 34, 6/29/79, pp. 8, 20.

[22]"Aid Agency 'Manipulates Cane Workers,'" National Catholic Reporter, v. 16, No. 4, 11/16/79, p. 18.

[23]Carole Collins, "'Church Meddling, Union Busting' Charged in Iowa," National Catholic Reporter, v. 16, No. 34, 7/4/80, pp. 5, 6.

[24]"Faces of Labor Priests," National Catholic Reporter, v. 16, No. 24, 4/11/80, p. 7.

A. Farah Manufacturing Company

1972

On May 2, 1972 the Amalgamated Clothing Workers of America (ACWA) struck the San Antonio, Texas, plant of the Farah Manu-facturing Company.[1] By mid-May 1972, the strike had spread to other Farah plants in El Paso, Texas, and in Albuquerque and Las Cruces, New Mexico. In late July 1972, Auxiliary bishop of the San Antonio archdiocese, Patrick Flores, announced his support of the clothing workers' strike. Noting that the clothesmaker paid only the minimum wage, Flores elaborated during a rally of approximately 200 strikers.

> This is why I'm here. This is why I think you have a cause. Nobody today wants to live by the lowest standards possible. . .
>
> I would say who in his common sense would go looking for work and say he will work for the least you'll pay? You want money, not because you're greedy, but because you need it. . .
>
> As long as people are underpaid, denied housing, equal educational opportunities, are not promoted in jobs, I believe they're stepping on our toes and cannot expect peace.

Flores, who also served as the chairperson of the Texas Commission on Civil Rights, noted that when individual efforts to improve working conditions fail, ". . . you have no choice but to join [a union]." Joining Flores was the archdiocesan Commission for Mexican-American Affairs and its executive director, Texas State Senator Joe Bernal. Both opened their remarks on the Farah strike with a reminder that they had been boycotting lettuce for some time in support of UFW. At the time of Flores' and Bernal's support for Farah strikers, endorsements came from the democratic presidential nominee, South Dakota's Senator George McGovern. The AFL-CIO executive council also endorsed the strike against Farah.

On October 31, 1972 the 70 year-old bishop of the El Paso diocese, Sidney Metzger, spoke in Spanish to some 2,000 El Paso strikers.[2] To those Farah workers, 95-98 per cent of whom were Mexican-Americans, Metzger said,

You are making a grand fight for liberty and
social justice. Even if you lose everything
you own, you will still have your honor and
dignity.

He added that people who did not understand why the Catholic
church spoke out in behalf of the strikers, ". . . do not understand that you are actually enslaved." According to George
McAlmon, chairperson of the El Paso Committee for Fairness at
Farah, a group associated neither with Farah nor ACWA, the
strikers effort to become unionized,

. . . is the most important local event in
the last 25 years. . . [and] could mean job
security, and in the long run, improvement
for miserably low wage bases.

Farah's spokespersons contended that the workers of El Paso's
largest employers were better paid than others in the city of
18,000 to 20,000 clothing workers. It was further contended
that, in face of foreign competition, Farah could not afford
"union interference."

During the strike and after, ACWA announced a national boycott of Farah-made men's slacks and jeans. Metzger, who had been
bishop of El Paso since 1942, received an inquiry from a priest
on behalf of another U.S. bishop. Metzger responded in a letter
to the priest. Copies of the letter were sent also to all the
U.S. bishops. The gist of the letter was to provide pertinent
information concerning "the difficult and complicated" Farah
situation in El Paso.

First, there was information about Farah's bitter and
adamant opposition to labor unions as expressed in the September
12, 1972 New York Times. The president of Farah was reported to
have sworn that Farah would never be unionized. That attitude of
Farah had been known in El Paso for years. The El Paso bishop
proceeded to develop some of the consequences of such an attitude. Farah found it virtually impossible to be objective or to
recognize the workers' basic right to unionize for purposes of
collective bargaining. Furthermore, the paternalism of the company was perpetuated and never got tested, because the company
"...uses all possible means to block" elections provided for by
federal law.

Second, Metzger analyzed the Farah image and presented his
own assessment of it. The attractive image Farah projected
publicly was accepted by sincere people who were ignorant of the
demands of social justice. The complaints of the "happy workers"
over the course of many years probably culminated in the strike.

Noting that Mexican-Americans had a way of coming to their parish priest with personal problems and that most of the Farah workers were women, Metzger indicated the sources of complaints he had received about the Farah situation in El Paso since 1967. Workers could not go to their personal doctor because the company did not want them to leave the plant. Nurses in the plant were careless about keeping professional confidences; sometimes they disclosed intimate phsyical problems of the workers. Workers complained about "stretch-out" in production quotas, absence of job security, erratic and confusing wage increases, inadequate maternity insurance, lack of illness leaves which would allow workers to return to their same jobs and the same rate of pay, and absence of negotiations about virtually all their demands. After citing some specifics about these complaints, Metzger expressed the hope that he was not wrong in asserting that there was a call for such provisions in the principles of social justice.

Third, Metzger responded to the Farah company's boast that they had more than 8,000 happy workers who would neither strike nor have any part of a labor union, since they were satisfied with their employment as it was. To this, bishop replied that in their simplicity many of the workers were not aware that their situation could be improved. The company repeatedly told the workers "they never had it so good" and exercised constant supervision over the workers lest they say the wrong things to outsiders visiting the plant. In addition, workers without job security and with high production demands lived in constant fear of being fired.

Fourth, Metzger talked about who had toured the Farah plants and what was discovered. Metzger spoke of his refusal to accept an invitation to visit the plant the next day for lunch and to be welcomed by the workers and entertained by a mariachi band. The bishop added that the reasons for such a refusal of such an invitation were obvious. When word got out that a local parish priest and the bishop gave approval to the strikers, "a delegation of 22 supposedly tried and true representatives from the company" met at the parish. The company "representatives" tried to discourage the parish priest from his support of the strike, but he gave his reasons for continuing his support of the strikers. In fact, one of the "representatives" later returned alone to express to the priest that her conscience bothered her because there were legitimate grievance over the company's dealings with its workers. Metzger also told of an inspection by a member of the El Paso office of the Texas Employment Commission. The bishop explained the results of such an inspection tour, as well as the reactions of some Farah executives to plant conditions. The local officials of the Texas

Employment Commission were suspicious that the workers were treated more like machines than people. Rather than allowing the officials to speak at random with the workers, the company selected certain workers who apparently were told what to say. The physical plant was known to be modern, clean and comfortable, but for the investigation of social justice conditions such anti-septic tours were deemed to be useless. A number of persons in higher company positions left because "they couldn't take it" - their consciences could not bear it.

Fifth, Metzger provided a lengthy comparison of the Farah pay scale to other plants in the surrounding era. Farah paid about the same as other nonunion apparel plants. In a very depressed area, where a living wage simply did not prevail, the wages in such a nonunion labor market were often passed off as "a living wage". Local Chamber of Commerce reports listed clothing as El Paso's number one industry and the average income of "the little people" among the clothing workers was $3,588 annually. This contrasted with an annual average of $7,500 for petroleum workers, $7,200 for metal workers and $6,100 for the food pro-cessing employees. The Amalgamated Clothing Workers of America contracts with Levi Strauss, Hortex Incorporated and Tex-Togs revealed a take-home pay each week of $102. Farah paid $69 per week. Hortex, Incorporated and Tex-Togs were local and smaller companies, so the bishop asked,

> If these smaller plants can live with a union contract and prosper why is it so impossible for gigantic Farah to do the same?

Sixth, Metzger explained that in El Paso an annual pay of $3,588 might be enough for a single person. However, for a family - many Mexican-American families were large - $3,588 was not an adequate wage in terms of social justice. That led to a discussion of the company's and people's perception of human dignity in the Farah situation. Metzger's initial statement was,

> Farah may be in good faith but in their pre-sent operations it seems they do not under-stand these demands and are ignoring them. The Mexican-Americans have a legitimate pride and are very conscious of their dignidad (dignity). And they consider many of Farah's practices an insult to their dignidad.

Metzger told of misdemeanor charges against more than 700 strikers being dismissed after federal courts declared unconsti-tutional an old Texas law which required pickets to remain at least 50 feet apart. Even though there was no violence or destruction of property, an out-of-court settlement forced Farah to "call off the dogs" trained as police dogs and used by Farah management to menace the pickets. The bishop concluded the discussion of dignity with a note about resentment building up within the workers since 1967 and a restatement of the sources of information. Most of the information had come over the years from the people and the parish priest. The ACWA representatives told Metzger nothing new. Farah either was not aware or did not want to be aware of the growing resentment expressed in the strike of more than 3,000 of its workers. In listening to the people over the years "...one gradually became aware that things at Farah were not actually as they were made to appear."

Seventh, and last was Metzger's recommendation that the inquiring bishop make a formal request that a retail outlet not re-order Farah clothing.

> The strike has assumed national importance and is supported by persons of national prominence. Our own "little people" in El Paso would be crushed if it were not for this national support. His Excellency will of course weigh what I have written and decide what he deems best.

A little more than a month after Metzger's letter, approximately 1,000 persons attended a rally in Chicago supporting the Farah workers.3 One of the speakers was Rev. Jesse Munoz, who represented Bishop Metzger from El Paso. Munoz declared,

> God has sent us many sumpathizers to be with us. . . Your interest has restored our faith in humanity. . . Your brotherhood has added hope that brightens their spirits. . . Our nonviolence is due to the fact God has been with us. . . Our faith has superseded physical force.

Another speaker, Sol Brandzel, Manager of ACWA's Chicago Joint Board and an ACWA vice president said,

> In El Paso, the church has understood the moral issues involved and has given great strength and support to the workers. . . Bishop Metzger has come to the aid of the strikers and has courageously withstood the pressure of the company and the community pressure the company has tried to generate.

By mid-February 1973, Metzger's letter was reprinted as an ad in the New York Times, the Washington Post and other major newspapers.[4] The ad was paid for by ACWA and permission to use the letter was given by Metzger. The ad, three quarters of a page, included a call for support of the Farah boycott signed by former U.S. Attorney General, Ramsey Clark; author and leader of Democratic Socialists, Michael Harrington; former New York Mayor, John Lindsay; New York Democratic Congressman, Herman Badillo; U.S.C.C. Urban Affairs Director John Cosgrove; Msgr. George C. Higgins; AFL-CIO President, George Meany; New Mexico Democratic Senator, Joseph Montoya; and others.

Also, by mid-February 1973, an endorsement of the Farah boycott came from the bishop to whom Metzger addressed his letter four months earlier - Bishop Joseph Hogan of Rochester, New York. Hogan explained his delay,

> In spite of the strong stands taken in favor of the boycott by many credible people and organizations, I personally felt obliged to spend four months gathering information.

> We were in direct consultation with representatives of both of the conflicting parties. Third parties, in particular the bishops of the dioceses involved in Texas, were consulted. My position is not an a priori affair, but the result of serious and honest study.

Hogan continued by urging retailers and consumers,

> . . . to examine their roles in this dispute as a moral issue. . . [Yet] this is not the sort of stance that the church can claim to be infallible.

> My support of the boycott is in no way an order to other members of the church to take a similar stand, but rather it is a witness to the sort of concern the gospel demands of all of us. This witness will be marred by any attempt on the parties in this dispute to use my position to harass local retailers and consumers.

Again, in mid-February 1973, at two rallies of almost 700 of the 2,000 striking Farah workers, in our Lady of the Light Church in El Paso, Cesar Chavez and 70 members of UFW expressed their solidarity.[5] In his address to the strikers, Chavez said,

> The struggle of workers in El Paso is the same as in California and Arizona, the struggle for dignity.
>
> The ingredients are right in El Paso for success. Pressure can be exerted on officials to bring about progress. It is always a difficult fight. You must sacrifice and sacrifice and sacrifice. But through that sacrifice your people will grow.

By the February 1973, the Farah Company had responded to the ACWA ad in several major U.S. newspapers.[6] One of the company's spokesperson stated that the union simply had failed to convince the Farah workers, despite the fact that wages at two unionized pants-manufacturing plants in El Paso were considerably higher. It was asserted that so much national attention was unfair without knowledge of local "facts." In an editorial, the *America* editors commented on the Farah reply,

> The fact that they [Mexican-Americans] must now wage a bitter struggle to secure a right taken for granted by other American workers is another instance of the pockets of injustice to this particular minority group that continue to exist. National attention through boycotts seems to provide the most effective hope of eliminating them. . .
>
> Although his language might be less elegant, Mr. Farah would probably share the puzzlement of the W.S.J. when it confessed . . . that it could never understand why the "warmed over Marxism" of *Populorum Progressio* had anything to do with religion. Bishop Metzger's letter, reasonable in tone and specific in detail, spells out the claims of justice in a particular struggle. Totally undogmatic in manner, the letter is an admirable exercise of episcopal authority.

On February 20, 1973 there was an endorsement of the Farah boycott by the Texas Conference of Churches during its annual meeting.[7] The resolution submitted to some 280 delegates, from 15 Catholic and Protestant member groups, said the boycott would remain in effect ". . . until such time as union recognition is secured or until the union calls off this boycott." The submission of the resolution by the conference's Division of Church and Society followed an address from Bishop Metzger, which was heard also by observers from Baptist and other churches.

By early March 1973, there were reports of other Catholic bishops endorsing the Farah boycott.[8] At a meeting in Santa Fe, with priests' senators from the Santa Fe ecclesiastical province, the bishops of New Mexico and Arizona endorsed the boycott. Their resolution read in part,

> . . . so that the basic human rights of col-
> lective bargaining and unionization might be
> recognized and allowed to become realities
> for the workers and strikers of the company.

In a March 3, 1973 letter to all U.S. bishops, El Paso's bishop Metzger claimed that without a negotiated personnel policy in writing workers would have only insufficient assurance of job security, reasonable and negotiated production quotas, and a fair wage sacle. Metzger insisted,

> Without these three basic requirements there
> is no social justice. . . [If] the company
> were to meet the demands of social justice
> by collective bargaining, I am confident it
> would prosper wonderfully. . .
>
> . . . if I had refused they [the workers]
> would have been bitter, disillusioned with
> the church.

Of Farah's announcement that it would appeal a March 29, 1973 NLRB order to reinstate 19 Mexican-American employees engaged in union activities, Metzger called the ruling, ". . . absolutely fair. . . [but] possibly made him [Farah] more determined right now not to give in to any collective bargaining." Farah also had recourse to federal courts to overturn an NLRB bargaining order after the court refused to review the NLRB certification of ACWA as the bargaining agent.

The El Paso Citizens Committee for the Evaluation of the Farah Boycott According to Principles of Social Justice was formed at the request of Rochester's Bishop Hogan and chaired by an El Paso attorney, Frank J. Galvan. The committee received mostly newspaper clippings from Farah but no acceptance of their invitation to meet with Farah administrative officers. Galvan said the committee was interested in whether the Farah employees received social justice, not just in Farah's claims.

In mid-April 1973 also, Metzger explained to ACWA's Chicago Joint Board that he came to ". . . carry the message of the Farah strikers to all Americans who believe in the common man's right to justice and decency."[9] After his talk the El Paso bishop participated in a press conference. He stressed that the problems of capital and labor involved ". . . fundamental rights and justice . . . they are problems of religion and religion has a duty to concern itself and speak out about them." He emphasized that the seventh and tenth commandments ". . . direct the exercise of justice between man and man in the possession and use of property." He underlined that when alone workers were at ". . . a great disadvantage with a large business corporation" and needed a union to bargain for improvements.

In early June 1973, Rev. Robert Getz, social action director of the El Paso diocese, provided a summary of the support and role of Bishop Metzger on the Farah workers' behalf, as well as a glimpse behind the scene of the El Paso strike action and economy.[10] Getz noted that the struggle against the $160 million pants manufacturer, employing 9,000 workers, had drawn attention and support from the ranks of Congress. In July 1972 the national boycott of Farah goods began with the support of Senators Edward Kennedy of Massachustees and Gaylord Nelson of Wisconsin. In the fall of 1972 a New York Times story by Homer Bigart attracted more national attention. In October 1972 Metzger's letter had appeared in the New York Times, Philadelphia Inquirer, Catholic diocesan newspapers, and union periodicals throughout the U.S. In May 1973, additional support was received by the Farah workers when the bishop of the Syracuse, New York, released Rev. Donald Bauer to work for ACWA for six months, in order to travel throughout the U.S. promoting the Farah boycott. By the end of 1972 there was a $10 million decline in sales for the year. From a high of $49, Farah stock by June 1973 had dropped to $11, as the boycott continued.

On May 1, 1973 at the regional meeting of the southerwestern bishops at Mesilla Park, New Mexico, Bishop Metzger was cited in a special testimonial dinner presentation by the AFL-CIO for his support of labor over the years. Getz cited the record,

> In 1947, at Silver City, New Mexico, he opposed Communist organizing efforts in the Mine and Mill Union. Then came the union-ization question at a plastics factory in Deming, New Mexico, at the Peyton meat-packing plant in El Paso, and the strike of

the Hilton Hotel workers, where the Bishop refused to cross picket lines. He has also demanded only union builders in any church construction. The Bishop has not had the support of the local press in these issues, nor the support of prominent Catholics, nor all priests. In the Sunday collections, many priests have received notes of $0.00, indicating non-support for the Bishop and the church.

In the March 26, 1973 issue of Time there was an interview article "The Bishop Versus Farah." In February 1973, Metzger did an interview with Harry Reasoner for television. Metzger also addressed bishops of western states assembled in Denver, Colorado. Even though some observers noted the absence of the "Cesar Chavez Charisma" in the "border worker" cause, others pointed to Bishop Metzger as the "closest thing to charisma in the struggle." The 71 year-old native Texan provided the behind-the-scenes spiritual leadership. In addition to private meetings with the Farah officials, Metzger met with Chavez to find ways of settling the strike.

The endorsement of the Farah boycott on February 20, 1973 in Austin by the Texan Conference of Churches followed a controversial vote. Metzger was accused of being misguided in his support of ACWA which allegedly was using the Catholic church for publicity. However, the union's and the church's behavior and NLRB decisions indicated otherwise. In addition to financing the strikers with millions of dollars, ACWA backed a spontaneous strike, which it did not call and was not prepared for in any way. There was an immediate need for public and worker education. There was little local leadership from the strikers; so "Sister Josephine, a Dominican dynamo" managed the strike office and Rev. Jesse Munoz provided for union meetings in his parish church, Our Lady of Light. The strikers, with a $30 per week grant from ACWA, were quite consumed with finding ways to meet the next payment deadlines for all kinds of needs. There was no union violence. There were no attacks on Farah as a "sweatshops" or as any better or worse than any other local employer. Hopes that the annual Farah stockholders' meeting would produce some step toward a settlement proved overly optimistic.

Back in 1970, ACWA won an NLRB-supervised election in Farah's cutting section. The company appealed the outcome in 1973. Another election among the machine operators was held in January 1973 and was still under advisement by the NLRB. On March 29, 1973 the NLRB ordered Farah to reinstate with back pay 20 employees who were fired for union-organizing activities going back to 1969. The company was ordered also to desist from

harassing and pressuring employee promoting unionization.   On
April 23, 1973 the Supreme Court agreed to hear an ACWA challenge
to Farah's employment policies.   With Farah's opposition to free
NLRB-conducted elections for the other workers and the failure of
any approach to negotiations, the prognosis for the strike was:
slow and long.

However, the prognosis was also that the workers' struggle
would be won outside El Paso by the boycott and through the
courts.   Despite the Farah strike representing the "cause of the
underdog" in other parts of the United States, it inspired little
sympathy in El Paso, a border city of 350,000 people, 56 per cent
of whom were Mexican-American and largely Catholic.   Getz
mentioned how the Chamber of Commerce, business leaders and the
average worker - Anglo or Mexican-American - accepted the Texas
open shop, anti-union, etc. as a given and Farah   as an
enlightened employer.   The usual urban American working conditions and wage-scales, brought by a successful strike, would
blow up the exploitive "border economy".   If the apparel
industry - the largest in the area - were unionized, the local
business leaders would say in alarm "...where would unionization
end and where would we get cheap labor?" Maids continued to work
six days a week for $15 in almost every middle-income family and
the Farah "happies" continued their daily sewing with $1.70 an
hour for starts.   Very personal economic reasons and fears
deterred people from supporting a strike for unionization.

Hence, for Getz, the El Paso diocesan director of Social
Action, the real issue of the strike was the right of workers to
organize, as opposed to "the patron system" which company
president Willie Farah, through a tight, family-run operation,
favors.   For Getz, Willie Farah's contention that he knew what
was best, what his workers might wish in benefits, wages and
working conditions was the gordion knot to the struggle, locally
and nationally, between company - town and union - church forces.
Getz concluded his summary of the ACWA - Farah disputes by
saying,

> Farah seems ready to hold out forever rather
> than concede free elections and collective
> bargaining with the rights of represen-
> tation, recourse and job security.   These
> are the issues of dignity which, in Bishop
> Metzger's view, far outweigh the money ques-
> tion.

By mid-June 1973, the Farah boycott had been endorsed by
Boston's Cardinal Medeiros; the General Secretary of the
Massachusetts Council of Churches', Rev. Joseph Sprague; the

Social Action chairperson of the Massachusetts Board of Rabbis, Rabbi Jude B. Miller; and the Priests' Senate of the Archdiocese of Washington, D.C.[11] Also, the bishops of the eight dioceses in New York State requested the USCC to initiate a study of the Farah-ACWA dispute and to distribute the findings to all the U.S. Bishops.[12]

In mid-July 1973, approximately 600 Mexican-Americans filled to overflow the San Fernando Cathedral in San Antonio for the "Mass for the Cause of Unionism."[13] The concelebrants were San Antonio's Archbishop Furey and Auxiliary Bishop Flores, as well as Metzger. The eucharist was preceded by a rally and march in support of strikers at Farah, the Longhorn Steel Company, the Ingram Manufacturing Company and L.H. Packing Company. In his sermon, which was heard outside by another 100 people, thanks to loudspeakers, Metzger said the Farah struggle was the

> . . . greatest struggle I have been engaged
> in [and] . . . I will go on fighting at your
> side as long as God gives me life. If any-
> one doubts we will succeed, he is mistaken.

Afterwards, Bishop Flores complained that many Mexican-Americans who worked full-time were so underpaid that they needed government subsidies. "It is insulting," he said, "to a working man's dignity to have to depend on alms, charity and welfare when he is employed full-time."

By late summer 1973, there was an additional source of support for the Farah workers.[14] In Charleston, South Carolina, Bishop Ernest Unterkoefler, acting on a resolution of the priests' senate, forbade Catholic schools to do business with firms like Farah of El Paso that refused to enter into collective bargaining with its workers.

In November 1973, columnist William F. Buckley, Jr., lambasted any U.S. bishops who supported the nationwide boycott of Farah clothing products.[15] He called them "men whose social thought has not moved since the mid-thirties." Singled out was Bishop Metzger. Buckley said Metzger did not know what he was talking about when he charged that Farah denied its employees "social justice."

1974

In late January, 1974 an NLRB administrative law judge decided that the facts on Farah's behavior was a textbook case of how an employer, through interference with his employee's right to self-organization, could violate Section 8 of the National Labor Relations Act. The Farah Company termed the judge's language "sweeping and vindictive." The judge, Walter H. Maloney, Jr., was accused of wholesale disregard of the principle of due process and Farah pledged an appeal of the decision. With the NLRB decision in mind the editors of America responded to columnist William Buckley's November 1974 charge about Metzger:

> In the meantime, though, Bishop Metzger and his fellows stand vindicated. If their social thought has not moved "since the mid-thirties," how antiquated the social thought of their most vociferous critics must be.

On February 24,1974 the Farah boycott was called-off and on February 25, 1974 the first steps were taken to elect a committee to conduct negotiations, which actually began on February 28, 1974.[16] The election by a card count was agreed to by Farah and was conducted by El Paso's Mayor, Fred Harvey. The result: 4,761 of the Farah workers signed blue cards with a preference for ACWA and 2,492 workers indicated no preference. During the course of the strike, Farah closed two plants in San Antonio and its plants in Albuquerque and Los Cruces, New Mexico and in its Victoria, Texas plant. The Farah work force dropped from 10,400 to approximately 6,000 workers. Farah sales dropped from $165 million in 1972 and to $145 million during the first half of 1973.

At the time of commencement of negotiations, a joint-statement was issued by William Farah, the company's president, and Murray Finley and Jacob Sheinkman, the union's president and secretary-treasurer, respectively. The statement set forth several agreements. One, ACWA agreed to end the strike of 2,000 workers that began in early May 1972. Two, ACWA agreed to inform all retailers that the boycott was ended. Three, Farah agreed to admit ACWA as the bargaining agent for the employees in all Farah plants. Four, Farah agreed to rehire the strikers. Five, ACWA dropped its unfair labor practice suits against Farah before the NLRB. Six, Farah agreed to drop anti-boycott suits against ACWA in seventeen cities across the U.S. Seven, both ACWA and Farah agreed to pay the strikers $30 per week up to 10 weeks until all were rehired.

Several statements were issued by people involved in the struggle. Bishop Metzger called for an end of bitterness, hatred and the mistakes that occurred in the dispute. After urging both labor and management to work for the good of each other and the good of the community, he defended the church's role.

> It is the church's role to...appeal to the conscience of both labor and management as well as to the conscience of the community.

He also stated his intention of writing to all the U.S. bishops as he had done fourteen months earlier. The second letter would suggest to the U.S. bishops that they could recommend products of the Farah Manufacturing Company. Metzger concluded,

> Ours is the priceless opportunity to present a model in which management and labor . . . work hand in hand for the good of each other and the good of the community.

Crediting the help of the church as a major element, Cesar Chavez exclaimed,

> It's a great, great victory for the people . . . opens the door for a lot of organizing among the Spanish-speaking in the Southwest United States . . . proves the effectiveness of the boycott.

Speaking on behalf of the Texas Conference of Churches, which on February 20, 1974 reaffirmed the right of collective bargaining for Farah workers and urged elections ". . . in an atmosphere free from intimidation and coercion," was its president, Catholic Bishop Thomas Tschoepe of Dallas. Said Tschoepe, "It is my firm opinion that the business of the church is to bring about reconciliation between people of honest differences."

The editors of the National Catholic Reporter characterized the Catholic bishops as providing ACWA with the same kind of strength to win as given also to UFW. The editors continued,

> These stands . . . indicate that they are becoming increasingly involved in issues outside the strict confines of church institutions. Their involvement will not be welcomed or applauded by all segments of the general public, . . . It is good to see . . . that they are willing to take moral stands boldly, especially in behalf of human betterment for the poor.

The editors of _America_ said,[17]

> During the strike, Bishop Sidney M. Metzger
> and several of his fellow bishops were among
> the strikers' staunchest allies [despite]
> ... widespread criticism that they were
> meddling. . . In this particular labor dis-
> pute, the bishops plainly were not talking
> through their episcopal mitres.

On March 7, 1974 the members of the local of ACWA representing the Farah workers overwhelmingly approved a three-year
contract.[18] Bishop Metzger said the contract was a very good one
and hoped it would ". . . work out for the mutual benefit of
employers and the company. . . I'm sure they've done the best
they could." The major terms of the contract were as follows:
One, all employees would get raises up to 80 cents per hour over
a three-year period and some skilled would get as much as $4.75
per hour. Prior to the strike, pay ranged from $1.70 to $2.40
per hour. Two, there were to be neither strikes or lockouts, but
grievances would be submitted to arbitration. Three, union
representatives would be allowed to enter plants to check on production standards. Four, there would be annual paid-vacations up
to three weeks, as well as eight paid-holidays per year. Five,
there would be job security and seniority rights. Six, there
would be comprehensive insurance for workers and dependents, paid
by the company. Seven, there would be medical coverage with
maternity benefits and weekly sickeness and accident benefits up
to eighteen weeks. Eight, there would be time-and-a-half for
working overtime and Saturday and double-time for all Sunday and
holiday work. Nine, as many of the fired workers would be
rehired as possible.

In his annual Labor Day Statement for the USCC, Msgr. George
Higgins praised two significant steps achieved during 1974, the
Farah settlement and strong backing for the UFW. Higgins called
the settlement of the Farah strike,

> . . . only the first step in what ought to
> be and promises to be a full-scale organ-
> izing drive, especially among black and
> Spanish-speaking workers.

B. J.P. Stevens Company

1976

In the spring of 1976 Bishops Michael Begley of Charlotte, North Carolina; F. Joseph Gossman of Raleigh, North Carolina, and Ernest Uterkoefler of Charleston, South Carolina, began studying the issues in the Amalgamated Clothing and Textile Workers Union (ACTWU) - J. P. Stevens Company (JPS) controversy.[19] It was reported that those bishops and possibly the USCC were likely to endorse a boycott of Steven's products, even though the expec- tation was that the Stevens boycott would be more difficult, expensive and prolonged than the UFW and Farah boycotts.   ACWA, which had been involved in labor controversy with the Farah Manufacturing Company, merged with the Textile Workers Union of America in June 1976 to become ACTWU.   The J.P. Stevens Company, the New York-based and second largest textile company in the world behind Burlington Industries, had a long history of serious labor law violations.

At the annual meeting of the Catholic Committee on Appalachia (CCA) in November 1976 Scott Hoyman, an ACTWU vice- president, announced some of the boycott plans and presented the background of the ACTWU-J.P. Stevens labor controversy.   Hoyman explained ACTWU's accusation of bad faith bargaining by Stevens. He alleged that after 22 months of negotiations in Roanoke Rapids, North Carolina, a contract settlement had not yet been made and that the company refused to negotiate.   Mentioning that less than 10 per cent of approximately 700,0000 southern textile workers were unionized, Hoyman added that ACTWU's efforts to organize the J.P. Stevens' workers was only ". . . the tip of the iceberg."   At the CCA meeting one of its spokespersons said, ". . . if the Southern bishops recommend a boycott of J.P. Stevens' products, CCA will promote that boycott."

It was learned that three of Southeastern bishops - Begley, Gossman, and Unterkoefler were visited, in the fall of 1976, by Whitney Stevens, the company president.[20] In November 1976 five southeastern bishops met with a then ACTWU vice-president and later a deputy undersecretary of labor in the Carter adminis- tration, Howard Samuel.   Present at the meeting were Begley, Gossman and Unterkoefler, as well as Archbishop Thomas A. Donnellan of Atlanta and Bishop Raymond Lessard of Savannah, Georgia.   Msgr. George Higgins, USCC Research Secretary, and Msgr. Francis Lally, Associate Secretary for Social Development and World Peace of the USCC, in early February 1977 visited Roanoke Rapids, North Carolina.   It was the site of ACTWU's only election victory to represent workers in seven J.P. Stevens plants.   The report of Higgins and Lally would be sent to the area bishops with recommendations, before the five already mentioned and Bishop Walter Sullivan of Richmond, Virginia, would make any public statement or take any position. Both USCC staff members hoped to arrange a meeting with company officials in Stevens' New York headquarters. At such a meeting, they would outline to the J.P. Stevens' officials their experience with the farm labor dispute, where the bishops' committee was able to offer mediation services. Of such talks Higgins said,

> The name of the game is a settlement. A 1,000-word statement by the bishops will not revolutionize the situation. There are very few outside groups (such as the bishops) that can play the role of mediator. . .The union knows full well what we are doing. Haste is not all that important because everybody is gearing up for a long pull. Catholic groups don't have to wait for the bishops.

Alluding to increasing church support for the J.P. Stevens boycott, Higgins said, "I tell priests and nuns not to get involved if they think it's going to be a joy ride."

1977

Getting involved, at least with endorsement statements, were the National Coalition of American Nuns, the Boston Province of Notre Dame Sisters, the North Carolina Council of Churches Social Action Ministry and Thomas Gumbleton, Detroit's auxiliary bishop. Gumbleton, who had supported the 22-month strike of Farah workers, said he believed the J.P. Stevens controversy ". . . is the same kind of justice issue." In a late-February 1977 meeting the five dioceses that made up that Atlanta ecclesiastical province (Atlanta, Charleston, Charlotte, Raleigh and Savannah) had representatives of the priests' senates meeting in Atlanta to consider a boycott resolution. According to Rev. Charles Mulholland of Greensville, North Carolina - a textile center - many of the priests wanted the resolution passed so as to bring it to the March 1977 Louisville convention of the National federation of Priests' Councils.

Furthermore, according to Rev. Patrick Sullivan, C.S.C., Catholic Liaison for ACTWU in the Stevens controversy, many dioceses and religious communities were distributing information on the issues involved. Catholic involvement was encouraged, said Sullivan, because

. . . the church should do for these workers
what it did for immigrants at the turn of
the century. It's a question of freedom and
human dignity for working people not to have
their lives controlled economically and
socially by the company. It's important for
the church to be preaching the gospel about
this.

There was also support in the form of two stockholder resolutions
that were presented at the March 1, 1977 J.P. Stevens Stockholders Meeting in New York. The resolutions, demanding information about anti-union expenses incurred by the company and
about minority group representation in the J.P. Stevens work
force, were sponsored by the World Division of the United
Methodist Board of Global Ministries and four Catholic religious
communities. Working through the Interfaith Center on
Corporate Responsibility in New York, and voting Stevens' stock
in support of the resolutions, the original sponsoring groups
were joined by at least eight other religious communities.

However, there was also an ominous side to involvement in
the controversy. So said Rev. John Barry, a Glenmary Home
Missionary on leave of absence and serving as an ACTWU organizer
in Hamlet, North Carolina. Barry told of being "under
surveillance" as he visited workers from nine area-Stevens
plants. Barry elaborated,

They come up with surprising information. I
don't know how they got it - maybe their
guardian angels tell them. . . I haven't
seen any cars tailing me, but my license
plate number and background as a priest were
written up in the local Chamber of Commerce
newsletter.

In February 1977 also, ACTWU issued a brochure targeted for
Catholics.[21] Produced by Sullivan, ACTWU's Catholic Liaison, the
brochure said, among other things,

-Workers who have shown interest in organizing have been fired, harassed and intimidated by their superiors.

-When workers have organized, the company
has either closed the plant in Statesboro,
Ga.) or bargained in bad faith (in Roanoke
Rapids, N.C.)

217

-Workers who favor organizing have been subject to out-of-plant surveillance, the
denial of overtime, changed working conditions, and coercive investigation.

-The federal courts and the National Labor
Relations Board more than 15 times have
cited J.P. Stevens for unfairly obstructing
its workers' efforts to organize.

-J.P. Stevens settled out of court for
$50,000 in a civil suit filed against the
company for wiretapping a union organizer's
motel room.

-The Eisenhower-appointed National Labor
Relations Board chairman, Boyd Leedom,
declared, "J.P. Stevens is so out of tune
with the humane, civilized approach to
industrial relations that it should shock
even those least sensitive to honor,
justice and decent treatment."

These accusations as well as charge of discrimination
against blacks and unhealthy and unsafe working conditions were
documented from federal court or government agency sources. This
brochure and other campaign literature was aimed at publicizing
the necessity of the boycott in the two newly merged unions'
fourteen year campaign to unionize the J.P. Stevens Company,
which in 1976 had sales of $1.4 billion and a net income of more
than $40 million. The ACTWU rationale was that if one Southern
textile company organized, the rest would follow. The clothing
and textile industry was one of the least organized and, after
food production, the largest employer in the U.S.

J.P. Stevens asserted that the sole union victory in Roanoke
Rapids, North Carolina, - only 7.5 per cent of the company's
45,000 employees - indicated that the Stevens' workers did not
want a union. Hence, company chairman and chief executive
officer, James D. Finley, viewed the attempts to turn the boycott
into a social cause dimly and distressingly: "The forcing of
unions on working people cannot be made into a proper social
cause." More immediately, the company saw the boycott as a union
attempt to apply pressure at the bargaining table at Roanoke
Rapids. The negotiations for a contract - continuing for more
than 30 months - had two very significant areas of disagreement:
dues check-off and outside binding arbitration of grievances
unsettled through regular grievance procedures. The union
insistence upon dues checkoff being included in the contract

benefitted the union, while placing the onus of collecting the union dues on the company. According to labor relations experts, the absence of contract provisions for binding third-party arbitration would give the union no other recourse than a strike, in case of unresolvable disputes.

In June 1977, a pastoral planning conference on Appalachia, sponsored by the National Federal of Priests' Councils, resolved, "To be alert to regional issues such as . . . strip mining and the boycott of textile manufacturer, J.P. Stevens and Company."[22] Also in June 1977, both the J.P. Stevens Company and ACTWU responded to a June 6th public statement of the southeastern Catholic bishops.[23] In the statement the bishops offered their services as mediators. If the offer were declined, the bishops continued,

> We will feel obliged, in the exercise of our pastoral ministry in the geographical area most directly affected by the Stevens dispute, to review the situation and, within a reasonable period of time, to issue a more detailed and more specific statement on the dispute.

With a nod to the union, the bishops urged J.P. Stevens, ". . . give evidence of positive support for the right of workers to organize and . . . demonstrate a willingness to bargain in good faith." With a nod to the company and union, the bishops refrained from endorsing the year-old boycott but hastened to support its goal: union organizing and collective bargaining for the Southern textile workers. The signers of the statement, representing the areas where more than sixty of the 85 J.P. Stevens' plants were located, were: Archbishop Thomas Donnellan of Atlanta; Bishops Michael Begley of Charlotte, N.C.; Joseph Gossman of Raleigh, N.C.; George Lynch, auxiliary of Raleigh; Raymond Lessard of Savannah, Ga.; Walter Sullivan of Richmond, Va. and Ernest Unterkoefler of Charleston, S.C.

The company responded that third party intervention would be welcome in contract negotiations for the Roanoke Rapids plants. With specific response to the bishops' reference to union organization and collective bargaining, the J.P. Stevens' spokesperson said

> . . . if the statement is taking the position that union representation of Southern textile workers is desirable whether or not the employees desire it, then we must take

strong exception to the position of the bishops.

The company accused the union of refusing to approach the bargaining table at Raonoke Rapids.

> We believe that the most direct and most meaningful assistance which the bishops or which any other interested group could render would be to bring the union to the bargaining table with greater frequency than has been the pattern for the past 12 months.

Some observers characterized the replies of both sides, as simply accusations of each other's failure to bargain in good faith. On the other hand, ACTWU, while accepting the bishops' mediating services without qualification characterized the company's allegations of union unwillingness to negoitate as "calculated misrepresentations."

The next exact move of the Southeastern bishops was not clear. However, Msgr. Francis Lally, their chief staff person and USCC Associate Secretary for Social Development and World Peace, said the bishops would, ". . . see what they should do as interested third parties. Mediators probably would be too strong a word." In late May Bishop Gossman of Raleigh acknowledged that endorsement of the boycott ". . . is certainly a possibility." Bishop Sullivan of Richmond said, "My own interpretation would be that (if the offer is rejected) the next step in the process would be to accept the boycott."

In July 1977, there was Catholic reaction to the first "debate" between representatives of J.P. Stevens and ACTWU, as well as to some Southern press reaction to the June 6th statement of the Southeastern Catholic bishops.[24] The debate, held at the University of Pittsburgh, was not a real debate, for which ACTWU had been asking. Instead, there were 12-minute opening statements and responses by each side to a series of written questions. According to ACTWU J.P. Stevens' officials had stipulated. Representing ACTWU were: Rev. William Somplatsky Jarman, ACTWU's Protestant Liaison, and Eric Frumin, Assistant Director of ACTWU's department of Occupational Health and Safety. Representing J.P. Stevens were: James R. Franklin, its Director of Corporate Public Relations and Dr. Lee Polk, professor of debating at Baylor University in Texas. Asked why the company consented to appear, Franklin responded, "Nostalgia." Although Franklin told the audience that he was born and raised in Pittsburgh, "nostalgia" did not explain why Stevens sent along a professional film crew to record the event and unloaded several charges against ACTWU.

The first charge was Polk's. He described Somplatsky-Jarman as,

> . . . a man of the cloth, a minister of the
> gospel. . . with unclean hands, with the
> blood of little people across the country on
> him.

While Franklin did not repudiate Polk's remarks, Somplatsky-Jarmon characterized the remark a ". . . polemical, personal attack on me . . . the board of elders and the ministerial board of my church."   The son of a very active social-minded minister, Somplatsky-Jarman noted that before his ordination, the ministerial board of the Disciples of Christ had reviewed his commitment to the union struggle and ordained him with the knowledge that he would work with ACTWU.

The second charge was that textile workers in Pennsylvania were paid less than J.P. Steven workers in the Carolinas. William Patterson, an ACTWU campaign representative in western Pennsylvania, had not heard that charge previously and was curious about the company representatives' sources for such an accusation.   The third Stevens' charge was one often uttered and rejected.   Namely, that the union had been convicted of labor relations violations and that ACTWU had resorted to violence.

Reactions of union sympathizers to the program were mixed. Some thought the ACTWU speakers did not answer the J.P. Stevens' charges effectively.   Msgr. Charles Owen Rice, a veteran of many labor-management disputes, in Pittsburgh and across the nation, thought the company was well prepared and made the best presentation of a bad cause.   The union representatives had blown a good cause by a bungled defense.   Rev. Edward M. Bryce, Justice and Peace Director for the diocese of Pittsburgh, regretted the use of cliches and accusations "along the classic lines of owner-workers confrontations."   The social justice owed to people was delayed by such a performance, although Polks' attack on Somplatsky-Jarman was rated as "stooping" and likely to justify the charges levelled against the company.

Bryce added that the Pittsburgh diocese had not yet endorsed the J.P. Stevens boycott, even though the union credited the diocese's action in the Farah boycott with forcing a settlment. In 1974 many department stores in the May Company - a national chain - ceased purchasing Farah products, after the PIttsburgh diocese was instrumental in persuading the local May Store, Kauffman's, to stop buying Farah's products.

Still other union sympathizers related J.P. Stevens "case" to the Labor Reform Act (HR 77) then before Congress, which would have provided - if passed - that companies convicted of unfair labor practices be disqualified from receiving government contracts. For, Stevens continued to hold government contracts, even though the company had been convicted in 15 separate cases of labor law violations, with many others subsumed under the fifteen.

The attacks on the June 6, 1977 statement of the Southeastern bishops were typified by headlines in three South Carolina newspapers. In Columbia, Greenville, and Charleston respectively the headlines read: "Catholic Bishops Toy With Southern Jobs," "The Church as Union Organizer," and "Boycott Weapon Hits Workers and Economy." Specifically, according to the National Catholic (NC) News Service, the Charleston Courier and Post editorialized,

> The sweeping assumption of Vatican Council II that the workers of the world are united - or ought to be - against employers doesn't apply on this side of the Atlantic.

> While we respect the right and duty of bishops to concern themselves with both the spiritual and physical well-being of their flocks, we wish they would devote a greater share of their considerable talent and energy to nonsecular affairs and a smaller share to what less sympathetic critics might call meddling in things about which they may lack knowledge and understanding.

The Columbia State said,

> We wonder if those seven Roman Catholic bishops from this region . . . have the foggiest idea of what they might be doing to the employees and stockholders of the J.P. Stevens textile chain.

In response to the State's editorial, Rev. Thomas R. Duffy, vicar general of the Charleston diocese said,

> You forget to mention that in all of these cases (cited in the paper's editorial) it

222

was only after long periods of objective deliberation that the bishops took action. . . We might well ask just who is "toying" with southern jobs.

While the reaffirmation of the J.P. Stevens boycott by the Seventh Annual Convention of the National Assembly of Women Religious in New Orleans[25] and the initial endorsement of the National Conference of Catholic Charities Convention in New York[26] buoyed ACTWU and its supporters, the Catholics in North Carolina were split by the boycott and unionization action.[27] In the early fall of 1977, a public statement of support for J.P. Stevens' workers, "What Is At Stake In The Stevens-Union Struggle?" was issued by fourteen southern religious leaders. It climaxed an intensive investigation directed by Reverend Donald Shriver, President of New York's Union Theological Seminary and one of the authors of Spindle and Spies, a study of earlier textile unrest in North Carolina. One of the Southern religious leaders - the only Catholic - was Sr. Evelyn Mattern, Justice and Peace director of the Raleigh diocese.

Strongly divided feelings of North Carolina Catholics were evident over the controversy when Edward M. Tompkins of Salisbury, N.C., wrote to the North Carolina Catholic, newspaper of the Charlotte and Raleigh dioceses in September. He said,

> It greatly irritates me to know that my subscription money to the North Carolina (sic) is used to provide a public forum for an organized labor parrot like Sister Evelyn Mattern.

Nevertheless, five days after Tompkins' letter appeared members of many religious denominations met at the United Church of Christ community center, Franklinton, to discuss further boycott support.

There were several speakers. One was Scott Hoyman, an ACTWU vice-president and southern director. Hoyman revealed that textile firms employed four out of ten North Carolinians, that the state had the lowest industrial wage scale in the U.S. - $60 a week less than Northern counterparts - and that North Carolina workers were on the average more productive than other industrial workers in the U.S. A second speaker was Rev. Edward Fleming who worked 24 years for J.P. Stevens. He had become one of the few black supervisors only because he acted as an "Uncle Tom." When Fleming stepped out of that role, he said he was fired. There was also a panel of J.P. Stevens workers, who had been fired or retired through disability, including "brown lung" disease -allegedly caused by continued exposure to cotton dust in the J.P. Stevens plants. Another panel included members of Southerners for Economic Justice (SEJ), an interfaith and inter-racial group. Some SEJ members stressed the necessity of union-izing all the J.P. Stevens plants at once, so as to prevent retaliatory moves of J.P. Stevens, by selectively closing plants that might have become unionized on a sequential basis. One SEJ member, Rev. C. Charles Mulholland, pastor of St. Gabriel's parish in Greenville, N.C., stressed the need for religious leaders to confront their congregations with the injustices in the J.P. Stevens company. Mulholland reflected out loud, "When we do that, we have to be ready to suffer."

Although that conference's unanimous support of ACTWU's organizing and boycott efforts was evident, so was strong oppo-sition from a rival group called The J.P. Stevens Employees Educational Committee. Its president was Gene Patterson, who claimed a membership of 1,300 employees united to stop the J.P. Stevens boycott before it destroyed their jobs. In addition to alleging that the August 1974 union victory at the seven Roanoke Rapids plants no longer reflected the wishes of the employees, Patterson spoke of the church's entry into the ACTWU-J.P. Stevens controvery: "We don't think churches should get involved, unions use all churches for publicity." Other members of The J.P. Stevens Employees Educational Committee also spoke out. Dorothy France, a weaver-instructor, said, "We aren't against blacks. We train everyone who comes in, but the blacks never stay." Leonard C. his Bible, said, "I think unions are the tool of the devil. Just read Revelations 13, where it tells about the mark of the beast."

In November 1977, the seven Southeastern Catholic bishops renewed their offer "to mediate" between ACTWU and J.P. Stevens.[28] As in June, ACTWU immediately accepted the bishops' offer. A J.P. Stevens spokesperson said the offer was under "very careful consideration." The second offer "to mediate" pre-ceded by a few days the NLRB announcement of its intention to seek a nationwide court order stopping J.P. Stevens from vio-lating federal labor law. Only once in its history (founded in 1935) had the NLRB ever sought and obtained such a national injunction. In 1948 such a court order was issued against the International Typographical Union.

If there was pressure on J.P. Stevens, some interpreted the events as pressuring the bishops as well. In addition to public pressure from pro-management sources, especially in the Southern press, there was pressure from union supporters for an endorse-ment of the boycott. In their first "mediation" offer the Southerneastern bishops said that, if the offer was declined, they would ". . . issue a more detailed and more specific state-ment on the dispute." The bishops also urged J.P. Stevens to ". . . give evidence of positive support for the right of workers to organize and . . . a willingness to bargain in good faith." Some observers interpreted the statements and comments of bishops Gossman and Sullivan in May 1977 as "a veiled threat" to endorse the boycott, if the company did not accept the mediation offer. The ACTWU Catholic liaison, Sullivan, hoped the bishops would do exactly that.

By early December 1977 the J.P. Stevens Company and ACTWU representatives planned to meet separately with the Southeastern bishops.[29] The announcement was made by the bishops' chair-person, Thomas Donnellan, archbishop of Atlanta. Donnellan said the bishops intended to hear both sides of the controversy before taking a stronger stand than in their June 1977 statement. He added that the meeting was requested by the bishops because ". . . we can't sit back and watch." They hoped to find ways to bring "justice and peace" to the communities polarized by the bitter dispute. While J.P. Stevens spokespeople could not be reached for comment, the ACTWU secretary-treasurer, Jacob Sheinkman, did speak about the meeting, in which he would lead the ACTWU representatives. He saw the meeting as, ". . . a preliminary meeting to discuss the issues. . . There's a very easy answer. The company has to obey the law - it's as simple as that." Yet, fog prevented the scheduled December 16th meeting from taking place.[30] While some of the bishops were able to meet with ACTWU officials, other bishops and all the J.P. Stevens officials were unable to land at the Atlanta airport. Donnellan was attempting to reschedule the meeting with J.P. Stevens officials.

<u>1978</u>

The rescheduled meeting was held in Atlanta on January 20, 1978.[31] Among the bishops present were: Donnellan, Unterkoefler, Begley, Gossman, Lynch and Lessard. The bishops issued no formal statement after the meeting, although some indicated such would be issued when Donnellan returned from his vacation, which began shortly after the meeting. After the meeting with the company officials, Begley, Gossman and Lynch flew back to North Carolina on the J.P. Stevens corporate jet. Gossman had ". . . more than second thoughts about accepting the offer." However, he decided that a refusal of the offer would not be "appropriate" because there was still ". . . much to talk about" with the J.P. Stevens' representatives. He concluded, "We would have shown less good will by walking out." Begley's reaction was: "I had no problem. I talk to these people not as a businessman but as a churchman."

At the meeting the company representatives showed a film which the bishops described as propaganda. For, at one point in the film, a minister was saying that the gospel and religion should have nothing to do with unions. Said Unterkoefler, "I took exception to that. . . I said this is a very narrow concept of Christianity - that it doesn't extend to matters of justice." Gossman thought the bishops were deeply at odds with the Stevens officials, "They have a very tough, individualistic philosophy that we don't have."

After the meeting the bishops still hoped to arrange a meeting with both company and union officials, but J.P. Stevens continued its refusal of a joint-meeting. None of the bishops would speculate on the next move of the group. Gossman indicated a willingness to do more than continue the talks, "It was made very evident they don't want us to endorse the boycott. My conclusion is we can do nothing and talk forever, or do something dramatic." Unterkoefler said that the bishops made it very clear, ". . . we're for the workers," but added that dialogue and not action still seemed appropriate because, "I look at this as a long struggle. I don't think it will be solved during the 1970's." He concluded that endorsing the boycott was a possibility, ". . . if it seems appropriate at some time." Begley thought the meeting was successful because there was "progress on the horizon" and thought that a boycott endorsement would not be appropriate after the meeting. He explained, "In justice, if we're encouraging these kinds of conferences, we can't do that until someone breaks." Finally, the bishops said the J.P. Stevens officials asked them to urge that union elections be held in the eleven J.P. Stevens plants where union organizing activity was the highest. The bishops said they would consider it.

However, the ACTWU General Counsel, Arthur Goldberg, remarked about such a consideration, "Sure, they would like to get us into elections, terrorize the daylights out of our employees, and then say the workers voted and they don't want a union." Other union supporters indicated that such urging by the bishops could be interpreted as greater support for Stevens than the union. Still other union supporters had hoped the bishops would endorse the boycott. These supporters saw in such a move encouragement of endorsements by more Northern bishops - seen as key to increasing the boycott's success. Some other ACTWU sympathizers suggested that the Southeastern bishops might be duped by Stevens if they continued to encourage "dialogue" between J.P. Stevens and ACTWU, rather than taking any action themselves. ACTWU's Catholic Liaison, Sullivan, was quoted as

226

saying, "The company is doing its damndest to keep them [the bishops] from coming out with anything but talk." J.P. Stevens' officials refused to comment on their meeting with the bishops.

Shortly after the January 20th meeting, the company was cited by the NLRB in the Federal District Court in New York and a nationwide injunction was requested to stop its illegal anti-union tactics. Charging J.P. Stevens with a 15-year "massive multi-state campaign to deny its employees their rights to seek collective bargaining representatives of their own choosing," the NLRB laid out its reason for such unusual legal steps. The NLRB claimed that without broad judicial protection, ACTWU's efforts would be met by unlawful conduct which would include discharging and disciplining workers for supporting the union, as well as threatening dismissals and plant closings if the union were selected as a bargaining agent.

By mid-February the Southeastern bishops initiated work on a joint-statement on the J.P. Stevens - ACTWU controversy and one of them received a petition protesting his involvement.[32] Even though he had not endorsed the boycott, Bishop Sullivan of Richmond, was accused by 28 of the 45 families in St. Paschal parish in South Boston, VA, of having a "certainly biased" position toward the union. The members of the parish, located near J.P. Stevens largest plant in Virginia, said that Sullivan should not have interfered in the ACTWU - J.P. Stevens dispute because it was "not a church-related matter."

In his response to the petitioners, the bishop of Richmond said,

> The church has always upheld the right of the worker to collective bargaining and the popes have taken many stands against injustice in labor practices.
>
> These principles don't have any meaning unless we have the courage to apply them.

He and the other bishops of dioceses where J.P. Stevens plants were located continued to be under fire from both pro-management and pro-union forces. The former in the hotly anti-union Southern states said the bishops had no business getting involved. The latter said that the bishops should endorse the boycott if they intended to stand-up for social justice.

In early March 1978, ACTWU's Catholic Liaison, Sullivan, responded to the February 3rd _National Catholic Reporter_ article by Bill Kenkelen.[33] Sullivan gave an overview of the eight-month period since the Southeastern bishops offered to mediate the controversy, asserting that more had been accomplished than mere "talking." He elaborated,

> In their efforts to be ministers of reconciliation, amid very regrettable delays and J.P. Stevens' obstinancy, these bishops have revealed several important facts:
>
> -One, the controversy does involve many social justice issues, where the church does belong and intends to be involved.
>
> -Two, despite J.P. Stevens' 15 years of defiance, workers still have a moral as well as a legal right to unionization and collective bargaining.
>
> -Three, sophisticated efforts in appeals procedures make that right meaningless and labor law reform necessary.
>
> -Four, J.P. Stevens' contempt of moral teachers and federal laws, as well as of mistreated workers (black and white) and exploited towns (north and south) can be corrected only by severe economic sanctions - fines and boycotts.
>
> Let doubts about these facts be dispelled by reading about attacks on these bishops in some of the Southern press during June and July 1977.

Later in March 1978 J.P. Stevens stockholders and workers, as well as ACTWU supporters, converged on Greenville, S.C. for the annual J.P. Stevens Stockholders meeting, which in 1977 witnessed a significant pro-union demonstration in New York City.[34] The night before the meeting there was a rally for several hundred supporters of the union. The focus of that rally was a report entitled, "Human Rights Report on J.P. Stevens for 1977" and the vocal testimony of former J.P. Stevens employees about plant conditions, especially in Roanoke Rapids.

As the major stockholders assembled the next morning, they were met by union pickets and a few company supporters. The chairman of the board and chief executive officer of J.P. Stevens, James D. Finley, gave an opening address to stockholders, as well as union supporters who had gained admittance through proxies distributed by religious groups holding company shares. Finley reserved his comments on labor relations for the end of his report, charging, ". . . most people have seen through union propaganda. . . Incontestable proof of the failure of the boycott is our continuing profits." He did so, even though there was a report that dividends of $3.01 per share represented a 52 per cent decline over the previous year. Following Finley's report seven resolutions, sponsored by religious groups, were introduced to the meeting.

The resolutions were aimed at forcing the J.P. Stevens Company to disclose its policies regarding hiring, promotion and retirement, as well as management-labor relations, working conditions, benefits, and discriminatory practices against black women and other minorities. During almost three hours of discussion the religious groups who sponsored the resolutions were supported by ACTWU and several coalitions, such as Southerners for Economic Justice. As several speakers, many of them former J.P. Stevens employees, condemned the company practices, its well-dressed sympathizers among the stockholders sat impassively. John E. Mason, a black graduate of South Carolina State, spoke several times. On one occasion he spoke of being fired for union activity he undertook after he had been denied a management position. Mason declared, "The company didn't just fire me; they even escorted me to the gates." Another speaker, Rev. Gerald Conroy, an experienced Glenmary worker-advocate, reminded Finley that the company had failed to accept the Southeastern bishops' offer "to mediate" the controversy. Even though the resolutions lost rather decisively in the voting, the supporters were encouraged and promised to resubmit the resolutions at the 1979 stockholders' meeting. As company and union enthusiasts left the meeting hall, they were greeted by a small group of anti-union pickets.

Also in March 1978 there were several indications of support for the ACTWU's cause.[35] The St. Louis archdiocesan Human Rights Commission and Boston's Cardinal Medeiros banned purchases of J.P. Stevens' products by the archdiocesan institutions and recommended strongly the boycott to members of those archdioceses. Some observers deemed such endorsements largely ineffective as long as the Southeastern bishops deigned not to endorse the boycott. Many who hoped for such as endorsement in the Southeastern bishops' March 16, 1978 statement were alternately displeased and pleased. While that statement did not contain a boycott endorsement, it did contain stinging criticism of the company's labor practices. Prepared by the bishops and the USCC staff of Msgr. Lally and Msgr. Higgins, after the bishops' separate meetings with J.P. Stevens and ACTWU representatives in December 1977 and January 1978, the document was signed by

Archbishop Donnellan and Bishops Begley, Gossman, Lessard, W. Sullivan, and Unterkoefler.

The severe criticism relied heavily upon federal decisions against J.P. Stevens for very serious and frequent violations of NLRA. Based on these decisions, these bishops said,

> . . . any fair-minded observer is forced to acknowledge that the blame for the present social crisis lies heavily upon the company . . . [J.P. Stevens tactics] have taxed the patience of the workers and scandalized the public so much as to suggest that new national legislation must be passed to make such dilatory efforts impossible in the future.

The national legislation referred to was the 1978 labor law reform bill which was passed in the House of Representatives by a wide margin but died later in a Senate filibuster when the votes to invoke cloture were not adequate. The ill-fated bill was to streamline union organizing procedures and to strengthen penalties against employers violating the labor law.

Anticipating criticism, as experienced after their June 1977 statement supporting workers' right to unionize for collective bargaining, the Southeastern bishops asserted that J.P. Stevens' unlawful actions were ". . . irreconcilable with the clear demands of social justice in the Christian gospel." These bishops also made it clear, "We reserve the right, and indeed accept the obligation, of further review if some change in the present situation does not soon eventuate." As for the failure to endorse the boycott, the Southeastern bishops' chairperson, Archbishop Donnellan of Atlanta said, "We decided that wouldn't help at this time." Donnellan, refusing to speculate if "further review" might mean an eventual boycott endorsement, concluded that such an interpretation might have been seen as a ". . . threat . . . and we're not in the business of making threats."

On March 17, 1978 there was a meeting in Washington, D.C. of approximately 80 people from some 27 women's organizations to launch formally the National Women's Committee to Support J.P. Stevens Workers.[36] The day-long conference was jointly-sponsored by the National Assembly of Women Religious (NAWR), the Coalition of Labor Union Women (CLUW) and the National Organization for Women (NOW). All the attending groups signed a telegram to David W. Mitchell, chief executive officer of the Avon Corporation, warning him that their members - possible Avon customers - would be alerted to his being a J.P. Stevens board member. On March

21, the Dow Jones news wire reported Mitchell's resignation from the J.P. Stevens board. Mitchell's statement read, "I cannot permit Avon to be drawn into the conflict and to be subjected to the pressures which the union is exerting as a result of my Stevens board membership."

The women's coalition also agreed on March 17 to launch a letter writing campaign to chain fabric stores throughout the U.S. For, a survey revealed that 99 per cent of fabric store consumers nationally were women. Hence, said ACTWU's liaison to women's organizations, Passionist Sister Jeannine Maynard, "It's key to this campaign that we get to women across the country." While Maynard admitted the difficulty consumers had in detecting which fabric came from J.P. Stevens plants, she noted that ACTWU knew of five fabric store chains that dealt directly with J.P. Stevens. The March 17 meeting also urged letter writing campaigns to department store managements, requesting cutbacks and discontinuance of any stocking of J.P. Stevens products.

Finally, according to NAWR's chairperson, Sister of St. Joseph Kathleen Keating, the newly formed coalition sent a delegation to the Carter administration's representative for women's issues, Midge Costanza. The delegation asked Costanza why the Carter administration continued to allow government agencies to continue purchases of J.P. Stevens products. Maynard said the armed services - which had discretionary power forbidding them to contract with companies guilty of race or sex discrimination - had a $3 million contract with Stevens for uniform and the space program materials. Maynard concluded by saying that the White House assistant, Costanza, promised to talk with defense department authorities ". . . and report back to us by March 30."

In mid-April 1978 there was a conference - in Montgomery, Alabama.[37] It called together representatives of the National Federation of Priests' Councils, National Assembly of Women Religious, the Methodist Board of Missions, Disciples of Christ, United Church of Christ, other religious groups, and ACTWU. After an attempted visit to a J.P. Stevens plant and testimony from black J.P. Stevens' workers gathered in St. Jude's Catholic church, the inter-faith task force held a press conference. During the press conference it was emphasized that "moral suasion" was not enough. Also, in April there was announcement of the endorsement of the J.P. Stevens boycott by the United Methodist Women, which represented 1.2 million church women. In June 1978, the Hartford Archdiocese's Justice and Peace Office endorsed the boycott.[38] The announcement said the action was taken because J.P. Stevens ". . . is engaged in activity directly contradictory to rights of workers to organize."

In mid-September 1978, ACTWU scored a double-victory.[39] The J.P. Stevens chief executive officer and board chairman, James D. Finley, resigned from the board of New York Life, one of the largest insurance operations in the U.S. Also, the chairman of the New York Life board, R. Manning Brown, resigned from the J.P. Stevens board. The actions were related partially to ACTWU's corporate campaign to enlist the help of New York Life's six million policyholders in replacing Finley and Brown by the election of Sister of Loretto Ann Patrick Ware and Clarence B. Jones. Ware, a Catholic religious sister, was an interfaith affairs expert serving on the staff of the National Council of Churches. Jones, a black business excecutive, had an extensive background in communications, insurance and financial services. ACTWU's corporate campaign director, Ray Rodgers, said, "We consider it a victory, but we are not going to stop here. . . We are going ahead with other boards that have interlocking relationships with J.P. Stevens." Mentioned as future targets of the corporate campagin were stores selling J.P. Stevens products and, another J.P. Stevens board member, E. Virgil Conway of the New York Seamen's Bank for Savings.

In late September 1978, there were several letters in response to a September 1 National Catholic Reporter article on the national charismatic convention held in August at the University of Notre Dame.[40] One letter from Alan T. Cavanaugh of Mt. Sinai, New York, probed and mused about the charismatics. Cavanaugh said,

> Is the extent of their charismatic, evangelical concern fulfilled in the personal conversion of others? I sense the absence of a critique of the social system of our society - a society that embodies materialist values, ethos and structures, and which also misshapes the human social dimensions.

Another letter from Sullivan, ACTWU's Catholic Liasion, described the response of the attendees at the charismatic convention to appeals for support of the J.P. Stevens boycott. Sullivan said,

> In the course of two days 50,000 pieces of literature were taken home to read about the issues, strategies, products of the J.P. Stevens Campaign. The hospitality and courtesy of the national charismatic staff were surpassed only by their assigning the J.P. Stevens display and literature booth the best position they have ever had in a

232

large convention in the last two years.

How much or how soon the enthusiasm issues
into effective social action remains to be
seen. Hopefully, much assistance will be
given to J.P. Stevens' textile workers and
others suffering from socio-economic
injustice. Hopefully, also, the Charismatic
and Social Justice leadership will respond
to the example of Cardinal Suenens and
Helder Camara, as they strive to integrate
all the power necessary to create the
kingdom of God on earth, not just in
heaven. . .

<u>1979</u>

In April 1979 it was alleged that support for the J.P.
Stevens boycott from the Catholic community on the west coast, as
in other areas in the U.S. came primarily from individuals and
Diocesan Peace and Justice Offices.[41] Steven Burrell, ACTWU's
boycott leader in northern California, would not say the consumer
boycott had been ineffective. However, he did say ". . . you
can't depend on the goodwill of the people, you have to pressure
individual stores." While successes in persuading "important"
stores in northern California were few, Burrell reported that
boycott leaders had worked especially hard to drum up support
within the religious community during 1978. He added,

We want to emphasize that the churches care
because the corporations want to see this as
a labor issue, not a moral issue. So we
constantly stress religious support, and
it's paying off.

For example, a protest was led, against J.P. Stevens products in
the linen department of a major retail department store, by Rev.
William O'Donell, pastor of Oakland's St. Joseph the Worker
parish and veteran of UFW boycotts. In Washington, Oregon and in
southern California several "important" stores agreed to cease
sales of J.P. Stevens products. The ACTWU boycott leader in
Oregon and Washington, Artha Adair, said "solid" support from the
religious community in those states was critical to any success
the boycott had met. The Los Angeles boycott leader, Larry
Frank, said, "When they see religious leaders coming at them,
they think twice."

In New York, ACTWU leaders said Catholic support for the boycott could be crucial if the Southeastern bishops endorsed the boycott. The union leaders said they ". . . haven't heard a word" from those bishops in several months. However, ACTWU spokespersons admitted that the boycott had received a tremendous boost since the release of the film "Norma Rae." The film, released nationally by 20th Century Fox, depicted a union organizing effort in a contemporary Southern textile mill. Church Women United's National Board of Managers representing a membership of approximately 2,000 local chapters of Catholic, Protestant and Orthodox women, unanimously passed a resolution to support the J.P. Stevens consumer boycott. The ACTWU campaign against J.P. Stevens also received support from several additional judicial actions affecting union organizing in Milledgeville, Georgia, and West Boylston, Alabama. The Justice and Peace Commission of the archdiocese of Boston gave its support for the boycott.[42] It asserted that J.P. Stevens' law tactics,

> . . . not only violate public law, they contradict the historic teachings of the church with regard to the rights of workers.

In November 1979 the Southeastern Catholic bishops, through their chairperson, Atlanta's Archbishop Donnellan, asked J.P. Stevens officials to explain the firm's conduct during an ACTWU organizing drive in Milledgeville, George.[43] As a result of ACTWU's filing a suit in a federal district court against J.P. Stevens and others, it was learned that there was unlawful police surveillance of J.P. Stevens and other workers, as well as of ACTWU representatives. Donnellan indicated that there would be no further statement on the controversy from the Southeastern bishops, until the J.P. Stevens' response was examined. Other sources said the Southeastern bishops' statement probably would condemn J.P. Stevens' actions and encourage workers to organize. The same sources throught the issuance of such a statement was scheduled tentatively for late November or early December 1979.

Of the new revelations, NCR's Askin said,

> The Milledgeville incident provided the most dramatic evidence yet that Stevens uses illegal means to block union organizing. In a multimillion dollar lawsuit filed last summer, ACTWU said Stevens and other firms conspired with town officials to violate workers' rights.

234

In depositions filed in the suit, the town's
mayor and police chief said they let Stevens
use the local police department to spy on
union organizers, "bug" their meetings and
identify union supporters.

According to Askin, if these revelations of further illegal labor
practices by J.P. Stevens moved the Southeastern bishops to
endorse the boycott, they would join a half dozen bishops who
previously endorsed it and such Catholic groups as: the National
Conference of Catholic Charities, National Federation of Priests'
Councils, National Assembly of Women Religius, Catholic Committee
on Urban Ministry, National Council of Catholic Women, National
Assembly of Religious Brothers, National Catholic Conference for
Interracial Justice, the National Coalition of American Nuns, the
Leadership of Women Religious, and the Conference of Major
Superiors of Men.

1980

On March 4, 1980, more than 100 J.P. Stevens workers joined
social actionists from Catholic, Methodist, Presbyterian, United
Church of Christ, Baptist and other religious groups in challenging the J.P. Stevens labor practices during its stockholders
meeting in Greenville, S.C.[44] For the third consecutive year the
Interfaith Center for Corporate Responsibility (ICCR) proposed
the J.P. Stevens' stockholders establish an independent committee
to review their company's labor policies. The spokesperson for
ICCR was Sister of Mercy, Barbara Ayres. For the third consecutive year, the resolution suffered an overwhelming defeat.
Claiming record sales of $1.83 billion in 1979, the J.P. Stevens
new chairperson, Whitney Stevens, contended J.P. Stevens was
eager to sign a "just and equitable" contract with ACTWU in
Roanoke Rapids, N.C., despite NLRB charges that J.P. Stevens had
bargained in Roanoke Rapids, ". . . in bad faith and without any
intention of concluding a collective bargaining agreement."
Stevens, a descendant of the founding family, vowed to continue
the fight against ACTWU:

We in the management of the company do not
believe that a union has anything con-
structive to offer the company or its
employees. For this reason, we openly and
strongly oppose the union and its effort to
organize our employees, and we will continue
to do so with every legal and proper means.

235

As Whitney Stevens denied charges that J.P. Stevens illegally intimidated union supporters, a local priest challenged the chairperson. Rev. Steven Pavignano, associate pastor of St. Anthony's parish in Greenville, asserted that the J.P. Stevens' influence was so pervasive and its hostility to unions so intense that union sympathizers among the clergy were afraid to express their views. ACTWU circulated at the stockholders' meeting a report on union victories, intensified legal action for labor law violations, and new investigations alleging massive violations of occupational and safety regulations at J.P. Stevens plants in South Carolina.

On March 12, 1980 the Southeastern Catholic bishops released a statement, which endorsed the J.P. Stevens boycott and blasted the nation's second largest textile firm for violating workers' rights.[45] The bishops called the boycott, "a legitimate and effective instrument toward the promotion of justice." In support of their stand the Southeastern bishops cited Vatican Council II documents and elaborated,

> Among the basic rights of the human person must be counted the right of freely founding labor unions. . . of taking part freely in the activity of these unions without the risk of reprisal.

> These rights are discarded only at the risk of upsetting the fabric of a social order that places the highest priority on defending the dignity and worth of the human person. The anti-union activities by the J.P. Stevens company persuade us that the company has firmly made its choice to prevent the formation of employee organizations that can lead to collective bargaining.

As the only top Southern religious leaders to have endorsed the boycott at that time, the Southeastern bishops' statement may have been the most important declaration of religious support for the boycott since its inception in 1976, even though several national Protestant denominations and Reform Jewish groups endorsed at earlier dates. The importance of the Southeastern bishops' statemment was highlighted, also, because they looked beyond J.P. Stevens and the textile industry. Rather startingly the bishops asserted,

> . . . organizing into collective bargaining units may be in some circumstances an objective duty of each worker to his or her

236

co-workers. At present, this may be the only effective way of assuring the protection of human dignity and self-determination in the work place.

A third reason for the greater importance of the Southeastern Catholic bishops' statement than the previous pronouncements of religious leaders was the bishops' challenge to union leaders to make themselves worthy of the trust. A call was given ". . . to develop and protect true democratic structures" for internal decision making and actively to recruit women and minority group members for union leadership. Finally, union leaders were urged to,

> . . . provide educational programs that will enable workers to participate more fully and responsibly in the affairs of their own work place and in the union at large.

There were several commentaries on the statement by people close to or distant from the drafting process. One of the Southeastern bishops, F. Joseph Gossman of Raleigh, in addition to finding attacks on the signers "thoroughly predictable," emphasized what informed observers knew, "We cannot be accused of jumping in with both feet. We were very measured and restrained." His assessment of the process recalled the three-year effort by the Southeastern bishops to assist in settling the dispute. One of the bishops' chief staff members and NCCB/USCC Secretary for Social Development and World Peace, Monsignor Francis J. Lally, thought that additional support from Catholic social activists and statements from other bishops around the nation would be forthcoming. An another observer stated anonymously that the company had lied to the bishops, who were outraged and insulted. The pastor of the only Catholic parish in Roanoke Rapids, St. John the Baptist, also commented. Reverend Armand Proulux, a former provincial of the New England LaSalettes, described the local situation as very delicate. Most of the people in the parish would be pro-J.P. Stevens and opposed to the Southeastern bishops statement. Proulux hoped the people could view the statement as an opportunity to apply gospel values to the union question.

Another priest close to the bishops and the later stages of the process was Glenmary Jerry Conway, a social activist in the Southeast U.S. for several years. Conroy spoke of the Southeastern bishops' support for the duty of workers in the region to organize. He expected the debate to reach a higher level than in the past. Conroy saw the Southeastern bishops' statement challenging the commonly accepted view in the area that unions were evil or diabolical. For the Southeastern bishops to say that labor unions are basically good and that workers, under certain conditions, may have an obligation to join was shattering news.

Conroy's hopes were echoed by another Southern social activist Jim Sessions, executive director of Southerners for Economic Justice. The leader of the interfaith and interracial workers' rights education and action group, as well as a very earlier supporter of the boycott, called the Southeastern bishops' statement a measure for morally sincere people throughout the South. Sessions' hope was that the statement would challenge all religious people, especially Protestants who had so many more mill workers than the Catholics, to face-up to the injustices in southern industry.

The vicar general of the Charleston diocese, Rev. Thomas R. Duffy, noted the unpopularity of unions in the South. Such anti-union feelings, shared by Catholics as well as Protestants, emphasized the need to communicate clearly Catholic teaching on labor unions and social justice. Even though many thought the Catholic church had no responsibility to speak out, since most of the textile workers were not Catholic, the vicar general, was convinced that the Catholic church had to explain to its members, most of whom were in management, their responsibilities toward their employees.

Further away from the process and plants the voice of the editors of the <u>National Catholic Reporter</u> was heard in Kansas City, Mo.[46] They applauded wholeheartedly the Southeastern bishops' putting the Catholic church "on the line" by their calling textile and other exploited workers to unionize. The editors admitted that many middle-class Catholics distrust big unionism and added, "Rightly so. Unions at their worst are as bad as corporations at their worst. We're interested in seeing both at their best." The welcomed support and easy recourse to Catholic teaching by past generations of working U.S. Catholics was noted in the editorial and prompted the comments about the contemporary scene in the Southeast U.S. These editorial comments also included a challenge to the wider U.S. Catholic church,

> Today, particularly in the South, Catholics
> are more likely to belong to the managerial
> class. Will they feel the same thrill their
> parents and grandparents did when the church
> identified itself strongly with the workers?
> Probably not. And that is the reason the
> Southern bishops, and all those hourly wage

238

earners, need support from the rest of us in
the U.S. church.

We urge the other bishops to identify themselves with the Southern bishops. We urge
lay people, priests and religious - and
Catholic organizations to offer material and
personnel support as needed.

The opposition [textile and manufacturing
corporations] can easily marshal personnel,
money and media. They have, after all, the
resources gained from low-paid, nonunionized workers and from tax breaks from
government officials who are well nourished
by company political contributions.

From New York City, there were also words of praise - an
America editorial.[47] Mention was made of the Southeastern
bishops' earlier efforts to end the ACTWU-J.P. Stevens controversy. Very baldly and boldly the editors of America stated the
truth as they saw it: "Stevens persuaded them [the bishops] to
endorse the boycott." The defense of the editors' judgment was a
quote, from the Southeastern bishops' March 12 statement, which
defined the length of time for their endorsement of the boycott,

Until a time when the company will demonstrate that it has eliminated the mood of
fear and retaliation from its plants,
bargains in good faith in contract negotiations and responds to the rights of workers
to organize, we believe the boycott is a
legitimate and effective instrument toward
the promotion of justice in this matter.

As expected the Southeastern bishops' March 12, 1980 statement was met with silence, praise and criticism by non-religious
groups.[48] J.P. Stevens officials refused to comment on the
bishops' message. ACTWU welcomed their endorsement as a,

. . . vindication of the Stevens workers'
struggle . . . rallying point for continued
consumer action . . . encouragement to all
workers to put forth intensified efforts to
organize.

Several Charlotte business people sharply criticized the bishops
for the statement. One of them, Edward Dowd, president of the
Central Piedmont Employees Association, announced his protest by

239

resigning from the Diocesan Communications Committee. While asserting that other Catholic managers in the area would contact parish priests and Bishop Begley to protest the statement, Dowd phrased his own as follows:

> In this part of the country, union versus union-free is a very heated emotional debate. . .
>
> The bishops know very little about labor matters. Many of us feel they ought to stick to saving souls. . . and stay out of labor relations.

Later, Dowd commented further, "I don't think the bishops know their rear ends from their elbows about labor relations [and their statement was]...regrettable, ill-advised, ill-timed and divisive."[49] James Babb, the executive vice president of Charlotte's CBS-television station, WBTV, called the bishops "naive". Reverend Christian Hearing, an assistant at Charlotte's most prosperous church, St. Gabriel's, told of a local newspaper publishing the story of the Southeastern bishops' statement on March 8, four days before the embargo date and one day before the completion of the bishop's annual fund-raising drive. Said Hearing, "We got harpooned . . . Most of our people are in very high managerial positions." Dozens of them told priests that they were angered by the bishops' statement. The annual appeal contributions dropped to about $25,000 from $33,000 in 1979. However, in the adjoining Raleigh diocese, where the bishops' statement received little press attention, collections were up in 1980.

There were also many priests and religious upset, according to Rev. Edward Molloy, a member of the Charlotte Justice and Peace Commission and pastor of Queen of the Apostles parish in Belmont, N.C.

> Personally, I am overjoyed that they spoke out. . . But I honestly think that most of the priests, most of the sisters, and 90 per cent of the laity have no social conscience on this issue.

The negative responses of some underscored for others the importance of the bishops' stand. Rev. Joseph Kelleher, pastor of Assumption parish in Charlotte, expressed it as follows:

> I was proud of my bishop. . . The bishops are showing leadership in an area where they

have nothing to gain by it.   It makes me
proud to be a Catholic.

Reaction at Belmont Abbey, a Benedictine liberal arts
college near Charlotte was more mixed.   In late February a J.P.
Stevens' job recruiting day scheduled for early March at the
college was cancelled, one day after a member of the Charlotte
Justice and Peace Commission informed the college officials that
the bishops' boycott endorsement was imminent.   Although Rev.
Neil Tobin, O.S.B., president of Belmont Abbey College, insisted
that the timing of the cancellation was "coincidental," social
justice activists in the area believed otherwise.   However,
despite the last-minute cancellation, some   faculty members
organized their own "J.P. Stevens Day."   There were films shown
and discussions on the plight of the textile workers.

Bishop Begley of the Charlotte diocese was indicated when
Belmont Abbey College officials asked, "Why are you talking about
this, don't you know that people in management help our school?"
While the college officials denied any direct challenge of
Begley, they would neither support nor openly oppose the bishops
in interviews.   Nevertheless, the provost, Rev. John P. Bradley,
O.S.B., doubted,

> . . . bishops are qualified to analyze this
> kind of labor relations situation. . . I
> don't know enough to tell if Stevens is the
> kind of renegade company that steps over the
> legal line.

Bradley admitted that the boycott endorsement by the bishops
probably would hurt the college financially.   Some time prior to
the endorsement, Bradley had written a pamphlet on the "morality
of a union-free environment" for the National Association of
Manufacturers' union resistance arm.   He said employers had a
right to oppose unionization provided they did not use "immoral
or illegal" tactics.

Whatever the reactions among some of the laity, clergy and
religious, several parish priests and religious slowly were working with the bishops to bring the message about unionization to
parishes in the region.   A Glenmary Sister, Evelyn Gettling,
travelled throughout the South organizing parish workshops on
social justice.   She felt that the bishops' statement was a use-
ful starting point for lively discussion on workers' rights.   The
Raleigh Justice and Peace Commission met in March to discuss
plans for bringing the union question to parishes.   Raleigh's
bishop, Joseph Gossman, said he would discuss the bishops' statement with parishioners in Roanoke Rapids during Easter week.

Gossman's approach was to identify the J.P. Stevens' conflict as something more than a labor-management dispute. He elaborated,

> I don't particularly care about unions, but I care about human rights. I care about the right of people to freely decide whether or not they will have a union. I don't believe that Stevens workers have ever had a chance to decide without fear of reprisals.

There was, also, local reaction from a J.P. Stevens loom-fixer and leader of the ACTWU's Rockhill, S.C. in-plant organizing committee. James Lindsay said of the Southeastern bishops' statement, "It's a real inspiration when other people support our rights as Stevens workers." Local Protestant reaction was expressed, also, by Rev. S. Collins Kilburn, executive director of the North Carolina Council of Churches. Kilburn, a United Church of Christ minister and a longtime social justice activist, said,

> It is a remarkable statement. . . It is hard to imagine a group of Southern religious leaders at their level in any other church speaking out on this issue.

The unprecedented gesture, for Kilburn, was an important contribution to efforts by pro-union clerics to break the region's tradition of church abstention from labor struggles. Yet, Kilburn and other religious leaders agreed it was unlikely that Southern Protestant churches, whether "mainline" denominations of the middle and upper classes or the fundamentalist churches which claim the allegiance of most workers, would rush to follow the Catholic Southeastern bishops' example.

For those Catholic leaders to join a union challenge to the region's most powerful industry was a risky venture. The overwhelming majority of the region's Catholics were managers and professional people. Many were executives who came to the South with companies fleeing Northern union wages. Many a parish priest confessed that textile executives were his most generous financial contributors and working class people comprised only a tiny fraction of the Catholic church membership. Furthermore, nativist hostility toward Catholics was widespread until a few decades ago and had not been erased from the region in 1980. Hence, there should have been no surprise that the bishops moved slowly and cautiously toward a position destined to anger Southern Catholics and non-Catholics alike. In fact no one was surprised that in North Carolina, the heartland of the textile industry and the nation's least unionized state, the hostility

242

expected by the bishops had been the most visible public reaction.

On March 30, 1980 the J.P. Stevens public relations chief and a Catholic, James Franklin, sent his company's response to the March 12 statement of the Southeastern Catholic bishops.[50] The statement criticized them for ". . . adding their voice to the strident union propaganda campaign against the company." The statement, in substance, was a defense of J.P. Stevens labor policies and a dispute over the bishops' facts. The bishops were accused of basing their declaration on "false information" and "misleading allegations and inferences." J.P. Stevens contended, in its response, that the NLRB and federal courts found the company guilty of labor law violations only five times since 1978, not the 20 times alleged by the bishops. J.P. stevens insisted that ACTWU, not the company, was preventing the completion of contract negotiations in Roanoke Rapids. J.P. Stevens reiterated, the chairperson, Whitney Stevens' declaration at the early March 1980 stockholders' meeting in Greenville, S.C.,

> We openly and strongly oppose the union in its efforts to organize our employees and we will continue to do so with every legal and proper means. We sincerely believe that the great majority of Stevens employees are also opposed to unions. We are proud of this and intend to support them in their right not to be unionized.

The chairperson of the Southeastern Catholic bishops, Archbishop Donnellan of Atlanta, replied crisply and concisely, "We stand by our statement and are not interested in engaging in a feud with J.P. Stevens." A more detailed and revealing reply was given by the bishops' USCC staffer, Lally.

He observed that the company responded with old arguments which the bishops already had considered and rejected. Lally, who shared in the research prepared for the March 12 statement, said the company's count of unfair labor practice decision appeared to include only those which had been upheld all the way through the labor board's lengthy appeal procedures. The bishops' count included lower level decisions still being appealed by J.P. Stevens at the time. Lally claimed the company first accused ACTWU of stalling negotiations at Roanoke Rapids. His own examination of that charge found it to be untrue. He noted that he double-checked the facts after a March 10th visit of Whitney Stevens and James Franklin to Donnellan. The meeting was an attempt to convince Atlanta's archbishop not to issue the boycott endorsement. Finding J.P. Stevens failing to respond to the substantive issues raised by the March 12 statement of the Southeastern bishops, Lally said,

> I am amused by their quibbling over numbers and legalistic terminology. Even by their own count, the record of J.P. Stevens is pretty bad.

In early April 1980, there was a calmer rejection of the Southeastern bishops' statement by a top-level, but troubled, Catholic textile executive in North Carolina.[51] Robert Neff, the Michigan-born vice president for personnel at the 10 plant firm of American and Efird Mills, deeply respected Bishop Begley and was an active member of Queen of Apostles parish in Belmont, N.C. A man who did not trust unions, Neff explained why the bishops' endorsement of the J.P. Stevens boycott was such a troubling blow to him,

> I feel the Catholic church is in a teaching function, so it is difficult for me to understand why the church is taking a stand on what I see as a political issue. . . I'm a lector in my church. The statement made me wonder if I have any business up front, reading like a teacher, when I don't believe all of what's being taught. I can't see myself reading to the people from the Bible and then hearing the priest interpret what I read in a way I believe is wrong.

Neff explained some of his reasons for being anti-union. He cited experience as a teenager, thirty year earlier, while working first in a unionized supermarket and later in a non-union store. In the non-union store, he said,

> . . .there was none of the friction and tension between workers and managers I saw in the first supermarket, and if you worked harder you were rewarded for it, which didn't happen with a union.

Referring to the low-profit textile industry, he claimed unions would either fail to raise wages or, if successful, would force prices up. The consequences of increased prices would be loss of customers and suffering for the workers.

As for the NLRB findings that J.P. Stevens persistently ignored the labor law and the Southeastern bishops' charge that J.P. Stevens followed "a pattern of lawlessness," Neff felt the

244

accusations did not ring true. He elaborated on the motives for his disbelief,

> It is difficult for me to conceive of a company threatening or coercing workers to oppose a union. It's hard for me to comprehend how a company could be deliberately breaking the law, because people in management have to be honest and honorable. If they weren't, no one would have trusted them, and they wouldn't have gotten where they are.

While the reactions, responses, and replies crisscrossed and unravelled, there were others in the Catholic community busily ministering to the textile workers.[52]   Among them were a Dominican Sister and a daughter of the University of Notre Dame's Economics Department chairperson and member of the USCC Committee on Social Development and World Peace.   Sr. Mary Priniski, O.P., and Alice Wilber worked in Rock Hill, S.C., a town of 34,000 people and the site of two J.P. Stevens plants to assist the local ACTWU organizers. Both worked for Southerners for Economic Justice.   Wilber was a labor studies student on leave from Indiana University at South Bend.   Priniski worked for SEJ with the desire to ". . . stand with the least in the struggle for justice." An additional reason in late 1979 was the offer of the Oratorian Fathers at Rock Hill to assist a justice organizer in the area. The priests ministered to parishes in four surrounding counties and were Priniski's and Wilber's only local contacts upon arriving.

However, after quickly searching out the ACTWU organizers, the two women became valued allies in the organizing campaign. For, their services were varied and important.   They provided research assistance, contact with the media, and advice on finding one's way through bureaucratic mazes.   The SEJ staffers showed up at meetings, as the only white members of the Chester (a nearby town) Movement for Justice.   The group was formed by blacks in Chester who were angered by police inaction on a series of suspicious killings of young black men.   Priniski and Wilber again offered assistance when the Catawba Indians renewed their decades-old struggle to obtain compensation for 225 square miles of South Carolina land stolen from them by whites.   Included in the 225 square miles were sites on which the Oratorian Fathers and other church property stood.   Not only the assistance but also the very presence of these strangers demonstrated to the poor and beleagured people in the vicinity that they and their struggles were worthy of support. As <u>NCR</u>'s Steve Askin concluded,

. . . they, and SEJ, make their most dis-
tinctive contribution by working simultaneously in factory and community. Through
them, Chester movement activists have
friends to turn to for advice on coping with
workplace abuse. Conversely, they provide a
valuable connection between the organizing
campaign - which is sometimes hindered, as
are all Southern workplace organizing
efforts, by widespread community indifference or hostility toward unions - and its
most promising potential community allies.

Another social activist, Glenmary Father Les Schmidt of Big
Stone Gap, Va., spoke out for the Southeastern bishops in early
May 1980.[53] Quite active behind the religious scenes during the
J.P. Stevens-ACTWU controversy, Schmidt complimented the National
Catholic Reporter for its articles on the controversy. Referring
to the March 12 statement of the Southeastern bishops, he said,

. . . the bishops had little to gain.
Still, they took a stand with the workers in
their uphill struggle. Furthermore, the
bishops underlined the duty to organize
wherever the common good demands.

From late March until early May, 1980 there were significant
developments in both Catholic and Protestant groups in North
Carolina.[54] The Raleigh diocesan pastoral council, which
included several corporate officials, publicly in late March
seconded the Southeastern bishops' boycott endorsement. In
April, the parish council in the only Catholic parish in Roanoke
Rapids challenged the J.P. Stevens Company. The parish council
announced that it would join the boycott by sending a new carpet-
ing order to another firm, despite a J.P. Stevens' offer to
supply its products at a substantial discount. On May 7, there
was a labor workshop, at which North Carolina bishops Begley and
Gossman were featured speakers. Both signers of the March 12
bishops' statement said their experience with the J.P. Stevens-
ACTWU controversy had convinced them that the Southern churches
should address labor issues.

That was exactly what the North Carolina Council of Churches
did dramatically on the very same day in May. That body's House
of Delegates, comprised of representatives of North Carolina's
Catholic and mainline Protestant churches, voted to encourage
collective bargaining and to seek new ties with working people
and their unions. The council's action was a very important and
new gesture toward religion-labor cooperation in the nation's
least unionized and lowest wage state.

The House of Delegates' statement, repudiating a tradition of Southern church antipathy toward unions, contained several significant elements. First, there was the affirmation that ". . . responsible organization of North Carolina industrial workers into unions is a step toward justice at this time." Second, there was the challenge to both labor and management that both had ". . . a moral obligation to bargain with each other in good faith." Third, there was the promise to educate church members so that they would feel ". . . challenged to become involved in this struggle for economic justice." Fourth, there was the call to member churches to strengthen their ties with both working people and managers. Fifth, there was a careful analysis of the connection between North Carolina's poverty, its industries' power, and its workers' powerlessness. Sixth, there was the assertion that workers who did not have unions usually became ". . . poor, undereducated, isolated individuals facing a well organized, wealthy corporation." Seventh, there was a frank confession of past sins.

> Frequently we have cherished the company of the bosses and avoided the company of the bossed. We have relished the political power, the social prestige and the economic benefits that come from close association with the leaders of industry. We sinned not in loving them as people, but in loving them as people of power. We confess that we have had little concern for industrial workers.

The statement easily passed on a voice vote, despite opposition from delegates who voiced concern about union violence and corruption. Rev. S. Collins Kilburn, the executive director of the North Carolina Council of Churches, had expected more intense opposition. As a strong supporter of the statement, Kilburn was quite pleased with the vote. For, the statement reflected a growing attentiveness to labor concerns among Southern religious leaders. Even though North Carolina Protestants were not expected to follow the Catholic church into the J.P. Stevens boycott, the North Carolina Council of Churches made more than a statement. On May 29, it was to bring together religious leaders, labor leaders, management people in Burlington, N.C. for a statewide religion and labor conference. It was one of several attempts to create ties with organized labor.

In July 1980, there was news of J.P. Stevens boycott support in the St. Paul-Minneapolis archdiocese.[55] Its Urban Affairs

Commission was thrown into a quandry when it was discovered that the archdiocesan schools clothed many of their pupils in uniforms made from J.P. Stevens fabric. The inadvertence was revealed in a survey designed to implement the archdiocesan commission's endorsement of the J.P. Stevens boycott. According to the commission staff member, Ted Snyder, the schools responded favorably to the request not to buy products manufactured by J.P. Stevens. The uniforms made from J.P. Stevens cloth were manufactured by Stephen Uniform Company - no relation to J.P. Stevens.

The manufacturer's president, Stephen Perlman, was the only consistent supplier of the most popular uniforms - made from J.P. Stevens plaid polyester fabric. Perlman said other firms rapidly were withdrawing from the school uniform-material business and predicted that J.P. Stevens soon would be the only possible source. Snyder said the urban affairs commission was perplexed. Although the archdiocese actively supported the boycott, there was no desire to punish a small local firm which had served the church so well, because it had to buy J.P. Stevens fabric. However, ACTWU's religious community liaison, Rev. William Somplatsky-Jarmon, said the uniform dilemma had arisen in other dioceses. ACTWU merely urged school officials to ask uniform makers to find a different source for the fabric usually used, or, if necessary, to switch to other type fabrics more readily available from different fabric makers than J.P. Stevens.

By mid-October 1980, the J.P. Stevens-ACTWU controversy was over with the announcement that there was a settlement of the seventeen-year-old battle.[56] As expected, the contract was approved with a great roar by the J.P. Stevens workers gathered on October 19, 1980 in Roanoke Rapids High School.[57] The contract covering 3,500 J.P. Stevens workers at ten plants in four towns in North Carolina, South Carolina and Alabama was described by a worker and ACTWU official. The worker , Virginia Barton, said, "The union contract will give us more control over our lives. It will really build up the morale of the people, too." Scott Hoyman, ACTWU executive vice president, Southern director and chief negotiator, said the contract,

> . . . compares favorably with other Amalgamated Clothing and Textile Worker Union (ACTWU) contracts with Southern Textile companies . . . It regulates workloads and provides the security of a seniority system for job changes and promotions.

Two provisions of the contract were dubbed unique by ACTWU officials. First, J.P. Stevens had to offer the union similar contracts for any plants at which the union won representation, either through the courts or by election within the next 18 months. Such a provision could have added another half dozen to the ten already covered by the initial contract. Second, J.P. Stevens had to offer the union any company-wide improvements in wages or benefits granted in non-union plants. The contract included the following provisions. Immediate wage increases of 19.35 per cent to levels negotiated in 1978 and 1980. Back pay for those increases totaling $3 million or approximately $1,300 per full-time worker. Regular wage and benefit renegotiations as often as every six months, if desired. Maintenance and guarantee of benefits already in effect including vacation and holiday pay, pensions, profit-sharing, health insurance, etc. The right of union representatives, including the union's time study engineer, to enter the plants to investigate worker complaints. A joint health and safety committee. Union dues collected through pay check deductions. Plant-wide seniority to govern matters such as layoffs, job bidding, job transfers, training for higher skills. Arbitration procedures covering discipline, workloads, seniority, health and safety and benefit levels. A three-step grievance procedure. A prohibition against discrimination on account of race, sex, age, religion or union membership.

As the contract was being signed in Roanke Rapids, officials of J.P. Stevens and ACTWU signed another national agreement which pointed to the effectiveness of ACTWU's multi-faceted campaign against J.P. Stevens on the plant floor, in the marketplaces, in the courtrooms, and in the corporate boardrooms. ACTWU agreed to give up its consumer boycott, corporate campaign, court-ordered remedies (right of ACTWU organizers to operate in plant lunchrooms and rest areas), and primary targeting of J.P. Stevens in organizing activities.

Also noted was ACTWU's soft-pedaling the boycott's effectiveness in the South, lest the union be accused of causing layoffs. Yet, the boycott's effectiveness was evident from cancellations of J.P. Stevens' orders by many retail stores and one Wall Street insider newsletter contending that the profitability of J.P. Stevens' domestic goods line had dropped dramatically. Also, it was noted that ACTWU's attorneys, Arthur J. Goldberg and Joel Ax, systematically followed up J.P. Stevens' lawbreaking with a thicket of legal charges and ACTWU's corporate campaign directors, Ray Rogers and Edward Allen, found the weak points in the web of J.P. Stevens' corporate board connections.

The key to the victory really may have been the early retirement of James D. Finley, chairperson of the J.P. Stevens Board. He was regarded widely as the architect and overseer of the anti-union strategy of the company. Day-to-day operations of the company were handed over to Whitney Stevens, one of the descendants of the company founders. He was thought to be more flexible. However accurate the assessment of either man, top level talks were underway and workers reported less pressure in the plants on union enthusiasts. In concluding that ACTWU's victory over J.P. Stevens was a boost in the momentum of union organizing in the South, two well experienced Southern organizing chiefs were quoted. ACTWU's Hoyman said, "When workers win, word gets around." UAW's James Turner told the Wall Street Journal,

> Everyone has traditionally pointed to the Stevens situation and said it is futile to try to organize while that is going on . . . [The settlement] will ready open the way for more progress.

In the third week of October 1980 - the week of the settlement - several voices were heard from the religious community.[58] The first were at the 16th annual meeting of the Committee on Religion in Appalachia (CORA) at Harrogate, Tennessee. Meeting on October 22, the 19 body church group's chairperson, Don Steele, said, "We applaud the the tenacity of the workers in not giving up hope and being persistent in their demands for a contract." Representatives from Catholic, Episcopalian, Methodist, Presbyterian and Southern Baptist member-organizations expressed support of organization drives in the region by textile, sewing and furniture factories, as well as of the March 1981 mineworkers' contract negotiations. CORA, in addition, heard the former J.P. Stevens worker and spark for ACTWU's earlier victory in Roanoke Rapids, Crystal Lee Sutton. She said the day of the settlement was

> . . . a great day in my life. . . [but] the union will still have a hard time. . . [because] I don't believe Mr. J.P. Stevens is going to abide by the law.

Other voices - as cautious as Crystal Lee Stutton's - were some of the Southeastern bishops.[59] On October 20, 1980 the six bishops issued a short statement expressing "satisfaction" and acknowledging "obstacles." Among other things their declaration said,

> It is appropriate for us now to express our satisfaction in the recent turn of events and to salute those who, on both sides of the table, assisted in resolving the problems. For our part, we continue to offer our services to both parties if any efforts of ours might be of use.

250

To be sure, the J.P. Stevens Company
continues to oppose unionization but has
pledged itself not to interfere improperly
in the unionization efforts of the workers.
There will be a long road ahead before the
textile workers are fully unionized, if
ever, but many real obstacles have been
removed from the path.

In a telephone interview, Bishop Walter Sullivan of Richmond made
reference to a remark J.P. Stevens' chief executive officer,
Whitney Stevens, in an October 19 press conference: "We will
continue to oppose the unions." Sullivan said that type of attitude made him,

> . . . skeptical that there is going to be a
> real about-face of the company. . . Just
> because there is a victory in a few plants
> doesn't mean there won't be future
> difficulties.

Sullivan added that he and the other five bishops would continue
to monitor the J.P. Stevens-ACTWU situation.

Also, in late October 1980, the editors of _America_ referred
to the Southeastern bishops' 1979 endorsement of the J.P. Stevens
boycott and ACTWU's corporate campaign.[60] The corporate campaign,
however, was characterized as an even more effective tactic than
the boycott. The corporate campaign was described as sophisticated legal and fiscal maneuvers to put pressure on the banks,
insurance companies, and investment firms that were J.P. Stevens'
principal money partners and that shared interlocking director-
ates with J.P. Stevens. Looking to the future, the editors of
America concluded,

> . . . the tactic may prove an epochal
> change in labor practices and could be
> important in reversing the quarter-
> century-old downward trend in labor union
> memberships.

In early November 1980, there was notice of Bishop Ernest
Unterkoefler of Charleston and Crystal Lee Sutton being co-
recipients of the 1980 _Pacem in Terris_ Award of the Davenport,
Iowa, diocesan Social Action Office and the Quad-City Justice and
Peace Coalition.[61] Unterkoefler's accolade for his role in the
J.P. Stevens-ACTWU controversy, contrasted with Charlotte's
Bishop Michael Begley's embarassment at being caught in the
middle of another textile labor-management dispute in July

1980.[62] Begley's office in the Charlotte Catholic Center was picketed on July 3, 1980 by ACTWU workers striking against Woonsocket Spinning Company's Charlotte yarn factory since June 22, 1980. The union workers protested the placement by the Charlotte diocesan Catholic Social Service Office of six Laotian refugees in jobs with the Woonsocket Spinning Company. Two of the Laotians began work in May and four began after the strike started. All six crossed the picket line, escorted at times by volunteers or staff members of the Catholic Social Service Office.

Following the protest at the Catholic Center, the Catholic Social Service coordinator, Trinitarian Sister Frances Sheridan, said she would remove, reluctantly, the Laotians from Woonsocket and try to find them other jobs. Sheridan stated that the four additional Laotian workers were placed at Woonsocket only because someone she thought to be in the union said the labor-management dispute had been settled. Her informant, however, turned out to be a member of the Woonsocket management. According to National Catholic Reporter's Steven Askin,

> Some observers suspect, though they cannot prove it, that the church may have been maneuvered into that awkward spot by local "union busters" eager to embarrass a bishop who stood with the union against his region's most powerful industry. They note that Woonsocket's chief negotiator in talks for a first contract last year was Edward Dowd, head of the anti-union Central Piedmont Employers Association and Charlotte's most vocal public opponent of the Southern bishops J.P. Stevens statement (NCR, March 28 and April 4). In the current round, management is represented by Blakeney, Alexander and Machem, a law firm best-known for its work as J.P. Stevens' labor counsel.

[1]Joy Cook, "Flores Support Boycott," National Catholic Reporter, v. 8, No. 33, 8/4/72, p. 17.

[2]"Bishop Supports Mexican-American Striker," National Catholic Reporter, v. 9, No. 4, 11/17/72, pp. 1, 6.

[3]Jerry De Muth, "Rallies Show Support for Farah Boycott," National Catholic Reporter, v. 9, No. 9, 12/22/72, p. 2.

[4]"Ad for Farah Boycott Reprints Bishops' Strike Support Letter," National Catholic Reporter, v. 9, No. 17, 2/23/73, pp. 3, 4.

[5]"Chavez Gives Support to Strikers at Farah," National Catholic Reporter, v. 9, No. 17, 2/23/73, p. 4.

[6]"The Bishop and the Boycott," Editorials, America, v. 128, No. 8, 3/3/73, pp. 178-179.

[7]"Texas Conference Backs Boycott," National Catholic Reporter, v. 9, No. 18, 3/2/73, p. 3.

[8]"More Bishops Back Boycott," National Catholic Reporter, v. 9, No. 24, 4/13/73, pp. 1, 18.

[9]Jerry De Muth, "Metzger Takes His Support of Farah Strike to Chicago," National Catholic Reporter, v. 9, No. 25, 4/20/73, p. 5.

[10]Robert Getz, "Supporting the Pants Strike," Commonweal, v. 98, No. 13, 6/1/73, pp. 300-301.

[11]"The Boycott of Farah," Briefly, National Catholic Reporter, v. 9, No. 30, 6/22/73, p. 20.

[12]"New York Bishops Ask Farah Study," Reporter at Large, National Catholic Reporter, v. 9, No. 29, 6/8/73, p. 24.

[13]"Bishops Offer Mass for Cause of Unionism," National Catholic Reporter, v. 9, No. 32, 7/20/73, p. 7.

[14]"Public Issues and Nonpublic Schools," Current Comment, America, v. 129, No. 7, 9/15/73, p. 156.

[15]"A Matter of 'Social Justice,'" Current Comment, America, v. 130, No. 6, 2/16/74, p. 105.

[16]"Union and Farah Start Bargaining After Strike Ends," National Catholic Reporter, v. 10, No. 19, 3/8/74, pp. 1, 10.

[17]"Settlement of Farah Strike," Current Comment, America, v. 130, No. 9, 3/9/74, p. 162.

[18]"Labor Lauded for Farah Settlement, UFW Support," National Catholic Reporter, v. 10, No. 38, 8/30/74, p. 6.

[19]Jason Petosa, "Appalachian Catholics Discuss Boycott," National Catholic Reporter, v. 13, No. 5, 11/19/76, p. 3.

[20]Jason Petosa, "Bishops May Offer Mediation in J.P. Stevens Controversy," National Catholic Reporter, v. 13, No. 17, 2/18/77, p. 1, 36.

[21]Peggy Everett, "Second Largest U.S. Textile Maker is Target of 14 Year Union Campaign," National Catholic Reporter, v. 13, No. 17, 2/18/77, p. 36.

[22]"NFPC to Aid Appalachia Planning," National Catholic Reporter, v. 13, No. 32, 6/3/77, p. 4.

[23]"Stevens Sidesteps Mediation Offer," National Catholic Reporter, v. 13, No. 33, 6/17/77, pp. 1, 28.

[24]Patricia A. Moore, "J.P. Stevens Debates Textile Union," National Catholic Reporter, v. 13, No. 36, 7/29/77, p. 24.

[25]"NAWR Supports Vermont Nun," National Catholic Reporter, v. 13, No. 38, 8/26/77, p. 6.

[26]"Admit Women to Permanent Diaconate," News Desk, National Catholic Reporter, v. 13, No. 44, 10/7/77, p. 3.

[27]Lois Spear, "Boycott Unionization of J.P. Stevens Splits Catholics in North Carolina," National Catholic Reporter, v. 13, No. 45, 10/14/77, p. 5.

[28]"Bishops Offer Again to Mediate," National Catholic Reporter, v. 14, No. 9, 12/16/77, p. 3.

[29]"J.P. Stevens to Meet With Southeast Bishops," National Catholic Reporter, v. 14, No. 10, 12/23/77, p. 2.

[30]"J.P. Stevens-Bishops Meet Blocked by Fog," National Catholic Reporter, v. 14, No. 11, 1/6/78, p. 2.

[31]Bill Kenkelen, "Bishops-Stevens Meet: Talk Not Action-- Yet," National Catholic Reporter, v. 14, No. 15, 2/3/78, pp. 1, 18.

[32]"Bishop's Role in Textile Fight Annoys Parishioners," National Catholic Reporter, v. 14, No. 18, 2/24/78, p. 2.

[33]"Men of the Cloth," Reparatee, National Catholic Reporter, v. 14, No. 20, 3/10/78, p. 10.

[34]Lois Spear, "Stockholder Moves Lose in J.P. Stevens Voting," National Catholic Reporter, v. 14, No. 21, 3/17/78, p. 28.

[35]"Southern Bishops Lash Stevens; Silent on Boycott," National Catholic Reporter, v. 14, No. 22, 3/24/78, p. 2.

[36]"Stevens Board Member Quits; Women Take Credit," _National Catholic Reporter_, v. 14, No. 23, 3/31/78, p. 5.

[37]"Catholic, Methodist," News Cue, _National Catholic Reporter_, v. 14, No. 27, 4/28/78, p. 6.

[38]"The Hartford Archdiocese," _National Catholic Reporter_, v. 14, No. 33, 6/16/78, p. 6.

[39]Lydia Chavez, "Two Resign; Firm-Union Talk," _National Catholic Reporter_, v. 14, No. 42, 9/22/78, p. 4.

[40]"Boycott Spirit," Repartee, _National Catholic Reporter_, v. 14, No. 43, 9/29/78, p. 10.

[41]Bill Kenkelen, "Religious Labor Leaders Escalate Stevens Boycott," _National Catholic Reporter_, v. 15, No. 28, 5/4/79, p. 20.

[42]"Boston Boycotts J.P. Stevens," _National Catholic Reporter_, v. 15, No. 34, 6/29/79, p. 6.

[43]Steve Askin, "Bishops Join Stevens Boycott," _National Catholic Reporter_, v. 16, No. 6, 11/30/79, p. 4.

[44]Steve Askin, "Activists Take Union Fight to Stevens' Stockholders," _National Catholic Reporter_, v. 16, No. 20, 3/14/80, p. 4.

[45]Steve Askin, "Bishops Back Boycott: Urge South: 'Organize,'" _National Catholic Reporter_, v. 16, No. 21, 3/21/80, pp. 1, 5, 19.

[46]"Southern Bishops' Stance Tests Catholics Beliefs," Editorial, <u>National Catholic Reporter</u>, v. 16, No. 21, 3/21/80, p. 12.

[47]"Bishops Boycott J.P. Stevens," Editorial, <u>America</u>, v. 142, No. 12, 3/29/80, p. 255.

[48]Steve Askin, "Praise, Blame Trail Bishops' Stevens Rap," <u>National Catholic Reporter</u>, v. 16, No. 22, 3/28/80, p. 3.

[49]Steve Askin, "Pro-Union Bishops Anger Many Southern Catholics," <u>National Catholic Reporter</u>, v. 16, No. 23, 4/4/80, pp. 1, 22.

[50]Steve Askin, "Stevens Denies Charges But Bishops Stand Fast," <u>National Catholic Reporter</u>, v. 16, No. 24, 4/11/80, pp. 1, 28.

[51]Steve Askin, "Executive: 'Church's Stand Is Wrong,'" <u>National Catholic Reporter</u>, v. 16, No. 25, 4/18/80, p. 1.

[52]Steve Askin, "Two Share Skills, Time," <u>National Catholic Reporter</u>, v. 16, No. 25, 4/18/80, p. 20.

[53]"Stevens Stories," Repartee, <u>National Catholic Reporter</u>, v. 16, No. 38, 5/9/80, p. 12.

[54]Steve Askin, "North Carolina Church Body Supports Unions," <u>National Catholic Reporter</u>, v. 16, No. 29, 5/16/80, pp. 3, 20.

[55]Steve Askin, "Minnesota Activists Find Stevens Cloth In Schools," <u>National Catholic Reporter</u>, v. 16, Nol 35, 7/18/80, p. 19.

[56]Steven Agreement Reached," Nation, National Catholic Reporter, v. 17, No. 1, 10/24/80, p. 6.

[57]Gretchen Donart, "Stevens Contract Ends 17-Year Fight," National Catholic Reporter, v. 17, No. 2, 10/31/80, pp. 3, 4.

[58]Steve Askin, "Appalachian Religion body 'Celebrates,'" National Catholic Reporter, v. 17, No. 2, 10-31/80, p. 3.

[59]James W. Michaels, Jr., "Bishops 'Satisfied'; Warn of Obstacles," National Catholic Reporter, v. 17, No. 2, 10/31/80, p. 4.

[60]"New Labor Tactics," Current Comment, America, v. 143, No. 13, 11/1/80, p. 258.

[61]People, National Catholic Reporter, v. 17, No. 3, 11/7/80, p. 8.

[62]Steve Askin, "Charlotte, N.E., Textile Workers Picket Bishop," National Catholic Reporter, v. 16, No. 35, 7/18/80, pp. 19, 24.

Chapter VI - Coal Miners

A. Duke Power Company

In 1974, members of the United Mine Workers of America (UMW) were on strike against the mines of the Duke Power Company in Harlan County, Kentucky.[1] Several members of the Catholic hierarchy and clergy intervened in various ways to express their desire for a just settlement through collective bargaining. In June 1974, Msgr. George Higgins visited Harlan County and put together a special task force of bishops to assist in such a settlement. Higgins seconded the comment of UMW president, Arnold Miller, that the Harlan County Duke-UMW controversy was another "Farah." Msgr. Geno Baroni, formerly of USCC staff and later president of the Urban Ethnic Center in Washington, D.C. joined a citizens public inquiry panel, which included former Secretary of Labor, Willard Wirtz; Oklahoma Senator, Fred Harris; and labor management expert, Daniel Pollitt of the University of North Carolina Law School.

Among the hierarchy who spoke out were Bishop Michael Begley of Charlotte and Bishop Richard Ackerman of Covington, Kentucky, two of the many bishops who co-authored in February 1975, the Appalachian bishops' pastoral, "This Land is Home To Me." The widely acclaimed prose of the pastoral was quite challenging to mine owners and unions in the area. Begley appealed to Duke officials to turn on the water in the coal camp. Begley prepared the way for mediation by keeping the door open and by remaining in constant touch with UMW and Duke leaders. Ackerman wrote to Carl Horn, Jr., President of the Duke Power Company,

> ...[Exert] whatever influence you have toward the "bargaining table," so that the common good may be achieved and preserved.

As Duke Power Company stock went from $16 to $11 since the initiation of a boycott, some bishops notified Duke Power of their support of a stock boycott.

B. Appalachian Developments in National Negotiations: 1977-1979

During the 1977 UMW negotiations, plagued by wildcat strikes despite a "no-strike" clause in 1974 negotiations, comments were made about the relationships between mine workers and the Catholic church.[2] Unlike other industries, the coal industry had no significant Catholic influence in its organization by labor

unions.   In fact, save for a sense of justice and survival which
moved miners and their wives to periodic heroism, there was no
religious influence of any kind in unionization of the U.S. coal
fields.   The outstanding semi-religious figure was an early
United Mine Workers organizer, Mother Jones, who used to say,
"Pray for the dead and fight like hell for the living."   A successor to an early Catholic UMW president, John Mitchell, Arnold
Miller was nominated for the UMW presidency in a convention held
at Wheeling College, a Jesuit-founded-and-affiliated institution
and the only Catholic institution of higher learning in
Appalachia.   Miller ran a low-keyed campaign on the "Miners for
Democracy" ticket against the allegedly tyrannical W.A. "Tony"
Boyle--later convicted of the murder of an earlier opposing candidate, Joseph "Jock" Yablonski.   Miller won the 1972 election.
Under Miller, the the leadership shifted from autocratic to near
chaotic.   Frequently, the rank-and-file, as well as the district
presidents paid no attention to the new UMWU president. Some
regarded Miller's no-strike clause as a sell-out.   Although
Miller was re-elected in the summer of 1976, he appeared to have
done so only by distancing himself from the no-strike clause, as
much as he could.

However, Miller could not waffle in negotiations with the
Appalachian Bituminous Coal Operators Association, who knew of
many wildcat strikes protesting wages, conditions, fringe benefits and the no-strike clause.   For many miners, the only effective protest to unsafe mines or other grievances was a walkout.
One local strike could easily become contagious as dissatisfied
miners would send pickets to other mines.   Such wildcat strikes
almost depleted the UMW's health and pension funds. Unlike other
unions, the UMW's funds were replenished on the basis of
production--"No work, no production, no royalties."

In the 1977 negotiations, the UMW, under Miller's leadership, wanted to change such a predicament.   By December there was
a national strike, which lasted 100 days--until March 1978.
There was a possible invocation of mergency strike procedures by
President Jimmy Carter, who made coal the keystone of his long-
range energy plan.   Despite such a possibility and the coal
operator's willingness to meet UMW money demands ($100 a day), a
radical group was formed, being convinced that the strike power
was what the workers needed in a local and regional coal-based
economy.   So, the Miners Right to Strike Committee (MRTSC), based
in south-central West Virginia and attracting younger and
militant miners, escalated management-labor language in the coal
regions to national class struggle rhetoric.   On Labor Day 1977,
MRTSC joined with workers from other industries to form the
National United Workers Organization and agreed that the leverage

to unite all the nation's workers and minorities was the strike.
The new organization's proclamation was

> Between the working class and the employing
> class there can be only an organized and pro-
> tracted   struggle...and the rich   can be
> damned!

Such rhetoric, through neither liberation theology nor mainstream
UMW thinking, found fertile ground in the Appalachian coal
fields. Many thought the price of free enterprise too expensive,
especially when, said Askin, "...many big coal concerns are owned
by international oil companies that already reap obscene profits
from the energy crisis."

The Catholic Committee of Appalachia (CCA) and the interfaith Commission on Religion in Appalachia (CORA) had been fighting "King Coal's strip mining minions" in the mountains. Behind
the scenes they, with the Council of the Southern Mountains, had
helped the UMW organize some non-union miners.   Along with the
MRTSC, all these groups knew that UMW was a fragile voice for
labor.   Referring to the probable December 6, 1977 strike, NCR's
Petosa concluded,

> Christians who believe that stewardship is a
> sacred trust can watch those signals, listen
> to the winter winds, and pray for a miracle
> to make King Coal a merry soul.

On March 20, 1978 the Bishop Joseph Hodges of Wheeling, West
Virginia, called for a day of prayer and fasting for striking
miners.[3] In his public statement, Hodges asked miners to avoid
violence, although he conceded that "...few of your victories
have been accomplished without conflict."   He also appealed to
coal operators "...for leadership that responds in justice to our
people."   At the same time, Sr. Shawn Scanlan, the CCA executive
director, said that without a centralized effort to aid Miners,
"...people are doing what they can in their own areas."   In
Welch, West Virginia, the pastor of St. Peter's Catholic parish,
Rev. Joseph Dene, said there was a small contingency fund available to miners, if they needed help.   He noted that up to that
time many miners were able to get by on savings and that stores
and hospitals were extending credit to customers and patients.
Yet, he also noted deep-seated anxiety in the area:

> The people are fearful of bloodshed, the loss
> of pensions, the breakup of the United Mine

Workers Union and the hardship which they are sure will get much greater.

CORA had distributed funds to the hardest hit areas to buy food and other necessities for the striking miners and their families.

C. Blue Diamond Coal Company and Sterna

The Company

In 1915, Alexander Bonnyman founded the Blue Diamond Coal Company.[4] He was active in the National Coal Association and various labor and welfare commissions in the Appalachian mountains. A prominent figure in the Catholic church, Alexander Bonnyman was also a substantial contributor to Catholic charitable causes. For his many services, Pope Pius XII named him to the Sovereign Order of the Knights of Malta. From 1919 until 1953, when he died, Alexander Bonnyman served as president and chairman of the board of the Blue Diamond Coal Company. Over the years from 1919 until 1978, the company operated more than 20 underground mines in Kentucky, Virginia and Tennessee.

In 1953 Gordon Bonnyman assumed leadership when his father died. In 1977 the company, one of the largest independent firms in the Appalachian region, was a public corporation with more than 400 shareholders and 400,000 shares of stock. Gordon Bonnyman and his wife owned less than two per cent of Blue Diamond stock, although it was alleged the Bonnyman family controlled a much greater share through wills or trusts. In 1976 the Blue Diamond Coal Company -totally free of any long range debts-had a net worth of $76 million. In addition to its coal interests, the company owned a clay and mica mining firm in North Carolina, substantial portions of the nation's 11th largest steel producer - McLouth Steel Corporation - and 97.5 per cent of the stock of Pittsburgh's Heppenstall, Inc. Blue Diamond was also sales agent for two other wholly owned subsidiaries; operated several mines nears Hazard, Kentucky, which in 1976 produced one million tons of coal; and owned the Scotia Coal Company in Letcher County in Kentucky, which produced more than 650,000 tons of coal in 1976. In that same year, 26 men died in methane gas explosions ini Scotia's Imboden Mine. The $60 million lawsuit brought by their widows was tossed out of federal district court in eastern Kentucky and was still on appeal in early 1978.

The Controversy

On December 31, 1975 the Blue Diamond Company bought the Stearns Mining Company for a reported $9 million. The Justus Mine part of the newly-acquired company in McCreary County, Kentucky, included two seams of bituminous steam coal which produced an annual rate of 350,000 tons. Three months after the purchase (March 1976), the Justus miners voted 126 to 57 to join the UMW. However, the NLRB did not certify the election until July 17, 1976, when the miners voted 151 to 1 to strike. Gordon Bonnyman, an extremely private businessman, made no secret in the coal fields of his antipathy for the UMW. In the aftermath of the Scotia diaster and during the Stearns strike, he refused press interviews. The man whose responsibility was to grant interviews, Vice President Frank C. Thomas, and did not return NCR's Massey's telephone calls. Another Blue Diamond official, Herman Stallard, refused to answer questions with the quip, "Our business is mining coal--not getting into debates."

According to UMW spokespeople, an impasse had developed. Blue Diamond had stated that the key issues were the length of the contract, a no-strike clause and arbitration procedures. For the UMW, the major impasse was a provision in the national UMW contract calling for an elected safety committee of miners with powers to remove miners from working conditions where an "imminent danger" threatened life or limb. Miners charged the company with using faulty equipment, never conducting fire drills and failing to train miners in the use of self-rescue devices that filtered out poisonous gases following explosions. The miners also claimed that the Justus Mine, opened in 1970 and proclaimed by the McCreary County Record as a "model," was "gassy" in 1978 and had a bad roof. Prior to the strike, the Justus Mine was in operation 132 days in 1976. The company reported a disabling injury rate of 72 percent-higher than the national 1976 average, according to the UMW. Federal safety inspectors found 98 violations of mine safety laws in the six and-one-half months before the strike, as compared to 101 violations for the 12 months before Blue Diamond acquisition. According to William, "Doc" Coffey, 37, who worked for the Stearns Mining Company for 16 years,

> We have no more violations than any other normal coal mine . . . Safety wasn't an issue before the UMW came in . . . [We] go by the law 100 per cent and report everything from a scratch to a broken leg. Not all companies do that. In eight years of production, we've lost only two men.

263

In eastern Kentucky miners' strikes were rarely free of gun-fire and violence. The Stearns dispute was no exception, even though no one was killed. Nevertheless, union organizers said the Stearns strike was tougher and rougher than the six-months-shorter strike at Brookside in Harlan County, Kentucky, which ended only after the shooting death of a young miner. Coffey claimed that, a few weeks after the talks broke off in January 1977, strikers began to fire on the mine office and supply buildings from surrounding ridges. Union leaders dis-agreed with Coffey's story and so did the former McCreary County sheriff, Joe Perry. He said, "While the company was handling its own security, I didn't have any problems as sheriff." However, in March 1976, the Blue Diamond Company hired the largest secu-rity agency in eastern Kentucky. Their guards built bunkers from railroad ties. In front of the mine buildings there was a shield made from 3/8 of an inch sheets of metal. The miners, on the other hand, dug trenches in front of a make-shift shack on pro-perty a quarter of a mile from the mine buildings. For five months, guns blazed almost every night. News people from national networks reported from the miners' trenches, under fire from the bunkers. The shack and especially the building were riddled with thousands of bullet holes. Power and telephone lines were cut and railroad tracks dynamited. Seven persons were injured. Most of them were the security agency guards.

In mid-August 1976, Circuit Court Judge J. B. Johnson, Jr. issued injunctions against both sides, threatening to ask for National Guard assistance "to end the combat." An uneasy truce lasted until October 1976 when Kentucky State Troopers, who had been escorting company supervisory personnel, began to escort non-striking miners to and from the mines as well. The miners crowded the picket line in large numbers. A pickup carrying three non-union miners was damaged heavily and 16 UMW miners were charged with violating the court order. While the governor, Julian Carroll, had promised neutrality to the UMW, Judge Johnson expressed dismay with the company's move which the governor had condoned. Said Johnson, "I certainly would have influenced the company not to do it." There were several further scuffles, injuries, arrests and some imprisonment involving as many as 79 strikers at one time.

By February 1978, twenty-five miners crossed the picket lines daily--13 of whom originally had supported the UMW strike. The 25 strike-breakers were sufficient to produce coal from one or two sections of the Justus Mine. According to 59-year-old Mahan Vanover, a Stearns Mining Company employee for 36 years,

> We've got 140 men still out. In 18 months
> that's awful good. We've not been run off

yet, and we're not going to be. We'll be
here until we got a contract.

The strike cost UMW more than $2 million in benefits for strikers
and salaries for the organizers--a reflection of the importance
of the strike to UMW. Since previous leadership abandoned striking miners during a 1960 coal market slump and even though the
UMW held its own the later in Brookside elections, UMW organizers
felt that the outcome of the Stearns strike would be decisive in
subsequent organizing efforts in the eastern Kentucky coal
fields.

The Church

Consequently, in late August 1977, Chuck Shuford, a UMW
press aide, approached CCA with a request to support the striking
miners. Established in 1967 when CORA was organized, CCA was one
of the most democratic organizations in the Catholic Church.
Originally a "bishop-oriented" group, CCA later gave bishops,
clergy, laity and religious an equal voice and vote. CCA drafted
the February 1975 pastoral letter on powerlessness for 24 Catholic bishops in 13 Appalachian states. Titled "This Land is Home
to Me," the pastoral was hailed as one of the strongest statements ever made by a religious body on the social and economic
conditions of the mountain poor. Hailed also for their unequivo-
cal language, the bishops were praised for their public commitment to the struggle for justice and the end of inequity and
exploitation.   Although CCA later aided textile and other
workers, the UMW dispute with Bonnyman was seen as the first test
case of the pastoral and divided elements of the Catholic church
in Appalachia.

Several of the CCA members who played a key role in the pastoral viewed the strike as a "golden opportunity for the church
to come out on the side of the miners." According to Glenmary
Father Jerry Conroy, an experienced worker advocate, the economic
injustice, from which the gospel calls people in the area to
deliver the oppressed, raised an ugly head in Gordon Bonnyman's
absolute refusal to negotiate a contract, to respond to the
demands for safe working conditions and to recognize the workers'
right to unionize.   An added burden was placed on the Catholic
church, since Bonnyman was a Catholic.   For Conroy, Bonnyman's
mistreatment of the workers and refusal to abide by Catholic
social teaching was a public scandal. Al Fritsch, S.J., director
of the Appalachian Office of the Center for Science in the Public
Interest, found the management lacking good faith and responsible
for the complete stalemate.   Sisters Marie Cirillo and Yvonne
Nelson, community development workers for the Nashville diocese,
thought the strike was a "test case" of willingness to follow

through with the principles established in the pastoral. Nelson, despite her serious reservations about UMW, stressed that it was a time for the church to be on the side of the poor and people colonized by large companies. Conway echoed Nelson's reservation and dedication. He did not see the UMW as the necessary solution but would support the miners' decision to seek social justice through the UMW.

Another Glenmary Father and experienced worker-advocate, Les Schmidt, referred to Vatican II's support of collective bargaining as a basic human right and qualified his support for the Stearns dispute. He supported the people's basic human right, not the presence of violence and immorality--not even the UMW in itself. Schmidt was the first to meet with Bonnyman's bishop, James D. Niedergeses of Nashville, to ask his support for the miners.

Following a talk with Schmidt around September 1, 1977, Niedergeses telephoned Bonnyman to discuss the strike. While the bishop refused to discuss the conversation directly, he relayed the gist of it to Schmidt. After expressing his concern for the strike and the suffering of the mining community, the bishop asked if the church could help bring a solution to the conflict. Bonnyman told Niedergeses to "stay out;" the church had "no business" in the dispute; the union would use church involvement as another "gimmick" against Blue Diamond; there were various illegal and immoral union practices. Niedergeses repeated his desire to resolve a troublesome situation, but expected no beneficial results because of Bonnyman's attitude. Bonnyman insisted that the issues were too complex for the church to understand. Bonnyman told the bishop that, if he persisted, he would force Bonnyman out of the church.

In September, shortly after his conversation with Bonnyman, the bishop met with Cirillo, Fritsch and others and clearly was troubled, deeply hurt, and affronted by Bonnyman's attitude. According to Fritsch, Niedergeses would like to discuss privately with Bonnyman the pastoral letter on powerlessness. The bishop also felt that Bonnyman did not seem to have too much trust in anyone nor to involve the gospel in his decision-making. If Bonnyman was going to leave the church the bishop said, "...he's going to do it himself." Niedergeses told the group that he would never be responsible for excluding Bonnyman from the church. The bishop did not see the church as judge, but as reconciler, on the basis of gospel principles. He felt that if the church was to excommunicate everyone who did not live according to the gospel the church would have no members at all.

Niedergeses was asked by the group at the September meeting to consider concrete steps for siding with the miners. Among them, was issuing a pastoral on the general issues of the strike and/or an interdict of Gordon Bonnyman. The bishop was responsive to other views expressed and was agreeable to discuss with other bishops the value of a pastoral and interdict. Yet he differed with the CCA activists on practical steps in siding with the miners against Blue Diamond, not on the principles or issues involved. He saw two warring factions and thought the church should bring them together. However, the CCA view was that when one side is powerless and there are occupational health and safety issues involved, the church should stand by the powerless and stand up to such injustices.

After the September 1977 meeting with the CCA activists Niedergeses discussed the dispute with Archbishop Thomas J. McDonough of Louisville, in which archdiocese the Justus Mine was located. Earlier, McDonough had asked how he might be of assistance to Good Shepherd parish in McCreary County with regard to the Stearns dispute. The parish, which had 20 adult members, voted to remain neutral and asked McDonough to do the same. Both McDonough and Niedergeses chose neutrality. Both issued communiques to the union and the company, asking them to work for the "common good" and to refrain from provoking violence. Both bishops offered to do whatever they could "to bring a just strike settlement."

Following his meeting with the Nashville bishop, the Louisville archbishop talked with Kentucky Governor, Julian Carroll, on several occasions. The Louisville archdiocesan Justice and Peace Office met with Kentucky State Police. Claiming that in other earlier press accounts of the strike he had been misquoted, McDonough told reporters, "I'm not telling you anything." The chairperson of the archdiocesan Justice and Peace Commission, Msgr. Alfred F. Horrigan, said, "Our immediate concern was the threat of violence." Horrigan said he knew of no replies to McDonough's telegrams offering the church's mediation services to Blue Diamond, UMW, or Judge Johnson. A reflection of the bishops' position was an "open letter" about the dispute published in the November 21, 1977 issue of the Nashville diocese's newspaper,

> We are confident that a just and peaceful settlement to this dispute can be reached... we ask all parties in the Stearns dispute and those affected by it, which is all of us, not to look back and keep complaining about weaknesses and wrongs of the past. Let's start proclaiming human needs with mutual respect and responsible action.

There followed some exchanges between CCA members and others over Bishop Nidergeses' position. Glenmary Conroy spoke of the church, not as arbitrator or mediator, but as reconciler. Reconciliation might well demand a 80-20 type of settlement to undo injustices toward the workers. Bishop Niedergeses complained that there was no way to have justice or charity without the facts. He felt that the bishops were not in a position to get all the facts.

Glenmary Schmidt called Niedergeses' stand a rationalization for non-reaction. Without facts, one does not have to act and the situation only gets worse--"By that time, all the workers will be dead." Accusing McDonough of the same "copout," Schmidt did admit that Niedegeses was not in complicity with the likes of Bonnyman and would apply Catholic social teaching, without making any apologies, when he was forced to do so. Also, according to Schmidt, Niedergeses sought a face-to-face meeting with Bonnyman and on two different occasions the bishop offered to travel to Knoxville and meet with the coal operator after a Sunday eucharist. The meeting never took place and the bishop indicated the obstacle lay with Bonnyman. While Bonnyman did contribute to his parish and to the Campaign for Human Development and may have contributed to the Nashville diocese in the past, since Niedergeses became bishop Bonnyman did not contribute substantially to the diocese, if at all.

Cirillo and Fritsch agreed with Conroy that McDonough's and Niedergeses' offer to mediate the dispute ". . .fails to respond to the full spirit" of the Appalachian pastoral on powerlessness. Sr. Yvonne Nelson said the two episcopal signers of "This Land is Home to Me" had not ignored it, but she was not sure the issues were being addressed. Schmidt did not think the bishops indicated any determination to apply the principles of the pastoral in the Stearns situation. He allowed that there were alternatives in the manner of responding and reacting.

Insisting his stand was consistent with the pastoral, Niedergeses replied that the Blue Diamond-UMW stalement resulted from ". . . an unwillingness on both sides to have an intelligent compromise." He and McDonough were searching for ways to establish credibility with both company and union. Niedergeses stated that both he and McDonough were willing to become involved but were not able to force themselves on the parties to the controversy.

A bit earlier in November 1977, some 200 CCA members, including bishops Begley of Charlotte and Sullivan of Richmond, unanimously adopted a resolution supporting the miners and calling for a public prayer vigil on their behalf. Despite Niedergeses' and

McDonough's fear of further violence and urging a cancellation, an all-night prayer service was held the Friday before Thanksgiving. Also, on the day after Thanksgiving 150 people joined a service on the McCreary County Courthouse steps before escorting back to jail 10 miners who had been released for the holiday. There were no incidents. Although originally announced and perceived as a Catholic-sponsored event, the CORA board of directors endorsed the CCA resolution and individuals from other religious groups--including a local Baptist minister--participated in the vigil.

Like McDonough and Niedergeses, the members of the local Catholic parish of the Good Shepherd opposed the vigil. The parishioners even took out radio and newspaper advertisements to clarify their position. One parishioner and general manager of a radio station in McCreary County, Marc Beaudien, said the prayer vigil for "a peaceful settlement" was a "great" idea. However, he found everything supportive of UMW, "casting a shadow over the church." He felt that the parishioners did not think the church's responsibility was to say who was right or who was wrong. The parishioners did want to be on one side of a war pitting "brother against brother." Yet, the prayer vigil was too one-sided. Beaubien expressed the parishioners' anxiety that the predominantly Baptist community surrounding the Justus Mine would identify the Good Shepherd parish with violence and the UMW and cost the parish its gains in the county.

Conroy thought that such institutional self-interest belied the gospel spirit and that the violence had to be interpreted in light of the hidden but systematic violence the workers had endured for years. Beaubien replied that he had received telephone threats against himself and the radio station. He complained that activists like Conroy have good intentions but do not have a good grasp of the local situation. Furthermore, their actions have repercussions long after the activists are gone. Beaubien preferred that the activists seek the insights and respect the desires of local people before speaking out so freely.

Sister Marie Cirillo, chairperson of CCA, thought that the Good Shepherd did what the best of parishes would do--act from their own perspective and the realities that surround them. She complimented the parish's assistance to the immediate needs of the poor, most of whom were not miners. Such created an obvious conflict with CCA coalfield workers, who sought social change. Cirillo called for more communication between the parishes and the activists. However, she did not think increased dialogue alone would resolve the actual conflict. Beaubien, who had never seen a copy of the Appalachian Bishops' pastoral, "This Land is Home to Me," agreed that more communication was needed.

CCA members wondered what to do next. Their chairperson, Cirillo, had misgivings about the bishops, as well as the activists' excessive reliance on the influence the bishops could have brought to bear on the Stearns dispute. She admitted that CCA had no plans to follow through with the bishops, but she insisted that, while letters had been received from Niedergeses expressing his continued concern and prayers for a successful outcome, the bishops were not dialoguing with CCA in a meaningful manner. She felt that going to the bishops was the first, not the only, step for CCA and the church to take.

Schmidt and Fritsch suggested one way out of the impasse was for the miners to buy the Justus Mine. Schmidt pointed to the bishop of the Youngstown diocese, Malone, who ". . . is taking a leadership role in a campaign for some 5,000 striking steelworkers to buy their plant." Cirillo then referred to the CCA's commission from the Appalachian bishops to develop a "plan of action" for the implementation of their pastoral's principles. Although CCA had worked on the action plan for three years, it was not completed on February 24, 1978 during the Stearns controversy. Cirillo thought there were three groups in CCA. One thought that CCA's role was to tell the bishops and the church what to do. Another group thought CCA's role was to analyze and to strategize its many scattered activities. A third group thought that, if CCA had an action plan, CCA should not reveal it in its war with social injustice.

For National Catholic Reporter's Massey, the dispute would affect the future details of the action plan and CCA would have to determine to what degree the bishops and parishes should be involved in the controversial issues addressed by "This Land is Home to Me." Massey, also, thought the end of the Stearns strike was "nowhere in sight." Expecting property damage and conflicts as UMW strikers maintained and non-union miners crossed picket lines, Massey concluded his lengthy report. He surmised that the activists would continue to speak out and the parishioners would pray most fervently for the conflict to cease. Success in persuading Bonnyman and Miller or other representatives of Blue Coal and UMW to renew negotiations was not likely. "If that happens," said Massey, "the bishops will have accomplished far more than they might otherwise, had they sided with the strikers at the outset." Unlikely, also, would be the bishops' siding with the miners, given a possible, but not probable, positive response from UMW and the continued silence of Bonnyman.

In April 1978, the executive director of CCA, Sr. Shawn Scanlan, S.N.D., of Prestonburg, Kentucky, expressed appreciation for the National Catholic Reporter Massey's report on the Stearns dispute.[5] However, she expressed regret over "...the distinct impression given that the Catholic Committee of Appalachia (CCA)" was in conflict with Archbishop McDonough and Bishop Niedergeses. Scanlan did not judge the bishops' efforts to be mediators and CCA's efforts to support the miners to be at odds. She explained,

> CCA and both bishops have shared their common concern over the strike . . . and have tried to discern together the best stance to be taken. I believe as we work together for truth and justice that different bodies will discern their roles differently. This is most appropriate. This difference of perspective should not be immediately interpreted as conflict. It can reflect a common desire to be a healing force in the struggle while seeing different ways in which this can and should be done by different members of the same body.

One month later, CCA affirmed its support of the miners in Stearns.[6] The organization also severely criticized the Blue Diamond Coal Company's attempt to resume coal production by using non-union miners in the 21-month-old strike.

On May 22, 1978 there was a meeting of Archbishop McDonough and Bishop Niedergeses concerning the Stearns controversy.[7] Attempts by them to meet Bonnyman had been unsuccessful. One source said the two bishops "held open the possibility" of endorsing the strike. Another meeting of the two was scheduled for June 9, 1978 to discuss what actions they might take to end the strike. At that meeting they were to be joined by Msgr. George Higgins.

On Memorial Day 1978, Blue Diamond signed a three-year contract with the "Justus Employees Association." The 81 members of the association, who had been crossing the picket line in the course of the strike, ratified the contract by a 79-0 vote. the signing took place on the same day the company was to have met with UMW for the first time since the company-union talks broke off in January 1977. The contract with the opposing association called for a top daily wage of $74, about $20 more than what Blue Diamond told UMW they could afford to pay. In the contract there was no mention of a mine safety committee, a key demand throughout the strike. UMW attorney, Peter Mitchell, said these developments in the strike would have

> . . . no effect . . .The picket line is still up. The organizers are still there, and from our perspective, nothing has changed.

271

On July 15, 1978 some 500 people gathered for a second anniversary support rally for the Stearns miners.[8]   From as far away as San Francisco and Baltimore came representatives of steel workers, auto workers, other UMW locals, and community activists, as well as concerned supporters from neighboring communities and states.   A damp, cold day was offset in part by plentiful food, speeches of support and donations of much needed money to enable the strike to continue.   However, what drew the diverse people into a group with a sense of community was the singing of songs dating back to the "labor wars" as early as the late 19th century.   One of those was written in a coal strike in the 1920s by Florence Reese, entitled, "Which Side Are You On?"

In September 1978, Msgr. Higgins' visit to Stearns took place. It was a symbol of the efforts of McDonough, Niedergeses, and CCA to bring an end to the strike and to implement some of the principles of "This Land is Home to Me."   Although Bonnyman refused to meet with Higgins, the Catholic church labor expert thought that the strike raised the very significant and basic question about whether or not the company was violating the workers' right to select their own representatives for collective bargaining.   Higgins admitted his social justice bias that, when the majority of the workers select their own agency for collective bargaining, a company has no right to deal with any other group claiming to be the workers' representative.   It was hoped that Higgins' visit and report--expected in October 1978--would be the beginning of official church involvement in the strike, whose complex issues gained significance beyond Appalachia.

Whatever the possibilities of "official church" involvement through Higgins' report, some CCA members felt that being "neutral" was insufficient.   They felt the Blue Diamond Coal Company and UMW were not equal and church involvement might have served as an equalizer.   Some CCA members, in addition, raised the critical question of "community control" in a town, county and state where great wealth poured out of a region and nothing remained, except roads broken up by heavy coal trucks and streams polluted by run-off water from mines and colleries.   Add hillsides stripped of coal and top soil and there are great probabilities of flooding.   The whole scene only intensified the widespread poverty in the area.

The description was part of Catholic Worker Rochelle Linner's analysis of the socio-economic status of the Stearns and surrounding area.   She also noted that coal mining, despite federal health and safety regulations, through the Mine Engineering and Safety Administration (MESA), is one of the most dangerous occupations in the U.S. Linner went so far as to say, "Blue Diamond might well be one of the most dangerous coal companies to work for." She mentioned its most infamous mine complex, Scotia,

272

in Letcher County Kentucky. In the Imboden mine there, twenty-six miners were killed in two separate methane gas explosions, in March 1976. More than two years later, May 1978, Blue Diamond was charged with seventy-two counts of safety violations and fined $267,897 by MESA for the company's responsibility in the deaths. In July 1973, the U.S. Department of Labor formally issued a ban against governmental agencies buying Blue Diamond Coal. The reason was Blue Diamond's violations of the 1969 Coal Mine Health and Safety Act were so numerous and recidivist in nature. Linner also thought mine safety would become an even more serious issue if the price of coal increased dramatically, as then expected in light of Carter's call to double coal production. Linner feared the multiplication of small one-seam coal mine companies--the "Mom and Pop" setups of the coal industry. With the expected disregard of mine safety in such a phenomenon, the UMW-Blue Diamond controversy would take on national importance.

Even though safety conditions became the major issue initially in July 1976 in the UMW strike against at Stearns' Justus Mine, eventually the issue of violence became more important. Until October 1977 there was an uneasy truce as the company legally challenged the August 1976 NLRB certification of UMW as the bargaining agent and refused to sign the national contract in March 1977. On October 17, 1977, there was a violent clash between riot-equipped and heavily-armed State Police and 150 pickets at the Justus Mine as protest against the introduction of non-union miners. One observer was quoted in the Mountain Eagle, "I've been to civil rights demonstrations and and marches on Washington, and I've seen a lot, but I've never seen guys beaten by police with such relish." On April 20, 1978, one of the strike-breakers, Donald Watson, was shot and killed as he left the Justus Mine. As of September 1978 no arrests had been made in the case. Yet, physical violence in the dispute received much attention.

For Linner the ignoring of the "quiet" violence of deeply-rooted systemic injustice would lead to conditions in which passions would erupt. Linner contrasted the "great wealth" of McCready County's natural resources with its listing as one of the poorest counties in Kentucky. The Strike at the Blue Diamond Justus Mine--the largest employer in the county--had devasting economic, psychological and social fallout. Striking miners' average income had dropped from $50 per day to $100 per week. That minimal amount came from the UMW strike fund. With most of the families refusing food stamps, the two-year period of reduced spending ability had a ripple effect on the economy of the whole area. Linner continued,

More tragic though, has been the psychological effect of not working. A psychiatrist in the area remarked, "Men are coming to me because they have a need to work. Men who are used to working all their lives get very depressed when they don't go to work."
The town of Stearns has been divided by the question, "which side are you on?"--between striking miners, those miners who have gone back to work, and the local management of Blue Diamond. There has been extensive property damage. Most seriously. . . intimidation and fear are the predominant moods in the town. Marriages have been destroyed because of the pressure of the strike. Young children are placed on tranquilizers by local physicians to help control their fear. Schools, churches, friendships--all have been affected.

Furthermore, in Linner's estimation there was the impact of existing legislation. Because the Blue Diamond was a private company and not obligated to file with the Securities Exchange Commission, exact financial figures on the company were not known. Under existing NLRB provisions, Blue Diamond could agree to a May 1978 call by federal mediators to resume negotiations, announce the formation of a rival "company union," and not be called to hearings until the winter of 1978. Such facilitated Bonnyman's anti-union sentiments as expressed in the McCreary County newspaper's editorial,

Some observers have speculated that Gordon Bonnyman ... would rather close his mine than let the UMW get a foothold in his company. Bonnyman realizes that a union victory would more than likely mean unionization of his other mines--including Leatherwood and infamous Scotia.

Yet, despite the safety hazards, violence, and even regrets that ". . . unions have metamorphosized into conservative, impersonal institutions, often in seeming collusion with big business," Linner called on readers to support the UMW cause in Stearns. She reminded readers of one of the "tragedies of contemporary radicalism"--ignorance of the sacrifice, courage, commitment and idealism that were the hallmarks of the struggle for unionism. She viewed that struggle as one against, not only corporate business, but also its natural ally, government. She conceded that Stearns was a "test case" for UMW, that there was internal UMW dissension, and that there was little "special recognition" given to the unique Stearns situation during the coal strike. Nevertheless, she noted that massive and consistent amounts of UMW money made the Stearns strike's continuance possible. Linner stressed the miners' choice to become a UMW local, to work under a UMW national contract, and to persevere for 26 months on the picket line.

However, by early May 1979--three and one-half years after it began--the Stearns Justus Mine strike ended.[9] The national UMW headquarters agreed to a formula, which allowed all of the Justus Employees' Association to vote as members of the bargaining unit, but only 60 of 123 striking miners to participate. The vote was 110 to 0 against the UMW in the federally supervised election. The national UMW president, Arnold Miller, accepted the results by telegram before a regional NLRB panel had the opportunity to certify the election. In a meeting, a week or so later, the strikers voted to appeal the election decision and to file suit charging that their civil rights were violated by the company, State Troopers, mine security guards and the courts. Glenmary Father, Gerald Conroy, quite upset, said,

> The union was hell-bent to get out of Stearns, and the way they did it was to go through this legal charade . . .The men are saying that the union leadership has sold them out . . .

> Miller deep-sixed a group of men who had shown phenomenal solidarity for three-and-a -half years . . .

> One of the reasons local bishops and nationa church groups failed to respond any better was their awareness of the chaos in the union leadership. They didn't want to get themselves in a situation that wasn't likely to produce positive results.

Conroy, also, complained about a telegram which Miller sent the day after the election to the 123 out of the 126 original miners, still on the ticket roster and which cut off their $100 per week strike benefits. The cutoff, Conroy charged, was " . . .clearly a retaliation, because it is standard union policy to give miners a grace period of three to six weeks before stopping the checks."

In September 1979, three Catholic groups and eleven other activist organizations and individuals planned to promote reforms in Blue Diamond's labor, environmental and mine health-safety

practices.[10]   The groups   attempted to   do so   as   Blue Diamond
Company   stockholders.   The three   religious groups were: the
Jesuit   Appalachian   Ministry   of   Griffthsville,   West   Virginia,
which bought one company share in over-the counter sales   in late
1978,   and Kentucky-based   Sisters of Loretto   and Michigan-based
Sister-Servants of the Immaculate Heart of Mary who owned most of
158 shares of Blue Diamond stock.

However, the Catholic groups and the others had to file suit
against the company, charging it had refused to recognize them as
stockholders.   The lawsuit was filed in Delaware where   the Blue
Diamond   Company   was   incorporated   and alleged   that   the   firm
refused to register the stock in the owner's name.   Although company spokespeople declined comment, Loretto Sister   Marian McAvoy
vigorously denied an earlier Blue Diamond claim that   the Sisters
of Loretto continued," . . . a pattern of harassment initiated by
the   United Mine Workers."   The sisters   were indirectly charged
with   threats   and violence   against company   officials   and non-
striking workers.

D. Jericol Strike

In   May 1979 miners   were   on   strike   in   Harlan   County,
Kentucky, against the Jericol Mine.[11] Also in the same month, 15
Benedictine monks from Weston Priory in Vermont were   involved in
their annual retreat.   Part of the retreat included a trip   with
Glenmary Father,   Gerald   Conroy,   and   a School   Sister   of   St.
Francis,   Joanne   Klas--both   experienced worker advocates   in the
Appalachian coal region.   The group visited Kentucky craftspeople
and friendship   centers, sang and played with   Tennessee mountain
musicians and prayed at   a burnt-out shack used by   pickets until
they lost their fight   against the   Blue Diamond Coal   Company in
Stearns, Kentucky.

The   group also   planned   to visit   the picket   line   at the
Jericol Mine.   As the group approached, uniformed state police in
four   squad cars appeared.   According to   Conroy, this SWAT team
demanded their names and reasons for being near the   picket line.
The group was asked to move down the road because a court injunction   limited pickets to 20 people.   The monks   were followed by
the police and not allowed private conversations with the miners.
Conroy said   "...we told   them   there is   not a   single   miner or
striker in our group."   Klas, who   lived in nearby Williamsburg,
said, "The cops   were threatened   because we were   supporting the
people's   right to strike."   When one   of the group's three cars
was   slow to   move   away, an   officer   beckoned   to   Brother Elias

across the road to a squad car. The officer requested more identification and said, "The first two times we ask you nicely,
the third time it may not be so gentle." Police followed the
group's cars a quarter of a mile from the picket site and took
everyone's name. When one officer was asked why this was necessary, he replied, "I don't know why; I was told to get your
names." Then a "Giant pillbox" on wheels with sheet metal sides
and weapons slots parked near the group.

One of the monks, Brother Philip, said, "It was bizarre,
like something out of "Star Wars." Said Conroy, "We couldn't
believe our presence would be treated in such a repressive
manner." Conroy also explained that the armed vehicle remained,
as a police-escorted convoy of school buses left the mine. These
buses, with blacked-out windows, carried the "scabs" working the
UMW-struck Jericol Mine. Another of the Benedictine monks,
Brother John, said, "We didn't go as judges, we were there to
stand with some people who were powerless." When the convoy of
buses and squad cars left, the group went to the pickets and sang
and prayed with them. One of the pickets told the group, "You
were treated just like the strikers, like criminals."

[1]John Barry, "Strike in Harlan County: Churchmen Support
Kentucky Coal Miners, National Catholic Reporter, v. 10, No. 38,
8/30/74, p. 16.

[2]Jason Petosa, "Strike Will Show King Coal's Clout,"
National Catholic Reporter, v. 14, No. 8, 12/9/77, pp. 1,3.

[3]"Coal Miners' Needs Elicit Scattered Church Efforts," National Catholic Reporter, v. 14, No. 22, 3/24/78, p. 16.

[4]David D. Massey, "So You're Catholic. Which Side Are You
On?" National Catholic Reporter, v. 14, No. 18, 2/24/78, pp. 7-
11.

[5]"Catholic Mine," Repartee, National Catholic Reporter, v.
14, No. 26, 4/14/78, p. 17.

[6]"The Catholic Committee," News Cue, National Catholic
Reporter, v. 14, No. 26, 4/14/78, p. 17.

[7]David D. Massey, "Bishops Weight Stearns Strike Endorsement," National Catholic Reporter, v. 14, No. 33, 6/18/78, p. 2.

[8]Rochelle Linner, "Which Side Are You On?" "Catholic
Worker, v. 44, 10/11/78, pp. 1,3,4.

[9]David D. Massey, "Strikers Lose Stearns Fight," National Catholic Reporter, v. 15, No. 32, 6/1/79, pp. 1-8.

[10]David D. Massey, "Religious Groups Help Challenge Coal Firm," National Catholic Reporter, v. 15, No. 42, 9/28/79, p. 6.

[11]Pam Bauer, "Monks Meet Miners, Police Show Force," National Catholic Reporter, v. 15, No. 32, 6/1/79, p. 20.

Chapter VII - Steel Workers and Others

A. Youngstown Pastoral Council

More than five years before the creation of the widely publicized "Youngstown Coalition" on behalf of steelworkers, the
Youngstown Diocesan Pastoral Council issued a statement entitled,
"Peace: A Challenging Priority."[1] Issued on Good Friday 1973
and nine-months in the making, the paper called the main elements
of gospel's radical ethic--"solidarity, simplicity and sharing."
In challenging Christians to translate peace "from an abstract
ideal to a concrete reality," the document called them to accept
the fact that injustice in the world is a grave problem and that
the U.S. is part of the problem, to develop convictions consistent with basic Christian tenets, to resolve conflicts without
violence, to have a lifestyle marked by simplicity, to develop
the gentleness and tenderness modeled on Christ, to have a deep
reverence for life and a profound respect for every person, and
to feel a sense of solidarity and share any abundance with all
humanity.

There were some more specific steps asked. Catholics in all
areas of life should be more concerned with government action
having international implications and more conscious of the need
to build justice in corporate policies. The laity was asked to
establish peace in the home and family life, respect for women,
mutual respect between employers and employees, and continued
efforts for racial and ethnic understanding and harmony. Priests
were called on to be more active in preaching and teaching about
peace, to help develop parish and institutional programs on
peace, and to examine their personal lifestyles. Religious communities were asked to promtote peace within their own religious
houses, to witness to peace by making a public commitment in
behalf of just causes, and to open their doors to those who "need
a place of security, love and warmth." There was a challenge to
employees of international corporations to know the impact their
companies' policies would have on foreign nations and to make
those policies beneficial to the people of other nations. The
statement urged union members to be sure that the needs of the
rank-and-file are known to management and to be conscious of
international trade arrangements and the impact they have elsewhere.

The pastoral council's statement was inclusive enough to
have continuing and universal application to many groups. However, its call to international corporations, union members and
priests assumed a poignancy in 1977 when the Youngstown Steel and

279

Tube Company announced it was all but closing down its Campbell Works on the Mahoning River.[2] Such a move would affect some 12 percent of steel industry employment in the area that called itself "Steel Valley." The bishop of the Youngstown diocese, James Malone, noted that the diocese was intricately involved in the Western Reserve Economic Development Agency (WREDA), a group that attempted to retain the existing industry and to develop new industry in the area. One of the diocesan priests, Rev. Edward Stanton, was a board member of WREDA. He said its officials met in late September, 1977 with U.S. Commerce Department representatives, seeking solutions to the "Steel Valley's" economic problems. WREDA, along with Ohio Governor, James Rhodes, and United Steelworkers leadership, called for measures to curtail imports and ease anti-pollution guidelines.

B. Youngstown Interfaith Coalition

1977

Also, in late September, 1977, Malone and John Burt, bishop of the Episcopal Diocese of Ohio, held a meeting of local religious leaders to seek development for families of the 5,000 steelworkers who were unemployed already. The religious leaders sought answers as pay checks ended, the tax base dwindled, and the unemployed migrated elsewhere. Like the local politicians and business leaders, the religious leaders were unable to devise specific programs to counter a crisis that reflected, in part, serious trouble because of outdated mills, foreign competition and the continuing sluggishness in the world economy. Although the U.S. Labor Department ruled in late September that the laid-off Youngstown workers were eligible for extra unemployment benefits, due to the impact of steel imports, Bishop Malone was guarded, "What's possible for us to do as an ecumenical community remains to be seen."

Malone was known to know the difference between real power and powerful appearances because of one's physique or material trappings.[3] He was said to have a quiet assurance, to be soft-spoken and to administer with an iron will. In addition to being chosen as a member of the five-man executive committee of the NCCB, Malone stood behind his priests who marched at Selma and against the Vietnam War. Despite, perhaps because of, surviving cancer, Malone was ahead of most people in most social causes. Maybe it was because people sought his support and he responded to them. That exactly what he did when Episcopal bishop, John Burt, whose Cleveland diocese included Youngstown, called Malone. The two convened, with other religious leaders, a series of meetings.

Malone explained that some 250 ministers, priests and rabbis banded together because the people they saw in the churches and synagogues were hurting. This broad-based religious coalition wanted to establish a corporation to reopen the mill. Such a corporation would have several goals. First, retain the 5,500 jobs threatened by the announcement of the closing of the Campbell workers. Second, there would be community ownership from the "earnest money" put up by the workers and thousands of other citizens. Third, the corporation would be a showcase for federal efforts to revitalize the steel industry and to prevent the economic and social demise of the Northern states. Fourth, local areas would have greater control of their economic futures. Fifth, local areas would have a model with which to battle companies attempting to discard local plants and workers. Sixth, allow the local interfaith leaders to return fulltime to their regular ministry.

In planning for such a corporation the Youngstown Religious Coalition was quite cognizant of what created the Youngstown closing. Youngstown Sheet and Tube (S & T), established in 1902, produced a high quality product at copetitive prices, was well liked by customers, made a six to eight percent return on sales--a respectable profit margin in the steel industry, had good working capital, was rich in ore and coal, and slowly was modernizing its antiquated facilities. In the 1960's, when steel companies were takeover targets for conglomerate builders, Youngstown Sheet and Tool was not alert to a New Orleans Company, the Lykes Corporation, which had acquired a large block of S & T common stock. "Takeover, like merger," said NCR's Petosa and Winiarski, "is often a polite business expression of corporate rape," for Lykes was a smaller company on the make. Although its assets of $137 million were considerably less than S & T's $806 million, Lykes wanted S & T's $100 million annual cash flow. Lykes got it, despite a Justice Department report that denounced the merger.

In order to buy S & T, Lykes went heavily into debt. S & T's annual cash flow was used to pay that debt and interest, as well as to expand into other business. Hence, as a United Steel Workers of America brief filed with the Justice Department documented, Lykes' financial ventures left it without money to continue modernizing S & T's facilities. The deterioration of equipment and worker morale proved disastrous in the cyclical steel industry, where companies have to do well during boom years to carry them through the lean years. An analysis by the Ohio Public Industry Campaign stated that had Lykes not taken over S & T, the latter would have had enough money to continued modernizing its facilities, despite low profits in 1970-1973.

Lykes had no commitment to the areas, plants or workers. They were all expendable, except to increase profits.

Lykes became expendable to some major banks which had financed the takeover. By 1975 they tightened Lykes' credit and took their money elsehwere--to the Japanese steel industry. Having lost its ambitious gamble with S & T, Lykes had to cut its self-inflicted losses. On September 19, 1977, there was an announcement that part of the Campbell and Brier Hill works at Youngstown would be closed, as unprofitable. To cover up its own mismangement, Lykes blamed everyone but itself and its bankers. At closing time, S & T's president, Jennings R. Lambeth, blamed the loss of 5,000 jobs on low-priced foreign steel, steel in imported products and the government's failure "to react."

React and act, however, the Youngstown Relgious Coalition did. It reached beyond Youngstown to Washington, D.C.'s Institute of Policy Studies, a "consultation" of economic and political experts organized by Dr. Richard Barnet. One of the experts, Dr. Gar Alperovitz of its Exploratory Project on Economic Alternatives, met with a Youngstown delegation: Stanton, Rev. Charles Rawlings, an aide to Burt who made the contact, and Gerald Dickey, a steelworker who edited the newspaper for USWA LocaL 1462 at S & T's Brier Hill works. Dickey suggested community/worker ownership of the closed plant and the idea hit home with Alperovitz, who since 1972 had been working to develop pratical alternatives to the U.S. troubled economic system.

Called by some a "radical economist," Alperovitz did not like the label. Expressing his interest in institutional change and distate for micro-economic analysis. Alperovitz made it clear that, while he shared a lot of sympathies with Marxists, he was not one himself. In 1977, Alperovitz was backed by the heads of the House and Senate banking committees for a place on Carter's Council of Economic Advisers. Even though he did not get Carter's nod, Alperovitz did win the religious leaders' confidence.

The Washington meeting was followed by an October 9 memorandum. In it, Alperovitz stated that virtually he saw only the moral and political issues as significant. He saw little hope of significant action, in the absence of a powerful organization of the local and national relgious and community interest groups. His plan was to start with a "powerful local commitment" which would include a fund raising campaign to "Save Our Community," to stir up national religious involvement and to initiate a national campaign to communicate how unjust the destruction of the Youngstown community was. The message would be for Youngstown and the nation. Such should "fire the imagination of young people, the religious community, the media" for economic justice in the 1970's and the 1980's. Hopefully, the religious leaders in Youngstown would be stirred up with the fire of the 1960's crusade for racial justice.

On October 29, 1977, the religious leaders held a Steel Crisis Conference and decided to take four steps. First, a pastoral letter would be issued. Its purposes would be to lay out the moral and ethical issues and to focus national attention on Youngstown. Second, there would be two studies. An economic feasibility study on the reopening of the Campbell works was to be joined with a study on the possibilities of worker-community ownership. Third, the religious leaders would become involved in advocacy of a national policy to stop the flight of runaway plants from the Northern states. Fourth, there would be the formation of an inter-faith religious coalition.

An executive committee of the coalition was also established: Malone as chairperson, Burt, Rabbi Sidney Berkowitz, Methodist Bishp James S. Thomas of Canton, Rev. William Laurie of the United Church of Christ's Ohio Conference and Rev. John Sharick, the Presbyterian church's area executive. Each member of the coalition's executive commitee put $10,000 on the table. Malone also invested Stanton, who was released from his post as diocesan Social Action director, in order to work full time as the coalition's treasurer. As this "bunch of preachers," as Stanton called the coalition, got its act together, they prepared for a show down with the Youngstown "decision-makers." The latter included Lykes-S & T spokespeople, the Chamber of Commerce, steel companies, utilities, banks, and local politicians--who did not sound much different from the others lamenting the situation.

During November and December 1977, as professional studies were being conducted to test the coalition's ideas, the religious leaders were busy becoming more acquainted with and ministering to the needs of Youngstown people affected by the closing of S & T. Malone emphasized the wounds to the dignity of individual workers and their families which required a religious response. While affirming the plan--reopening the mill and pursuing corporate accountability--Malone referred to the declaration of the 1971 Roman Synod of Bishops: " . . . working for justice is a constitutive part of preaching the gospel." Malone, however, was quite conscious of ". . . the frustration that so little could be done to fashion a path out of the wilderness." Describing Youngstown as a community of ethnic people for whom close family ties and neighborhood living meant a lot and noting that Youngstown had more ethnic-centered churches per capita than any other U.S. city, Malone underlined that the fabric of family and cultural life would be ripped apart without jobs.

283

Episcopal priest Rawlings felt the religious leaders' answer was significant. For, there was a real interfaith coalition, presently at the leadership level. The lower leadership level was experiencing the ambivalence in the parishes and synagogues, where people were nervous over breaking new ground. A Lutheran pastor, Charles Lundquist, commented on the psycho-physical effects of the plant closings: hypertension, ulcers, alcoholism, and heart attacks. Lundquist appreciated the coalition's challenging everyone to think beyond the immediate problems of families and parishes. People were working together and getting to know and trust each other. Yet, some of the clergy were revealed for what they were--cowards afraid to stick their necks out. Some of the local religious leaders blamed the workers for bringing hardships on themselves, by demands for higher wages and provisions of less productivity. Some even thought the separation pay from S & T and federal relief money was quite a boon to the people and the area.

However, preliminary estimates of the Youngstown Planning Commission predicted that the closing's ripple effect ultimately would cost the Youngstown area 18,000 jobs, $146 million in retail sales, and eight percent of the population of the area. The little community of Campbell was hit the hardest. It expected to lose 80 percent of its revenue from income and property taxes. Such a loss would devastate its school system. According to its mayor, Michael J. Katula, the decision for most of the people--especially the young--was to stay and find a job or to relocate. A retired maintenance superintendent for a nearby U.S. Steel mill would tell his sons to move to Texas or New Jersey or to forget it--if they ever asked about being steel workers. Some families were stuck with large mortgage and auto payments. When asked about the coalition, Howard Broll, who had 30 years with S & T, said, "They're the only ones willing to do anything." John Zackasee, 27 years with S & T replied, "Right now there ain't nobody else to turn to."

On November 21, 1977, Rev. William Hogan, S.J., of Fordham University's Industrial Economics Research Institute published a study for a group of cities, including Youngstown, with troubled steel plants. Hogan, often consulted by the steel industry and the government had visited virtually every major steel mill in the free world. Hogan estimated that the building of a new plant's annual production capacity could exceed $1,000 per ton, the expansion at existing plants could be accomplished at $400 per ton. In terms of national and local economic development, Hogan thought the nations' most disadvantaged steel plants were valuable assets, indeed essential, in providing for the nation's future steel needs. He also described the existing plants--even the closed ones--as the keystone of many local economies.

Hogan's study also indicated rather widespread firings across the U.S.--nearly 22,000 during the first nine months of 1977. Two weeks later, on December 6, 1977, Hogan's ideas appeared in the report of President Carter's Interagency, Steel Task Force. Its chairperson and Under-secretary of the Treasury, Anthony Solomon, had met with the Youngstown Religious Coalition. In recommending that projects like the coalition's be funded, the Task Force's report to the president said

> We believe . . . community and/or worker takeover may prove to be realistic and economically viable if . . . accompanied by sufficient modernization.

As federal money appeared forthcoming and a moral crusade was forming, the coalition's first study was completed. On December 16, 1977, its author, George Beetle, a Philadelphia engineer, acknowledged that he was not able to investigate thoroughly enough prior to the time a firm decision had to be made whether or not to reopen the mill. If short term problems could be solved, the long term prospects would be good. However, by 1981 replacement facilities had to be built as the existing facilities were no longer usable. The serious difficulties to be overcome in the short term were: a good price for the closed plant, the replacement of primary facilities, low operating costs after production, and markets that would buy the plant's products at decent prices. The grand total of costs was estimated at $535 million, with 40 percent available in the first two years. The costs breakdown were as follows: buying from Lykes and restarting production in stages--$120 million; renewing the plant, over and above maintenance--$65 million; improving the company's product image, now badly deteriorated, through new equipment and quality controls--$30 million; cost reduction improvements--$40 million; replacement of major facilities, including coke plant and blast furnaces--$160 million; environmental protection measures--$40 million. However, listed as an "essential requirement" by Bettle's study was a back-breaker. Operations had to resume in nine months or lose a position in the steel marketplace.

The "preachers" realized what they were up against: create a corporation, secure management, arrange supplies of raw materials, establish financial relationship to support the one-half billion dollar investment--all in nine months. The "preachers" were undaunted. The scene was set with a tough pastoral letter in December 1977, to clarify the moral issues and to list specific sins in the steel industry along with "chicanery." The pastoral was much more than a clarion call. Malone had asked John Carr, former USCC urban affairs coordinator, to assist in drafting the pastoral. Carr said, "They were angry and they showed it." He was amazed what the coalition members did to his initial draft. Unlike the usual religious documents, the pastoral of the Youngstown Religious Coalition spoke in specifics, not in generalities.

Stating plainly that the Youngstown Crisis ". . . is not in any sense a purely economic problem," the pastoral stressed the crisis reached beyond the Mahoning or "Steel" Valley, to "other cities across the nation." The problems of the steel industry were acknowledged. There was the workers'

> . . . excessive concern with higher and higher wages and better and better fringe benefits. Perhaps production costs have been raised by the failure of railroads to overcome their jurisdictional and territorial conflicts as well as work regulations which make efficient . . . transportation of steel and raw materials impossible. Nationally the failure to formulate a comprehensive national policy to retain and support the manufacture of basic steel is a serious failing. . . . Internationally, the willingness of some foreign steel producers to "dump" steel at below market prices into the U.S. has contributed to our difficulties.

Although, the coalition was not sidetracked "on a search for scapegoats," Lykes and other steel companies did not escape guilt in the coalition's pastoral,

> We were disturbed by the Lykes Corporation's attempt to focus responsibility for their action upon environmental laws, imported steel and governmental efforts to keep down the cost of steel. While these factors may have contributed to this decision, it is worth noting that the amount of steel imported into the U.S. has remained relatively constant for the past 10 years.

> We also understand that industry expenditures on pollution abatement equipment as a percentage of total capital expenditures has remained relatively constant over the past five years and that steel prices have risen more rapidly than the consumer price index.

The Youngstown pastoral set down moral priorities--
". . . human beings and community life are higher values than
corporate profits"--and ethical guidelines. The priorities and
guidelines were the ground rules for corporate decision makers:
communitarianism, rather than full fledged socialism. Corporations must take into account the effects their decisions have on
local communities. Otherwise, corporations must reckon with the
community's wrath. Several reasons were provided for steel
companies closing plants. Among them was,

> . . . a strategy of concentration and reduc-
> ing productive capacity in order to take full
> economic advantage of steel needs in the
> future and make the industry more profitable.

Such was no longer excusable. Industrial investment decisions,
the pastoral proclaimed,

> . . . ought to take into account the needs
> and desires of employees and the community at
> large. In its refusal to invest in new
> equipment or necessary maintenance, the Lykes
> Corporation failed to do this. . . [The]
> economic decisions ought not to be left to
> the judgment of a few persons with economic
> power, but should be shared with the larger
> community which is affected by the decisions.
> In the suddenness, the totality and the
> secrecy of this decision (to close its
> plant), the Lykes' Corporation ignored this
> principle. Corporations have a social
> responsibility to their employees and to the
> community, as well as . . . to shareholders.

The pastoral also drew the battle lines with other steel companies. They were asked,

> . . . to pledge publicly, community and
> employee consultation in future economic and
> investment decisions affecting employment and
> community life. The failure of Lykes to
> share its problems and options with the com-
> munity and its abrupt decision to shut down
> cannot be repeated.

With the pastoral publicized, the Youngstown Religious
Coalition struck up specific steps directed at specific targets.
First, the coalition struck the "Steel Valley" and the nation
with a "Save Our Valley Campaign." The coalition persuaded local
banks to set up savings accounts into which people could put no-

risk "earnest money." Such money signalled the community's willingness to support a corporation which would re-open the steel
mill and put the jobless back to work. Malone and Stanton
spelled out the two-fold strategy. Bishop Malone would look for
federal assistance to the extent that the area could demonstrate
that it was special. Father Stanton said that the coalition
sought help from national denominations, religious congregations
and orders, and such particularized organizations as the NCCB
Campaign for Human Development.

The School Sisters of Notre Dame joined the coalition's
crusade by filing a stockholder resolution to pressure the Lykes
Company into cooperating with the coalition's plan to re-open the
mill. The religious community owned 7,000 shares of Lykes stock.
The Presbyterians were supposed to devote 10 percent of their
national stock portfolio to high-risk people-oriented projects,
such as the Youngstown Religious Coalition's proposed worker/com-
munity owned corporation. By late April 1978, the coalition
would appeal to 40 officials of religious groups in New York.
Responses would come from several groups. The Presbyterian Board
of Pension would provide $200,000. A nationally known Presby-
terian clergyman would say, "This is the beginning, not the end
of our support." There was speculation that the Presbyterians'
financial leadership would extend to an additional $500,000
later. The Methodists' National and Women's Divisions of their
Board of Ministries would pledge. The Episcopalians gave $60,000
and New York's Riverside Church would contribute $100,000. The
coalition's public information director, John Greenman, would
expect ten or fifteen other denominations to respond to the
appeal once they were contacted by the coalition.

Second, the coalition struck Lykes' planned merged with LTV
(owners of Jones and Laughlin Steel Company) by filing anti-trust
charges. In November 1977, the coalition authorized its legal
counsel to discuss with the Justice Department its opposition, in
a desire for restitution. Serious atonement by Lykes would
reduce a large amount of the $535 million needed for a Youngstown
worker/community. By January 23, 1978, the United Steel Workers
of America (USWA) officials were to meet with the government's
legal arm to express its concern about the Lykes merger with the
Dallas-based LTV. Both the coalition and USWA would argue that
the merger could lead to further shutdowns in Youngstown and
elsewhere. In the first quarter of 1978, LTV was to lose $20
million, with 60 percent of the red ink coming from its Jones and
Laughlin Steel Company. Business Week was referred to about a
grand scheme to make one company out of two of the weakest
companies in the steel industry. It depended upon the elimination of duplication, waste and inefficiency. Lykes would
acquiesce to the pastoral's request for minimal maintenance of
the closed mill until efforts to re-open it were completed.

However, Lykes was to balk in 1978, when the coalition pressed the company to sell all its facilities in the Youngstown area. Such included a seamless tube plant, reportedly the second most profitable operation of its kind in the U.S. Owning that plant would make the community/worker owned corporation much more financially viable. Yet, Lykes would agree to provide financial data to an analyst advising the coalition. Paul Marshall of Putnam, Hayes and Bartlett of Newton, Mass., would advise on an equitable sale and other things necessary for the new corporation. When Stanton was asked if the coalition's opposition to the proposed merger forced Lykes into a reluctant cooperation, he would respond, "It's certainly made them take us more seriously." Another coalition member would say that Lykes asked for the delay because they were afraid of losing their case. Lykes would return with an offer more acceptable to the coalition.

Third, the coalition struck an accord with USWA. In November 1977, informal meetings began between coalition and union leaders. In December 1977, there was a formal meeting of coalition people with the USWA district and local leadership, in order to develop a consensus on appropriate action steps proposed by the coalition's background papers. Stanton's rapport with Youngstown unions, frequent mediation of labor-management disputes, and negotiation of contracts with the lay teachers in the diocesan schools, according to one source, made him a person to be trusted by both sides. Such a person was rare in Youngstown, especially for the unions.

The meetings went well. Area union leaders assured the coalition that rank and file members would eliminate much of the goldbricking and theft that occurred in the steel mills. Worker productivity would increase by at least 15 percent, according to Alperovitz. There would also be several million dollars available in "earnest money" from the USWA--maybe as much as $1,000 per worker. Stanton noted that USWA would support a community/ worker owned corporation, but would maintain its traditional bargaining role and not be part of ownership. James Smith, assistant to the president of USWA, explained, that by law the union was not able to invest in any business with which the union bargained or which competed with other firms with which the union bargained. Nevertheless, as a large, powerful and rich union, USWA knew how to lobby in Washington. Its Youngstown district had been especially helpful to the coalition's interventions with the Justice Department over the proposed merger of Lykes and LTV.

Fourth, the coalition struck a posture of political neutrality, thereby neutralizing and extracting cooperation from the local and national politicians. Initially, in Youngstown the

289

"preachers" called the shots and the "decision-makers" went along. One well placed local official said of the decision-makers, "They're afraid they'll look bad if they don't cooperate." Rev. Richard Fernandez, a United Church of Christ minister, hired by the coalition for community organization, said, "We have the only boat in the river." Stanton quoted from the pastoral to show that the coalition generated public confidence because people believed its boat would not be pirated,

> We in the religious community attempt to respond to this crisis with no vested interests or hidden concerns other than the welfare of our community. It is our intention to provide a common ground and impetus for community efforts. . .

> We do not wish to take the place of leaders of industry, union leaders, business representatives and government officials.

Malone, also, tried to put the coalition's role in perspective. The coalition existed only because there was no investor available yet to buy the mill and put 5,000 people back to work. The coalition, far from being a savior, would go out of existence once such an investor appeared. Another religious leader noted that effective social action or participatory democracy required exactly what the coalition had in its local groupings--an existing network of neighborhood centers.

Nonetheless, such statements of Malone and others did not ease the frustration of Youngstown's new mayor, Phillip Richley. He seemed impatient with the coalition and like other "decision-makers" did not seem to think the coalition could pull it off-- given who they were and what they attempted. To their efforts he said "God bless them," as he proceeded to tick off the politicians to reach Washington for help. Richley indicated the tasks of persuading the General Services Administration to send in procurement grants, obtaining Title 9 Economic Development Administration funds for steel-impacted towns, and getting disaster units. However, Richley also complained, "We're not getting a hell of a lot of help. We're getting meetings."

Backing from the federal government was the coalition's fifth target. On December 20, 1977, a contingent from Youngstown met in Washington with officials of the Commerce Department and the Housing and Urban Development Department. In addition to Malone, Stanton, Alperovitz and WREDA's president Walter Sullivan, in attendance were Richley, Democratic Congressman Charles Carney, and Charles W. Minshall of the Batelle Institute in Columbus who was preparing a study for Carney's committee of

290

"decision-makers." HUD had $300,000 to fund a study of the Youngstown situation but only if the Youngstown contingent presented a united front. It was federal pump-primer and showdown time. If the HUD-sponsored study showed re-opening of the mill would be feasible, then a well-spring of federal funding could come with its implementation. Would the "decision-makers" or the "preachers" control the HUD grant?

On December 21, 1977, the Youngstown contingent met in Carney's Washington office, with Malone presiding. Malone stated the coalition's case briefly. Carney spoke for half an hour in the "decision-makers" behalf. When he finished, soft-spoken and iron-willed Malone said, "Gentlemen, as I was saying. . . " Although the conclusion of the meeting was a compromise of sorts, the coalition would handle the grant. The money would be gotten by the coalition from Alperovitz' Center for Economic Alternatives. Under the direction of the coalition, the center would manage the planning process. While the existing group of decision-makers, The Mahoning Valley Economic Development Committee (MVEDC), would focus on attracting new industry and converting abandoned facilities to other uses in Youngstown. However, MVEDC also would review, suggest, and advise with regard to the coordination with other studies. MVEDC also would give support in the organization of whatever implementary steps were appropriate. Concurring in the agreement were Ohio's U.S. senators, Howard Metzenbaum and John Glenn, along with the USWA's district president, Frank Leseganich. On December 30, 1977, HUD approved the grant.

True, the federal government would continue to invest in Youngstown by unemployment insurance, welfare premiums and disaster relief programs. However, high-level Carter administration officials preferred to support a self-help plan that would save productive skilled jobs and the community's tax base as the coalition's background papers had already stated. HUD Undersecretary, Jay Janis, told Alperovitz that HUD would like the Youngstown project to be a showcase of self-help and community involvement. An example for the rest of the nation! As the director of the feasibility study, Alperovitz noted that HUD had commissioned his study as a test of the realism of concepts of worker-community ownership as a solution to some urban problems, not as a response to the steel crisis.

The coalition's strategy was to ask the federal government for grants, loans, and loan guarantees, in order to make up the difference in the $535 million from the goals of the "Save Our Valley" campaign. That goal was between $11 million to $18 million. In its first three months, the campaign raised approximately $1.7 million in some 1,700 local accounts. Yet, WREDA's Sullivan did not believe the federal government would give enough for the coalition's plan to succeed. He noted that the biggest stock of dollars--$300 million--was for renewing a source of hot metal pig iron and steel. Sullivan thought that viability would be more likely if there was another option to retooling--blast open or basic oxygen furnaces.

Coincidentally, Hogan, S.J., of Fordham was in the process of studying for WREDA, with sponsorship of five area steel companies (including S & T), the feasibility of a joint-venture hot metal facility. In the report to President Carter, Solomon's task force advocated such joint ventures. Both Sullivan and Stanton saw Youngstown caught in the steel industry's ongoing "strategy of concentration," as expressed in the pastoral. The companies were trimming marginal operations--their capacity for steel-making--to prepare for an expected high demand for steel in the early 1980's. The concentration had diminished already the nation's steel-making capacity by three percent. In his study, Hogan said such concentration was detrimental to the national interest.

The coalition's sixth target was the other steel companies, as well as Lykes. Although they had not spoken for or against the plan of the Youngstown Religious Coalition, they sought Washington's assistance in modernizing their plants, combating foreign compeition, and easing pollution standards. They did so, even though since the late 1940's, few U.S. companies invested enough money to make their facilities competitive with Japanese and German mills built since World War II.

For example, in 1977 the U.S. Steel's Pittsburgh plants violated pollution standards. Edgard Speer, its chairperson, put ads in the newspapers with thinly veiled threats to close the plants, if the pollution restrictions were not loosened. Eventually, a compromise was reached. When the coalition's pastoral called for community consultation prior to any further plant closings, Speer told a reporter that he would not spend more money to keep U.S. Steel's Youngstown mills going. U.S. Steel tried to back step from Speer's gloomy statement by issuing the usual, "no immediate plans at this time." In April, Speer was quoted in Fortune, "There are a lot of places where they would love to have our money and get some jobs. And then we'll sell to the U.S. market." Here, the rub for Speer was the failure of the federal government to devise trade policies less favorable to foreign steelmakers. Yet, it was known that U.S. Steel had plans to build on the shores of Lake Erie, sixty miles north of Youngstown, a four billion dollar complex to show the world what the U.S. steel industry can do when it has the will to do so. When asked if U.S. Steel pledged to consult with the community before big decisions that might have affected Youngstown people, a company spokesperson answered in two ways. First, he said the company had not been asked, even though there were full page newspaper ads with the pastoral's publicity. Secondly, he remarked that such decisions are business decisions. U.S. Steel made such decisions within the company.

Such an arbitrary attitude toward decision-making by business throughout Ohio provoked a law (SB 337) under consideration in the Ohio Senate. Proposed by the Ohio Public Interest Campaign and introduced by Senator Michael Schwarzwalder, Democrat of Columbus, it would have required large corporations which planned to close plants or relocate them out of state to provide two years advance notice to the communities affected and pay into a special fund for community redevelopment. The law was opposed strongly by the business lobby as inhibiting free enterprise and viewed with mixed emotions by labor.

USWA's Smith thought that business would be tempted to relocate in less progressive states or overseas. Such laws at the state level only placed progressive states at a serious disadvantage. The same effect followed the state anti-pollution laws. In testimony before a Senate anti-trust subcommittee, in May 1978, Smith would lobby for laws that would prevent companies from crippling the economy of whole areas of the U.S. He would refer to the Mahoning Valley and other areas in the Northeast and Midwest that were suffering from mergers, buyouts and take-overs of some major companies.

Ira Harris, a Solomon Brothers investment banking partner, spoke of European companies having to contribute to national interests as well as company interests. He was not sure how long the U.S. business world could enjoy its present freedom from government dictation about public interest balancing company interest. Harris cited one of his European clients predicting the end of U.S. capitalism within twenty years. The various social, familial, and personal costs of free enterprise were cited, as well as accountability demanded by such laws as: occupational health and safety, public health and ecology, consumer protection, fair trade and labor practices.

Bishop Malone was convinced that every instance of human suffering could be documented from real life in the Mahoning Valley. He cited specifically strains on marriage and family life, depression, alienation, alcoholism drug abuse and crime. Nevertheless, Malone thought the benefits of the proposed Ohio legislation remained a bargain, despite the fact that business usually passed on the other costs to consumers, tax payers, and victims. For, an ounce of prevention was still worth a pound of cure for the "story of human anguish" behind each "dry statistic."

293

Corporate accountability was viewed by some business people with alarm, as "creeping socialism." Some business people in Youngstown opposed the coalition because to them a community/worker owned company smacked of socialism. Other business people in Youngstown publicly said that the religious leaders were being seduced by their socialist allies, such as Stoughton Lynd. The former Yale historian, anti-war Quaker and lawyer would be portrayed in early 1978 by Newsweek as a Marxist. Few U.S. clergy leaders wanted to overthrow the whole capitalistic system said religious historian, Martin Marty, during an NCR interview. In Youngstown the religious leaders' talk reflected a desire not to condemn ". . . a capitalism kept within bounds," according to the American hierarchy's desire for more than 65 years. Nevertheless, by raising corporate responsibility to new visibility and by proposing a worker/community-owned company, the Youngstown Religious Coalition challenged the U.S. mystique in which free enterprise had been intertwined with democracy, capitalism and Christianity.

The re-opening of the Youngstown mill was defended on moral grounds. The pastoral said

> . . . the idea of worker and community owner-
> ship is not foreign to our religious and
> national traditions. It ought to be explored
> as a creative response to abandonment of the
> mill by outside interests. . . Our tradi-
> tional teaching points out that economic
> decisions ought not to be left to the judg-
> ment of a few persons with economic power,
> but should be shared with the larger com-
> munity which is affected by the decisions.

Stanton spoke of the coalition being concerned about what such shutdowns do to people, as a pastoral concern. Religious leaders could not look the other way when people are thrown out of their jobs.

1978

Nevertheless, since the November 1977 pastoral the Youngstown Religious Coalition leaders said scarcely a word about the community's right to share corporate investment decisions that greatly affected the community's well-being. Coalition officials indicated that a re-opened mill was the first step toward corporate accountability. Reverend John Sharick, the Youngstown area Presbyterian executive, remarked that the coalition's executive and steering committees had not set corporate accountability as a priority. However, he thought that the pursuit of the re-opening of the Campbell works might be construed as dealing with one of its moral and ethical implications--corporate accountability. One priest involved in the coalition said, "In tactical terms, it's essential now to keep a single focus." Even though Malone did advocate strongly for corporate accountability laws in the U.S. Senate, the coalition did nothing to support the Ohio Public Interest Campaign's (OPIC) for such a law in the Ohio legislature. One minister said of the coalition, "If we get in league with OPIC, we'll lose support from local corporation people." Another minister, noting that governing boards of many churches were weighted with people from corporate management, thought the coalition could not afford to alienate them. The best that could be hoped for was to neutralize them. Reverend Robert Campbell, a Presbyterian minister on the coalition steering committee, thought that realistically the closest the religious leaders could come to encourage corporate accountability would be to exercise their traditional role of conscience-raising. Instead, Campbell spoke of the coalition launching the war for people to control their own economic destiny.

The other side of the corporate accountability coin was challenging the union and the workers. While pushing management on one hand, the coalition also would have to push union leaders to be more socially responsible for their decisions which affect the community's well being. Sharick noted that union accountability had not been raised as an issue. He thought that the coalition did not know how to approach such a touchy issue. Worker productivity--an honest day's work for pay--was a key factor for the re-opened mill's success. Soon the coalition would have to talk about accountability to the workers. Gar Alperovitz thought the workers would be receptive, on the basis of discussions with steelworkers. Their ownership position, plus their confidence in management working for their interests, would bring about significant improvements in efficiency. His experience elsewhere had taught him the same.

Whatever the reluctance to push either aspect of accountability, the Youngstown Religious Coalition' strategy moved forward. In early May 1978, Alperovitz was to complete the HUD-funded feasibility study on re-opening the mill. The coalition leaders' expected the study would confirm the preliminary findings Alperovitz released in April 1978--that a worker community owned mill could operate successfully under certain conditions. There were five basic conditions. A suitable price for the mill and markets for the mill's products were the first two conditions. Their fulfillment could be affected by the Justice Department's decision of the Lykes-LTV merger, which was expected in the summer of 1978. The three other conditions included: federal procurement of steel from the re-opened mill, federally

295

guaranteed loans to modernize the mill, and federally guaranteed loans to test experimental technology. Commerce and HUD were to decide on these three conditions in the fall of 1978 after an evaluation of Alperovitz's study.

In the meantime, Alperovitz warned that the coalition's national campaign had to ensure that the mill would be viewed as a unique project, but with special relevance elsewhere. To be convinced were the federal government, national religious leaders and other interested parties. The project had to be valued as worthy of special and unique effort--a national demonstration site.

After describing the drama of Youngstown in some detail, NCR's Petosa and Winiarski added several editorial comments. With integrity and toughness the Youngstown Religious Coalition showed adroit political maneuvering with civic governmental and industrial leaders. Even if the coalition leaders had not time enough to make history by making corporate accountability a practical reality in their community, history would judge not just their political skill, but the depth of their integrity as preachers precisely on the issue of corporate accountability. Some of the coalition leaders might have conjured up that social justice principle, without understanding its implications for themselves, but not Malone. One well-placed priest talked of Malone as one of the few bishops who understood the full implications of the documents he signed at the Second Vatican Council.

The coalition leaders' unclear stance on corporate accountability as a wider project than Youngstown was probably a handy bit of leverage for the coalition in June 1978. To have pushed corporate accountability then would have jeopardized the efforts to reopen the mill and risked the corporate managers' countering with the issue of union/worker accountability. For the Youngstown religious leaders to push it further at that time would have been also particularly difficult, knowing that prophets are not popular with their people and championing forceful attempts at social ministry complicates pastoral ministry. Yet, with the pastoral letter and the attempt to re-open the mill, the religious leaders were exploring their power to influence the socio-economic equations that touched the lives of their people. Neither the religious leaders, nor their people, nor the Youngstown people could ever be the same again.

In stressing that the moral issue was corporate responsibility, there was no demeaning of the relief for the jobless: the enormous work of mercy in trying to re-open the mill, the terrible risk and daring in raising people's hope when it seemed there was nothing for which to hope. The religious leaders were testing the meaning of the peculiar service they were giving to the community. As they learned step-by-step what they could and should do, with their people's trust, they exacted cooperation from vested interests and gave the Youngstown community a boost toward greater control of its economic destiny.

Their scheme for corporate accountability offered a much needed conscience in the form of protective vigilance and changed people's expectations about the real and ethical behavior of corporations toward communities in which they are located. Nationally, the coalition's educational-fund raising campaign might tap the slowly growing sensitivity of religious leaders to the average person's frustrating impotency in the face of social inequities built into business-as-usual. Locally, the coalition relieved a feeling of powerlessness that might otherwise have become little more than grousing, whimpering and lamenting the Youngstown community's fate. The coalition also was a belated reproach to union leaders, politicians and religious leaders--in Youngstown and the nation--who had tolerated business-as-usual while knowing full well that at the corporate bottom line, the workers were expendable. Martin Marty, the Lutheran theologian, remarked that religious leaders cannot blame workers. Religious leaders are skilled and trained as change agents, workers are not. Religious leaders are trained to give people the kinds of symbols by which they can revolt--like Martin Luther King did.

There were other NCR comments in early June 1978 by the editorial staff.[4] The editors pointed the finger of blame for the Youngstown crisis very specifically at J.T. Lykes and Frank Nemec of the Lykes Corporation; officials of the Justice Department and/or Nixon Administration; and officials of Chemical Bank, Chase Manhattan Bank, and Citibank; individual as well as institutional stockholders and depositors; and voters and legislators. All these people and groups were the focus of the prophetic voice and action of the Youngstown Religious Coalition. NCR's editors concluded,

> By publicly declaring that companies are accountable for the social costs of their investment decisions, and that the priority of those decisions must put people ahead of profit, the clergy have highlighted the conflict between a Christian value system and a capitalistic value system. The clergy, in the tradition of papal encyclicals, have kicked at the Achilles heel of capitalism-- the amoral or immoral lack of concern about anything beyond profit and the protection of investment. . .

297

> If visiting clergy in Selma helped ignite the
> civil rights struggle for individuals, it may
> be that local clergy in Youngstown, with help
> from friends around the country, can launch a
> civic rights struggle for communities. To
> date they have raised the issue of corporate
> accountability to new visibility. They have
> escalated the struggle for social justice in
> the marketplace--an appropriate North Ameri-
> can direction for liberation theology.

NCR's editor in early 1978, Arthur Jones, explained why the
editorial decision was made to look at Youngstown as a case history in moral economics.[5] The NCR saw the drama of Youngstown in
microcosm "the drama of worldwide corporate responsibility--or
irresponsibility." The editorial board expanded,

> Is a story such as Youngstown worth all this
> time and effort and space? We at NCR hope
> so--because only by facing up to the com-
> plexities, the political realities, the
> social nuances can concerned Americans begin
> to understand the dimensions of the economic
> system of which they are a small part.
>
> For North American Christians, an understand-
> ing of the system, complicated as it is, has
> to be acquired in order to press for just
> changes. That is what Petosa and Winiarski
> were reaching for with this article--a pre-
> sentation of the problem that will enable the
> reader to see the situation as it is.
>
> Then, perhaps, we all can begin to press for
> changes in the system that can prevent a con-
> stant repetition of the Youngstown drama.
> Economics may bore people, but we no longer
> live in a world or society in which people
> can take the easy way out and simply worry
> about their own money, their own jobs and
> their own lives.

On June 21, 1978, however, the Youngstown Religious
Coalition suffered a setback with Attorney General Griffin Bell's
announcement of the Justice Department approval of the unconditional merger of the Lykes and LTV Corporations.[6] Bell's noti-
fication read,

> The department is concerned with the efforts
> of the ecumenical coalition . . . to acquire

certain facilities in the Youngstown area. While we cannot judge whether these efforts will ultimately be successful, the Department of Justice views the coalition's efforts as fundamentally important. Thus, we anticipate that the LTV Corp. will bargain in good faith with the coalition's representatives.

A further statement by Bell mentioned that the Justice Department investigation of the merger proposal

. . . led me to conclude that Lykes faced a grave probability of a business failure in the near future and that the prospects for turning the situation around, absent the proposed merger, were highly speculative.

According to a Justice Department spokesperson, the announcement made it clear the merger was believed to be anticompetitive but Bell said Lykes' financial failure also would be anticompetitive and would cost jobs. The transaction was approved because the Lykes Corporation fell under the "failing company" exception to the antimerger provisions of the antitrust laws. Bell's comments were deemd to carry no compulsion but said the Justice Department spokesperson,

We hope the company will give it no compulsion [but to set conditions] . . . we felt would put it in a regulatory rather than a law enforcement position.

Reaction to Bell's decision and commentary was mixed. One observer remarked about the Justice Department statement noting, unusually, that the antitrust division staff and Assistant Attorney General, John Shenefield, agreed. Another observer speculated that there was an attempt to satisfy both big business and the consumer. The Carter administration could point to the Bell decision as pro-business, while Shenefield's antitrust could say it supported competition. Still other observers expected the merger to mean the loss of some 1,000 additional jobs in the Youngstown area, as the merged corporation closed older facilities there in favor of newer facilities in Aliquippa, PA. A spokesperson reportedly said such a move would take at least 18 months.

Reactions of coalition leaders was more positive than might have been anticipated, given the coalition's hopes that any approval of the merger would have set conditions, such as mandatory bargaining with the coalition regarding ownership of the closed Campbell works. Stanton said that, if LTV reneged

". . . the pressure of public opinion would crucify them." Noting that the coalition's economist was studying corporation books
to write a plan to bargain for the Campbell facilities, Stanton
concluded, "A hell of a lot more was gotten than if we hadn't
screamed." Alperovitz, the coalition economist said,

> Now that the Carter administration has
> increased the concentration of power in the
> steel industry, it must appropriate aid for
> competition [such as the ecumenical
> coalition].

About six weeks after Petosa's and Winiarski's extensive
investigative report, NCR readers reacted--mostly favorably.[7]
Stephen A. Mallard of Nutley, New Jersey, congratulated NCR.
Yet, without excusing any of the irresponsible actors in the
Youngstown mill closing, cited by the NCR editors, he listed
several other culprits not mentioned in the early June 1978
issue. Irresponsible activists, who posed as self-appointed pro-
tectors of the public interest, advocating zero growth and return
to pristine environment and who used endless procedural ploys to
frustrate industrial development. Irresponsible judges, who
played the procedural game with the activists. Irresponsible
legislators, who passed panacea laws that resulted in excessive
government interference in everything, damage to the economy, and
skyrocketing taxes. Bureaucrats, who mindlessly interpreted laws
(for instance, those protecting the environment and worker
safety) and whose actions resulted in little or no increased
improvements but in enormously increased costs. Workers (certainly not all workers) who stalled and cheated on the job, driving up the price of American goods so that they could not compete
on the world market. The public, which tolerated all this nonsense and failed to hold these scoundrels accountable--"both
those on your list and my list."

Anne Costello of Philadelphia thanked Petosa and Winiarski
for making her read about economics, which she found boring. She
was glad to learn for the first time that the fault was not the
USWA' workers who had lost their jobs. Rather, she appreciated
that the Japanese were willing to work harder and better--and for
less money. She asked the writers to teach people how to change
the system and to let her know, "Do the Russians have multi-
nationals?" Her question was answered somewhat, without tongue-
in-cheek, by Fritz Marti of South Bend, IN. He asked NCR to
state more clearly that the economic-political system which rules
the communist countries is state capitalism. That is much worse
than the private capitalism NCR was criticizing. Marti emphasized that free enterprise required capital but would fall back
on the "profit motive"--sheer power--without religious respect
for justice, which could lead to a truly free society. Marti

disagreed with NCR's writers that the question was ". . . the conflict between a Christian value system and a capitalistic value system." For Marti, the question was ". . . justice versus profits . . . religosity versus 'business as usual'", even if rabbis were not involved in the Youngstown Religious Coalition.

There were many more totally positive and non-critical letters. One was the pleasure of Mary R. Kohner of Winona, Minnesota, who sighed with relief that, through the leadership of Bishop Malone, the corporal works of mercy were being implemented. Another was the keen and attentive appreciation of the former president of the National Federation of Priests' Councils, under whose tutelage the NFPC did quite notable things for social justice also. Frank Bonnike of Park Ridge, Il., commended NCR. For, it had presented dramatically one of "American Catholicism's finest hours," the very best of Vatican II, and one of the reasons "why we need the National Catholic Reporter." Finally, a long-time social activist, Sr. Mary Hegarty, P.B.V.M., of Brooklyn, New York, wished dozens of Catholic newspapers would have such a story. She appreciated economic development that restored democracy as exemplified in Youngstown and the difficulty of putting one's body where one's mouth is. Hegarty ended with reference to remarks she had heard from Ralph Nader. It seems that in earlier days, Nader encouraged community organizers to be prepared for federal funds that would be available for all sorts of activities. Later, Nader saw no hope from either political party. The only way to have any real success, in Nader's mind, would be to have leaders who were elected on the backs of the people. Putting Nader's ideas and Youngstown together, Hegarty concluded, "I see people feeling their strength--along with their moral responsibility--in endeavours like Youngstown and then going."

In late July 1978, there was good news about money promised and provided for the coalition.[8] The Campaign for Human Development, as well as New York City's Riverside Church, gave $100,000 to the coalition. The Presbyterian Board of Pensions gave $200,000, the Episcopalians $60,000 and the American Baptist National Ministries $25,000.

Very shortly, however, the money-news for the coalition became mixed, given little cooperation from Lykes, an attack from the chairperson of U.S. Steel, and less than enthusiastic nods from the Carter administration.[9] Since the Justice Department approval of the Lykes-LTV merger, the coalition's purchase negotiations with Lykes hit snags. Lykes-LTV indicated it would close additional Youngstown facilities 18 months after the merger was completed. Lykes-LTV also refused to commit itself to purchase from the "re-opened" mill's steel products previously absorbed by its steel companies. The coalition and the USWA had

301

asked for these conditions in briefs filed with the Justice Department before Bell's unconditional approval of the mergers. A coalition spokesperson claimed Lykes-LTV ". . . only paid lip service to Bell's. . . " request for cooperation with the coalition. Malone felt that Bell's decision made it more difficult for the interfaith coalition to regain the jobs for the area.

During the summer the coalition sought help from Massachusetts Democratic Senator Edward Kennedy, chairperson of a Senate subcommittee concerned with the social-economic effects of mergers. Kennedy was considering special hearings on the Lykes-LTV merger in October 1978 and his staff was trying to get the research papers on the Lykes investigation from the Justice Department. In mid September 1978, the Youngstown _Vindicator_ revealed that one member of the subcommittee, Ohio Democratic Senator Howard Metzenbaum, contacted Bell after coalition negotiations with Lykes-LTV collapsed. Bell called J & L president, Thomas Graham, and urged resumption of negotiations. Graham then contacted the coalition. Said the coalition's Fernandez, ". . . the first time Lykes-LTV has taken the initiative." According to Stanton, negotiations would resume as soon as both sides could get their people together.

Up to that time, steel industry leaders had not applauded the coalition's efforts to re-open the closed mill and to re-employ the workers. Those leaders either "pooh-poohed" the coalition effort or suggested it was socialistic. However, on June 19, 1978, in a speech to the McKeesport Pa. Chamber of Commerce, the coalition was mentioned. Speer chairperson of U.S. Steel, asserted,

> . . . the whole concept of community owned facilities is the same as communism--particularly where the profit of a facility will go for the social benefit of the people. This is communism.

Soon after the speech, Malone wrote to Dr. Phillip A. Potter, general secretary of the World Council of Churches. Malone accused Speer of denouncing the coalition's work ". . . as nothing short of a communist take-over." Malone discovered that the real threat was not from the government proposal. The ". . . opposition of powerful corporate interests in the U.S. economy. . ." was the real problem. Malone judged that directing part of corporate profits to the common good was ". . . consistent with Christian principles and American ideals of justice." Stanton chuckled over the reaction of the U.S. Steel's leader to the worker-community ownership plan,

> . . . when Edward Speer calls us communists,
> you know we got their attention . . . Every
> time they want to shut down a mill, they're
> afraid of having a bunch of preachers chal-
> lenging their responsibility to the com-
> munity.

In mid-September 1978, Alperovitz released the report of HUD-funding, which asserted that the more than half a billion program of the Youngstown Religious Coalition depended very heavily on support of Jimmy Carter. One recommendation was the appointment of a top level person from the president's or vice-president's staff to head a federal task force and to work with the coalition. A second recommendation was that a $300 million federal loan guarantee sought by the coalition be set aside while the coalition arranged financing for its program. A spokesperson for the National Center for Economic Alternatives in Washington, D.C., which prepared the report under coalition supervision said the loan guarantee

> . . . should not be earmarked for any other
> purpose until the president decides whether
> he will support the Youngstown effort.

A fourth recommendation was that there also be a project to develop and demonstrate new steel technology. That project, estimated to be profitable in the long run, would cost $30 to $50 million and would take about four years to fully establish. It would be attached to the re-opened mill and be "working scale." The project was initially proposed by the civic and business people's Mahoning Economic Development Committee and would bene-fit the entire industry. A fifth recommendation of Alperovitz's report was that $15 million be given "immediately" to purchase the closed mill, which then could be turned into a national "showcase" project demonstrating how a local community could combat the urban blight caused by runaway industry. The money could be financed by Urban Development Action grants. It would be used to hire a management team and to support staff and con-sultants for engineering and market research. These people would form the nucleus of a new community-owned company and allow the religious coalition to begin diminishing its role.

This recommendation also suggested that much more money was available from other sources: suppliers to a re-opened mill, various federal and state agencies, private banking and invest-ment groups, religious organizations, and individuals. Solomon Brothers and New England Merchants indicated they would be inter-ested in Youngstown investments. As wisdom for all such funding sources, Alperovitz noted

This is an alternative to make-work and welfare. By doing nothing, the government loses
$45 million in the first three years alone in
welfare, trade adjustment allowances, etc.
Every year after that it loses $6.5 million
in taxes. Taxes alone justify $75 million in
government funds for direct equity
investment--not just loan guarantees.

Yet, such funding sources sought more than wisdom. They had to
be convinced that their investments would be "safe." Only the
Carter administration and federal agencies could provide such
"security."

Even though federal funds were to augment the coalition's
own $4 million pledged by approximately 4,000 local individuals
and religious groups, as well as by some national religious
groups, administration support was in doubt. Carter had been
scheduled to visit Aliquippa, Pa., steelworkers laid off by the
J & L Company and to stop in Columbus, Ohio, for political meetings on September 16, 1978. Coalition leaders, who had been trying to see Carter for some time, sought a meeting in Columbus.
The leaders were prepared to call a Columbus press conference and
"voice displeasure" if the meeting with Carter did not ensue.
The coalition also scheduled full-page newspaper ads in
Washington and Columbus, calling on the president to deal seriously with the Youngstown endeavours. The ads were signed by
more than 1,200 Ohio bishops, clerics, laity and rabbis.

Episcopal priest, Rev. Charles Rawlings of Cleveland, called
the ads ". . . an unprecedented joint-venture for our state."
Coalition staff member and United Church of Christ minister,
Richard Fernandez, commented, "Ohio was a big state for Carter in
'76 and Youngstown was the district that won it for him."
Cleveland's Episcopal bishop, John Burt, sent Carter a telegram,
noting that J & L ". . . will be making the steel not made in
Youngstown." Burt also reminded Carter that his Attorney General
had created problems for the coalition. However, these plans
were made before the White House could reply to Burt about
Carter's cancellation of his travel plans to Pennsylvania and
Ohio, because of the super-secret Middle East summit at Camp
David, Maryland, with Begin of Israel and Sadat of Egypt.

According to some coalition people, Carter's backing might
have been obtained more easily if the USWA were more enthusiastic
about the efforts of the Youngstown Coalition. Union officials
at the Pittsburgh national offices were reported to be suspicious
about what the Youngstown community/worker ownership plan might
have done to the USWA's successful bargaining formula. Also, the
Youngstown USWA district had voted against the USWA's national

president, Lloyd McBride. Some Youngstown steelworkers thought that election had made McBride less enthusiastic about helping their laid-off union members. At any rate, as of September 1978, the USWA's national headquarters had been officially neutral.

On September 27, 1978, there was a meeting of approximately a dozen coalition representatives, Ohio politicians, and Carter administration officials.[10] The coalition sought $15 million to purchase and re-open the Campbell steelworks and $300 million in loans for continued operation until the community/worker-owned plant became profitable. Visions of a national model project for a steelmaking community were entertained by the Mahoning Valley Economic Development, which consisted of politicians and business leaders and which supported the coalition. Among the Ohio politicians present were Democratic Senator John Glenn and Democratic Representative Charles J. Carney. Representing the Carter administration were Jack H. Watson, assistant to the president for Inter-Governmental affairs, and Robert Hall, Commerce Department assistant secretary for Economic Development. Also present were national religious representatives, including a U.S. Catholic Conference representative.

The meeting was the occasion for an administration announcement that $100 million in guaranteed loans would be available for "economically feasible" steel projects in the Youngstown area. Also announced was an administration study of the coalition's plan to purchase and re-open the Campbell Works. The study was to be directed by Hall and was to determine the Carter administration support of the coalition plan. Watson told reporters that he was skeptical about,

> . . . the utility of national models. . .
> However, I have very little doubt that some-
> thing can be done for the Mahoning Valley.

Watson also mentioned that the Hall Report findings would be available by mid-October 1978. The coalition's Stanton claimed the report was due the day before the coalition recommended Purchase negotiations with Lykes. Stanton noted that Watson had received a report from Carter's Secretary of Labor, Ray Marshall, and "was very well informed."

While Youngstown awaited the results of government study, there were reports in national business publications and on television that most of the 5,000 steelworkers laid off from Youngstown's Campbell Works were employed at other jobs.[13] Stanton called such reports misleading,

> It all depends on how you interpret the unem-
> ployment rolls. Some guys get temporary jobs

and go off the rolls for a month or so. Others simply give up and are living on savings or early retirement. And some have taken any jobs they could find, like sacking groceries; but what do they make? Not enough to support a family. And about 500 have left town.

Stanton also noted Lykes-LTV's announcement that additional Youngstown workers would be laid off in 1979. Stanton added, "We've certainly got our work cut out for us. But we're going to keep the pressure on the politicians and the White House." In that connection, the coalition sent telegrams, in mid-October 1978, to all political office holders and candidates for office in Ohio. The politicians were asked to inform the coalition, by return telegram, where they stood on the coalition's requests for help from the federal government. The politicians--and indirectly the White House--were told that the coalition would relay their responses to religious leaders throughout the state. The state's religious leaders, in turn, would inform 400,000 households where the politicians stood.

On the other hand, in mid-October 1978, the White House had a message for the Youngstown Religious Coalition. As promised in September, the White House answered the coalition in three weeks time. Yet, Watson's telephone call and letter to Malone was not the kind of "progress report" for which the coalition had hoped. Instead of the $15 million for the plant purchase and the $300 million in loan guarantees for plant operations, the White House gave the coalition $93,000 for additional market analysis. That analysis was deemed necessary to estimate the potential market for a re-opened mill's steel products--a very sensitive point in Youngstown. The coalition held Carter's Attorney General, Griffin Bell, responsible for Lykes-LTV refusal to agree to buy the steel produced by the re-opened, community/worker-owned Campbell works.

In the mid-October 1978 message, Watson said any White House boosting of government steel procurement from the Campbell Works to make up for the Lykes-LTV loss would have to wait on a Justice Department clarification on the legality of such a large share of the mill's output going to federal agencies. Another White House caution was raised over the coalition's lack of a firm purchase price for the mill. The next negotiation session between the coalition and Lykes was set for November 3, 1978. Watson also told the coalition that its request for a center to research steelmaking technology--attached to a re-opened mill--was referred to Lehigh University.

The people there, already studying the development of such a research center, were instructed to look at Youngstown as a possible site, according to Stanton. He added,

> Of course, Lehigh is located in Bethlehem, Pa., the home of Bethlehem Steel (the nation's second largest steelmaker). I don't know if we'll get a fair shake.

Indicative of the coalition's disappointment at the news but preparation for battle, was the comment of Rev. John Sharick, the head of the Presbyterian church's Youngstown district.

> Once again Youngstown waits while absentee decision makers hundreds of miles away determine whether men willing and able to work will have that opportunity.

From October 22-25, 1978, the Catholic Committee on Urban Ministry (CCUM) meeting on the campus of the University of Notre Dame with approximately 500 participants--mostly veterans of more modest social action thrusts--regarded the Youngstown Religious Coalition as decidedly good news.[12] The high regard was based on institutional religion in Youngstown making a bold assault on a serious human problem, the partnership of all the city's major denominations and the results already achieved by the effort. One speaker on the coalition developments was Youngstown's James Malone. After summarizing developments, he expressed some disappointment and uncomfortability. The disappointment was White House's "less than definite response." The uncomfortability was

> . . . that it is the ordained members of the Christian community who are leaders of this undertaking. . . [which] rightfully belongs to the non-ordained.

Malone's discomfort was a non-intended response to another speaker at the CCUM meeting, Ed Marciniak. He and several others had released a "Statement of Concern" about clerical domination of Catholic social action efforts throughout the U.S. Yet, another lay person, James Smith, assistant to the USWA's president, praised the coalition without qualification. For Smith, the effort had a profound impact, precisely because it was spearheaded, ". . . not by a group of left-wingers but by the established bishops of the community." Smith also predicted that the Youngstown campaign would not succeed without considerable pain and struggle. For the religious leaders were ". . . challenging the right of property owners to not operate a plant." That right had never before been restricted.

307

By the middle of November 1978, the Federal Trade Commission had declined to review the Lykes-LTV merger.[13] In rejecting the suggestion of Democratic Senator Edward Kennedy of Massachusetts, the FTC said it normally would not duplicate a Justice Department investigation. By the end of November, 1978, a representative of the Lykes Corporation put a price of $16 million on the closed portions and an additional $7 million for the facilities it planned to close in 1979. Stanton, the coalition's executive secretary, said the coalition did not want all the closed facilities. Along with USWA representatives the coalition would determine exactly what facilities and equipment would be needed. There was to be a response to the Lykes offer before mid-December 1978. Meanwhile, the coalition was preparing applications for grants and loans it hoped to receive from the federal government to re-open the mills.

By mid-December 1978, however, the coalition did not simply issue a response to Lykes, but also made an appeal for a probe by the Senate Judiciary Committee's anti-trust and monopoly sub-panel on the Justice Department's endorsement of the Lykes-LTV merger.[14] In seeking to examine all the documents the Justice Department had available for its decisions, the coalition denied that it was pressuring Lykes-LTV to lower its selling price and to be more cooperative in negotiations. Stanton expanded,

> The selling price is negotiable and we're getting good cooperation now. The appeal is part of the coalition's desire to look at the moral and ethical concerns of the situation here--which is why the coalition started in the first place. We want to see if anti-trust laws and procedures are working for people's benefit, not just for the good of corporations. And we want to know if there is something in the documents from Lykes-LTV that would alter our assumptions about the desirability of reopening the mill.

1979

By late January 1979 Lykes-LTV announced the closing of more Youngstown facilities--laying-off some 1,500 workers--in the fall of 1979.[15] In the meantime, the coalition was to submit a grant application to HUD for $17 million. Of it, $12 million was to purchase the closed mill and $5 million to hire a management team, set up an independent corporation, and secure long-range financing. Expecting a decision from HUD by April 1, 1979, Stanton said a positive response and success in other coalition efforts would mean readiness and partial production and rehiring of approximately 2,000 workers in August. Of the April 1 date, Stanton asserted,

> Then it's go or no-go for us. . . But we'd
> also have to get the $100 million in federal
> loan guarantees which the White House said
> was available.

The deadline was met by the last week of March 1979 and the decision seemed to come from an abrupt change of heart.[16] The door was closed on $257 million in grant and loan guarantee funds. The coalition was informed during a Washington meeting between some of its leaders and Watson, as well as through a Commerce Department letter available in the White House office. The letter said,

> -Government regulations do not allow more
> than $100 million in loan guarantees for any
> one project.

> -The economic feasibility of the coalition's
> plan is questionable.

Watson told the coalition leaders that Carter empowered him to deny the funds. A White House press aide said, "Yes, the president was aware of the decision and he concurs in it." Watson also said that $100 million in loan guarantees was kept in reserve, ". . . for a viable steel project in the Youngstown area." However, in a later press statement, Watson made no pledge to the coalition specifically, but spoke of developing ". . . a more diversified (economic) base for the area"--a strategy that could exclude the coalition's plan to re-open the mill.

Watson was accused of reneging on a commitment the coalition claimed he made in the fall of 1978 if certain standards were met. Malone and Burt, the coalition's co-chairpersons, in a telegram to the White House, expressed outrage and surprise at the rejection because ". . . we were misdirected in our efforts and reliance." The telegram also called the administration's reasons for denying the funds "unacceptable." Malone and Burt said the administration had not mentioned such problems in the March 21, 1979 meeting. The two bishops said the letter showed "appalling insensitivity" to the unemployed.

Other coalitions mentioned that they had long been aware of the $100 million limit. Yet, in September 1979, Watson had told them the $300 million proposal was not outlandish and could be worked out. There was an October 18, 1978 White House letter to the coalition which could be interpreted as fudging on the $300

million figure. Furthermore, in all discussions since the fall
of 1978, the figures involved were much higher than the government limit stated in March 1979. Since the fall, also, the
coalition had refined its economic feasibility to conform with
standards set by administration officials. The final proposal of
the coalition was a $17 million grant to buy the mill and a $245
million in loan guarantees to operate it. The mill was expected
to show a profit in three years. Just days before the administration's bad news, the USWA headquarters announced its support
for the coalition's idea to increase the mill's productivity.
Such initially would lower costs of vacation pay and pension benefits and use hourly incentive pay with which the workers could
buy stock in the mill.

Coalition officials were uncertain of the motives behind the
Carter administration's change of heart. Stanton commented,
"Anything we say is just speculation." Noting that in September,
just before congressional elections, the administration supported
the coalition's plan, Stanton mentioned, "In March, after the
elections, they could say 'no' and get us out of their hair."
Sharick agreed that the election motive was speculative,

> . . . but that's the way it would look. . .
> it's possible the president has changed his
> priorities about urban policies.

Both Stanton and Sharick agreed that the coalition had left
several unanswered questions, in writing, for the administration
to answer. One question was why the coalition was not kept
informed of developments that may have changed the administration's view of the proposal. Sharick noted, "It's possible
that their decision was made long ago." When asked whether the
coalition's interest in increasing the accountability of companies to communities had accomplished anything, Stanton
responded that he could not really tell, ". . . but I have a gut
feeling we have put some fear of God in the companies." Sharick
agreed that within the community some increased support developed
for corporate responsibility, particularly among workers. However, he said it would be easier now for ". . . the business community to adopt an I-told-you-so stance."

As for the next steps, the coalition was scheduled to meet
during the first week of April to decide what, if anything, they
could still do to help re-employ the jobless workers. One dis-
couraged coalition leader said, "We have about the same chance
[for success] as going ice skating in hell." Stanton said the
$100 million in federal loan guarantees could be used to re-open
just the rolling mill portion of the steel-making facility. Such
an operation would employ about 1,600 workers. There was also
talk of the coalition drafting another pastoral letter. A

spokesperson from Burt's Episcopal diocese said a coalition official there was urging people ". . . to bombard the White House with letters of anger and disappointment."

In late May 1979, Commonweal ran an article by Robert Howard, staff associate of the New Republic, which gave an overview of the Youngstown crisis with several twists about the workers, the union, the government, and the coalition.[17]

> The equally dramatic efforts of area clergy to save the 4200 jobs lost there has been proclaimed as a model for citizen action to confront those economic problems shared by cities throughout the northeast. Youngstown's Ecumenical Coalition of the Mahoning Valley has mobilized church groups throughout Ohio and the nation behind the goals of corporate accountability and economic self-reliance. It has created what amounts to a political machine to demand state and federal aid in the massive task of resurrecting the closed Campbell Works.

Despite the Commerce Department's rejection in late March 1979 of the coalition's request for federal loans to guarantee the community/worker owned palnt, Howard thought it would be a mistake to assume that the last had been heard of Youngstown. He explained that all the publicity missed the most lasting feature of the Youngstown drama--the response of the Mahoning Valley steelworkers themselves. Howard deemed the crisis as economic and cultural. The Youngstown working class was witnessing the breakup of the partnership of big government, big business and big labor that was forged during World War II. Howard saw the workers caught between the desire to save what they had cherished and the realization that change had to come.

Several people in the area expressed it well. A local union official heard the words of politicians, businessmen and lawyers. However, ". . . no one has any ideas." Joe Lukas, politically conservative and formerly a foreman at the Campbell Works, thought the government was ". . . just selling us down the drain." Even though others might think it sounded communistic, Lukas did not think ". . . the people had enough control." Although no one seemed to know why, Lukas saw all the things he knew all his life, ". . . just like sand castles washed away." George Limberty was 48 years old and had worked in the Youngstown Sheet and Tube for eleven years. He found the loss of jobs very frustrating. Forgetting about no way to fight against management just did not work. It only came back to haunt him in his dreams. The benefits were like burial money and the free time

311

was getting to him after a year. He saw no help from USWA, "The guys that are runnin' the union now are from the old school. They're working hand in hand with the management against us."

Howard thought Limberty's judgment unfair. Even though USWA's president, Lloyd McBride, reportedly claimed at one meeting that the mill closings were outside the boundaries of collective bargaining, Howard was certain there was no labor-management conspiracy against the coalition's program. Historically outside the labor-management experience in the U.S. have been worker-community ownership and control questions and solutions. Such have confused, not facilitated, the collective bargaining procedures which normally are quite clear-cut and patterned.

Like most union leadership, the USWA officials were not familiar with such complex and novel challenges. In fact, some of the officials were quite suspicious of the worker-community ownership plan of the coalition. One example was Russell Baxter, senior president of the locals and member of AFL-CIO council in the Youngstown area. He claimed close relationships with the USWA headquarters in Pittsburgh. His local--2163-was hardest hit by the layoffs. He complained of the younger union members' lack of appreciation and commitment and was at odds with the leaders of the rest of the locals in the area. His verbalized support of whatever the coalition could get for Youngstown was judged to be an obsessive caution and cynicism. He expressed his cynicism of the local leaders, ". . . those sons o'bitches were just happy their local didn't get hit," of the young workers, ". . . who don't know what hard times are," and of the coalition which, ". . . is offerin false hope." Baxter had no solutions, other than reiterating how tough things were in the depression and how much he was doing for his local through his contacts with the USWA international headquarters in Pittsburgh. Of lay-offs, plant closings and the problems of the valley's steel industry he said, with a mixture of humor and self-depreciation, "These are deep subjects and I'm just a dummy."

Ed Mann, one of the most militant in the USWA, was a founder of RAFT--the "Rank and File Team"--a movement for internal democracy within USWA in the 1960's. He was also a strong supporter of dissident candidate Ed Sadlowski in his challenge to McBride for the USWA presidency in 1977. Sadlowski carried the Youngstown district. When the Brier Hill facility was to close in late 1979, Mann would lose all his local membership. He was torn between the disillusionment among the workers in the mill, who had similar experiences years before in the coal mines of Pennsylvania and West Virginia, and the inertia of the USWA international headquarters, which had no responsible plan but tardy reaction. However, Mann was determined to seek alternatives. The local (1462) leadership had asked assistance from the coalition and demanded a meeting with Jones and Laughlin officials to discuss shut-down mechanisms. "I've never been frightened of an idea in my life," exclaimed McMann, "But a lot of people are. And a lot of them are in the higher echelons of our union." As an explanation of why the USWA headquarters came out in full support of the coalition in late March 1979, when USWA president McBride urged Carter to grant the federal financing, McMann referred to rank and file pressure from Youngstown locals. Coalition leaders referred to success in getting a qualified management team. Jim Smith, McBride's liaison to the coalition, referred to the realism of the detailed worker-community ownership proposal.

Howard, the staff associate of the New Republic, thought there were several reasons that nudged the USWA headquarters, not to take a leadership role necessarily, but to get caught up in a new and necessary experience and learning process. One, the Youngstown experience had contributed to the international a new awareness of the multiple and deeply rooted problems of economic dislocation. Two, the agreement on labor costs was a precedent for USWA. Three, there was a recent conference of the international headquarters on the relative costs and benefits of building new plants compared to rehabilitating the existing ones. Howard felt it was impossible to determine if initial support of the coalition from the international headquarters would have made any real difference in reopening the Campbell Works. However, he was convinced that new kinds of questions were being asked. He thought the consequences of such probing would be seen in future years.

For Howard, there were other steelworkers who chose neither migration in search of new jobs nor cynicism about maintaining the old ones. They were usually lower level union officials-- grievance committee members, safety representatives, or recording secretaries like Gerald Dickey. Referring to the day of announcement of the plant closing, Dickey said,

> If you wanted to have a revolution in there,
> the day to do it was Monday. Those guys were
> mad enough to try anything. . . The problem
> is you've only got a short time-period to do
> somethin'.

Referring to the day at Youngstown's Stop Fine Mill when armed company police fired on the strikers and USWA's "Flying Squadron" in the organizing efforts of the 1930's, Dickey said, "When you think of what those guys had to go through, and yet they won . . . Maybe we'll win too."

Howard explained the meticulous anf flexible efforts of the coalition before Carter's refusal of government funds. By March the technical questions, raised by the feasiability study, had been answered. A survey of over 600 potential purchasers of the steel within 200 miles of Youngstown revealed a good market. The requisitions for loan guarantees had been reduced from $300 million to $245 million. The local union had negotiated on the labor costs. The president of a major U.S. steel company agreed to serve as chairperson of the worker-community ownership venture. The assembling of a competent management team was underway. Technical consultants drew up a 20-year forecast, which saw profits within three years.

Although feeling betrayed the coalition leaders had to face the fact that May 31, 1979 was the expiration date on the coalition's option to buy the Lykes' Campbell Works. Consequently, the leaders prepared a pastoral letter drawing the moral implications of the government's decision, technical consultants tried to formulate an alternative plan on a smaller scale, involving less government money and employing less workers, and there were reports of using the weight of labor support to pressure the Carter administration to reconsider.

Howard saw time getting very short, no signs of how such a strategy might work, and Youngstown's crisis only getting worse. The government's decision only fueled the workers' anxiety, discontent and mistrust. The traditional markers of their social world--mill, job, union--had proven unsure and the old systems no longer met their needs. In certain publications of the national press and among opponents of the coalition it was said that the steelworkers did not support it. Bill Sferra, a sociologist at Youngstown State University, said so too. "The coalition is all leaders and no followers." Howard thought such judgments hid as much as they revealed. Ed Mann explained that if the workers were restrained in active support, they were also anxious to see the coalition succeed,

> Workers aren't aggressively activists. We've been taught over the last thirty years that movements aren't clean. You can't expect dramatic changes in that attitude over the course of one year.

Some examples were cited by Howard of the "passive support" of the steel workers. One worker, speaking of those in retirement willing to help, said, "They'll come back in you see, their family is here; this is home." Another worker thought that what was necessary for support was "a company we can trust."

Because Youngstown's crisis was in so many ways a crisis of traditional values, Howard saw the coalition as the defender of the traditional working class culture in the face of far-reaching economic change: a sense of community, financial security, a job with which the working class could identify. However, to sustain such values, Howard insisted that local culture itself had to be open to change, new ideas, new practices and new institutions. Howard thought that in the turmoils of social change were the seeds of social innovation. For him, that was the tremendous potential of the coalition. Its potential would not fade away any more than the potential of the unemployed workers. For Howard, Youngstown's last chapter might also be its first. For, ". . . it is built into the pain and promise of social changes which will be with us for a long time."

Ironically, less than two months after the Carter administration's refusal of the coalition's grants, there was news of the steel industry being on the government dole.[18] Import quotas boosted profits and employment. Setting "trigger" or minimum prices for imported steel so decreased imports and allowed domestic producers to increase their own prices that domestic mills were operating in mid-1979 at nearly 95 percent of capacity. Loan guarantees, like the more than $100 million given the Wheeling-Pittsburgh Steel Corporation, tended to prop up firms at the expense of competitors. Although Europe poured in massive subsidies, negotiated quotas and attempts to impose strict price controls, the U.S. did not have to be so forceful. The European industry was older, more price competitive and more dependent on exports. The U.S. consumer had borne most of the costs through high prices, profits and wages. Yet, the government role was unmistakable.

> The government--through its loan-guarantee program--is acquiring an increasingly large steel investment that it will need to protect. Industry and labor are eager for that protection, and urge it through a variety of administrative and technical proposals. We will continue to have the mantle of free enterprise, and the reality of government control.

By late June 1979, there were reports that the Youngstown Religious Coalition had not met for some time, was without a goal, was in repose, and had not taken on any new projects since the Carter administration refused federal funding.[19] The coalition's executive director, Stanton, reported that some coalition members had begun new efforts "under the umbrella of the coalition, although not every coalition member is a participant." One such effort that was coordinated by Rev. Eugene Bay, a Presbyterian, was a gathering of labor, business, and industrial leaders concerned with the image of Youngstown's labor. It was reported, also, that coalition leaders had discussed three followup actions: a report of the coalition's steel project, a political statement over the name of Malone, and a new pastoral statement.

Tensions within the coalition, threatening such actions, were threefold. First, there was a resident/non-resident tension. Some felt that members, such as Cleveland's Episcopal Bishop John Burt had little stake in Youngstown. Second, there was the establishment/non-establishment tension. Some were critical of Stanton, who had been given credit for much of the coalition's local political quarterbacking. As one ". . . welcome in all the innermost circles," Stanton was judged as unable to confront such people effectively. Third, there was the intra-church tensions. One source claimed that several high-ranking churchmen involved were "catching heat" from more conservative church members. Stanton had to deny rumors that he was leaving the priesthood or in conflict with his bishop, Malone. Stanton stated that he planned to work with private sector interests, out of the public eye.

Several persons emphasized that the coalition had established a reputation for credibility, which could still be used. Said Rev. John Sharick, executive presbyter of Eastminster Presbytery, "We need to provide a moral, public voice and keep calling the attention of the valley. . ." to problems. According to Rev. Robert Campbell of the First Presbyterian Church, "The coalition is alive and well if another crisis hits. We have a body ready to move." However, most observers described any coalition efforts to come as "diffuse" or "without the energy" of the plant-opening project, until the next "crisis."

By the end of November 1979, shock waves affected communities in seven states, due to U.S. Steel's closing of 15 steel plants and mills.[22] Some of the other U.S. Steel plants closed were in New Haven, Connecticut; Fairfield, Alabama; Pittsburgh, Pennsylvania; and Torrance, California. However, the impact was greatest in the "Steel" or Ohio's Mahoning Valley, still suffering from the closing of the Campbell Works in 1977. Youngstown expected some 3,500 layoffs immediately as a result of U.S. Steel's closing of a basic steel plant and a finishing mill and some 1,400 when the Jones and Laughlin Steel Company (part of the Lykes-LTV Corporation) closed in January 1980.

The November 1979 closings shifted attention to the Youngstown Religious Coalition again, not simply because U.S. Steel was one of the steel companies that lobbied vigorously against the individual/community ownership plan--calling it "communistic"--but also because even the area's Republican congressman, Lyle Williams, sent a telegram to the coalition, asking it "to do something." Stanton said the communities' reaction to the combined loss of another 4,900 jobs was "stunned silence." He added, "Everybody's still kind of punchy and nobody knows what to do." Stanton mentioned that of the 4,100 people who lost their jobs in 1977, about 500 took severance pay and moved out of the area, another 1,100 took some sort of early retirement, and about 1,000 to 1,100 found other work, often in less-skilled and lower paying jobs. Stanton continued,

> That left about 1,500, whose benefits have run out. They're just hanging out there becoming poor and eventually will live on food stamps and welfare.
>
> My guess is that a bigger portion of the 4,900 new unemployed will find themselves with this last group.

1980

In February 1980, it was learned by the coalition leaders' use of the Freedom of Information Act that the Carter administration had never taken them seriously.[21] The coalition leaders obtained a long series of internal government memoranda expressing doubts about the plan, doubts which had never been shared with the Youngstown Religious Coalition. On the other hand, the government's file on the more than $100 million loan guarantee to Wheeling-Pittsburgh Corporation, the nation's ninth largest steel firm, contained, according to Rawlings, ". . . 12 inches of correspondence, criticism and exchange of views." Rawlings concluded that the government always opposed the community control of a steel mill. Big steel's clout--the government money for steel investment--would be monopolized by private industry.

C. Karen Silkwood Case

On November 13, 1974, Karen Silkwood, a 28-year-old laboratory analyst and organizer for the Oil, Chemical and Atomic Workers International Union, was found dead in her Honda Civic off Oklahoma Highway No. 74.[22] Her father, several sympathizers and the Quixote Center--a Catholic-oriented and Washington, D.C. based social justice group--in 1976, spearheaded a civil rights suit. They alleged a conspiracy between a nuclear power corporation and the Federal Bureau of Investigation, to prevent Karen Silkwood from organizing a union local to improve safety standards at the Oklahoma plutonium factory of the Kerr-McGee

Nuclear Corporation. The suit alleged that 22 Kerr-McGee Nuclear
Corporation employees and four FBI operatives were involved. The
suit also charged Kerr-McGee with negligence in plutonium handling.

Just before Silkwood's car ran off the highway and smashed
into a concrete culvert, she was on her way to an Oklahoma City
Holiday Inn to give a New York Times reporter documents allegedly
incriminating to the Kerr-McGee Cimarron nuclear facility in
Crescent, Oklahoma. Her documents were never recovered.   Suspi-
cion still lingered in 1976 that Karen Silkwood was murdered,
even though her father's and the Quixote Center's suit was the
third attempt to unravel facts behind her contamination by plutonium and her death.   Her union spent seven months pushing the
U.S. Justice Department to investigate, but in May 1975 that
official probe was discontinued without much notice.   At that
point the National Organization for Women (NOW) lobbied for a
congressional investigation.   In 1976, the House Energy and
Environment Subcommittee held hearings. They failed because, for
the most part, the Justice Department refused to cooperate and
because the House of Representatives would not authorize funds to
hire its own investigators. There were many questions still outstanding from the House of Representatives hearings.   First, how
and why was Silkwood's apartment contaminated?   Second, where
were Silkwood's missing documents?   Third, did Silkwood fall
asleep at the wheel or was she forced off the road?   Oklahoma
highway patrol officers contended the former, but an independent
investigator contended the latter.   Fourth, how much plutonium
was missing from the plant?   Fifth, how safe were the six-foot,
pencil-thin plutonium fel rods manufactured by the Kerr-McGee
company for the fast-breeder reactors?

Karen Silkwood's father had wanted to file a civil suit
after the Justice Department closed its case. He could not raise
the minimum $25,000 lawyers needed to prepare a case.   He was
introduced by Sarah Nelson, a labor task force coordinator and
fund-raiser for NOW, to Daniel Sheehan, a Harvard law school
graduate with a reputation for tackling the government in court
and winning. Silkwood asked Sheehan if he would take the case.
Timing was essential.   A two-year statute of limitations would
take effect in November 1976.   Sheehan, 32, worked in the Jesuit
Social Ministry Office in Washington, D.C., served as a Jesuit
volunteer, and had asked for admission into Society of Jesus.
The director of the Jesuit Social Ministry Office at that time
was Rev. William Davis, S.J., who regarded the Silkwood case as
an important social justice issue. Said Davis,

> No one else was about to take it up.   Over
> and above the specifics of the case, which
> stands on its own merits, we felt a number of

important public policy issues were involved.
The incredible health hazards in the plutonium industry;
The woeful inadequacy of the regulatory
agencies;
The liaison between big business and government agencies like the FBI.

Both Sheehan and Davis voluntarily left the Jesuit Social
Ministry Office in June 1977. Davis explained, ". . . The Jesuit
Office of Social Ministry was established primarily to serve
Jesuits . . . I resigned so I could continue pursuing issues like
the Silkwood case." So, the Quioxote Center adopted the Silkwood
case. The Quixote Center was founded in 1976 and described
itself as a, ". . . gathering of people who will work and pray
with laughter, to reach for the stars that seem too distant to be
touched or too dim to be worth the effort." To aid, at no cost,
complaintant William Silkwood, Karen's father, were three of its
seven full-time staff. From its annual budget of $95,000--raised
from fees, contributions, talks and donations--the Center paid
the subsistence salaries of the Silkwood case workers: Davis,
Nelson and Sheehan. For the civil suit donations came from a
variety of feminists, labor supporters and environmentalists.
Rolling Stone magazine raised substantial sums for the case
through four investigative stories by Howard Kohn.

Sheehan's victories over the federal government included the
Pentagon Papers and the Wounded Knee suits. In the Silkwood case
he would try to establish three precedents. One, an illegal conspiracy existed between big business and the FBI. Two, the Kerr-
McGee Corporation should be convicted, under the 1964 Civil
Rights Act, for violating the rights of workers to organize.
Three, any off-site contamination of private citizens is the
responsibility of a nuclear corporation. Among twelve specific
complaints against Kerr-McGee, Sheehan charged that the corporation had conspired in six ways. First, the corporation illegally
had the telephones of Silkwood and other organizers bugged.
Second, the corporation had illegally collected dossiers on the
private lives of Silkwood and other organizers. Third, the
corporation hired "operations agents" to endanger citizens'
physical safety. Fourth, the corporation ordered its employees
not to talk to the media, under threat of being fired. Fifth,
the corporation fired or transferred persons from the Cimarron
facility as a punshiment for pro-union activity. Sixth, the corporation falsified official reports to investigators from
agencies such as the FBI, the Atomic Energy Commission and the
U.S. Congress.

The trial was planned for spring 1978 in Oklahoma City. Two
key witnesses were journalist Jacqui Srouji, a self-described

FBI undercover operative, and Lawrence Olson, an FBI field agent, allegedly Srouji's control and director of the Silkwood field investigation. In 1976 hearings, Srouji startled a House of Representative hearings by stating under cross examination that she had 1,000 pages of FBI Silkwood documentation. Among that documentation were "letterhead memos" from Olson to the Justice Department suggesting that Silkwood had been contaminated by plutonium smugglers operating out of the Cimarron facility. FBI agent Olson and his superior, Theodore Rosak--also named in the complaint--had asked the Justice Department to investigate a possible black market plutonium ring. The Justice Department refused and Rosak was transferred to Denver, Colorado. Srouji, Olson and Rosak reportedly were part of an illegal FBI counterintelligence program (COINTELPRO). Between 1963 and 1967, as a reporter for the Nashville Banner, Srouji allegedly infiltrated civil rights and student groups for the FBI. Allegedly Olson bugged Martin Luther Kings' bedrooms and allegedly Rosak burglarized the Socialist Workers' Party Office in several cities.

Sheehan's suit charged that the trio came to believe Silkwood was contaminated intentionally and driven off the highway. However, the trio was uncertain who was responsible. Sheehan alleged that the trio protected Kerr-McGee security officers, including a former FBI agent, from possible indictment for illegal surveillance. Sheehan alleged that the FBI "colored" the investigation in favor of Kerr-McGee. Sheehan alleged that Olson perjured himself during the House hearings. Finally, Sheehan alleged that the FBI directed Srouji to smear Silkwood as "mentally distrubted," and to testify that the union contaminated Silkwood to make her a martyr.

As Daniel Sheehan prepared the federal court case, William Davis laid the groundwork for shareholder action against the Kerr-McGee Corporation.[23] During a meeting of the Inter-Faith Committee on Corporate Responsibility (ICCR) in New York, Davis brought up the Silkwood case. At the meeting, concern about doing something helpful was expressed by Brother Robert Taylor, associate treasurer for the Atonement Friars of Graymoor, New York. The religious community held 2,400 shares of Kerr-McGee stock.

So, on January 1977, Taylor filed a stockholders' resolution asking whether Kerr-McGee's Cimarron, Oklahoma, personnel between 1972 and 1975,

> -Violated any Atomic Energy Commission and Nuclear Regulatory Commission regulations governing the storage, possession of, handling of, access to and security of nuclear material;

-Violated worker safety regulations;

-Took steps to harass or punish workers who tried to organize to remedy abuses.

The resolution quoted from Congressional testimony and asked for a full report within two months after the 1977 shareholder's meeting. The resolution for full disclosure on the allegations behind the Silkwood case was never voted on by the stockholders. For, Kerr-McGee routinely appealed the resolution to the Securities and Exchange Commission (SEC), which passes on admissability of stockholders' resolutions, and lost. However, arguing that, because the Cimarron facility was closed, the requested report was no longer germane, Kerr-McGee appealed a second time and received a favorable SEC ruling.

In early October 1978, the civil rights portion of the Silkwood case was dismissed when a federal district court judge ruled that the 1964 Civil Rights Act did not protect labor unions from harassment, wiretapping and surveillance.[24] Still intact was that part of the case dealing with complaints of injury, contamination and negligence on the part of the Kerr-McGee Corporation. Daniel Sheehan, co-director of the Quixote Center and attorney for the case, stated he would appeal the judge's "narrow" interpretation of the 1964 Civil Rights Act, as applying only to racial discrimination. At a press conference, Sheehan added,

> We will ask for an expedited appeal and ruling so as to keep both halves of the case in a single trial to be held in January.

[1]"Youngstown Statement Asks Soldiarity, Sharing," National Catholic Reporter, v. 9, No. 26, 4/27/73, p. 19.

[2]"Churches Ask Job Aid for Steel Valley," National Catholic Reporter, v. 13, No. 44, 10/7/77, p. 2.

[3]Jason Petosa and Mark Winiarski, "The Drama of Youngstown," National Catholic Reporter, v. 14, No. 32, 6/2/78, pp. 3-7, 14-15, and 20.

[4]"When Profits, Not People, Count," Editors, National Catholic Reporter, v. 14, No. 32, 6/2/78, p. 1.

[5]Arthur Jones, "When Money Talks . . . People Listen," National Catholic Reporter, v. 14, No. 32, 6/2/78, p. 10.

[6]Mark Winiarski, "'Work With Coalition,' Steel Told As Merger Approved," National Catholic Reporter, v. 14, No. 34, 6/30/78, pp. 1, 18.

[7]"Youngstown: 'The Best of Vatican II,'" Repartee, National Catholic Reporter, v. 14, NO. 35, 7/14/78, pp. 10-11.

[8]"$100,000 CHD Grant Goes to Youngstown," National Catholic Reporter, v. 14, NO. 36, 7/26/78, p. 20.

[9]Jason Petosa, "Youngstown Fight 'Needs Carter's Aid,'" National Catholic Reporter, v. 14, No. 42, 9/22/78, pp. 1, 4.

[10]Mark Winiarski, "Youngstown Could Get $100 Million in Loans," National Catholic Reporter, v. 14, No. 44, 10/6/78, p. 3.

[11]Jason Petosa, "More Money, More Studies, But Steel Mill Still Closed," National Catholic Reporter, v. 15, No. 2, 10/27/78, pp. 5, 26.

[12]Robert McClory, "Cheers for Youngstown, Boos for Higgins' Firing," National Catholic Reporter, v. 15, No. 3, 11/3/78, p. 5.

[13]Jason Petosa, "Steel Mill Price Set," National Catholic Reporter, v. 15, No. 7, 12/1/78, p. 16.

[14]"Youngstown Coalition Asks Merger Probe," National Catholic Reporter, v. 15, No. 10, 12/22/78, p. 3.

[15]"Youngstown Group Seeks $17 Million," National Catholic Reporter, v. 15, No. 16, 2/9/79, p. 3.

[16]Jason Petosa, "Carter Denies Youngstown Plea for Steel Funds, National Catholic Reporter, v. 15, No. 25, 4/13/79, pp. 1, 20.

[17]Robert Howard, "Going Bust in Youngstown, Commonweal, v. 106, No. 10, 5/25/79, pp. 301-305.

[18]Robert J. Samuelson, "Steel on the Dole," National Catholic Reporter, v. 15, No. 32, 6/1/79, p. 15.

[19]"Interest Down, Tension Up in Youngstown Coalition," National Catholic Reporter, v. 15, No. 34, 6/29/79, p. 5.

[20]"Steel Mill Closings Jolt Youngstown," National Catholic Reporter, v. 16, No. 7, 12/7/79, p. 16.

[21]Steve Askin, "Washington Double-Cross," National Catholic Reporter, v. 16, No. 18, 2/29/80, p. 6.

[22]Richard Rashke, "Catholic Center Probes Union Organizer's Death," National Catholic Reporter, v. 14, No. 4, 11/11/77, pp. 1-4.

[23]"Stockholders Defeat Friars' Appeal for Silkwood Data," National Catholic Reporter, v. 14, No. 4, 11/11/77, p. 4.

[24]"In Silkwood Case, Civil Rights Act 'No Protection,'" National Catholic Reporter, v. 14, No. 45, 10/13/78, p. 3.

Chapter VIII - Example to U.S. Society?

A. Evaluative Framework

To be an example for other people or groups, is to present a representation, type or model of meaningful behavior. Here, an attempt is made to indicate the examples offered to the U.S. society, in terms of the goals, tactics, actors, and reactions operative in U.S. Catholic involvement in some prominent labor-management controversies from 1960-1980. An attempt has been made to arrange these goals, tactics, actors and reactions according to a hierarchy based on the reading of papal and national church leaders' statements on labor-management relations, the documents and commentaries of the Second Vatican Council, and the literature of management theorists and humanistic psychologists. (cf. Appendix, "Evaluative Frameworks") The arrangement is tentative and in need of substantive documentation. The hope is that others will be spurred to such analysis. That hope is based on the firm conviction, not only that authoritative dicta too frequently are ignored, but also that the time has come for a theoretical and operational integration from the theological and behavioral literature about labor-management relations.

Whatever one makes of Michael Maccoby's critique of theorists or psychologists like Abraham Maslow, there are many who would commend Maccoby's call for,

> . . . a kind of managerial mutant, a new corporate type, the gamesman who develops his heart as well as his head, and who could become examples of leadership in a changing society where the goal is economic dependency and the humanization of technology.[1]

Echoing Maccoby's call is Jesuit Joseph Joblin, who served for more than twenty years as Vatican representative on the staff of the ILO. Joblin said on May 19, 1982 in a personal letter,

> The topic of your research seems to me very important, especially as you concentrate on the years 1955-1980 which are the turning point of a civilization. Your introduction may compare what Pius XII said on Labor Relations to the Governing Body of the ILO in November 1954 and how Paul VI had touched the question before the ILO Conference in 1969 (10 June). In the first case, you are con-

fronted with "the" doctrine of LMR; in the
second case there is something else. The
problem has changed: 1) the industrial world
is not anymore limited to the western
capitalist countries, 2) The structures
required for negotiations are not perfect in
other economies, 3) there is need of insisting on the "organic participation" of the
workers (you find the expression twice in
Paul VI), 4) the object of the negotiations
has to be enlarged--with environment,
vocational training and all aspects of life,
economic considerations (note here the reference to the indirect employer in <u>Laborem</u>
<u>Exercens.</u>) Under these circumstances, I
would ask myself how and whether Catholicism
and other organized religions have seen the
changing society and encouraged the evo-
lution. Labor Relations has not lost its
importance but under the same words we discover a new reality. What will be the consequences especially in Labor Education?[2]

Some dimensions of Joblin's questions and Maccoby's search are
addressed here in an evaluation of the U.S. Catholic Church's
goals, tactics, actors, and reactions as it was involved in some
prominent in labor-management controversies from 1960-1980.
Other dimensions await others' research!

B. Unanswered or Unasked Questions

Fairness in any type of evaluation must allow for pertinent
data missed by the evaluator and qualifying the judgments. Such
caution is even more appropriate when discussing data gleaned
from periodical literature--subject to so many subjective factors
from editors and writers--and from a time period elapsed more
than five years before publication. Such caution is most fitting
in presenting data on controversies such as those of labor and
management. For, legalities and strategies, impinging on either
party, limit the content of communications during the controversy. So, either party may not have had the opportunity nor
desire to "tell all" when the periodical literature was reporting. Consequently, any evaluation of the U.S. Catholic Church's
involvement in some prominent controversies, as well as labor's
and management's actions, must be qualified. One must leave room
for questions not asked and not answered in the Catholic periodical literature from 1960 to 1980, as well as data presently
available but missed by the present evaluator, one of whose aims

is to provoke such additions or omissions for the record's greater reliability.

C. Recommendations

No expertise is pretended in recommendations to scholars organizers, administrators and activists. What is suggested simply springs from my personal experience and research findings!

Chapter I-IV. Labor-Management Relations in Agriculture

1. Unasked or Unanswered Questions

a. Migrants and Braceros

What lessons learned from the battles over "braceros" legislation can help us in assessing current efforts to respond to needs of migrant and undocumented workers? Were there other growers who deserved praise for expressing as honest an analysis on the bracero and migrant problems? Who were they, where did they live and why were they not more effective among their peers? In assessing the church's ministry to migrants and braceros, how did it differ from the later ministry to farmworkers unionizing in California, Texas, Arizona, the midwest, and elsewhere?

What is the realism of convening a conference of growers, canners, labor leaders, religious leaders, academic experts and public officials today, as the Chicago Council on Working Life did by its late 1959 National Conference to Stabilize Migrant Labor--especially in light of FLOC, Texas Farmworkers, Iowa canning workers, sugar cane workers, and other unorganized food laborers? What assessment can be made and lessons learned, in light of several meetings of Hispanic ministry workers focusing attention on the plight of the migrants and braceros? How many other examples are there like the Salvatorian Sisters' Divine Savior Hospital and the diocese of Madison establishing La Clinica in Endeavor to minister to the health needs of migrants and braceros? Has the appearance of regional bishops' pastorals on agricultural life, "Guests and Strangers" and "This Land Is Home To Me" made any difference in the farmers' knowledge of Catholic social justice teaching and their response to the problems elaborated in such pastorals?

b. Cesar Chavez and the U.F.W.

What kind of assistance did union organizing before Chavez receive from the church--especially the efforts of the founder of NFWA, Ernesto Galarza? Is there data on private consultations between church leaders on the one hand and growers and public officials on the other hand? How would McCarthy's statement, "Cesar Chavez . . . has been called by his friends the walking embodiment of the principles in the Church's social encyclicals," be received today? In addition to the words of Chavez and Worship are there other analyses of proper and non-manipulative liturgies during social justice causes? What is now known about the March 1966 letter of directors of Rural Life Offices of eight California dioceses not becoming a California Bishops' pastoral letter on the Delano farmworker controversy? Could the USCC Bishops Committee on Farm Labor have come into existence earlier and have broadened its scope to other states where farm worker controversies were appearing? What lessons can the Catholic church learn from the national and local work of the Migrant Ministry sponsored and supported by the National Council of Churches? Has there been any detailed study on Catholics involved in opposition to the church's role in the farmworker controversies, e.g. denunciations, threats, financial and other forms of pressure? Why did it take so long to correct or to retire obstructionist clergy.

What is the justice in Krebs' criticism of the late 1968 California Catholic Bishops' statement because it did not include support of the grape boycott and because the Catholic bishops had less to lose then the NCC which endorsed the boycott earlier? In the context of Patrick McNamara's study "Social Action Priests in the Mexican Community," (from which the hierarchy of actors and reactions was adapted) is the involvement of priests and religious, for social justice purposes, in non-church institutions--especially labor unions and government human service agencies--the same as involvement in elected or other appointed government offices? How much of church indifference and/or non-cooperation with union organizing throughout the U.S. was based on the church's thrust for legitimation in terms of secular prestige, financial enhancement, expanding membership, and societal influence? How fair was Fr. Mark Day, OFM in criticizing the behavior of most of the Catholic clergy in Delano? How much of the failure of some activists and publicists to understand or accept the "bridge-building" role of the church in labor-management relations is due to conscious or unconscious socialist leanings, negativism toward corporations, or strategic inexperience? Has anyone taken seriously the suggestion of Fr. Holleran, O.F.M. to make a social justice case study out of the church's involvement in the agricultural workers' controversies?

Would not an interesting study be a comparative analysis of the process and impact of the three major U.S. religious groups' involvement in the farmworker processes?

In terms of the effectiveness of the labor movement today and in the future, what are the implications of Chavez's finding repugnant the thought of eventually becoming "one of the biggest union leaders in the country?" What are the details behind Chavez' early high praise for the Protestant's California Migrant Ministry and heavy criticism of Catholic priests and bishops? What kind of early warning system would make possible prompt, continued and effective Catholic church response to Chavez' and other social justice leaders' call for the Catholic church's presence and sacrifice for social change--"We don't ask for words. We ask for deeds. We don't ask for paternalism. We ask for servanthood?" What "behind-the-scenes" activities account for the Catholic church's later deeds and service? How much has Chavez, other farmworker leaders and the Catholic church heeded San Antonio Archbishop Flores' 1970 advice to face up to automation challenges and retraining needs in agricultural work? Is there any basis in church teaching on labor-management relations for the criticism of CHD grants to UFW since money "which was designated for anti-poverty groups, ends up in the hands of a labor organizing committee already funded from various sources?" How did Bishop Clinch of Monterey respond to the letter of 104 people, representing some fourteen parishes, that he denounce the CHD grants? Did the parishioners, with four priests, actually withhold funds from the diocesan development campaign?

What were the factors behind the USCC Social Development Committee's endorsement of the UFW boycott of head lettuce, given the earlier outcry about the committee's silence on UFW boycotts? Given the success of earlier behind-the-scenes interventions of the Bishops' Labor Committee, what accounted for the five or so months it took in 1973 to resolve the UFW-Teamster jurisdictional battle? Has there been a detailed analysis of the process employed to turn out such massive support of the call for those free elections, during the summer of 1973? What are the implications today of Dorothy Day's words that summer, in the context of opting for the poor and the oppressed? Should farm-activists wait for her words to be fully heeded before assisting in other worker-causes? What dynamics were at work in the support UFW received from corporations like Safeway Stores and National Food Stores--support that went beyond boycotting? Has James J. Magee, Coordinator of Social Work at the College of New Rochelle, updated his late November 1973 analysis of the church's involvement in the farmworkers' cause, especially as to any implementation of his suggested action steps? What are the organizational implications of Magee's suggested action steps, especially with regard to undoing the migrant system and vested interests of the agribusiness, to supporting the non-judgmental stance of the Bishops' Farm Labor Committee and his call for interfaith collaboration in resolving the farmworker problem?

Why did Bishop Clinch of Monterey oppose the July 1974 visit of religious major superiors to Salinas? Given the success of the church's military ordinariate but the very slight impact of the church on the American black population (for which a separate vicariate was refused after the Civil War) is Fr. Virgil Elizondo's 1975 call for a separate migrant vicariate a wise experiment to be undertaken today? During negotiations and ALRB activities what were the operational understandings between the NCC Migrant Ministry and the Bishops' Farm Labor Committee? Whatever happened to the California's Proposition 14 and what is the present impact of California's ALRA? What would be some other situations, in which direct government work, such as Bishop Mahony's in California, would "implement social justice"? What steps could be taken effectively by the church to implement a need expressed by Bishop Mahony--that growers organize to deal with the "middlemen" who squeeze their profits? Is there any data that NCRLC could have served as an intermediary for greater collaboration between the UFW and the leaders of the 1977 striking farmers, whom the NCRLC supported?

c. Other Food Laborers

What major church groups have endorsed the FLOC boycott? What evidence is there for migrant worker support of FLOC's organizing? How many diocesan school systems had discontinued Campbell "labels for education" campaign and why?

In addition to personality and jurisdictional aspects, was there outside pressure on Bishop Tracy to remove Fr. Vincent O'Connell, S.M. from any identification with the diocese? What was meant by the diocesan statement that O'Connell's words "appeared to be harmful to the interest of the people" and Bishop Tracy's earlier assertion, "I find no need to explain to Father O'Connell or to anyone else the rationale for this decision?" Has there been any assessment of O'Connell's contribution and controversy in the Southern Mutual Help Association? How does Sr. Lorna Bourg's assessment of the church's involvement in sugar cane workers' plight compare to that of Thomas Becnel's in Labor, Church and the Sugar Establishment? What happened to Henri Pelet, who housed O'Connell and worked more than 35 years organizing sugar cane workers? How many more lay union officials have similar stories to tell of their sugar cane endeavours?

What were the conclusions of the 1980-81 study of labor-management controversies conducted by the Social Action and Catholic Charities directors of the four dioceses in Iowa? What was the supportive or other roles of the national AFL-CIO head-quarters and the Grain Millers international headquarters in the Clinton Corn workers struggle? How true were the charges of Marxist influence in Local Six? What were the roles of Mary Ellen Eckelberg, Fr. William O'Connor and the Catholic Worker house in Davenport during the controversy? How valid is the charge of indifference and non-cooperation of the local Catholic clergy? Why were the alternatives of the "pastoral task force" never accepted? Why did Iowa bishops fail to do what New York State bishops did in the 1973 Farah-ACWA controversy--ask USCC to study the controversy?

2. Evaluation

The Catholic periodical literature from 1960 to 1980 pre-sented a record of much church involvement in some prominent labor-management controversies in the agricultural industry. However, almost overshadowing the assistance rendered the migrant, bracero, FLOC and Iowa Corn workers was the tremendous help given Cesar Chavez and the United Farm Workers. According to the evaluation hierarchies employed here, the record for the church's involvement for all agricultural workers is as follows.

Overwhelmingly, the most frequent goal sought was the self-actualization sub-goal of the right to organize for collective bargaining. The next most frequent were the survival-safety sub-goals of adequate wages, employment and improved health con-ditions. In terms of tactics, the overwhelming frequency was of demonstrating and imprisonment in the "presence" strategy and fasting in the "liturgy" category. Such is attributable largely to the presence of so many members of the clergy and religious communities at Delano in the early 1970's. Also quite frequent were the boycott and legislative sub-goals in the "power" strategy, in the "proclamation" strategy the endorsements--mostly of UFW strikes and boycotts--and dialogue in the "reconciliation" category. In terms of actors, the most frequent were bishops, clerics and religious in various institutional leadership posi-tions. Also, quite frequent were clergy, religious and lay social action types. With a favorable response to calls for volunteers, the number of lay socially-interested was very strik-ing. As for the reactions of labor and others to the Catholic church's involvement, there was much approval by the labor move-ment, save some segments of the Teamsters' union. Among manage-ment there was much indifference, save for heavy opposition among growers and some cooperation among some national and local food companies that cooperated with the boycotts and other efforts. Due to the massive turnout in Delano in the early 1970's the most frequent reaction was legal actions of arrests and jailings prompted by violations of injunctions of which growers were supportive. The next most frequent reaction of management and some Teamsters was verbal attack. There was also some instances of non-cooperation, insults, and physical violence. As for the church leaders' reaction to church members' involvement, there were some instances of non-cooperation and a few instances of other reactions--usually directed at social action priests.

3. Recommendations

The National Catholic Rural Life Conference should be supported in its efforts to assist the remaining small family-farmers to cope with the control of the agro-industrial complex. Such efforts should be coordinated with efforts to help the migrant and permanent black, hispanic and other farm workers. For these purposes the NCRLC and other national church groups should convene a meeting to assess the issues, accumulate the data, and coordinate the necessary resources. Rural dioceses should identify growers and processors, of private and public corporations in the agro-industrial complex who have insight into the issues, concern for social justice, competence to cope with the complexities and commitment to improve the agro-industrial workers' lot and complex development--in face of overseas needs and competition, international trade and technological advances, governmental regulations and subsidies, and fantastic costs. Evaluate the implementation of "This Land Is Home to Me" and "Guests and Strangers" and compare the suggestions on agriculture in the U.S. Catholic Bishops' Pastoral, Catholic Social Teaching and the U.S. Economy." Support some immigration bill with provisions for grower penalties, workers' identification cards and other effective measures for greater justice to migrant and U.S. farm workers and a minimum of discrimination.

Collaboration between the NCC Migrant Ministry and NCRLC should be encouraged. NCRLC should be in consultation with the AFL-CIO organizing and industrial union departments about farmworkers--migrants, UFW, sugar cane, FLOC and others--in the hope of closer cooperation in efforts to improve their lives and enhance their civil and human rights. CHD should evaluate its grants to smaller disparate farmworker groups, in light of the need to use funds more effectively in CHD's aim to empower people. A U.S. church "umbrella-office" for labor-management relations should be available for unions and for companies like Gallo, Campbell, Libby, Heinz, and Standard Brands for hard mediation resources placed at their disposal for settlement of labor controversies. Attention to effective structures and policies should be given in the agriculture section of the U.S. bishop's pastoral on the U.S. economy.

Chapter VII - Labor-Management Relations in Clothing & Textiles

1. Unasked or Unanswered Questions

Is there any valid difference between priests and religious working full or part-time for a labor union, corporation or political organization and the priests and religious who worked for UFW in the California controversy, ACWA in the Farah controversy, ACTWU in the J. P. Stevens controversy, or the UMW in coal mining controversies--before or after these controversies were "declared" bona-fide social justice causes? What are some of the similarities and contrasts between church-labor-management relations in the UFW, ACWA, ACTWU, and UMW organizing campaigns? What were the similarities and contrasts in any formal or informal action of the NCCB/USCC or its committees in the UFW-California Growers, ACWA-Farah, ACTWU J. P. Stevens, and UMW-coal mining controversies? How can one convince people that church support for the right of workers to organize is as valid social justice teaching today as it was in "the mid-thirties"? Aside from an insulting remark that Bishop Metzger did not know what he was talking about, were there other attacks on Metzger and other church leaders not reported in the Catholic periodical literature from 1960-1980?

Why did it take almost a year for the study of the ACTWU-J.P. Stevens controversy issues, before a statement of concern and offer of mediation from the Southeastern bishops? Given the impact of the bishops' intervention in the earlier UFW-California Growers and ACWA-Farah controversies were Higgins' cautions about "gearing up for a long pull" and Catholic groups not having "to wait for the bishops" warranted? Was the delay in the first statement due to labor union predictions of a long struggle, the need to thaw out J. P. Stevens opposition, internal union problems, insufficient USCC staff for labor-management work, or fear of antagonizing the small but largely management-oriented Catholic population in the Southeastern textile area? How much influence did the three Southeastern bishops' statements have on getting the union and company officials together for secret talks during 1978 and 1979?

Were the other members of the U.S. hierarchy asked, or only expected, to refrain from endorsing the J. P. Stevens boycott until the Southeastern bishops had done so? Why was there a general reluctance of some traditionally activist national church organizations either to endorse the J. P. Stevens boycott or to become heavily involved in promoting the boycott? How much was this reluctance due to deference for the local bishops or to the complaints that ACTWU had failed to build the strong community grassroots support which these organizations experienced in the UFW-California Growers controversy? What are the implications for the interfaith collaboration in labor-management relations in the realization that in March 1980, the Southeastern bishops were the only top southern religious leaders to have endorsed the J. P. Stevens boycott? What concerted efforts could interfaith leaders in the Southeastern U.S. be making to assist the very troubled textile industry? Could Southerners for Economic Justice be a quasi-successor on an interfaith and interracial basis to the old Catholic Committee of the South? Six years later, in the midst of worldwide economic crisis, what are the conditions of J. P. Stevens workers and prospects for the textile industry?

2. Evaluation

Even though there has been a long history of low wages and miserable conditions in both the garment and textile industries, the Farah and J. P. Stevens controversies were the first in which Catholic leaders played such a prominent and sustaining role. Compared to their role in the UFW-California growers controversy the church's role in the later campaigns was relatively short and small. This was due partially to the dynamics and time-line of the earlier controversy. Yet, the church's role in both Farah and J. P. Stevens struggles was acknowledged generally as important. In terms of goals, again the church's most common was the self-actualizing right of workers to organize. References to tactics were mostly to the "presence" subtactic of demonstrating, less so the "education" subtactic of news coverage, and even less so to the "proclamation" subtactic of endorsements and the "power" subtactic of boycotting. Noticeable, however, was the introduction of stockholder action in the form of worker resolutions. The most frequent actors were institutional--bishops and clerics--and less frequent were religious in the social action category. Noticeable were three Catholic clerics and two Catholic religious women serving on ACWA and ACTWU staffs, full-time. As for reactions of labor or management to church involvement in the Farah and J. P. Stevens controversies, there were some instances of non-cooperation, verbal attack and insults--mostly in the J. P. Stevens campaign. In the Farah controversy there was some sprinkling of violence, outside the plant.

333

3. Recommendations

Since the "Sunbelt" of the U.S. experiences so much anti-union activity, dioceses there should identify and contact Catholic managerial officials in the area, who are able to move beyond the opposition to church teaching on the right of workers to join a union of their own choosing and address the other labor-management issues. Sought would be people who would balance their concern for the belonging-esteem goals with concern for the survival-safety goals and some openness to the self-actualization sub-goals of worker co-management, worker co-ownership and industrial-economic planning by management, labor and government at various levels. Dioceses in "sunbelt" states should think and act collaboratively on labor-management relations and join coalitions of interfaith nature--especially the Southerners for Economic Justice. Sunbelt dioceses should attempt to have input in the various chambers of commerce, trade associations and industrial planning groups. Understood is that the sunbelt dioceses will be in touch with any national church umbrella organization recommended above, Catholic institutions of higher learning and the regional or national church groups -- NCCC, NCCIJ, NFPC, CMSM and LCWR. Such regional and national church collaboration should be stressed in the U.S. bishops' pastoral on the U.S. economy.

Chapter VIII - Labor-Management Controversies in Coal Mining

1. Unasked and Unanswered Questions

Given the very obvious poverty of the Appalachian coal region and the greater prosperity of the Southeastern states and given the almost total absence of Catholics in Appalachia and the small but wealthy Catholic population in the Southeastern states, is there evidence available to illustrate a patterned difference among church leaders' response to labor-management relations in the two areas? If the church were to reinstate an earlier recourse to interdict and excommunication, what would be the net effect of such a practice in labor-management controversies--on the culprits, the church, and the labor-management ministry?

What were the evidences of illegal and immoral actions in union practices alleged by Bonnyman, what bearing did they have on a union election and contract, and why did Bonnyman not bring his "case" to the public and the courts? What were the reasons for UMW's failure to respond to McDonough's offer of mediation assistance? What would Bishop Niedergeses construe as forcing church involvement and did he consider other alternatives? Was there any consultation between McDonough and Niedergeses on the

334

one hand and Begley and Sullivan on the other hand--seeing differences over backing the miners and a public prayer vigil? Did the disagreement highlight the absence or breakdown of any implementing process for the Appalachian pastoral? What contributed to the apparent dissent among the CCA membership over the strategies and goals in the Appalacian pastoral "action plan" and over the action to take in the UMW-Blue Diamond Company? What changes would the leadership--locally and nationally--have to make to stir greater involvement by the local bishops and national church groups? How can church leaders and activists effectively prompt necessary changes in unions or companies when approached for church assistance in a labor-management controversy? How can church leaders and activists effectively prod unions or companies to document alleged immoral or illegal behavior for legal authorities and the public?

2. Evaluations

Given the relatively short period of time involved in the controversies in the coal mining industries reported by the Catholic periodical literature 1960-1980, there was little church involvement. Perhaps, such involvement was small also, due to Blue Diamond's intransigence and UMW internal troubles. Perhaps, also, that small involvement was greater than early church involvement in earlier controversies in the nation's coal fields. Again, the church's most frequent goal was in the self-actualizing category right of workers to organize for collective bargaining. Noteworthy was the interest in miner-ownership of the Justus Mine, however aborted at conception. The most common tactic was demonstrating in the "presence" category and endorsements as "proclamation." Next in frequency was prayer in the "liturgy" category. The most frequent actors were "social action" types, equally spread among clerics, religious and laity--due largely to the nature and organizing of CCA. Among reactions to church involvement there were some verbal attacks, insults and non-cooperation--mostly from the Blue Diamond Company.

3. Recommendations

The efforts should continue to build implementing structures and processes for the Appalacian pastoral. Dioceses in which much coal mining takes place should identify and contact management officials who can move beyond opposition to unions and sort out with union leaders and members--with interfaith prodding--the necessary changes for the common good of the coal industry. A national church umbrella could be of some assistance to such regional groupings of dioceses, in terms of research, multi-national dimensions, and successes elsewhere. Collaboration on an interfaith basis should spread to other coal mining regions, after the example of CCA and CORA in the Appalachian region.

Chapter VII - Labor-Management Controversies in Steel and Other Industries

1. Unasked and Unanswered Questions

How many dioceses work in collaboration with local or state economic development agencies as Youngstown did with WREDA? With all the plant closings in the Midwest and Northeast and the "give-aways" in the sunbelt, what is being done on the diocesan and national U.S. church levels to analyze, protest, and remedy so many local regions' exploitation by governmental and corporate officials? Why was the national religious crusade, envisioned by the Youngstown Religious Coalition, never successful? Who has done serious and extensive theological and ethical analysis of "plant closings"? Are any other dioceses or national church organizations pursuing with such centers as Gar Alperovitz's Center for Economic Alternatives the action implications for "reform of the economic system" in Pope John Paul II's encyclical On Human Labor or the U.S. bishops' pastoral on the U.S. economy? Were any church leaders pursuing with national political, corporate and labor leaders the kind of help the Youngstown Religious Coalition so badly needed to be successful? Why were reports on Catholic "earnest money" for the re-opening of the Campbell Works so scarce? In the analysis of the coalition's early failure to inspire rank-and-file, parish and neighborhood support, how much attention has been given to the role of local religious leaders, who did not serve in the coalition? Was there real failure to communicate effectively with them or were they not hearing, due to everyday cares in running a church or synagogue or to a theology that did not grasp fully the social justice dimensions of corporate responsibility and reform of economic structures? How extensively did the coalition leaders seize upon the "communist-smear" to relate to their people the Catholic, Jewish and Protestant support for worker co-ownership and co-management?

How can one develop effective lay involvement in socio-economic issues and yet not overlook the influence of religious leaders or decision-makers in business, government and labor? What were the behind-the-scenes role of other Catholic lay leaders in business, government and labor, after the example of Ted Kennedy? What were the details of the coalition's tensions: resident/non-resident, establishment/non-establishment, and intra-church? Using the Youngstown Religious Coalition as a case study what can be learned of interfaith dynamics--cooperation, competition, communication, ecclesiology, social justice teaching, etc.? What were the weaknesses and strengths, the reality and promise of each? Was a second pastoral ever published by the coalition?

2. Evaluation

As in the coal mining industry, the church's involvement in the steel industry was relatively limited, in light of the industry's history and crisis. In terms of goals, the self-actualizing sub-goals of co-ownership and planning were most prominent. The most prominent concern in the survival-safety category was for employment. In terms of actors, the most influential were Bishop Malone and his assistant Rev. Edward Stanton, executive director of the coalition. Quite numerous were socially interested and social action clerics. What they did, aside from belong to the coalition was left unsaid. The most common tactic was educational--news coverage by press conferences and newspaper stories. There was much "service" and "power" tactics. Statements and pastorals were present by way of "proclamation." The reaction of labor at the international level was mostly non-cooperation and indifference. The reaction of management, except for a few verbal attacks and one insult, was mostly non-cooperation. The reaction of government was more supportive locally and in the U.S. Congress than the national executive, which was deceptive and hostile.

3. Recommendations

As in the agricultural, clothing, and mining industry, dioceses should identify and contact managerial officials in the steel industry, who can move beyond opposition to unions and dialogue with religious, political and union leaders about the common good of the workers and other aspects of the steel industry. People who already are conducting such dialogues should be publicized and encouraged. The assistance of a national U.S. church umbrella, should be sought. A national U.S. church umbrella office should be in continuing consultation with academicians and consultants, expert and interested in the reform of economic system, such as Gar Alperovitz's Center for Economic Alternatives. Some competent theologians, economists, political scientists and activists should undertake a thorough analysis and evaluation of the Youngstown Religious Coalition. Publications and seminars should be made available to encourage other such interfaith coalitions, since the Youngstown Religious Coalition-- with its tensions and shortcomings--was not a failure! It was the most recent and ambitious interfaith coalition to implement long-time dreams and hopes of effective interfaith collaboration in labor-management issues, which today's world so badly needs. The Youngstown Interfaith Coalition should be most instructive and encouraging to the framers of the U.S. bishops' pastoral on the U.S. economy--especially with regard to industrial planning, policy or whatever more diplomatic term can be created. Failure to do so will not only slight papal insistence but also ignore an absolutely essential international socio-politico-economic need!

Conclusion

References has been made several times, in passing to a national U.S. Church umbrella to assist. Let me explain!

Whether at the USCC, NCCC or some specially created umbrella, the U.S. church should have a permanent office for its role in labor-management relations. The staff should be small but experienced and professional. Its objectives should be: to keep other national and diocesan officials informed of labor-management trends and controversies; to be available for providing or locating the expertise needed for church input in labor-management controversies in terms of dialogue, mediation or other action; to collate information on significant programs, studies, personnel, finances and other resources to assist other church people with labor-management controversies and to communicate the church's position to society. These objectives assume utilization of Catholic and other higher educational institutions, labor-management schools, arbitration and mediation offices--both public and private, as well as any organization interested in better labor-management relations. There should be policy clarifications, about minimum expectations of coalitions the church might join in behalf of labor-management relations, and social justice clarifications, about the church's tradition in labor-management relations--perhaps along the lines of the goals-hierarchy used here. Such an office also might aid the implementation of the U.S. bishops' pastoral, "Catholic social teaching and the U.S. economy."

[1]Michael Maccoby, The Gamesman: The New Corporate Leaders, N.Y.: Simon and Schuster, 1976, p. 244.

[2]Joseph Joblin, S.J., in a personal letter to the author from the Pontifical Gregorian University in Rome, May 19, 1982.

[3]Michael Maccoby, in loc. cit., p. 219.

Chapter IX - Interfaith Implications

If this book serves any worthwhile purpose at all, my fond hope is that it will encourage others to fill out the record of Catholic church involvement in labor-management controversies. A fonder hope is that others will do the same for the Jewish and Protestant record. Yet, my fondest hope is that, with the record of current involvement of the three major U.S. religious bodies in place, Catholic, Jewish and Protestant leaders and activists would join together, at all levels of society, to bring labor and management into greater cooperation for the long-term betterment of their own separate interests and the common good. Whatever the labor-management involvement record of Jewish and Protestant leaders and activists from 1960-1980, the former probably will experience activity similar to that of the latter. The Jewish and Protestant leaders and activists also will look to the future in ways similar to Catholic leaders and activists. Only the complete record can say with some surety. However, the Catholic experience from 1960-1980 does provide some hints of the criticisms, actors, tactics and goals to expect.

While the language varied, there was management criticism-- especially in the UFW-California growers' controversy, the ACTWU- J.P. Stevens controversy and the UMW-Blue Diamond controversy-- that the church did not belong, did not understand the complex issues, and was easily taken in by union propaganda. My surprise was that the Catholic periodical literature from 1960-1980 had so few details of such management criticism. My surprise also extended to finding so few references in the literature to union criticism of the church. Criticism of the church in the earlier years of the UFW-California controversy was stronger than in the later period. I surmised that muted criticism was expressed by hopes for earlier endorsement in the ACTWU-J.P. Stevens contro- versy. Criticism of the church from other than management and union sources was clear in the UMW-Blue Diamond controversy and muted in rumors of later dissension and failure to reach the rank-and-file during the Youngstown Religious Coalition. My sur- prise pleasantly extended, also, to finding so few complaints from any source about negative reactions of Catholic church leaders to involvement of its activists in the labor-management controversies. The exceptions were in the earlier periods of the assistance extended to agricultural workers. Perhaps, a more complete record of Catholic involvement would make Jewish and Protestant leaders and activists expect greater criticism. As will be clear below, management complaint that the church favors unions too much is understandable in terms of the Catholic Church's insistence that workers, like any other group in society, have the human right to organize themselves to represent

339

their interests collectively. A right neither church nor management should deny!

Among the Catholic actors involved in labor management issues, clerical institutional actors were most prevalent. The laity were most frequent as social action actors. Save for the absence of religious, the Jewish and Protestant experience would seem to follow suit, although only the complete record will tell for sure about the types of actors. Yet, one hopes for greater lay involvement than in the Caholic record.

With respect to tactics used in the Catholic involvement experience, there were the large number of people fasting while in jail and demonstrating during the UFW-California growers' controversy. The most common tactics were endorsements in the "proclamation" category. The next most prevalent were implementing the UFW boycott and legislative action for the benefit of agricultural workers in the "power" category. Also quite common were news coverage in the "education" category. Save for the fasting, Jewish and Protestant experience would seem to expect the same. Again, only the complete record can tell with greater surety. Yet, one is curious about ways to achieve better use of religious institutions, resources, people and symbols.

As for goals of the Catholic involvement experience, save for the Youngstown Religious Coalition, the overwhelmingly prevalent goal was assistance to ensure the workers' right to organize for collective bargaining. Of course, implied in collective bargaining support rendered by the Catholic church are the survival-safety goals of employment, wages, fringe benefits, health and safety. In the Youngstown Religious Coalition experience the focus on worker/community ownership and planning also included employment. The Catholic church championing of workers' right to organize for collective bargaining may tell--more about the times we live in than the Catholic church's fulfillment of part of its teaching. As has been shown in my U.S. Catholic Institutions and Labor Unions (University Press of America 1985), administrators in Catholic institutions fell into the same trend as management opposition to unions. Only the full record can tell how much of the Catholic church's success in telling others in management to respect the workers' right to organize was due to conviction about the teaching among the faithful, the charisma of people like Chavez, the concern for other Catholics' plight, or the communication and organization skills of the Catholic leaders and activists. Most likely a mixture of all factors is closer to the truth. Equally interesting to speculate in a fuller record would be the distraction such institutional opposition caused from more concern about the belonging-esteem goals (training and retraining, job description, job accountability,

340

grievance procedures and affirmative system) and the other self-actualization goals (self-determination and participation in a duly elected and certified labor organization, worker co-management, worker co-ownership, collaborative planning by management and labor and government at all levels industry, area, nation, world). An excellent, immediate and interfaith beginning for such speculation would seem to be the Youngstown Religious Coalition experience.

Allow me to explain! Perennially religious groups are faced with swings or cycles concerning the involvement in the world. Preaching and teaching, books and periodicals, synods and councils convey extremes or shades about the religious groups' "wordly" involvement. One or another person or group, at one time or another, will opt for a clear choice or a combination of the following: remain aloof, help persons, educate behavior of citizens, formulate societal norms, remove causes, or create a new society. Past histories and current news detail religious turmoil, successes and failures in a single thrust or in combinations. While most mainline religious groups have rejected the aloofness and attempted more than educating loyal citizens, various sect-type religious groups have remained aloof and attempted to create their own little world in isolation. Some mainline denominational spokespersons or groups have had grand schemes or patch-work borrowings from secular ideologies to formulate societal norms, to remove causes, or to create a new society, so great has been their concern for correcting socio-economic injustice. Most mainline spokespersons or groups in Catholic, Jewish and Protestant tradition have offered principles forcefully and applications gingerly, so aware are they of the limitations of religious teaching and the complications of the socio-economic sphere. Throughout the later twentieth century history of Catholic, Jewish and Protestant bodies there seems to have been a consensus, with degrees of difference and detail, on the goals used here: survival-safety, belonging-esteem and self-actualization.

The Youngstown Religious Coalition seems to me a sincere, traditionally grounded, and pragmatically guarded response to a socio-economic crisis in one area. The coalition was not perfect. It was crisis-oriented, top-heavy with clergy, late in arriving, hasty in planning, ineffective in arousing a national coalition, unaided by the power of the labor movement, and undercut by the Carter administration. Yet, the coalition had accomplishments. It showed that a religious coalition reached out to those in need, tried to formulate societal norms about plant closings, and addressed some of the causes of plant closings. It provided a case study from which the other local religious coalitions can draw invaluable lessons about the need for continued knowledge of socioeconomic factors at work in an area; continued contact with business, labor, and government leaders in an area; continued wider national and international organizational influence; continued relationship of socio-economic issues to faith and worship; and continued effort to develop its rank-and-file in its communication and decision-making processes. It addressed several dimensions of an exten-sive and increasing socio-economic curse--the threatening demise of communities because of plant closings.

While the Youngstown Religious Coalition did not address measures to remedy unfair foreign competition, tax inequities favoring corporations, government subsidization of some indus-tries, and the tremendous power of transnational corporations, the coalition did surface these as factors in the crisis. Despite the Youngstown Religious Coalition's tremendous time limits and great resource restrictions, the pressing need and promising benefits of continued, intelligent, informed, organized and cooperative interfaith attention to local and regional, national and international socio-economic issues have been demon-strated strikingly. As much as the interfaith collaboration in Cesar Chavez' farmworkers cause and Martin Luther King's civil rights crusade in their time, the Youngstown Religious Coalition deserves genuine respect and serious study in our time. More importantly, it calls for the same kind of interfaith coalitions on the reform of our economic processes and structures, from labor, management and government at all levels.

In highlighting so much of the socio-economic principles of Catholic, Jewish, and Protestant tradition, interfaith coalitions like the one in Youngstown reveal that the very dangerous and perplexing socio-economic crises of our times call for more than union organizing of an industry and touch more than the minori-ties of a nation or world. Without sanctifying detailed approaches, which are beyond their ken, and without embracing a capitalism or socialism, which are beyond their province, inter-faith coalitions should be busy nudging and cajoling, encouraging and inspiring labor, management and government to get on with Macooby's economic democracy and the humanization of technology and Joblin's organic participation of workers and negotiations that embrace the environment, vocational training and all aspects of economic life. Indeed, a fuller record of Catholic, Jewish and Protestant involvement and a broader vision of interfaith coalitions will reveal not only that under labor-management rela-tions today there is a new reality but that Pope John Paul II's call for reform of the economic system and for economic planning resonate as well in Jewish and Protestant challenges to labor, management and government.

Among the many recommendations this book has offered the Catholic leaders and activists, two are offered to begin a national interfaith coalition, more radical and universal than the work of those who assisted Chavez and King. One, create and/or adapt national umbrella offices for socio-economic issues. Two, meet very soon to consider on an interfaith basis the action implications of the U.S. Catholic bishops' pastoral, "Catholic Social Teaching and the U.S. Economy." The successes with Chavez and King and Youngstown were not complete. Neither were they futile. The only failure is not to try! That failure could be the harbinger of worse. Little people might be overwhelmed by powerful forces when they expect their religious leaders to confront, inspire and instruct. Instead, these people may find their religious leaders bereft of the spirit of prophets, psalmists and judges. Such little people then might leave more altars alone, spires ignored and lights out. For their priests, ministers and rabbis failed to hear the Lord's call and to summon God's people!

The summons to God's people, however, is for the big as well as the little people, the laity as well as the clergy--to come on the passage themselves and to assist others as well. Hence, every Catholic, Jew and Protestant--whether in labor or management, government or ministry--must face the risks of Abraham and Moses, Jesus and His disciples, buoyed by the faith in a living and loving, provident and powerful God. No hidden hand or increasing imponderables, no past precedents or present predicaments should deter them from making the creative changes in attitudes, processes, structures, practices and laws to bring labor and management and government to greater cooperation for their own long-term interests and the common good. They might well ponder the message on the desk of Lane Kirkland, AFL-CIO president, which might just as easily be on the desk of executives or people in ministry who should be Noahs in our time,

> A ship in harbor is safe.
> But that is not what ships
> are built for.

1. Hierarchy of Goals

The hierarchy of goals uses some of the language and levels of needs of Abraham Maslow's "self-actualization theory." It was employed as part of the NCCB-NORC study of the U.S. priests in the late 1960s. It would seem as appropriate for study of ministry to workers. Aware of Maccoby's criticism of Maslow's work as a humanistic psychological theory, the goals-arrangement here is employed more as "a traditional humanistic concept."[3] For, the goals gleaned from the sources indicated above are presented there as related to human nature or revelation in greater or lesser degrees--Maslow's theory speaks of psychological needs in human development. The present arrangement speaks of goals for achievement by religious and other human groups in labor-management relations. Maslow has five levels of needs, arranged from lowest to highest: pysiological, safety, belongingness-love, esteem and self-actualization. The goals hierarchy here has three levels, moving from the most necessary to the most desirable: survival-safety, belonging-esteem, self-actualization. The sub-goals for "survival-safety" are adequate employment, wages, fringe benefits, health conditions, and safety conditions of work. The sub-goals for "belonging-esteem" are: training, communication, job description, job accountability, grievance procedures, and affirmation in work. The sub-goals for "self-actualization" are: the right to organize for collective bargaining, self-determination and participation in a duly elected and certified labor organization, worker management, worker co-ownership, collaborative planning by management, labor and government (industry-wide, area-wide, nation-wide, world-wide). There is no presumption that lower sub-goals are always either steps toward or achieved before higher sub-goals.

I might note an article by the Notre Dame economist and member of the staff of the bishop's commission on the U.S. economy, Charles K. Wilber. In volume 2, number 1, 1985 of Notre Dame's Journal of Law and Public Policy, Wilber wrote an article entitled. "Economics and Ethics: The Challenge of the Bishop's Pastoral Letter on the Economy." Wilber laid out three specific goals for an economy: "Life sustenance" (necessary, enhancement and luxury goods), "esteem and fellowwhip," and "freedom," (consumer sovereignty, worker sovereignty, and citizen sovereignty). In concluding his section on social goals, Wilber said,

> These three social goals...embody the core of
> Catholic social thought and express much of

what is best in the American experience. Acceptance of these goals will require the creation of a new social consensus to replace both the reigning free market philosophy and the presently discredited New Deal/Keynesian consensus.

2. Hierarchy of Tactics

The hierarchy of tactics attempts to indicate a progression from less to more influential and costly involvement. Again, no presumption is made that one level is a step toward nor effective before a higher level. In any given labor-management situation, the issues and process at work would be so complex that generalizing here for church involvement tactics would be rash. The levels of tactics are: education, reconciliation, liturgy, service, proclamation, presence and power. The "education" subtactics are: news coverage, lectures, seminars and workshops. The "reconciliation" subtactics are: dialogue, mediation and arbitration. The dimensions of "liturgy" include: prayer service, eucharist, fasting and processions. The "service" subtactics are: financial assistance, provision of personnel, counselling and social work. The "proclamation" subtactics are: editorial support, resolutions for specific actions, and endorsement of arbitration or strike or boycott. The "presence" subtactics are: demonstration presence, picketing presence, and imprisonment. The "power" subtactics are: stockholder action, boycott action, legislative lobbying, introduction of litigation, joining coalitions for joint-action.

3. Hierarchy of Actors

The hierarchy of actors attempts to indicate a progression from informal to formal and from unorganized to organized involvement. There are four levels of clerical, lay and religious actors: socially interested, social action, institutionally approved or appointed, personally chosen and engaged. The "socially interested" act or would be revealed in occasional donations, services and actions. The "social action" actor would be revealed by publicity in the secular and Catholic press and by sustained activity over a comparatively long period of time. Examples of "institutionally approved or appointed" actor would be officials in Justice and Peace Offices, Catholic Charities, Campaign for Human Development, etc. Examples of "personally chosen and engaged" actors would be direct involvement in instructing, demonstrating, picketing, organizing, etc. for labor or management.

345

4. Hierarchy of Reactions

There are two hierarchies of reactions, usually progressing from the more simple and nonchalant to the more complex and determined. The first hierarchy of reactions by labor, management or others to church involvement, include: indifference, non-cooperation, verbal attack, insult, financial pressure, rights violations and legal action. The second hierarchy of reactions by church leaders to involvement by other church people, include: indifference, non-cooperation, verbal attack, silencing, prohibiting, transferring, rights violation and legal action.